Flyfisher's Guid

EASTERN TROPHY
TAILWATERS

40 Great Trout Waters from Maine to Georgia

TOM GILMORE

Fishing Titles Available from Wilderness Adventures Press, Inc.™

Flyfishers Guide to™

Flyfisher's Guide to Alaska
Flyfisher's Guide to Arizona
Flyfisher's Guide to the Big Apple
Flyfisher's Guide to Chesapeake Bay
Flyfisher's Guide to Colorado
Flyfisher's Guide to Connecticut
Flyfisher's Guide to the Florida Keys
Flyfisher's Guide to Freshwater Florida
Flyfisher's Guide to Idaho
Flyfisher's Guide to Mexico
Flyfisher's Guide to Montana
Flyfisher's Guide to Michigan
Flyfisher's Guide to Minnesota
Flyfisher's Guide to Missouri & Arkansas
Flyfisher's Guide to Nevada
Flyfisher's Guide to the New England Coast
Flyfisher's Guide to New Mexico
Flyfisher's Guide to New York
Flyfisher's Guide to the Northeast Coast
Flyfisher's Guide to Northern California
Flyfisher's Guide to Northern New England
Flyfisher's Guide to Oregon
Flyfisher's Guide to Saltwater Florida
Flyfisher's Guide to Tennessee
Flyfisher's Guide to Texas
Flyfisher's Guide to the Texas Gulf Coast
Flyfisher's Guide to Utah
Flyfisher's Guide to Virginia
Flyfisher's Guide to Washington
Flyfisher's Guide to Western Washington Lakes
Flyfisher's Guide to Wisconsin & Iowa
Flyfisher's Guide to Wyoming
Flyfisher's Guide to Yellowstone National Park
Flyfishing Northern New England's Seasons

On the Fly Guide to™

On the Fly Guide to the Northwest
On the Fly Guide to the Northern Rockies

Best Fishing Waters™ Books

California's Best Fishing Waters
Colorado's Best Fishing Waters
Idaho's Best Fishing Waters
Montana's Best Fishing Waters
Oregon's Best Fishing Waters
Washington's Best Fishing Waters

Micro SD Cards with GPS Waypoints

Montana's Fishing GPS Maps
Colorado's Fishing GPS Maps
Washington's Fishing GPS Maps

Anglers Guide to™

Complete Anglers Guide to Oregon

Angler's Guide to the West Coast

Saltwater Angler's Guide to Southern California

Field Guide to™

Field Guide to Fishing Knots

Fly Tying

Go-To Flies™

Flyfishing Adventures™

Montana

Trout Adventures™

North America

Flyfisher's Guide to™

EASTERN TROPHY
TAILWATERS

40 Great Trout Waters from Maine to Georgia

INCLUDING GPS

Tom Gilmore

Flyfisher's Guide to™ Series

Wilderness
Adventures
Press, Inc.™

Belgrade, Montana

Published by Wilderness Adventures Press, Inc.™
45 Buckskin Rd
Belgrade, MT 59715
866-400-2012
Website: www.wildadvpress.com
email: books@wildadvpress.com

Printed in South Korea

ISBN: 978-1-940239-05-7

Table of Contents

Dedication

To Joanne
My wife, lifelong partner, and best friend.
Joanne has always supported my passion for fishing and the outdoors. She has partnered in every book I have written, in every step of the way, from booking guides as surprise birthday presents to reading and editing drafts, then questioning, editing, and re-reading text. This book would not have been possible without her loving help, wisdom, and support.

FOREWORD

BY ED JAWOROWSKI

Increasing population density, urbanization, residential subdivisions, industrial and commercial development, combined with recreational activities like kayaking, tubing, and angling place ever-increasing demands on freshwater resources from Maine to Georgia. Shrinking water tables and warming temperatures affect not only fish, but also the aquatic fauna on which trout and other fish feed. The numbers and variety of macroinvertebrates diminish along with the available waters themselves. But all is not doom and gloom for anglers seeking additional trout fishing opportunities. Tailwaters represent perhaps the most important means for ensuring the future of our sport.

While providing water for thirsty populations and preventing natural disasters, both water supply and flood control dams, when properly managed, simultaneously have the potential for preserving, reclaiming, or establishing coldwater fisheries. By keeping downstream waters cooler, maintaining consistent flows, and encouraging macroinvertebrate proliferation, they create miles of great fishing, even near metropolitan areas in some of the most densely settled regions of the country. Anglers in and around urban centers like Boston, Atlanta, New York, Philadelphia, Pittsburgh, Baltimore, and Washington already reap the benefits of tailwater fisheries.

Wilderness Adventures Press has wisely selected one of the most qualified writers in the game to make flyfishers aware of the benefits of these man-made enhancements and to direct them in their search for these angling meccas. My association with Tom Gilmore goes back more than 40 years, from the day we first met at a meeting of the Main Line Fly Tyers in the Philadelphia suburbs. We have been steadfast friends and fishing companions ever since. His business management skills at the Schuylkill Valley Nature Center and the Philadelphia Zoo, followed by a 29-year stint as President and CEO of the New Jersey Audubon Society - during which time he garnered awards and accolades as a front runner in conservation and environmental areas - attest to his interest in and love of the outdoors.

Gilmore's *Flyfisher's Guide to the Big Apple* (Wilderness Adventures Press, 2011) which followed two groundbreaking books on saltwater flyfishing, established his credentials as one of the finest writers of flyfishing guides in the sport. He has all the necessary qualifications and he's been through it all. He is an accomplished fly angler in fresh and salt water - from trout to tuna - a remarkable fly tier, and has traveled extensively throughout the country and abroad. I know of no one more thorough and relentless in his research and attention to detail. I realized early on in our friendship that he was as tenacious as a bulldog, whether raising funds for a conservation cause, or inducing a trout to rise to his fly. He has left no stone unturned in digging out information about the rivers included in this work, and he's personally fished them all. You'll find an enormous pool of information about tailwater fisheries in New England, the Mid-Atlantic, and the Southeast. Gilmore has focused on the most important major fisheries, but included some lesser-known gems that will offer you opportunities for exploring new waters. Those selected for inclusion in this book have all been subjected to rigorous standards. Only the best make his list. You will discover up-to-date information about the fish and fishing, recommendations on tackle, flies, and techniques, plus related travel and support services to help you enjoy excursions afield. *Eastern Trophy Tailwaters* represents that ideal combination of a timely and important topic, explored and expounded by the person perfectly suited for the job.

Ed Jaworowski at the Lefty Kreh Fly Fishing Trail on Big Gunpowder Falls River.

Acknowledgements

Over the years a great many people have contributed to my knowledge and enjoyment of the sport of flyfishing and to the production of this manuscript. I wish I could thank every one of them, but time and space does not allow.

I wish to extend my deepest gratitude to Ed Jaworowski – friend, mentor, and life-long fishing partner. Whether it's casting, fly tying, entomology, photography, writing or preparing presentations, Ed takes it to another level, and I am glad he pushes me to do the same. Ed, thank you for the hundreds of hours we spent fishing and photographing *Eastern Trophy Tailwaters*.

Special thanks to the following:

Lefty Kreh, Bob Clouser, and Bob Popovics, not only for the killer fly patterns you have given us, but also for your willingness to share your knowledge. There aren't three better ambassadors for any sport; they're real pros who enjoy nothing more than helping novices improve their game.

Rick Pope and his team at Temple Fork Outfitters for their help as support in obtaining great rods used to do "the field research" for this project.

Beau Beasley, for the many hours we spent on the road searching out tailwaters, for his photographs, for his writing skills – which I try to emulate in my writing – but most of all for his friendship. See you on the water.

Ed Janiga, who first urged me to put down the fly rod and pick up the pen. Ed, thanks for your confidence and encouragement. You have created a monster!

Fishing partners Joe Darcy, Joey DiBello, and Rick Steven – they possess all of the qualities of great fishing partners. They enjoy every moment of every trip (good or bad), they have great senses of humor, and they are the first to pitch in and help.

Lee Hartman – for his work to protect the coldwater resources on the Upper Delaware, and for the photos and text he provided for the Upper Delaware Section.

Al Caucci – for his work to protect the Upper Delaware and for unlocking the mysteries of the Delaware hatches, and for generously sharing his knowledge with others.

Darren Rist, a great guide and flyfishing instructor. Darren, thank you for showing me your home water, the West Branch of the Delaware, and for giving me a West Branch 101 lesson and guiding me to my first West Branch wild browns.

Chuck Swartz, for guiding me on the Upper Delaware and for giving me the "Cliff Notes" version of the history of the Delaware River trout fishery.

Aaron Jasper, for the many photos he provided, for his advice on the Croton Watershed streams, and for reviewing the section on the Croton Watershed. Aaron guides on the tailwaters of New York and Connecticut, and he catches more trophy trout than anyone I know.

Bruce Felmly for sharing his knowledge of the fishery at Upper Dam in western Maine, and for allowing me to reprint his story "The Day" - Columbus Day at the Upper Dam.

Bob Romano, for giving me the lowdown on the fishery and history of the Upper Dam and the Magalloway River, and for lending me his library of books on the history of the Rangeley Region of Maine. Bob himself is a gifted writer and I urge readers to pick up his beautifully scripted books on western Maine.

If I could fish only one eastern tailwater, it would be the South Holston in Bristol, Tennessee – it's just that special! And if I could stay at only one lodge, it would be the South Holston River Lodge overlooking the river. Special thanks to Bill Anderson, owner, Jon Hooper, general manager, and his assistant Tony Marcucci. You guys are great hosts and great friends.

Bill and Lang Wilson, for hosting Beau Beasley and me at your beautiful cabin on the banks of the Jackson River in Covington, Virginia. What a day – catching and releasing rainbow trout, red wine around a campfire, and a great grilled steak dinner with all the trimmings.

I want to thank all the anglers who shared their photographs for this project and, while he will be recognized in the photo credits, I wanted to especially recognize professional outdoor writer and photographer, King Montgomery, for generously allowing me to use several of his magnificent photos taken on Grand Lake Stream. Speaking of Grand Lake Stream, I want to thank Jeff McEvoy and Beth Rankin, who own and run Weatherby's Lodge and their manager, Frank Lepore, for the wonderful job they did hosting our group at Grand Lake Stream. Jeff even fixed the flat tire I got on a local logging road while I was catching landlocked salmon – Jeff, the patch is still holding.

Thanks also to the dozens of guides who shared their knowledge, photos, experience, and the hot spots which formed the foundation of this book. Guides who shared their knowledge and/or photos and time on the water include: Harold Harsh, Robert Duport, Todd Towle, Brett Damm, Kris Thomson, Greg Ingis, Lisa Savard, Tom Harrison, Christopher Jackson, Bryan Lynch, Rob Nicholas, Torrey Collins, Dean Druckenmiller, Joe DeMarkis, Micah Dammeyer, Teo Whitlock, Dane Law, Steve Lamb, Tom Hopkins, Bob Borgwat, Eugene Shuler, Davie Crawford, Blaine Chocklett, Jake Jordon, Josh Wohlforth, Brian Williams, Tom Hopkins and Michael "Rocky" Cox.

Anglers who contributed their knowledge and/or photographs to this guidebook include: Jack and Bryan Radigan, Jeff Poor, Nate Dickinson, Mike Cole, Rob Creamer, Dick Turse, Bob Powell, Rob Nicholas, Steve Vorkapich, Ken Oakes, Dave Skok, Richard Procopio, Teddy Patlen, John Roetman, Lee Schisler, Steve Murphy, Jim Quinn, Joe Johnson, Mandy Sanasie, Tony Macchiarola, Don Helms, Bill Dickson, Bob Bryan, Pete Douma, Tim Geist, Mike Simoni, John Alan Barthelemy, Ina Inglersall, Joe Johnston, Art Watkins, Jerry Plisinski, Don Campbell, John and Aidan Park, Howard "Woody" Woodbury, Dave Moore, Ted McKenzie, Larry Bucciarelli, Lenny Maiorano, Charlie Knight, Tom and Mark DeAngelis, Jeff Kurt, and Brian Cowden. Thanks for the good times and the memories.

In memory of former fishing partners who have moved on to fish the big rivers in the sky: the late Bill Ryan, Jim Ambridge, Joe Keegan, Bruce Gould, Dan Schnabel, Bob Davoli, and Jack Sebzda.

Thanks to fishery management professionals Greg Burr, Robert Van Riper, and David Boucher for their help with the Maine chapter. For help with the Maryland chapter, Keith Lockwood, recreational fisheries outreach coordinator, and Dr. Robert Bachman, the former director of Maryland's Freshwater Fisheries. For help on the Middle Yough, I'd like to thank Pennsylvania Fisheries Biologist, Rick Lorson.

Also Bill Dawson, for his support and help in obtaining the great tackle used to do the "field research" for this project. And I'd like to thank Walter Koenig for his crisp edits of my early drafts.

I am grateful to Chuck and Blanche Johnson and Josh Bergan, of Wilderness Adventures Press for their continued support of my work and for giving me the opportunity to join their family of the best flyfishing guidebooks in America. Their books have enhanced my fly fishing trips throughout North America, from Alaska to the Florida Keys.

Also thanks to my three lovely daughters - Jennifer, Julie, and Chrissy - and my sons-in-laws -Bryan and Jim - great kids and great friends. To my adorable grandchildren and hopefully future anglers – Jack, Ashley, Reagan, Paige, Morgan, and Brooke – thank you for making every family get-together a joy, and for the beautiful artwork which decorated my draft manuscripts.

Most of all I want to thank my wife, Joanne. As my lifelong partner, Joanne has always generously supported my passion for fishing and the outdoors. She partnered in this project every step of the way, from booking guides as surprise birthday presents to reading and editing drafts, then questioning, editing, and re-reading the text. This book would not have been possible without her loving help, wisdom, and support.

Preface

Eastern Trophy Tailwaters will introduce you, the reader, to the "world-class" tailwaters close to all of our major eastern cities. You will learn that you don't have to get on a plane to fly to the Rockies or even more exotic destinations in search of trophy trout – the book will reveal where to find them, practically in your backyard. During his research, the author explored over one hundred eastern tailwaters and eliminated all but what he felt were truly "world-class". In the pages that follow you will discover the secrets, hotspots, hatches, and areas of easy access to the East's best tailwaters. You will be guided by the author's first-hand fishing knowledge and information from his detailed stream logs, stretching back over four decades. The author shares his experiences, anecdotes, detailed descriptions, and directions to public access, as well as tips and tactics for flyfishing success on tailwaters. While the book is written from a fly angler's perspective, the information will be just as helpful to all trout fishermen.

RATING SYSTEM

I determined how many stars a water rates by five criteria: Public access, the ability to hold trout year round, fishable populations of wild trout, scenic beauty, and overall fishing experience. The rivers were ranked from one to ten for each criterion. Five-star rivers earned a score of 45 or better. Four-star rivers earned a score of 40 to 44. Rivers with a score below 40 were not included in the book.

Introduction

I started my love affair with tailwater trout on the Upper Delaware River in New York State. However, that love affair was very short-lived – at first. On the evening of June 6, 1980, I landed my first tailwater trout - a big, heavy, beautiful wild rainbow. It was my first tailwater experience, and the fish was at the time my largest wild trout. It took a dry fly and leaped and ran like crazy. That evening I thought to myself, no more small freestone streams for me – tailwaters equal big trout. I was hooked! Well, my next half dozen trips to the Upper Delaware produced zilch, nada, el skunko! I realized that I had a steep learning curve to conquer if I was going to be successful on our eastern tailwaters. I would need to learn and monitor water temperatures, reservoir discharge flow rates, and tailwater hatch schedules. I also learned that, for the most part, especially close to tailwater dams I would be fishing smaller flies, especially small mayflies and midges as they are the dominant tailwater insects.

Our eastern trout streams continue to suffer negative impacts from overdevelopment, groundwater withdrawals, flooding, droughts, non-point source pollution, and climate change. Tailwaters are becoming an increasingly important part of our coldwater fisheries and if current trends continue, they may become an even more important part of the future of flyfishing for trout. How important are tailwater rivers to our coldwater fishing opportunities? Taking a quick look through John Ross's *Trout Unlimited Guide to America's 100 Best Trout Streams*, you will see that 55 of the 100 streams are tailwaters; more than freestone and spring creeks combined.

Most anglers would agree that dams are a mixed blessing. They provide drinking water supplies and electrical power for our major cities and water for crop irrigation for a great many of our farms. However, they have certainly had a negative impact on our migratory fish species; blocking access to historic spawning grounds for species like American shad and Atlantic salmon. Fortunately, rivers that are below dams which release cold water from deep in their reservoirs have the ability to support large populations of aquatic insect life and high numbers of large trout. Dams provide cold water and near constant temperatures year round; in fact, many of our tailwaters can be fished year round. Not only can they be fished 12 months of the year, but due to the near constant temperatures, the fish continue to grow all year and reach sizes not found in our freestone streams. In addition to providing cold water, tailwater reservoirs filter out sediment which sinks to the bottom, leaving the water below the dam much cleaner than the water flowing into the reservoir. While I hope no more free-flowing rivers get dammed, where the dams already exist, I'll gladly fish tailwaters.

I have had the pleasure of fishing some of the West's "world-class" tailwaters including the Bighorn in Montana, the Wind in Wyoming, Henry's Fork of the Snake in Idaho, the Green in Utah, and the South Platte in Colorado, but I can tell you from first-hand experience, you don't have to hop on a plane to experience world class tailwater flyfishing. No matter where you live on the East Coast, this guide will introduce you to "world-class" tailwaters practically in your backyard. In the pages that follow I will take you to the best eastern tailwater rivers from Maine to Georgia, all of which I have personally fished in addition to interviewing fisheries biologists, anglers, and guides who target these great rivers.

Eastern Trophy Tailwaters Locator Map

Maine
1. Grand Lake Stream
2. West Branch of the Penobscot River
3. Rapid River
4. Upper Dam Pool
5. Magalloway River
6. Kennebec River

New Hampshire
7. Upper Connecticut River
8. Upper Connecticut River – Trophy Trout Section

Massachusetts
9. Deerfield River

Connecticut
10. Housatonic River
11. West Branch Farmington River

New York
12. Mainstem of the Upper Delaware River
13. West Branch of the Delaware River
14. East Branch of the Delaware River
15. Neversink River
16. Mongaup River
17. Esopus River
18. East Branch Croton River
19. West Branch Croton River – West Branch Reservoir Outlet
20. West Branch Croton River – Croton Falls Reservoir Outlet
21. Muscoot River

Pennsylvania
22. Lehigh River
23. Pohopoco Creek
24. Lackawaxen River
25. Clark's Creek
26. Youghiogheny River

Maryland
27. Big Gunpowder Falls River
28. North Branch of the Potomac River
29. Savage River
30. Upper Youghiogheny River

Virginia
31. Jackson River
32. Smith River

Tennessee
33. South Fork Holston River
34. Watauga River
35. Clinch River
36. Hiwassee River

North Carolina
37. Nantahala River
38. Tuckasegee River

Georgia
39. Toccoa River
40. Chattahoochee River

EASTERN TROPHY TAILWATERS LOCATOR MAP

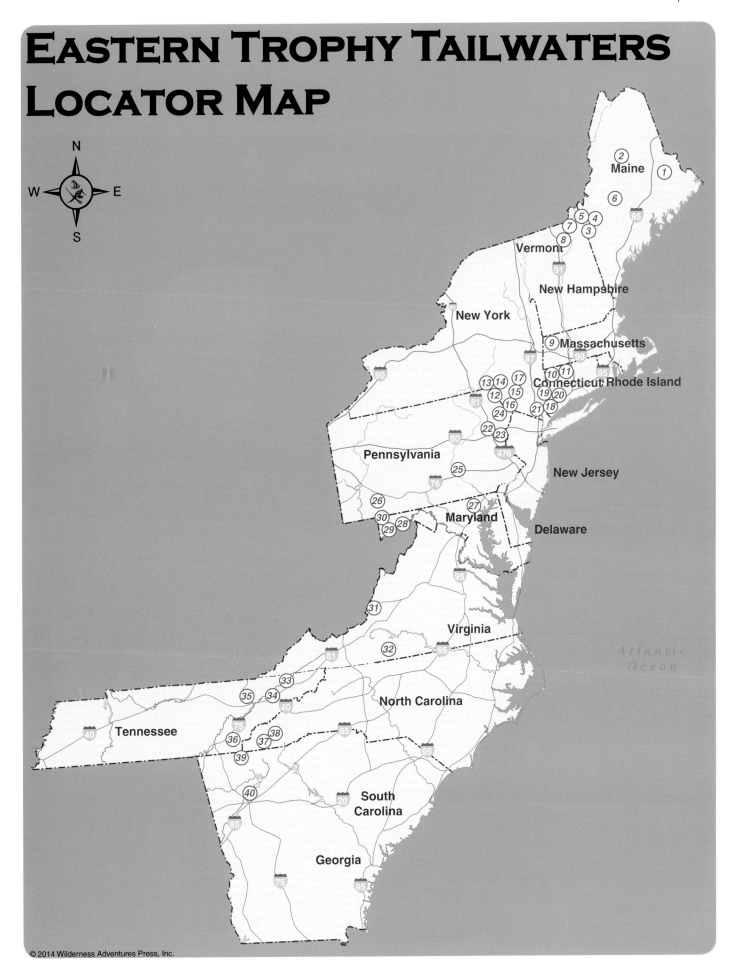

© 2014 Wilderness Adventures Press, Inc.

The tailwaters of Maine and New Hampshire offer shots at landlocked salmon. Photo courtesy King Montgomery.

An Angler's Approach to Tailwater Trout
Anatomy of Tailwater Rivers

WHAT IS A TAILWATER?

For the purpose of this book, I'll define a tailwater as a section of river below a dam that releases water from deep in the reservoir, creating or enhancing a coldwater fishery. Depending on the depth of the release, the water temperatures can be in the 40-to 50-degree range. Tailwater release temperatures are very constant year round, which means the fish have a 12-month growing season. Growth rates can be phenomenal, with some trout experiencing growth rates of up to one inch per month. Some anglers liken tailwaters to spring creeks, and it's a good comparison – tailwaters are in many ways man-made and controlled, simulated spring creeks.

Dams and tailwaters are invariably linked. Today, dams are built for two principal reasons: water detention and diversion. Water detention reservoirs store water either for electric power generation, flood control, or water supply. Water diversion reservoirs are used to send water in a different direction, usually for irrigation but occasionally for water supply.

ELECTRIC POWER-GENERATING RESERVOIRS

The East has more than its fair share of tailwaters, particularly in the Southeast. This is the result of a need to bring power to our expanding rural areas, especially in Virginia, Tennessee, North Carolina, and Georgia. In addition to delivering power to these rural areas, as a bi-product, the dams also brought some world-class trout fishing to the region.

Hydroelectric tailwater rivers are the most difficult and generally the most dangerous to fish. Hydroelectric dams need to release water to generate power. They usually run their generators during the daytime on weekdays, often in the afternoons to meet peak demand for power. Generation does not occur as often on weekends, when demand for power usually drops off. During power generation the flows are often increased dramatically, which is known as "bouncing". One hydroelectric tailwater I fish has daily summer flows of 30 cubic feet per second (cfs) in the morning, bouncing to 800cfs in the afternoon. It is critical for anglers to know a river's release schedule and also to know that officials don't always follow the schedule. Always be alert for rising water levels. On some rivers you need to know the release schedule to increase your fishing time and success rate. On others, knowing the release schedule is critical to your safety.

WATER SUPPLY RESERVOIRS

Water storage reservoirs which are used for water supply can be more consistent in their water releases than dams constructed for hydroelectric power generation. For trout, the ideal situation is to have stable flow rates. On some rivers, increased release flows can cool down the river. This can cut off a hatch and often shut down feeding until the trout acclimatize to the colder temperature. Yet on other rivers, an increased flow can increase food availability for the trout by washing scuds, sow bugs, and midge larva out of aquatic vegetation, triggering a feeding spree – this is when you have the best chance of hooking a monster trout. Conversely, a decrease in release can raise water temperatures and trigger a hatch and feeding spree or shut it down. Like tides in the ocean, there is no one-size-fits-all when it comes to the best flows for fishing. It is advisable to check with local fly shops and outfitters to see what flow regimen produces the best fishing conditions.

FLOOD CONTROL DAMS

Flood control dams only need to release a great deal of water when a weather event is predicted so, during normal weather patterns, they can have release regimen which are more regular and stable – ideal for trout growth and angling.

TAILWATER FLOWS AND RELEASE SCHEDULES

A river's flow or volume, as mentioned, is measured in cubic feet per second (cfs). Because of variables like a river's depth, width, and gradient, you can't compare one river's cfs to that of another. A discharge of 400cfs on one river might be a very low flow and on another river 400cfs might result in a flood stage. The United States Geologic Survey (USGS) provides current information from stream gauging stations for most tailwaters. In addition to cfs, the

USGS often provides water temperature and the height of the river at the gauging station. It also provides historical data which is especially helpful in understanding the stage or height of a river compared to its historical norm. Most tailwaters have toll-free numbers which provide taped recordings giving the release schedule, and websites which show the predicted release schedule. Check power generation schedules in advance; as noted earlier, normal schedules are not always adhered to.

SAFETY

Every season we lose anglers to wading accidents and, unfortunately, tailwaters have a disproportionate amount of these accidents. I use extreme caution when wading and I still have had several scares on tailwater rivers. A few years back, on my first visit to the Hiwassee River in southeastern Tennessee, my friend Joe Darcy and I really had to hustle close to 100 yards back to shore in rapidly rising water to avoid a bath – at best. We had fished in the morning on an upstream section of the river near the dam. We arrived about two hours before the scheduled release. Our plan was to fish close to shore until the flows began to rise and then to drive downstream to a section we were told it would take about three hours for the flows to reach. The first part of the plan worked pretty well. We were into fish almost immediately and easily waded to shore when the dam's warning alarm went off. As planned, we drove downstream to the next section of river, thinking we had a good three hours to fish before the rising water levels reached us. We waded out about 100 yards to the channel which was close to the far bank. Again we were into fish in short order and I was really focused on fooling the trout rising in front of me. I really hadn't taken the time to study my surroundings and didn't notice the water starting to rise. Fortunately, Darcy had done what you must do when fishing a tailwater – when he got into casting position, he studied his surroundings. After a while, he noticed that a nearby rock which had been dry when he started fishing was now six inches under water. We really had to hustle back to shore as the river's flow rose quickly. Tailwater safety tips:

- Check power generation schedules in advance (but as noted earlier, they don't always stick to their schedules).
- Be aware of your surroundings – notice the water level on the rocks around you.
- Look for water turning murky or debris in the water, which can be an indication of rising water.
- If you are wearing waders, wear a wading belt around your waist.
- Wearing a floatation device is a good idea.
- Carry a whistle and flashlight.
- Use a wading staff.
- Wear studded wading boots.

TAILWATERS:
THE GOOD, THE BAD, AND THE UGLY

Historically, dams have taken a major toll on fish populations by blocking anadromous fish spawning migration runs. This is especially true for American shad and Atlantic salmon. Getting rid of such dams is something that, in my professional career and personal life, I have always supported and worked toward. Thirty years ago, if you told me that someday I would be writing a book extoling the virtues of fishing tailwaters below dams, I would have told you that day would be when hell freezes over. I grew up in the Philadelphia area and have fished the Delaware River for over 40 years. I worked as a volunteer to oppose the proposed Tocks Island Dam project just north of the Delaware Water Gap. The proposed dam has since been taken off the drawing board, leaving the main stem of the Delaware River from Hancock, New York 321 miles down to the mouth of the Delaware Bay as the longest free-flowing river in the East.

I had always loved fishing the river for smallmouth bass and shad. However, after dams were built in the mid-60s on the Delaware's two main tributaries - the East and West Branches - my preferred target species in the Delaware River became wild rainbow and brown trout which grow to massive sizes in the cool, nitrogen-rich tailwaters created by these two bottom-release dams. Tailwaters are a relatively new addition to our trout waters; they are the result of dam building, but with a new twist. Unlike older dams - many of which were built to provide power to mills and which spilled warm water over their tops - most of our newer dams have the ability to release cold water from the bottom or lower sections of the dam. Some of the best trout fishing we have in the East has been created by bottom-release dams, which give the river downstream a strong shot of very cold water. Many of the modern bottom-release dams have release gates at different water levels, or they have mixing towers so they can release water at different levels to provide optimum water temperatures for trout. Tailwater rivers have many of the same characteristics as our limestone spring creeks, except they are managed by humans, not Mother Nature. Tailwater releases tend to be rich in nutrients from all the organic materials which flow into the reservoirs and find their way to the bottom. These nutrients are the major food source for the aquatic insects which thrive in tailwater conditions and are the forage base for the trout, promoting phenomenal growth rates.

Tailwater temperatures are relatively consistent even on the hottest and coldest days of the year. Because tailwaters generally do not get ravaged by floods like our freestone streams, their insect life is more abundant. I emphasize more abundant, not more diverse. Studies by aquatic biologists on tailwater streams and rivers show that, due to the cold flows, fewer species of insects can survive close to the dam, but due to the nutrient-richness of the releases, tailwaters produce weed-rich river floors and promote a high biomass of aquatic insects for trout to feed on. As you move downstream from the dams, the diversity of insect life increases and it can be as diverse as or even more diverse than in our freestone streams. Author and entomologist, Al Caucci, reports that the Delaware River and its two branches have almost all of the East's significant hatches. Caucci has authored numerous flyfishing articles and several books on aquatic insects, including his milestone work *Hatches*. He also developed the "Comparadun" fly series and is the former owner of the Delaware River Club. He was also one of the early pioneers of this great fishery starting in the early 1960s, and over the years he has discovered about 30 "super hatches" of mayflies in the system. His research and writing have benefited thousands of tailwater anglers.

As previously noted, year-round water temperatures don't vary much in tailwaters compared to freestone streams. The only exception is during periods when the reservoirs are "spilling". This happens when we have high water caused by heavy rains or big snow melt, causing reservoirs to fill and overflow the tops of their dams. Sometimes a little spilling will improve the fishing – this is especially true in the early spring when the releases are still very cold and the spill raises the water temperatures while often washing baitfish from the reservoir over the dam and into the river.

FREESTONE STREAMS

In the East, we have three types of trout streams. In addition to tailwaters, we have freestone streams and limestone spring creeks. The most common of these are freestone streams which – unlike limestone spring creeks, which largely rely on springs for their flows – are dependent on rain and runoff from their watersheds. Freestone streams have to overcome several obstacles if they are to remain viable trout waters. On most of our freestone streams, it is either feast or famine, particularly when it comes to water supply. Freestone streams suffer the most from the extremes of floods and droughts; both extremes can have a devastating impact on the insect life. There are often long periods of time when our freestone streams are not fishable due to either warm low-water or high-water or flood conditions.

LIMESTONE STREAMS

Limestone streams are the most reliable of our three types of streams. Their sources are limestone springs. Therefore they are less affected by runoff, as their watersheds are not as vast as freestone streams. They have higher alkaline or pH (alkaline) levels than freestone streams, making them better able to deal with the effects of acid rain. A higher pH also enables limestone streams to sustain tremendous levels of aquatic life. Underground springs keep their waters cooler in the summer and warmer in the winter than their freestone counterparts. Limestone streams rarely freeze and, in fact, I have caught trout on dry flies every month of the year on Pennsylvania's Little Lehigh River near Allentown.

Because water temperatures in limestone streams are very constant year round, they are very popular with the flyfishing community and they receive a lot of fishing pressure. Limestone streams as a general rule have a higher percentage of wild and holdover trout than large freestone streams. When you fish a limestone stream, you can be confident that the fish are educated, well-fed, and highly selective. Long leaders (12 feet and longer) with fine tippets of 6x to 8x will improve your success rate. I tend to fish the limestone streams more in the summer, when most of the larger freestone streams are beginning to warm. Most of the summer limestone spring creek hatches I encounter are smaller mayflies, usually sulphurs, olives, and tricos. In addition to these flies, I carry an assortment of midge patterns, dries and larva and pupa, as well as scuds, shrimp, sow bugs, and an assortment of terrestrials, especially ants – trout love ants. These patterns make up a large part of my tailwater selection, which will be covered in the next chapter.

Biology of Tailwater Rivers

TAILWATER TROUT

The family *Salmonidae* includes great fly rod game fish. In addition to salmon and several species of trout, it also includes chars and grayling. Only two species in the *Salmonidae* family are native to the eastern United States, brook trout and Atlantic salmon. The East also has two species of trout which were introduced and now reproduce in many of our tailwater rivers: brown trout introduced from Europe, and rainbow trout introduced from the West Coast of North America. In addition to landlocked salmon and brook, brown, and rainbow trout, also stocked in some of our eastern tailwaters are cutthroat, golden rainbow, and tiger trout.

BROOK TROUT *(SALVELINUS FONTINALIS)*

Brook trout are native to the eastern United States from Maine to Georgia. Often called "speckled trout" or "specs", the brook trout is not a true trout but rather a char. It is also the smallest of the region's salmonid species and the least tolerant of human encroachment in its watersheds – they need the cleanest and coldest water of our trout species. Brook trout are the aquatic version of the canaries in the coal mine. Miners used to take canaries into mine shafts to serve as a warning when the air was unfit to breathe – if the canary died, the miners knew it was time to get out of the mine shaft. Similarly, brook trout populations (or a lack thereof) serve as an indicator of the health of our watersheds.

In the 1880s, eastern brook trout averaged between 9 and 10 inches, 12- to 14-inch fish were not uncommon, and an occasional fish reached a length in excess of 20 inches and a weight of up to five pounds. By 1900, nearly all of our eastern primeval forests were logged, causing the warming and siltation of the region's trout streams. Logging combined with poor farming practices, dam building, and industrial discharges extirpated or greatly reduced brook trout populations in our rivers and streams. The final blow to our native brook trout came around the turn of the century when states and private fishing clubs started stocking German brown trout to supplement the declining brook trout populations. Brown trout grow larger and are more aggressive than brook trout, thus driving them out of prime habitats. Brook trout prefer colder water than brown trout, and for the most part, brook trout now exist only in our smaller headwater streams – the exception being in northern New England, where on some of the better rivers, anglers landing four-pound brook trout is a daily occurrence.

Recognizing the need to address a whole host of issues impacting native brook trout populations, a group of public and private entities formed the Eastern Brook Trout Joint Venture (EBTJV) to work cooperatively to halt the decline of this species. EBTJV is a fish habitat partnership operating under the National Fish Habitat Action Plan. The EBTJV coordinates efforts to improve native brook trout habitat. Seventeen states are working to prioritize policy changes and on-the-ground actions to improve water quality and restore brook trout habitat and populations using incentive-based and non-regulatory programs.

Brook trout can be distinguished from other trout by the white leading edge on their black and orange fins and also by their backs, which are olive with worm-like markings. They spawn in the fall, traveling upstream to headwaters. In these small streams, sexually mature fish may only be five or six inches long but in the tailwater rivers of northern New England three- and four-pound fish are not uncommon and five-pound fish still exist. Brook trout are relatively short-lived, with few fish living longer than five years.

LANDLOCKED SALMON *(SALMO SALAR)*

Landlocked salmon are the freshwater form of the sea-run Atlantic salmon. While they are a sub-species of the Atlantic salmon, there are no physical differences between the two salmon except that landlocked salmon do not get as big as their ocean-going counterparts, averaging 16- to 18-inches. Salar is Latin for "leaper." Landlocks have a tendency to go airborne, making several "electric leaps" when they feel the hook. In the United States they were originally found in just four Maine lake systems: Sebago, Green, Sebec, and Grand. Today, Maine hosts the largest sport fishery for the species in the world, with 44 rivers and streams supporting landlocked salmon.

Landlocked salmon are very silvery with a slightly forked tail and small dark x-shaped markings on their upper sides and backs. Mature males develop a "kype" or hooked jaw during the fall spawning season.

BROWN TROUT (SALMO TRUTTA)

Brown trout are native to northern Europe and were imported to this country from Scotland and Germany in the late 1800s. These trout are considered the most difficult trout to catch on a fly. They grow substantially bigger than all other salmonids. Larger browns feed in low-light conditions and many become nocturnal feeders, especially in the warmer months. They are more tolerant of high water temperatures, siltation, and pollution than brook and rainbow trout. Stocked browns hold over better than stocked brook and rainbow trout because of their ability to adapt to different conditions, and they are the most difficult to catch because they can be very selective feeders. They can be distinguished from other trout by their brown to dark tan backs and their white to yellow bellies. The spots on their backs and sides are black, orange, and red. The best way to distinguish them from brook trout is that brown trout have dark spots on a light background while brook trout have light spots on a dark background. Like brook trout, browns spawn in the fall and during that time, egg patterns can be very effective trout flies. Brown trout eat aquatic and terrestrial insects, crustaceans, fish, small mammals, salamanders and frogs. They can live up to 12 years and grow to tremendous sizes. Brown trout grow to be the largest of our tailwater trout – the world record brown weighed 40 pounds, 4 ounces and was landed in the Little Red River tailwater below Greer's Ferry in Arkansas in 1992.

RAINBOW TROUT (ONCORHYNCHUS MYKISS)

Rainbow trout are a western North American species, native to the Pacific slope from California to Alaska. Around the turn of the century, rainbows – like browns – were introduced on the East Coast to supplement the declining brook trout populations. They spawn in the spring, and today they reproduce in all of the states covered in this book. However, on the Eastern Seaboard rainbow trout are not nearly as successful at reproducing as brown and brook trout. Their distinguishing marking is a pink or reddish lateral stripe running the length of the fish. They have dark green backs with scattered dark spots and silvery white bellies. Rainbows are a great fighting fish; they often provide spectacular aerial displays when hooked.

GOLDEN RAINBOW (ONCORHYNCHUS MYKISS)

Golden rainbow trout are not sterile hybrids – they are a color variation of rainbow trout whose origins are from West Virginia. They should not be confused with the golden trout from California and the Rockies. The first golden rainbow trout originated from a single rainbow trout, and was spawned in the fall of 1954 in West Virginia. This trout's body color was a chimera of golden and normally-pigmented tissue. "Chimera" is a term used to describe an organism, or part of one, with at least two genetically different tissues resulting from a mutation. When this fish was crossed with a normally-pigmented rainbow, the light-colored offspring were called palomino trout. It took selective breeding for several generations to result in the development of a true breeding golden rainbow trout. These trout are more brilliant than the palomino rainbow trout. Golden rainbow trout have a deep gold-orange or yellow body color, but with the red lateral strip so distinctive of rainbow trout. They prefer the same habitat as rainbow trout and because they are so easy to spot, they are a help to anglers in finding rainbows.

I was first made aware of the relationship by Maryland guide, Harold Harsh, on a float trip down the North Branch of the Potomac. Harold would spot a "banana fish" as the locals call them, and position our boat so we could drift nymphs towards it and, more times than not, we would hook up with a rainbow, although occasionally with a golden rainbow. In 1963, this fish strain was popularized as the West Virginia Centennial Golden Trout. Today they are stocked in Maryland, Pennsylvania, and West Virginia.

CUTTHROAT TROUT (ONCORHYNCHUS CLARKII)

Native to the Pacific Northwest and the Rocky Mountains, cutthroat trout are found in only one watershed covered in *Eastern Trophy Tailwaters,* the North Branch of the Potomac on the Maryland and West Virginia border. They are stocked in the North Branch by the state of Maryland, mostly as fingerlings. I have been fortunate enough to land them on several of my visits to the North Branch. They can be distinguished from all other trout species by the distinctive red "cutthroat" marking under their lower jaw. *Oncorhynchus* means "hooked nose", referring to the hook or "kype" which develops on the lower jaw of breeding males. *Clarkii* is named after William Clark of the Lewis and Clark Expedition to the Rockies. They are related to rainbow trout and it is not uncommon for them to interbreed with rainbows, producing a sterile hybrid called a "cut-bow". I have caught numerous cut-bows in the Yellowstone River watershed, but I am not aware of any being taken in the East.

TIGER TROUT (SALMO TRUTTA X SALVELINUS FONTINALIS)

Tiger trout are the sterile hybrid of a female brown trout's eggs that were fertilized by the sperm of a male brook trout. Their backs and sides have a dark maze of tiger-like vermiculations and their bellies are a yellowish-orange color. Due to their very aggressive nature and the fact that it is extremely rare for them to reproduce in the wild, several states use tiger trout to control "rough" fish populations. They combine the voraciousness of brown trout with a brook trout's willingness to eat a fly. While I have only landed a handful of tigers that I believe were hatchery-raised, I was impressed with their fighting ability. Because tiger trout do not reproduce, all of their energy goes toward feeding, enabling them to grow larger and faster than most trout.

HATCHES AND THEIR IMITATIONS

Most anglers start their dry fly careers chasing one of the large and famous hatches like Hendricksons, March browns, or green drakes. My first flyfishing mentor, Phil Wagner, was a Pennsylvania limestone stream junkie, and that is how he got me started in flyfishing in 1971 – diminutive flies, usually midges and long, gossamer leaders were the order of the day. The first flyfishing book I purchased was Ed Koch's pioneering work *Fishing the Midge*, published by Freshet Press in 1972. It was the first book devoted entirely to tying and fishing midges. Koch developed his patterns, skills, and techniques on many of Pennsylvania's famous limestone spring creeks, like Penns, Big Spring, Falling Springs, and the Letort, all of which harbor some of the country's wariest trout. With the help of Koch's book and Phil's guidance, my first few years of flyfishing were also spent on many of the same limestone streams that Koch fished.

The flies we fished in my formative years on Pennsylvania limestone spring creeks were midges, midges, and more midges – larva, pupa, and adults. Most of the patterns we fished were developed by Koch. We only strayed from midges during mayfly hatches, which on Pennsylvania's limestone spring creeks were on the small side. Sulphurs, blue-winged olives, and diminutive tricos were the main mayfly hatches we encountered. We rounded out our limestone fly boxes with scuds and terrestrials.

On my "home water" - the Little Lehigh in Allentown, Pennsylvania - midges produce dry fly action 12 months of the year. My roots prepared me well for my education and humbling experiences as a tailwater angler. Long leaders, gossamer tippets, and tiny flies are still the major part of my tool chest. Back then, having not had much experience with dry flies larger than size 18 – I considered fooling a trout on a large mayfly a greater challenge than on a midge – as the trout got a better look at any tying imperfections I made on my large dry flies, I soon learned that there is no greater challenge in trout fishing than targeting enormous trout on large tailwater rivers with minute flies and gossamer leaders. Tailwaters are where the trout separate the men from the boys.

My log shows that I have taken many tailwater trout on large dries like March browns, green drakes, and slate drakes – but almost always a good distance downstream from the tailwater release area. Tailwater releases are often in the 40- to 50-degree range, and insect diversity by tailwater dams is limited but increases as the water warms downstream from the dams. Hydroelectric dams have great irregularity in flows, which impacts the diversity of aquatic life. Midges, crane flies, and scuds are the dominant forage species close to hydroelectric dams as these species can tolerate greater fluctuations in flows than most aquatic insects. On some tailwaters, midges make up over fifty percent of aquatic life and a trout's diet. These tiny two-winged flies are part of the order *Diptera* of which there are over 3,500 species in North America. Midges have three to five broods a year, so they are available for trout all year long and provide the number one food source for trout from late fall into early spring.

To be a proficient tailwater angler, you need to recognize and have a range of fly patterns for each stage in a midge's life cycle. The larva stage of a midge's life cycle is often overlooked by anglers. Larva patterns can be fish killers, especially in the morning before any hatching activity begins. Larva bodies are long, thin, and uniform in shape, and deadly patterns can be made by simply wrapping thread or wire on a hook and twisting a second thread tied as a ribbing to give the body a segmented look. Larva look even more realistic when tied on a curved hook. A midge larva doesn't have much of a thorax, so I don't use a bead or other material up near the eye of the hook. Midge pupas on the other hand, are short and squat, as the adult's developing wings are in the pupa's thorax area. On most days, a midge pupa will out-fish midge larva and adult stages. The pupas are slow to emerge, making them available to trout for longer periods of time. My favorite midge pupa imitations are beadhead Zebra Midges and Pat Dorsey's Black Beauty. Dorsey puts a Spirit River Quick Silver bead on his Mercury Black Beauty to imitate a pupa's gas bubble. An emerging pupa can be identified as the wings become more and more prominent, and the wings should be tied into your flies. Rim Chung's RS2 and John Engler's DW-40 are good imitations of emerging midge pupa. When trout are feeding on emerging midge pupa in the surface film, anglers are often fooled into thinking they are taking the adult midge or dry fly. It is always a good idea to seine the water to see what insects are available to trout and what stage of their life cycle they are in before you select the flies you will fish. In most cases, an emerging midge pupa will out-fish an imitation of the adult midge. When in doubt, I'll fish an adult pattern with an emerger tied to the bend of the dry midge, with 12 to 18 inches of tippet. Adult midges are easy to imitate with a simple thread body and two turns of hackle. On most of my midge dry flies, I use a grizzly hackle but I'll also tie some with cream, tan, or black thread bodies and hackle. A Griffith's Gnat is an excellent midge dry fly imitation, and tied in larger sizes it represents a midge cluster. You will need to become the master of the minutiae to constantly succeed on tailwaters.

THE HATCHES

Knowledge of your region's hatches and a good selection of flies to match the naturals are very important tools in our sport. Below is a comprehensive hatch chart for the East Coast and suggested flies to match the naturals. Common names can vary from region to region, so I think it's important to also list scientific names so we know we are talking about the same insect. While I rigorously researched this chart, it would not have been complete or accurate without the review and editing of Greg Hoover and Ed Jaworowski, both excellent flyfishermen. Greg is a professor of entomology at Penn State University and Ed is the retired chair of the Classics Department at Villanova University in Pennsylvania where he taught Latin and Greek. Due to vast geographical differences and seasons, I did not put hatch dates on the master hatch chart. While hatch dates will vary from region to region, the order of the hatches will remain constant. (Note: The scientific names given were current at the time of this writing, but they do change from time to time.)

Massachusetts' Deerfield River is one of the best trout fisheries in the Northeast.

Master Hatch Chart for Eastern Tailwaters

Common Name (Scientific Name)	Fly Patterns	Hook Sizes
Early Black Stonefly	Black Elk Hair Caddis Dry	16-18
Taeniopteryx nivalis		
Early Brown Stonefly	Brown Bi-Visible Dry	14-16
Strophopteryx fasciata	Stimulator Dry	14-16
Little Black Caddis	Black Elk Hair Caddis	16-18
Chimarra atterrima		
Little Blue-winged Olive	Parachute Adams	16-18
Baetis tricaudatus	Parachute BWO	16-18
(Formerly *Baetis vagans*)		
Blue Quill	Blue Dun Dry	16-18
Paraleptophlebia adoptiva	Blue Quill Dry	16-18
Paraleptophlebia spp.	Blue Quill Nymph	16-18
Quill Gordon	Quill Gordon Dry	14
Epeorus pleuralis	Hare's Ear Wet	14
Hendrickson/Red Quill	Hendrickson Dry	14
Ephemerella subvaria	Red Quill Dry	14
Black Quill	Black Quill Dry	12-14
Leptophlebia cupida		
Tan Caddis	Elk Hair Caddis Dry	14-16
Hydropsyche spp.	Leonard Wright Caddis Dry	14-16
***March Brown**	March Brown Dry	12
Maccaffertium vicarium	Gray Fox Dry	12-14
(formerly *Stenonema vicarium*)	March Brown Wet	12
Blue-winged Olive	Blue-winged Olive Dry	14
Drunella cornuta		
(formerly *Ephemerella cornuta*)		
Pale Evening Dun	Pale Evening Dun Dry	14-16
Ephemerella invaria	Sulphur Spinner	14-16
Grannom	Brown Elk Hair Caddis	12-14
Brachycentrus fuliginosus.	Wright's Fluttering Caddis	12-14
	Sparkle Pupa	12-14
Apple Green Caddis	Wright's Fluttering Caddis	14-16
Brachycentrus appalachia	Sparkle Pupa	14-16
Great Brown Stonefly	Stimulator Dry	8-10
Acroneuria lycorias	Golden Stone fly Nymph	8-10
Light Cahill	Light Cahill Dry	12
Stenacron interpunctatum	Light Cahill Wet	12
(formerly *Stenonema canadense*)		
(formerly *Stenonema interpunctatum*)		
Sulphur	Pale Evening Dun Dry	16-18
Ephemerella dorothea	Pale Evening Dun Spinner	16-18
Pink Lady	Pale Evening Dun Dry	14
Epeorus vitreus	Pale Evening Dun Spinner	14
Green Drake	Green Drake Dry	8-10
Ephemera guttulata	Coffin Fly Spinner	8-10
Brown Drake	Brown Wulff Dry	12-14
Ephemera simulans		

Slate Drake	Slate Drake Dry	10-12
Isonychia bicolor	Adams Dry	10-12
Isonychia sadleri & harperi	Gray Wulff	10-12
	Leadwing Coachman Wet	10-12
Little Yellow Sally	Yellow Elk Hair Caddis Dry	14-16
Isoperla bilineata	Stimulator Dry	14-16
Tiny Blue-winged Olive	Parachute Adams	20-24
Acentrella turbida	Parachute BWO	20-24
(formerly Pseudocloeon)		
Blue-winged Olive	Blue-winged Olive Dry	14-18
Attenella attenuata		
(formerly Ephemerella attenuata)		
Yellow Drake	Yellow Drake Dry	10-12
Ephemera varia		
Golden Drake	Golden Drake Dry	8-10
Anthopotamus distinctus		
(formerly Potamanthus distinctus		
Tricos	Trico Spinner Dry	22-26
Tricorythyodes allectus		
Tricorythyodes stygiatus		
White Fly	White Wulff Dry	12-14
Ephoron leukon		
Flying Ants	Flying Ant Dry	16-20
Ants	Parachute Ant Dry	16-20
	Black Wire Ant Wet	16-20
	Foam Ant Dry	14-20
Beetles	Foam Beetle	12
Grasshoppers	Dave's Hopper	10-12
Inchworms	Deer Hair Dry	12
Geometridae	Green Weenie Wet	12
October Caddis	Orange Stimulator Dry	10
Pycnopsyche ssp.	LaFontaine's Sparkle Pupa	10

Year-Round Aquatic Insects

Midges		
Chironomidae		
Adult midge	Griffith's Gnat Dry	18-22
Emerging midge pupas	RS 2	18-24
	DW-40	18-24
Midge pupa	Mercury Black Beauty	18-24
	B.H. Zebra Midge	18-24
Midge larva	Blood Midge Larva	18-22

Crustaceans

Scuds (Cress Bugs)	Dorsey's UV Scud	12-18
Mysis shrimp	Rodger's Freshwater Shrimp	12-16

*Stenonema fuscum (Gray Fox) is now considered the same species as *Maccaffertium vicarium,* formerly *Stenonema vicarium* (March Brown)

My Deadly Dozen Tailwater Flies

I currently have an assortment of over 100 different fly patterns, but I know that with about a dozen patterns in various sizes and colors, I can cover over 90 percent of my flyfishing situations. My favorite of these is the Adams – I have taken and continue to take more trout on an Adams or Parachute Adams than on any other dry fly pattern. Many years ago while fishing a remote stream in north-central Pennsylvania, I ran into a local flyfisherman. He was an elderly gentleman and he clearly was a no-frills angler. He wore hip boots, no vest, and had one fly box he kept in the pocket of his flannel shirt. I, on the other hand, looked like I had just walked out of Abercrombie and Fitch – new chest waders, wading staff, chest box, vest, and close to a dozen boxes of flies. As I walked past him he smiled and asked, "Any luck?" I had been fishing for several hours with no luck, but my pride got the best of me. "Just started", I replied, "How about you?" "Having a good day, the trout are looking up – they are keyed in on the early grays", he responded. At that time I had not heard of "the early grays" (quill Gordons, blue quills, and Hendricksons) so I asked him what fly he was using and he replied, "Quill Adams". He reached into his shirt, took out his fly box, and gave me several. He went on to say that he only fished three dry flies: a Quill Adams, a yellow Adams, and an Adams – Adams (which is the standard gray-bodied Adams) in various sizes. Over the years, I've come to realize that over 50 percent of the time that trout are surface-feeding, these three flies in the appropriate sizes will work. The take-home message here is that if a fly of the right size, shape, and color is presented properly, it will usually produce trout. The Quill Adams in various sizes is a good pattern for the "early grays and olives", the yellow Adams can be very successful during sulphur and Cahill hatches, and the Adams – Adams works very well for various olives, dark caddis, and slate drakes. An Adams can be difficult to see in low-light conditions, especially on overcast or rainy days. There is a simple solution to this problem – fish a Parachute Adams with a visible post. On large tailwaters you want to fish the foam lines, as that is where the current is delivering the naturals. But the foam lines usually have white foam bubbles, making a standard white post Adams or Olive Parachute hard to see. The solution here is to tie some parachutes with brightly colored posts.

My second go-to dry fly is Leonard Wright Jr.'s Fluttering Caddis, although Al Troth's Elk Hair Caddis is a very close second and I am never on the water without both of them. Wright's Fluttering Caddis is a style of tying; it can be tied in various sizes and colors to match any adult caddis or stonefly. Wright's ground breaking work *Fishing the Dry Fly as a Living Insect,* published by E. P. Dutton & Co., Inc in 1972, rocked the flyfishing community by suggesting that dead drift dry fly fishing was not always dead right. And while he was a student of Frederic Halford – who is generally accepted as "the father of modern dry fly fishing" and was a proponent of long, drag-free floats – Wright's theory of movement of a dry fly was almost considered "heresy" by many dry fly purists at the time his book was published. In a trout stream we have aquatic insects, twigs, berries, leaves, evergreen needles, and other debris of the size and shape of trout food. Wright in his writings points out that trout have to distinguish between flotsam and aquatic insects, and he concluded that "movement helps trout distinguish between the wheat and the chaff".

Wright tied the Fluttering Caddis with an extremely thin, dubbed-fur body. This enabled him to tie in spade hackle fibers so that they would lie nearly parallel to the hook shank. He positioned them in small bunches along both sides of the hook shank and up over the top of it, producing a very realistic-looking caddis wing. He finished off the fly with a traditional hackle collar wrapped behind the eye of the hook. As to its floatability, Wright wrote, "The fly floated perfectly even after it had been twitched, for the wing itself, which was twice as long as the body, acted as the floatingest tail a fly ever had." I substitute mink guard hairs for the spade hackle down wing; it helps the fly ride higher, skitters better, and is more durable than the hackle fibers. When fishing the slower pools and runs, I clip the hackle collar flush on the bottom for a more realistic low-riding fly.

My third and final go-to dry fly is a Griffith's Gnat. This small, dark, high-floating fly produces well when small caddis, midges, and blue-winged olives are on the water. In larger sizes it is a good representation of a midge cluster, and can also serve as a good strike indicator or locator fly.

In addition to these three dry flies, I carry a large assortment of traditional Catskill-style "match-the-hatch" dry flies in various styles. Recently on tailwaters, I have been fishing more low-riding dry flies tied with Cul De Canard (CDC) feathers in addition to Al Caucci's Comparaduns and parachute-style dry flies. I find that these low-riding style dry flies out-perform traditional dry flies when fishing over selective tailwater trout, especially in pools and slower-moving runs. Traditional Catskill-style dry flies still have a place in my fly boxes and in my heart. I fish them in moving water with good success.

Fishing wet flies is a lost art. It doesn't have the cachet that dry fly fishing does, but it does produce fish! Wet flies can imitate all of the stages of an insect's life cycle – a nymph, an emerger, a drowned adult or spinner, even

An angler plying the waters of the West Branch of the Delaware River at Hale Eddy on a hot July morning.

a terrestrial. When I'm fishing a good-size stream, if no trout are rising, I'll usually search the water with wet flies – I can cover more water with wets - and on most days they produce well enough that I don't need to switch to nymphs or dries. Even when trout start to rise, I generally stay with wets as they often work better at the beginning of a hatch than a dry fly. I fish the wet flies down and across the stream. When I see a trout rise, I cast my wet flies about three feet above the fish. As the fly approaches the fish I'll twitch it, and more times than not the twitch will trigger a solid strike. Always fish wet flies until they complete their swing to the surface at the end of a drift. Often, as the fly starts to rise toward the surface like an emerging insect I'll get a strike. My go-to wets are the soft-hackle patterns popularized by Sylvester Nemes in his book *The Soft-Hackled Fly*. My favorite soft-hackled pattern is the Partridge and Herl. It suggests many forms of insect life. I

find it a particularly effective searching pattern, and it can be deadly during caddis hatches. I tie these on sizes 14 and 16 heavy wire hooks. My other favorite wet fly is a black gnat tied with a crow fiber for the body with a fine wire rib and a starling hackle collar. I tie the starling and crow pattern on sizes 16 to 20 wet fly hooks. It is a good representation of early black caddis, midge pupa, and drowned terrestrials. I always fish two wet flies, the larger one on the point and the smaller one off a dropper on the leader.

Ninety percent of trout feeding takes place below the surface of the water and the majority of that time they will be feeding on mayfly and stonefly nymphs, caddis larva, pupa, aquatic worms, and crustaceans like scuds, sow bugs, and freshwater shrimp.

On freestone streams, my number one nymph is a Golden Stonefly. Unlike mayflies, stoneflies have two- or three-year life cycles, so there are always stonefly nymphs available to trout. However, stoneflies are not as dominant in our tailwaters, especially up near the dams where the predominant mayflies are blue-winged olives, sulphurs, and tricos so my number one tailwater nymph is Frank Sawyer's legendary Pheasant Tail in sizes 18 to 22. It is a good representation of most of our small mayfly nymphs.

Another must-have fly is a caddis pupa. Caddis have a three-stage life cycle: larva, pupa, and adult. I mentioned earlier that for the adult, I have a slight preference for Leonard Wright's Fluttering Caddis over Al Troth's Elk Hair Caddis, but they are both killer patterns. For sub-surface caddis fishing, I prefer the pupa over the larva as the pupa stage - when they are emerging - drifts for long distances, providing an easy meal for trout.

The most productive pupa pattern I have found is green, size 14 LaFontaine's Sparkle Pupa. The late Gary LaFontaine was the true master of caddis behavior and patterns and his definitive work, *Caddisflies,* occupies an important place in my flyfishing library.

Midges, midges, and more midges – as I mentioned earlier, North America has over 3,500 species of aquatic *Diptera,* more than mayflies, stoneflies, and caddis flies combined. Two families of *Diptera* are important to flyfishers: *Chironomidae* or midges and *Simuliidae* or black flies. In many tailwaters, especially near the dam, all three stages in a midge's life cycle - larva, pupa and adult - are the trout's most important food source, making up as much as 50 percent or more of a trout's diet. Midges have multi-broods – as many as five in a year - and they are available to trout 365 days a year. While all three periods of the life cycle are important to trout, the pupa is most important. My favorite midge pattern is Pat Dorsey's Mercury Black Beauty. It is a great imitation for a midge pupa, and the plain Black Beauty (tied without the glass bead) is a good imitation of the black fly larva. The silver-lined glass bead on midges of the Mercury Black Beauty imitates the gas bubble on the pupa as it emerges.

When midges are hatching, the pupa suspend themselves just below the surface film and drift long distances before emerging as adults. This gives trout an easy meal, but it is easy for the angler to think the trout are taking adults. During the adult's emergence I like to fish two flies, a heavily hackled Griffith's Gnat, which represents a midge cluster and can serve as the "indicator" fly, and a small pupa pattern tied to the bend of the Gnat's hook.

Midge larva are wormlike in shape and are generally found near the bottom of our tailwaters. They are available to trout in the greatest numbers when tailwater release flows are increased. This often knocks larva out of vegetation and can start a feeding frenzy. Midge larva are found in many colors, including red, olive, gray, and black, but the most common color is red. A red or "blood" midge larva is my choice for imitating the larva stage of a midge. My tie is simple: a body of red 70-denier UTC thread ribbed with the same thread, which I twist before I use it as a rib. I tie it on a size 18 to 22 curved shank hook to produce a more realistic look than a standard hook gives. As I mentioned earlier, my favorite adult midge pattern is a Griffith's Gnat dry.

Streamers! I love fishing streamers because of the jolting strikes they bring from trout. My top streamers are Marabou Muddlers in white, yellow, and black, both unweighted and cone head. If I could only fish one fly, it would have to be a Woolly Bugger with an olive body and black marabou tail and black hackle. It's a great searching pattern – it has produced well for me with both stocked and stream-bred trout. I tie it both unweighted and cone head, but more and more I am leaning toward weighted streamers. Weighted flies are always moving – when you strip line they rise up and when you pause, the weight of the fly makes it dive like a wounded minnow. Buggers can also be productive when fished dead drift as they can be taken for crayfish, leaches, and big stoneflies.

Well, that leaves me with one more fly in my "deadly dozen" – a terrestrial. It is hard to beat an ant – ants are trout candy! My favorite ant pattern is the McMurray Balsa Wood Ant in black and cinnamon, but sinking ant and flying ant patterns also have a place in my fly box. (Note: As we go to press, McMurray Ants were no longer commercially sold – a foam ant is a good substitute.) Small ants can be difficult to see at a distance. There are three things you can do to improve your ability to see your ant pattern. You can tie a small piece of white or red polypropylene on the back of the ant, put a small drop of brightly colored paint on the top of the ant body, or tie on a second, more visible dry fly a short distance above the ant as a strike indicator.

My deadly dozen have served me well on tailwaters from Maine to Georgia, but there are many regional patterns that will out-produce my deadly dozen on the region's local streams. For example, the South Holston has a great sulphur hatch that runs from late April into November and I would not fish the South Holston without CDC, Comparadun, or Puff Daddy sulphur patterns. These are discussed in the section on Tennessee's South Holston. By the same token, it would be a crime to fish the Rangeley area of Maine without tossing a few of Carrie Stevens' Gray Ghost or Herbie Welsh's Black Ghost streamer patterns which are described in the chapter on Maine under the section on Maine's Upper Dam.

TIMING AND FISHING THE HATCH

In addition to knowing hatch dates, you also need to know the time of day the hatch starts. You will have better success if you fish the beginning of the hatch. As the hatch progresses, the fish get more and more selective. With hatches that go on for several weeks, like the tricos, the trout can get super-selective and they can become next to impossible to catch. It is important to plan your trip near the start of the hatch date. In addition to fishing near the beginning of the hatch start date, you want to fish each day as the hatch starts because, as the hatch progresses during the day, the trout will have more naturals to feed on and they will get more selective. In the early season, most hatches occur mid-day when the water warms up to 50-plus degrees. For example, quill Gordons and blue quills begin hatching around noon, and they continue for about three hours.

Several years back I fished a blue quill hatch on Kettle Creek in north-central Pennsylvania. The first day I didn't arrive on the water until 2:00pm and the hatch was in full swing. I fished several pools which were loaded with rising trout – all but a few refused my offerings. The next day I was on the water at 11:00am and the first trout rose about noon, as the hatch was starting. During the first hour of the hatch, the first eleven fish I cast to readily took my fly, and most of them came to the net. Over the next few hours only a handful of fish took my fly – they had gotten re-educated to the naturals and become much more selective.

By late May and throughout the summer, most hatches are either very early in the morning or late in the evening, when many anglers are having breakfast or dinner. If you want to catch fish at this time of the year, you need to arrive early and/or stay late. When I fish the trico hatch, I like to arrive at first light and be the first angler to fish over each trout. For nearly two decades I fished the trico hatch on the Little Lehigh in Allentown, Pennsylvania. I would arrive at first light and fish downstream from the hatchery for about a half mile. This usually allowed me to be the first one to present my fly to every fish that was rising. When the action slowed, I'd walk back upstream past anglers who were complaining about the fish having lockjaw. Many of the "lockjaw" trout were the fish that I had hooked earlier.

Daylight Savings Time now begins in early March. The older hatch charts were made using Eastern Standard Time and therefore the hatches actually begin an hour later than most charts and books show.

FOUR SEASONS OF TAILWATERS

WINTER

While it is impossible to compare the seasons on tailwaters over the large geographic area covered in this book (Maine to Georgia), I can make a few generalizations which have helped me increase my seasonal success. While you can't fish Maine tailwaters in winter's subzero weather, North Carolina, Tennessee, and Georgia's tailwaters on the other hand offer excellent fishing all winter long. When the weather lets you get out and fish, winter fishing is going to be mostly nymphs and streamers. Winter streamer fishing can be especially productive during high-water periods, especially when water is "spilling" over the tops of dams, often sending baitfish over the dam to the tailwater trout. Most of your winter fishing will be sub-surface. However, several of our eastern tailwaters provide excellent winter dry fly fishing, especially with midges. As I write this, Don Butler who works and guides out of Upcountry Sportfishing on the banks of Connecticut's Farmington River, holds a record 83 months in a row of landing a trout on a dry fly in the Farmington River.

Blue-winged olives (*Baetis*) are the last mayflies to hatch in fall and the first to appear in the spring – on some tailwaters, olives hatch all winter. Olives are multi-brood insects and the most common mayflies on many of our tailwater rivers. In winter, your best bet is to fish during the warmest part of the day. Look for fish suspended in the water column – the fish on the bottoms of rivers are not looking to feed. If no trout are rising, drifting small midge larva, pupa, and mayfly nymphs to suspended fish is a good winter tactic. However, if you want to target trophy trout, fish big streamers deep with a sink-tip fly line. The biggest tailwater trout of the year are often taken on large streamers fished slow and deep in the winter.

SPRING

The first spring mayfly hatches after the blue-winged olives are the early grays, blue quills, quill Gordons and Hendricksons, but you won't find these up near the dams as the water is too cold for them to survive. Biologists' studies show time and again that tailwaters have less diversity of species but high biomass close to the dam. As you move downstream on tailwater, the diversity of bugs increases but the biomass often decreases. In the early spring, look for the early grays in the lower sections of the trout portion of tailwaters. Once you find them hatching, as with all of our eastern hatches, you can follow the hatch upstream as the water temperatures rise. As spring progresses, some of our largest mayflies - like March browns, light Cahills, and brown and green drakes - begin to show on the lower reaches on many of our tailwaters. While most anglers really get excited around drake time, my favorite late spring hatch is the March browns. Like the drakes, March browns are a big meal and can bring up some of the largest trout in a river. March browns, however, hatch over a longer period of time – weeks rather than days like the drakes. March brown hatches are very sporadic and can last for hours each day – I find that in these conditions the trout do not get as selective as they do on insects which have short-lived "blizzard hatches".

SUMMER

Most of the summer hatches on tailwater streams are the smaller mayflies, usually sulphurs, olives, and tricos. However, some tailwaters have excellent summer slate drake hatches. Every article or book I read about summer fishing talks about the importance of terrestrials, ants, inchworms, beetles, and hoppers – they are not just summer insects, especially ants. Look for them in spring, summer, and fall whenever the temperature is above freezing. My good friend, Ed Jaworowski, has been telling me this for years, but the message really sank in a few years ago when I fished Mud Run in early April. Mud Run is a wilderness trout stream in Hickory Run State Park in one of the coldest mountain regions in eastern Pennsylvania. As I sat on the back bumper of my car putting on my waders, a colony of large black ants swarmed all over me, and while that was an issue to deal with in itself, I decided to see if the trout would feed on them so early in the season. Streamside, I rigged a dry dropper combination with a floating ant as an indicator and a wet ant tied to the bend of the dry on two feet of tippet. Well, it was like stealing candy from a baby. One trout after another took the ants, most took the wet ant but several took the dry. You should have seen the looks I got when I responded to anglers asking, "What are you catching them on?"

FALL

Most anglers don't realize just how spectacular fall fishing can be all along the East Coast. The crowds are gone, the foliage makes for a beautiful backdrop, and the trout are on the feed to prepare for the long winter. The enormous October caddis hatches, often called the pumpkin caddis, can give anglers some of the best fishing of the year. Gary LaFontaine felt that this hatch is one of the top four aquatic insect hatches for giving flyfishers a shot at trophy trout. Tremendous blue-winged olives and slate drake hatches continue well into the fall. As an added bonus, brown and brook trout are wearing their beautiful fall spawning colors. Note: Egg patterns are very effective during the fall spawning season. Please be careful to avoid the trout's spawning redds. The only down-side of fall fishing is foul-hooking leaves that fall into the water. I try to time my fall fishing to before the leaves start falling or well after they are done.

A gorgeous Chattahoochee River wild brown trout.

READING THE WATER

Learning to read the water is critical to knowing where and how to present your fly so that it drifts into a trout's feeding lane. Reading the water is as important to an angler as reading a green is to a golfer. For trout to survive and grow to trophy size, it is critical for them to choose strategic locations – locations that offer protection from predators, relief from current, and access to a food supply. Trout often "stage" at seams where fast water and slow water come together. These areas can often be easily identified by white foam or bubble lines on the surface of the water. Often these seams are created by structure – rocks, tree roots, logs, and gravel bars. Because foam lines or bubble lines are generally white – I avoid using white posts on parachute flies and white strike indicators.

The best lies for trout are the ones that deliver both concentrations of food and shelter from predators. It is not uncommon for trout to have two lies, one that provides shelter from predators and one that delivers a good food supply. Shelter lies would include undercut banks, logs, under rocks, and at the bottom of very deep pools. Feeding lies are usually seams, runs, and riffles which deliver food. When sight-fishing to a large trout in a feeding lane, survey the water and identify potential obstacles the trout is likely to flee to in an effort to escape.

Plan how you will fight the fish to avoid these obstacles and where you will land the fish. All this before you even cast to it. I often find that when I first set the hook on a big trout, I usually have a few seconds before the fish realizes it is hooked, gathers its wits, and heads for its shelter lie in an attempt to break free. This is the time to aggressively play the fish. You should play big fish off the reel. However at the beginning of the fight, when a trout is disoriented, is the time to aggressively strip line to shorten the distance between you and the fish and lengthen the distance between the trout and its shelter lie. If you can get the trout to a safe distance from structure you can confidently play them off the reel. With a good and properly set drag, you can cushion sudden surges by the trout late in the fight. This is especially common when the fish sees the net.

RISE FORMS

The ability to read and interpret different types of rise forms trout make when feeding on or near the surface can dramatically improve your choice of flies and fishing success. While there are whole books devoted to the subject of rise forms and selectively feeding trout, for the purposes of this book I will highlight five of the most basic rise forms.

A sipping rise form indicates the trout are feeding in a leisurely manner. The insects the trout are targeting are not able to easily escape. The trout become slow and deliberate in their feeding motion. They slowly rise up to the surface and only slightly open their mouths to suck in the insect, leaving only a faint ring or rise form. A sipping rise form is the most difficult to detect, and even when detected, many anglers mistakenly think the diminutive ring was caused by a very small fish. Don't be fooled; some of my largest wild trout have been taken when they were sipping insects off the surface of the water. Sipping rises are usually caused by trout feeding on small duns, terrestrials, or spent-wing spinners which are floating in the surface film of the stream.

A head rise form is very easy to see and identify because you can actually see the trout's head as it breaks through the surface of the water to take in an insect. A head rise is a sure sign that the trout is feeding on a good-sized insect, usually a mayfly, which should be imitated by a dry-fly pattern.

Splashy rises are a sure sign the trout are chasing down their meal. This indicates that their prey is moving either very fast or erratically. This is usually a sign that they are feeding on caddis or stoneflies, but on a windy day they could also be chasing down mayflies being blown around. I find that when I see trout rising in this manner, twitching the fly as it approaches the trout often brings a solid strike. It's a good idea to fish a slightly stronger tippet when trout are feeding this aggressively so as to avoid break-offs during the hook set.

A dorsal and tail rise form is the most difficult to read and it can be the most frustrating to fish. Anglers see the surface of the water break and the resulting "feeding ring" and assume the trout is taking insects off the water's surface. From a distance, a dorsal and tail rise can be confused with a head rise. When trout are feeding in this fashion, you can throw every dry in your fly box at them without success. These trout are feeding on nymphs or emergers an inch or two below the surface or in the surface film, and it is their dorsal fin and tail which are breaking the surface, not their heads.

Boils or bulges are top-water disturbances without the surface being broken. These are caused when a trout is rising toward the surface to chase down an emerger and its body mass pushes water upwards, causing an upwelling near the surface.

One final word on rise forms. You should cast your fly upstream of a trout's feeding position, which is different than the location of the rise. When a trout sees an insect, it begins to rise up to inspect it and as it does, the insect and the trout are drifting downstream to a point where the trout either takes or rejects the insect. The trout then returns upstream to its feeding position. The drift can be very short in fast water and several feet or more in slow-moving pools.

Tailwater Tackle and Techniques

RODS

As I mentioned earlier, as a novice, the first flyfishing book I purchased was Ed Koch's *Fishing the Midge*. Koch was introduced to the "midge rod" by Carlisle rod maker Ed Shenk, and like Shenk, Koch became an instant disciple of the midge rod. I had the pleasure of meeting both Shenk and Koch on the banks of the Letort, and they both were fishing one-piece, 6-foot midge rods made by Shenk. The only rod I owned at the time was an 8-foot fiberglass rod. Shortly after meeting Koch and Shenk, I purchased a 6-foot glass rod. These two rods served me well for several years. I used the "midge rod" on Pennsylvania's limestone creeks and small freestone streams and the bigger rod on the region's larger freestone streams.

Once graphite rods came on the market, I really took a shine to them. They were a lot lighter than glass or bamboo and, because of their light weight, I started moving up in rod length until I got to 9 feet. I feel that longer rods have many advantages over shorter ones. Longer rods give you more control of your fly line when mending and dead-drift nymph fishing, and since trout feed sub-surface 90 percent of the time, I do a lot of nymphing. A longer rod means less line on the water, which helps reduce drag and, because of this, I recently purchased a 10-foot, 4-weight rod.

For a tailwater float trip I'll pack two rods, both 9-footers. The rod I'll use most frequently is a 9-foot, 4-weight rod with a weight-forward floating line for light-weight nymphs and dry flies. My back-up rod is a 9-foot, 6-weight for chucking big streamers and weighted nymphs with a weight forward floating line. I also carry a back-up reel with a 6-weight sink-tip line for dredging the bottom of deep runs and pools with streamers.

REELS

When I started flyfishing for trout, conventional wisdom was that fly reels were simply a tool for holding line. That is still largely true for the many of our eastern freestone streams, particularly our small mountain brook trout streams. But when fishing tailwaters, you always have the possibility of hooking a trophy trout, and you should fight big fish off the reel. You need a reel with a very smooth drag system, especially when fighting fish on light tippets. I also prefer an exposed spool on the reel so I have the option of adding additional pressure by palming the spool.

YOU NEVER FORGET YOUR FIRST

In early June of 1980, I joined a group of anglers from the Main Line Fly Tyers fishing club and headed up from Philadelphia, Pennsylvania to Roscoe, New York for a week of sampling the rivers of the Catskills' "charmed circle." It was on this trip that I took my first tailwater trout from the Delaware River on the evening of June 6 – and what a trout it was!

We had rented two cabins on the banks of the Willowemoc Creek behind the house and fly shop of legendary Catskill tyer, Harry Darbee. After having had good success on the Beaverkill and Willowemoc during the early part of the week, we decided one evening to drive over the mountain and fish the Delaware in the hope of landing a few of its big wild trout. Prior to that trip, the only fly reel I owned was a Pflueger Medalist model 1492, their smallest trout reel. It contained very little backing – backing that at that time had not seen the light of day. That spring, having read articles about the large wild Delaware River trout, I purchased a larger Pflueger Medalist reel and put 100 yards of backing on the spool. While it didn't have a smooth drag system, at least it had the capacity to store backing.

Notes from my flyfishing log indicate that we fished near a cemetery a few miles upstream from Kellams Bridge. I was joined by fishing partners and club members, Bill Ryan and Jim Ambridge. Upon arriving on the banks of the river, we hurriedly donned our waders and headed down to the river in eager anticipation of tackling some big stream-bred trout. Nothing happened during the first two hours. The river seemed devoid of life. We saw no insects and no fish. As the sun dipped below the hemlocks on the river's west bank, a few fish started to rise on the far side of the river, well out of our casting range. I tried to cross the river several times, but each time I found the water deeper than the top of my waders.

About an hour before dark, another angler came down to the river. After we exchanged pleasantries, I told him that a few trout had been rising along the opposite bank out of our casting range. He told me that he knew a safe route across the river and invited me to follow him. I took him up on his kind offer and followed him across. Upon reaching the west bank, I thanked him and suggested that he fish the head of the large pool where the trout were rising while I'd fish the tail of the pool, a good 200 feet or more downstream from him.

While there were a multitude of insects hatching, no fish were working in the tail of the pool. The sun was setting to the west below the evergreens behind me and dusk was fast approaching. After a while, I decided I had better start working my way back before it got too dark for me to safely wade across the river. As I started to reel in my line, I noticed a single rise not 30 feet in front of me. I paused and after a few moments the trout's feeding intensified. There was just enough light that I could see that it was a big fish, certainly bigger than any trout I had ever taken. The majority of the flies on the water were small sulphurs, but there were a few March browns. I couldn't tell what the trout was feeding on, but I knew at that time I didn't have the experience to land a trout of that size on the size 18 Sulphur Dun which was attached to my 6x tippet. I cut the fly off, cut my leader back to about 4x, and tied on a size 12 March Brown Dun. Ready with the stronger tippet and larger fly, I tried to time the fish's rises. It was difficult to wait, but I knew my best chance of getting this fish to take my fly would be on the first cast. With hands trembling and knees knocking, somehow my cast was right on target about three feet above the fish. As the fly drifted toward the trout, it stuck its nose up through the surface of the river and inhaled my fly. The moment I set the hook the trout was airborne. In what seemed like only a second the trout made three tarpon-like jumps and started racing downstream – taking me deep into my newly-installed fly line backing. The fish was using all of its power and that of the river's current to plow downstream.

I could hear Bill and Jim screaming encouragement from the far bank. What I didn't notice at that time was that the angler above me had started cursing as he waded back across the river. I stumbled awkwardly back out of the river to the bank and then started racing downstream after my trophy. After a few minutes, I had the fly line back on the reel and eventually worked the fish into the shallows. I had forgotten my net, but fortunately I was able to beach the fish on a wet gravel bar. The trout measured just under 20 inches, and as I turned to show Bill and Jim my trophy, I could see that they were being berated by the formerly friendly angler. He complained to them that he had come over to the Delaware River from Roscoe to get some solitude and we had taken his spot and his fish. Apparently, the fact that we had arrived two hours before him and that he had invited me to join him in crossing the river had been forgotten by the unhappy angler.

By then it was almost dark. I could barely see, and I had no idea where the crossing spot was. As I gingerly waded back across the river, the water started getting very close to the top of my waders, so I tightened my waist-belt and pushed forward. At about mid-stream, the water started seeping in over the top of my waders and I was being pushed downstream by the current. I was getting wet but

wasn't in any real danger – the water in this section of river wasn't more than chest-deep.

When I safely reached shore, I was greeted by my buddies with high fives and a cold beer. We toasted that great fish and the river, and then headed back to the cabin for some serious celebrating. Today that fish still stands as my largest wild rainbow trout from the Delaware River. (Note: If you keep a fishing log, moments like this will last a lifetime.) If I had been using a lighter tippet, I don't think I would have landed that fish because of my reel's awkward drag system. If you are going to target big fish, your reel's capacity for backing and its drag system are critical to success. Our tailwaters contain double-digit trout, and I am talking pounds, not inches. Consider the former world-record brown trout which weighed an astonishing 40 pounds, 4 ounces, landed on Arkansas's Little Red River tailwater below Greer's Ferry Dam. Now, I have never taken a 10-pound trout and the odds are I never will, but if I am lucky enough to hook one, I want to have the tackle which gives me the best chance of landing it. Never gear up for your average-size fish or all you will ever land is an average-size fish. Gear up for the fish of a lifetime and be prepared to land it if you are fortunate enough to hook it.

FLY LINE CARE

A clean, well-dressed fly line casts easier and farther, floats higher, and lasts longer. I clean my lines every few trips by soaking them in warm water with some mild dish soap and lightly wipe them with a cloth, rinse, and let dry. Once dry, I'll coat the lines with AgentX or Glide. In the off-season if I am not fishing, I'll store my lines on large-diameter spools made by Reel E Good Products, Inc. to minimize the coiling.

LEADERS

I have always been an advocate of fishing long leaders, especially when fishing dry flies. Fishing long leaders helps keep your fly line farther away from the trout, which minimizes your chances of spooking fish; and it is easier to get a long drag-free float with a longer leader. When you cast a fly, you don't want your leader to completely straighten out or you will immediately get drag. If you're fishing a 9-foot leader, your fly line might only be five or six feet from the fly. You will spook a lot of trout fishing dries on a short leader. When I started flyfishing, most commercial leaders came in two sizes, 7.5 and 9 feet. Wanting to fish longer leaders, I purchased a leader kit from Orvis and tied my own knotted leaders. Using Ed Koch's leader formulas, I was able to tie 10- and 12-foot leaders. I prefer to use knotless leaders, as hand-tied knotted leaders can accumulate weeds and other debris on their knots. Today you can purchase knotless leaders up to 15 feet in length. I'll carry an assortment of leaders ranging from 7.5 feet to 15 feet in sizes from 2x to 6x. The first thing I do when I open a new leader is add 24 inches of 3, 4, 5, 6, 7, or 8x tippet. This way when you change a fly you shorten your tippet section, not your leader, and tippet is much cheaper to replace than leader. You can carry an assortment of leaders in a leader wallet or a small zip-lock sandwich bag.

TIPPET – FLUOROCARBON VS. MONOFILAMENT

I ended my internal debates on fluorocarbon vs. monofilament during my research for my book *Tuna on the Fly*. Despite the fact that fluorocarbon is much more expensive than monofilament, commercial rod and reel tuna fishermen invest their money in fluorocarbon, feeling the return in terms of their harvest is worth the extra money. Fluorocarbon is nearly invisible to trout, it sinks slowly, thus minimizing the surface shadow, and I prefer to use it in nearly all situations. The fact that it sinks is a little bit of a handicap for dry fly fishing, especially with small dries. As I said, I prefer it in nearly all situations – the one exception is when fishing dry flies size 16 or smaller; then I'll fish with monofilament.

WADERS

When I started flyfishing, the only wader option we had was a "boot foot" wader. These were one-piece waders being sold by shoe size, not height or waist size. At that time I was thinner and, while my foot fit, my waders were twice as wide as I was. Being only five foot eight inches, the tops of the waders almost came up to my eyes. The boots were heavy, clunky, hot, and without the option of felt or studs on their soles – making it difficult to safely wade in. To improve traction, I would purchase golf rubbers with studs on the bottoms one size larger than my wading boot. After I placed the rubber securely over the wader boots, I would tape the mid-portion of the golf rubber around the boot so it would not come off. For many years this system served me well.

Today we have quite an assortment of wading options in quite a range of prices. For me, the best option is stocking foot waders, which come without a boot. This option enables you to get the wading pants and the boots separately, so you will be able to get the right fit in both the wader and boot. Today's wading shoes are comfortable, light-weight, and come with various option soles for added traction. They give you much better mobility and balance than boot foot waders. The pant portion of the wader allows you to get a pair of light-weight, breathable waders for comfort in the heat and neoprene waders for cold weather and coldwater wading.

If you are only going to purchase one pair of waders, I would recommend a lightweight, breathable type. You can layer your legs with long johns and fleece wading pants under your waders for coldwater wading. Due to the spread of invasive algae (see below), many states are banning the use of felt-sole wading shoes, which can easily transport algae from one watershed to another. I own two types of boot foot wading shoe: one pair with spikes or cleats which I use for all my wading, and a pair with "sticky rubber" soles, which I wear when fishing from a driftboat.

DIDYMO

Didymo, also known as rock snot, is an invasive algae that forms a mat and can cover long stretches of a stream's bottom. It can choke out many of the organisms that live on the stream bottom, thereby reducing the food supply for trout. There is no known way to control or eliminate didymo. It is easily spread by wading birds, ducks, anglers, kayakers, canoeists, tubers, boaters, and other water-based recreational activities. The microscopic algae can cling to waders and fishing tackle and remain viable for several weeks. Felt-sole boots, due to their ability to absorb didymo cells and stay damp for prolonged periods of time, are a major factor in spreading didymo. I strongly recommend the elimination of felt on waders. Many manufacturers are already doing so, and many states now ban the use of felts. It is important for anglers to take precautions against spreading didymo. The New York State Department of Environmental Conservation recommends soaking your equipment in a mixture of two percent bleach with water - that would be 13 ounces of bleach in five gallons of water.

WADING STAFFS

There are very few rivers and streams that I would now fish without a wading staff. Age, perhaps wisdom, knee replacement, and more than a few dunkings have made the wading staff an indispensable part of my fishing gear. A wading staff is like adding a third leg on the water – it greatly improves your balance. It can also be used to probe for rocks, holes, and other submerged obstacles, especially in discolored water. Like everything else in the flyfishing world, wading staffs are made with every conceivable material and for every budget. I started out in my younger days with a simple broomstick and a piece of clothes line to attach it to my wading belt. I later moved up to an old ski pole, and today I use a folding aluminum staff connected with a shock stretch cord. It fits into a holster when not in use and it attaches with a cord to my wading belt.

Vests, Chest Packs, Boat Bags

I strongly prefer a shorty vest, as it allows me to wade deeper without soaking my vest and everything that is in it. I fish with a combination of a vest and a small chest box. My vest is stuffed with everything I'll need for an extended fishing trip. It may be overkill and I may look like a pack mule, but I am never without what I need on the water. My vest check list includes:

Spare pair of polarized sunglasses – to cut sun glare, which enables you to see more fish and, more importantly, see the bottom for safer wading.

Waterproof, floating fly boxes. Believe me, they are worth the extra money to keep your flies dry when you drop the box or it falls out of your vest – or when you take a dive.

- Raingear – I never fish without having raingear in my vest.
- Light fleece – a must for tailwater anglers.
- Leaders.
- Tippets.
- Tippet threaders.
- Split Shot.
- Strike indicators.
- Forceps – (for releasing fish).
- Whistle – in case I get in trouble.
- Flashlight.
- Dry shake for CDC flies.
- Dry fly floatant.
- A BIG landing net.
- Nippers.
- Stream thermometer.
- Insect repellent.
- Sun screen.
- Water bottle.

Anglers often ask me why I wear a vest and a chest box. The answer is simple: for convenience and speed. Before every outing, I'll place in my chest box the tackle I will need for that day on the water. I generally use a four-tray box – the top two trays with dividers and the bottom two trays with foam inserts. In the top tray I'll place all the dry flies I plan to use for the day. In the second tray I'll place all the nymphs and wet flies I plan on using, plus a bunch of split shot and a few strike indicators. The foam inserts in the third tray hold my streamers. Finally, in the bottom tray

I place a few leaders, two tippet spools, and a few "tippet threaders" – a great aid for tying on small flies with my aging eyes. Finally, my fly floatant clips into a small holder on the outside of my chest box. Changing flies or rigs is simple and fast. Everything is right in front of me. Both hands are free to tie knots, and if I drop a fly, it usually falls right back into the chest box.

Boat Bags

If you fish tailwaters frequently, chances are you will be doing a fair amount of float trips. I spent years and a fair amount of money trying to get the perfect boat bag. You want one that is big enough to hold everything you will need for a day's fishing – remember, on a float trip there is no going back to the car to get something you forgot. But the bag can't be so big that the guide has to store it in some inaccessible location on the boat. I want my bag and everything that is in it at my fingertips. I currently have four boat bags, and it has been years since any of them have seen the light of day. I used to take everything out of my vest and stuff it into my boat bag – then, after the float, restock my vest – a lot of senseless work, and inevitably something got lost in the shuffle. If you are using a boat bag and you get out of the boat to wade, your "stuff" is back in the boat. Since everything I need is already in my vest and my chest box, I eliminate the middleman (a.k.a. the boat bag), wear my chest box, and place my vest over the back of my boat seat. Everything is at my fingertips, flies, tippet, split shot, etc., and in the same position whether I am floating or wading. No rummaging through a bag to get to fly boxes or tippet.

Bug Juice

Forgetting insect repellent can ruin a day's fishing. Mayflies are not the only insects that show up during the "evening hatch" – all types of biting insects come out to play, and you need to be prepared. On many occasions I have seen anglers leave rising trout because they were being "eaten alive". My insect repellent never leaves my vest. While there are many types and brands of repellent, I strongly recommend the roll-on type. They come in small containers, and you can pinpoint where you want to apply it. No creams to get on your hands, flies, and fly line. No spray going into your eyes, nose, and throat.

Landing Nets

Big landing nets are more important on tailwaters than

freestone streams, due to the size of the trout and the lighter tippets you will be fishing. I can't tell you how many stories I have heard or read about where fish were lost at the last minute because the angler didn't have a net or the net was too small. Why in god's name would you carry a net that is too small to land a potential trophy trout? Use a big net. No guide worth their salt would ever have a net too small to land a client's fish – why would you? The only reason I can think of for having a small net is to make your fish look bigger – not a good reason. I am partial to nets with clear rubber bags rather than the traditional "mesh" bag. Brodin's solid rubber "Ghost" net fits the bill nicely. It practically disappears in the water and therefore is less likely to spook trout than a mesh net. The rubber net bag gently cradles the fish, causing less harm than traditional nylon bags and the trout's gills will not get caught in the net (and neither will your hooks). In addition to successfully landing more fish, by using a net you don't have to handle fish or remove them from the water. Using a net also increases the likelihood that the fish will survive.

STRIKE INDICATORS

When I started flyfishing in 1971, strike indicators were virtually unknown. When they started to arrive on the market they were scorned by many seasoned anglers – it was like fishing with a bobber, not requiring the skill or "sixth sense" to detect the subtle take of a trout. Dead-drift nymphing without the aid of a strike indicator can take anglers months if not years to learn. I had so much trouble detecting delicate strikes while nymphing in my first few years of flyfishing that I decided one year – if trout were not rising I would only fish nymphs. I went a whole year without using wet flies or streamers – just nymphs (unless trout were rising to dry flies) in an effort to develop the nymphing "sixth sense". Back then conventional wisdom was to nymph with a short line and watch the leader/line connection for the subtle take. I tied my own knotted leaders and I would paint the knots red at the top of the leader for additional help in detecting strikes. It took years for me to develop that "sixth sense". I worked hard to become a "nympher" – having paid my dues when strike indicators were not on the market. When they did arrive on the scene, I didn't want to lower my standards and give in to using indicators. Since then I've done a 180-degree turnaround on the use of indicators. Fishing with strike indicators has greatly improved my effectiveness and success rate when nymphing. They allow you to detect subtle strikes which would otherwise go undetected, and they can enhance your control of the depth at which your nymph suspends in the water column.

I am overwhelmed at the number of strike indicators there are on the market. They are made of every conceivable type of floating material on the planet – plastic, putty, yarn, closed-cell foam, and balsa, to name a few. For such a simple concept – basically a bobber – how could the flyfishing community make something so simple into something so complicated? After all, we humans are supposedly at the top of the evolutionary ladder and all we are trying to do is outsmart an animal with the brain the size of a pea.

In advance of writing this section, I wanted to learn everything I could about strike indicators. So I turned to the man who walks, talks, eats, drinks, and dreams strike indicators, Steve Vorkapich, the founder and owner of Float Master Products. Vorkapich was gracious enough to grant me an interview and answered my many naive questions about "flyfishing with a bobber". I learned a great deal during my hour-long interview with Vorkapich – who must have the only honorary Ph.D. in strike indicators on the planet. Below I share a fraction of the wisdom I gleamed from Vorkapich (for more information, go to his website (www.floatmasterco.net).

Unsatisfied with the indicators on the market, Vorkapich developed his own indicators for personal use. They were so popular with his fishing buddies that he was making them for an ever-increasing army of "friends". Local tackle stores started to push him to make them commercially, and before he knew it he had his own business.

Indicators can and do spook fish, especially in the slower-moving, long, clear pools so frequently found on tailwaters. This can happen when the indicator splashes down on the water during the cast, or because of the flashy colors often used so that the angler can see the indicator. One solution to the color issue is to fish a white indicator, as our rivers are loaded with white bubbles and foam lines in the trout's feeding lanes. The problem with a white indicator fished in a foam line is that it is very hard for the angler to pick out the indicator from the foam line. Float Master products were the first I believe to develop a line of two-color indicators. The tops have visible colors like red, chartreuse, and yellow and the bottoms have more subtle colors like white for fishing a bubble line or a seam in relatively clear water, a gray bottom for overcast days, and a black bottom when there is a fair amount of debris in the water.

Before purchasing one, decide what you want in a strike indicator. For most situations, Float Master indicators work well for me; however, for nymphing slow pools I prefer yarn indicators. They can detect the slightest take, offer very little wind resistance, and make little or no disturbance when landing.

This is what I look for in a strike indicator:

- Ease in putting on and taking off the leader, even when the leaders are rigged with flies and weight.
- An indicator that won't slide up and down the leader when fishing.
- An indicator which lands softly so as to minimize spooking of fish.
- An indicator that won't leave kinks in the leader when removed.
- An indicator that lets you quickly adjust the depth in the water column.

To fish a nymph near the river's bottom, the distance between your fly and indicator should be about 1.5 times the depth of the water. Over the last few years I have been using strike indicators more and more, and they have enabled me to greatly increase my catch rate. This is particularly true when fish are taking small flies sub-surface, as a good indicator will detect the slightest take. Using an indicator also enables you to nymph with a long line.

WEIGHT

There are many ways to sink a fly. You can use flies which have weight wrapped on the hook shank before the body is tied. This can work well on large nymphs, but is problematic in smaller flies and especially with slim patterns like midge larva. Beadhead flies are very popular and effective, especially on smaller nymphs. You can also sink your fly by adding split shot or tungsten putty to your leader. When using split shot, I prefer several small shot spread out on the leader over one large shot to avoid the "hinge" effect while casting. I'll start with one or two small shot and add more if necessary. Lead putty is also a good option. It is easy to remove, you can determine just how much you want to use, and it is easier to adjust on leader than split shot.

RIGGING TANDEM FLIES

Fishing two (or more) flies has lots of advantages. In addition to doubling your chances for a hook-up, you can fish different stages in an insect's life cycle. Before a hatch, I'll often fish the nymph and emerger together. Once the hatch gets under way and I see surface activity, I'll often switch to a dry fly and emerger tandem rig.

DRY DROPPER

Often when fishing small nymphs, I'll suspend them under a larger dry fly rather than a strike indicator. I am surprised how often I have trout take the indicator dry fly over the nymph. After tying on the dry fly, I'll add 18 to 24 inches of tippet to the bend of the hook on the dry fly with a clinch or improved clinch knot and tie the nymph onto the tag end of the tippet.

I also find a dry dropper rig effective when fishing small dries, terrestrials, and spinners, which are hard to see. I follow the larger fly and if a fish rises within two feet of the larger fly, I'll set the hook. One deadly rig when fishing dry-fly midges, tricos, and ants is to use a large Griffith's Gnat as the indicator fly. They float well, are easy to see, and represent a cluster of midges. Tie the smaller fly off the hook bend on the gnat.

TRADITIONAL BRACE OF WET FLIES

During non-hatch periods which are frequent, I like to fish multiple-fly rigs. One of my favorite systems is the traditional brace of wet flies. I fish them down and across the current with an occasional twitch. Most takes are at the end of the drift as the flies start to swing up and appear to be emerging toward the surface. I don't see many anglers fishing with classic wet fly patterns in the traditional wet fly style, but it is still a deadly way to fish. The rigging I use for this type of fishing is to tie the heaviest wet fly on the point – the very end of my leader. I'll start with a 7.5- or 9-foot, 2x leader and extend it with two feet of 3x fluorocarbon tied on with either a blood knot or a surgeon's knot. I'll leave about six inches of the 2x tag to tie on the dropper wet. I have fished three wet flies this way, but it is generally not worth the extra tangles. When fishing streamers, I find I get better results by tying a small wet fly on the dropper and the bigger streamer on the point. I think the sight of a streamer "chasing" another critter can often be the trigger mechanism for a feeding trout.

TANDEM NYMPHS

When fishing close to tailwater dams, I'll often suspend two small nymphs under a strike indicator. Good combinations include midge larva and pupa, and Pheasant Tail nymph and a scud pattern. When I fish two nymphs, I'll tie the heavier nymph on first and then tie the lighter nymph on the heavier nymph's bend in the hook with 18 inches of tippet.

PRACTICE CATCH-AND-RELEASE

More and more anglers are practicing catch-and-release fishing, which certainly helps the resource and leaves more trout in our rivers and streams. A recent joint study by the Pennsylvania Fish and Boat Commission and Penn State

University indicated that Pennsylvania's trout anglers have both a high catch and a high release rate. A spring trout landing survey indicated that anglers averaged slightly over one trout per hour of fishing and 63 percent of those fish were released.

Do released trout survive? The short answer is yes! A study by scientists from Idaho State University and the U.S. Fish and Wildlife Service found the survival rate of released cutthroat trout on the Yellowstone River's catch-and-release section near Buffalo Ford was an astonishing 97 percent. During the study season they estimated that the average trout was caught 9.7 times. Admittedly this study was done on a flyfishing-only, catch-and-release section of the river. Many other studies have shown that fish caught and released on artificials have a better survival rate than fish caught and released by anglers using bait.

TIPS FOR SAFELY RELEASING TROUT

Most of my non-fishing friends and relatives don't understand why I release fish. It just doesn't make sense to them – I spend all that time and money to catch trout and then I release them. I finally have resorted to using Lefty Kreh's classic response: "Do golfers cook their golf balls after a game?" Here are some tips which should help you to release trout with an improved survival rate:

- The most important thing is to play the fish quickly so that it is not totally exhausted.
- Whenever possible, leave the fish in the water when removing hooks.
- Turning fish upside down when unhooking them often calms them and makes releasing them easier.
- Keep hand contact to a minimum and always wet your hands before you touch a fish.
- Don't fish when the water temperature is 68 degrees or higher, it will put too much stress on the fish.
- Have your hook-release tool handy (I use forceps).
- Fish barbless hooks or pinch the barbs down on your hooks.
- When you release a fish, point it into the current and wait for it to swim away.
- Use a landing net.

DOCUMENTING YOUR CATCH

With the increase in catch-and-release fishing, many anglers are carrying cameras to memorialize their catches. Photos usually result in more handling of fish and more time that the fish are out of the water. I believe that there is a higher mortality rate on fish that are photographed than those which are not, so please minimize the number of photos you take and plan them in advance. Several of the trout Internet sites that I browse have anglers who report catching a dozen trout and post photos of all 12. If you want to take quality photos and minimize the stress on the fish, you must plan ahead. The person who wants to take the photo should have the camera ready and the photo planned before the fish is landed. How many times have we seen others, or been guilty ourselves, of landing a fish and then deciding to take a photo? If you have to hunt through your vest, and then hand over your camera to a partner, and instruct them on how to use it, just don't take the shot. In these circumstances, you're most likely going to be disappointed with your photo, and you will have put the fish at risk.

I have been fortunate over the last 40 years to have Ed Jaworowski as a mentor and close friend. In addition to being a world-class fly caster, instructor, and outdoor writer, Ed is also a professional photographer. My den walls are filled with great shots of fish, courtesy of Ed's talent and generosity.

If you are not lucky enough to have your own "camera-man", plan the photos you want well in advance. Instruct your partner on how to use your camera before you begin fishing or better yet, have your partner use their own camera. As a general rule, I don't takes photos of a friend's fish with their camera, I use mine – I am familiar with the settings on my camera, it is always at the ready, and with the technology we have today it is simple to distribute the photos after a trip. When the fish is hooked, I'll plan the photo based on the location of the sun and the background I want in the photo. Today there are many excellent small water-proof cameras on the market, and I always carry one in my vest.

North Carolina's Nantahala River during a white water release.

While in grade school I took up fishing with a passion. My home stream was Philadelphia's Wissahickon Creek located in Fairmount Park. This is where I caught my first fish, a sunny, and my first trout, a brown. The Wissahickon flows through a beautiful section of Philadelphia's Fairmount Park. The park exists in large part due to the vision of the city forefathers and the generosity of the Houston family who donated much of the land to the city. My grandparents worked for the Houstons and lived in a cottage on the Houston estate overlooking the Wissahickon Valley, and I fished with my grandfather on almost every visit.

When I was in the sixth grade, I contracted whooping cough and was confined to my home for several months. My teacher went out of her way to send home assignments, puzzles, math problems, and science experiments to help fill the day and to keep me up with my class. Even with all the extra credit work I still had many idle hours.

In an effort to fill my day with more than school work, my parents purchased subscriptions to outdoor magazines for me. In the mornings and early afternoons before my home work was delivered to my door by a classmate who lived down the block, I would ply the pages of *Field and Stream*, *Outdoor Life*, and *Sports Afield*. I salivated over pictures of the cabins, lodges, canoes, campfires, and big

An angler landing landlocked salmon at the Dam Pool of Maine's Grand Lake Stream. Photo by King Montgomery.

trout at remote wilderness fishing destinations. Back then, the magazines had small ads which you could clip out, put your name and address on them, and mail them to various lodges, fish camps, and fishing guides for information. It wasn't long before the daily barrage of letters, brochures, and flyers from all over North America started arriving at our door – all addressed to Mr. Thomas J. Gilmore. Little did they know they were offering a grade school student the opportunity to buy land in Alaska, the Rockies, and the Great North Woods or to go on wilderness fishing adventures.

I spent many an hour daydreaming of someday traveling to one of these remote fishing destinations –

sitting around campfires, fishing from canoes, and catching wild trout, salmon, and bass.

When I turned 16, my parents let me buy a car – it was a 1946 Chevy coupe that my uncle sold to me for $125 dollars. The year was 1962. Once I had transportation, my best friend, Rich Calvanese, and I meticulously planned a week-long camping and fishing trip to the Hickory Run State Park in Pennsylvania's Pocono Mountains. Hickory Run has 15,500 wild acres and is surrounded by five state game lands. The park offers anglers a high quality fishing experience for native and stream-bred trout in a wilderness setting. We purchased a large camp tent, sleeping bags, and my first Coleman stove.

On the last Friday in June we packed the '46 Chevy with all of our camping and fishing gear and food supplies – which included a disproportionate amount of Coca-Cola and chocolate candy. Our plan was to rise early on Saturday and drive a hundred miles to Hickory Run, set up camp, and start a week of fishing. Neither of us got much sleep that night – we were off at first light on our "wilderness adventure". About half way through our journey, the car's engine erupted in a maze of smoke and developed a loud, continuous knocking noise. We limped along the Pennsylvania Turnpike to the next exit and turned into the first gas station – its patrons and the attendant who could hear and see us coming did not seem very sympathetic to our predicament. There was a mechanic on duty – remember when gas stations had mechanics? It didn't take him long to diagnose the problem and blurt out the grim news, "Well boys, you threw a rod – the engine is dead!" To say we were disappointed would be a gross understatement. My father, who had to pick us up with all of our gear, didn't seem to share our disappointment on the way back home.

It didn't take long for our next attempt at a wilderness adventure. By the next spring, Richey had purchased a used VW Beetle and we were again planning a trip. This trip was to be more ambitious and adventurous – a trip to Maine's north woods to Woodie Wheaton's Lodge, whose logo was, "Fishin Not Wishing at Wheaton's". This time the car made the trip. The Wheatons were great hosts, and the meals were out of this world. By day our guides got us into the best smallmouth fishing of our lives, plus trophy brook trout and landlocked salmon. During the mid-day breaks our guide would cook up a delicious shore lunch finished off by Mrs. Wheaton's freshly baked pies. There were many firsts on that trip – first moose sighting, first landlocked salmon, first brook trout over 15 inches, first smallmouth over 20 inches, and first shore lunch. I promised myself that none of these firsts would be my last. And I have kept that promise. I try to return to Maine every year and on a good year, I'll make both a spring and fall visit.

New England's tailwaters covered in this section not only give you the opportunity to fish for trophy rainbow and brown trout, but in the north woods of Maine and northern New Hampshire, you have the opportunity to target truly trophy-size native brook trout and landlocked salmon. Eleven New England tailwaters made the grade of four or more stars, qualifying them for inclusion in this book. Six are from Maine, three are in Connecticut, and one each from New Hampshire and Massachusetts.

Rick Steven with landlocked salmon on the Rapid River.

MAINE

MAINE STATE FACTS

State Abbreviation: ME
Area: 35,387 square miles – 39th largest in the U.S.
Population: 1,318,301
State Fish: Landlocked salmon

TROUT FISHING LICENSE

Maine Department of Inland Fisheries & Wildlife - www.mefishwildlife.com
Annual resident fee: $25.00
Annual non-resident fee: $64.00
Non-resident 15-day fee: $47.00
Non-resident 7- day fee: $43.00
Non-resident 3-day fee: $23.00
Non-resident 1-day fee: $11.00

STATE RECORDS

Landlocked salmon, 22 pounds, 8 ounces by Edward Blakely / 1907 / Sebago Lake

Brook trout, 9 pounds, 2 ounces by Patrick Coan / January 8, 2010 / Mousam Lake

Brown trout, 23 pounds, 8 ounces by Robert Hodsdon / March 3, 1996 / Square Pond

Rainbow trout 6 pounds, 8 ounces by Steve Day / June 5, 2007 / Androscoggin River

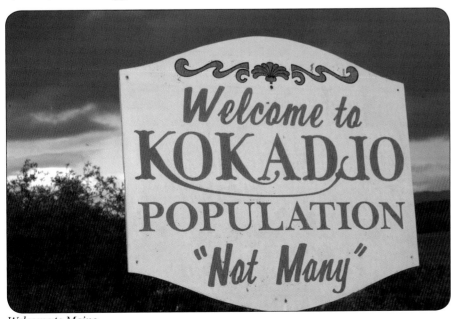

Welcome to Maine.

Maine has a rich history and tradition of welcoming outdoor enthusiasts, anglers, hunters, campers, hikers, and whitewater rafters. This tradition dates back to the mid-1800s when several private Maine sporting camps opened for the public's enjoyment. Today the tradition continues, as several of the original camps are still in operation and have been joined by newer, more modern facilities.

Many towns and villages in Maine's "Great North Woods" boast of having more moose than people. When I travel to the north woods I am always rejuvenated. It's so beautiful. Everything is unspoiled and natural – no parking meters, no red lights, no rush hour, just mile after mile of never-ending forests of spruce and pine sprinkled with hardwoods – aspens, birches, and maples, which turn the woods into a blaze of reds, yellows, and oranges every fall. Maine's north woods have 10 million uninhabited acres – that's 15,600 square miles without a single permanent resident, more unpopulated open space than any other state except Alaska.

The state fish is the landlocked salmon (*Salmo salar*). The silver leaper is one of two inland *Salmonidae* which are native to Maine. The other of course is the brook trout (*Salvelinus fontinalis*). Today, Maine supports one of the largest landlocked salmon sport fisheries in the world. Landlocked salmon are found in close to 300 lakes and 44 rivers and streams. Many of Maine's lakes were formed by Ice Age glaciers which scoured the land as they migrated toward the ocean. Post Ice Age, when the glaciers melted and retreated, the salmon became landlocked in deep, cold lakes which provided ideal habitat for them.

Maine also hosts the largest population of native brook trout in the United States. It is estimated that Maine supports 93 percent of the remaining wild brook trout in the continental United States. It also supports one of the best smallmouth bass fisheries in the nation. In this chapter, I cover six Maine tailwater rivers, and all but one earned my five-star rating.

GRAND LAKE STREAM

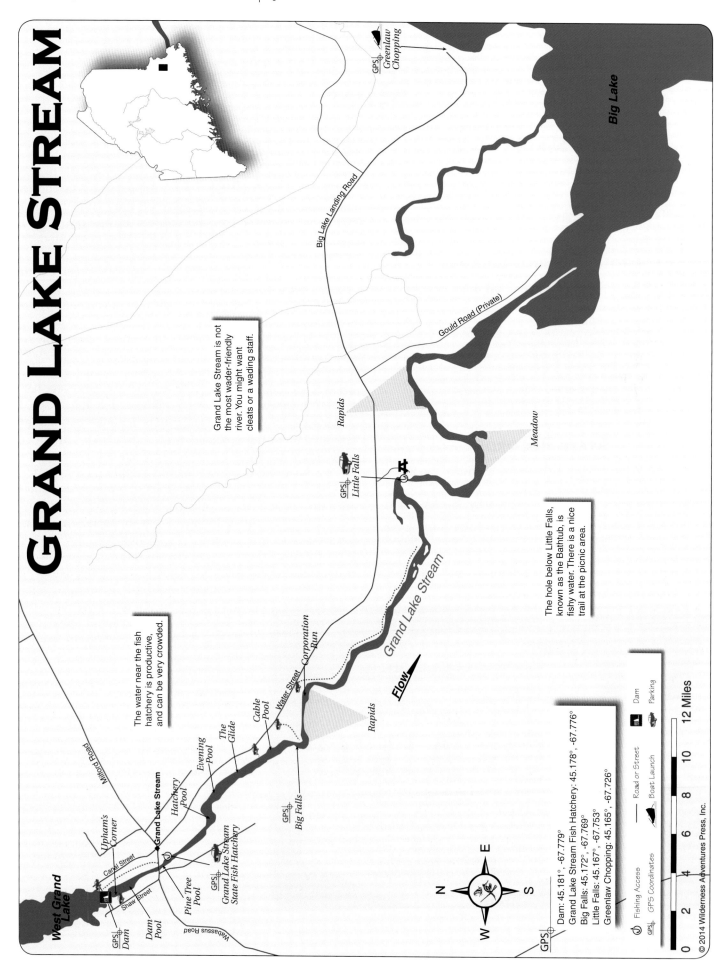

Grand Lake Stream is not the most wader-friendly river. You might want cleats or a wading staff.

The water near the fish hatchery is productive, and can be very crowded.

The hole below Little Falls, known as the Bathtub, is fishy water. There is a nice trail at the picnic area.

GPS| Greenlaw Chopping

Big Lake

Big Lake Landing Road

Gould Road (Private)

Meadow

Rapids

GPS| Little Falls

Little Falls

Grand Lake Stream

Flow

Rapids

Water Street

Corporation Run

Cable Pool

The Glide

Evening Pool

GPS| Big Falls

Hatchery Pool

Upham's Corner

Grand Lake Stream

Milford Road

Canal Street

Pine Tree Pool

GPS| Grand Lake Stream State Fish Hatchery

Shaw Street

Dam Pool

GPS| Dam

West Grand Lake

Wabassus Road

Dam: 45.181°, -67.779°
Grand Lake Stream Fish Hatchery: 45.178°, -67.776°
Big Falls: 45.172°, -67.769°
Little Falls: 45.167°, -67.753°
Greenlaw Chopping: 45.165°, -67.726°

N E S W

Fishing Access
GPS| GPS Coordinates
Road or Street
Boat Launch
Dam
Parking

0   2   4   6   8   10   12 Miles

© 2014 Wilderness Adventures Press, Inc.

GRAND LAKE STREAM (FIVE STARS)

In the 1850s and 60s, word of the great landlocked salmon fishing at Grand Lake Stream (GLS) began to spread. Back then, the only way to reach Grand Lake Stream was by boat. In 1855, William Gould built a boat landing on Big Lake at the mouth of Grand Lake Stream, and anglers started to come by boat to Grand Lake Stream to sample the landlocked salmon fishing. The anglers' only way to escape from the elements was to tent along the river. Gould built a makeshift wagon to carry their gear and supplies up the old tote road along Grand Lake Stream from Big Lake up to West Grand Lake. Every spring and fall, tent villages would be set up to accommodate the sportsmen.

In the late 1870s, a tannery was constructed in the Grand Lake area. By the 1880s, it employed over 150 men and was the life blood of the village of Grand Lake Stream. The tannery superintendent built a beautiful home overlooking the river. The townspeople nicknamed it the "White House". In March of 1898, the tannery – the very foundation of the village of Grand Lake Stream and its economy and the biggest employer of its residents – closed. By 1900, half of the town's residents had left to find employment elsewhere. What emerged was a new and now long-standing tradition for the area which continues today: hosting "sports" who come to the region to fish and hunt in the Great North Woods.

In an effort to enhance their experience, the Maine Legislature established a licensing fee ($1.00) for qualified guides. Fly Rod Crosby, a female guide from the Rangeley area, was the first to receive such a license. By the early 1900s, sports could take a train to Princeton, Maine and then continue 12 miles by stagecoach to Big Lake, cross Big Lake by boat, and take a buckboard from the landing to the White House for lodging. In the 1930s, the Weatherbys purchased the White House and opened Weatherby's Camp to host outdoor enthusiasts.

Grand Lake Stream has been fished by the likes of baseball super stars Ted Williams and Stan "The Man" Musial and United States Generals Jimmy Doolittle and Matthew Ridgway, as well as angling legends Curt Gowdy, A.J. McClane, and Joe Brooks.

Weatherby's is a large part of Maine's rich angling history. Today the newest Weatherby's owners, Jeff McEvoy and Beth Rankin, are writing the next chapter in its rich history. Before purchasing the camp, Jeff guided in the region for some 22 years. He apprenticed with head guide Woodie Wheaton during the 1980s on East Grand Lake in the Upper St. Croix watershed, learning the guiding profession in the Grand Lake tradition. McEvoy so loved the area that he and Rankin decided to purchase the camp. Weatherby's is continuing the great tradition of Maine

sporting camps and has an international reputation for its first-class experience. The history of Weatherby's, written by Arthur W. Wheaton, can be viewed on the camp's website (www.weatherbys.com). As mentioned, Arthur's father Woodie Wheaton guided in the region and later operated his own sporting camp in Forest City. I had the pleasure of fishing with Woodie in the late 1960s. He was the first guide I ever fished with, and his knowledge of the fishery and the ways of the North Woods set the bar high for my subsequent guides.

Today, getting to Grand Lake Stream is simple – it is an easy two-hour car ride northeast of Bangor. However, my first trip to Grand Lake Stream to sample some of its legendary landlocked salmon fishing turned into quite an unplanned adventure, thanks to a few moose and a GPS unit on crack. It started with a grim weather forecast of cold rain, heavy at times, for the next week to 10 days. My start was delayed a day due to a few last-minute business meetings. Since we had already rented the cabin on the American plan, I told my three fishing partners, Rick Steven, Joe DiBello, and Joe Darcy, to head up without me and I would drive up after my meetings.

I had originally planned to drive up with Darcy, so I started out a day late and a partner short on what was to be 12 hours of hell on wheels – hour after hour of torrential downpours with a few exciting thunder claps and lightning strikes thrown in for good measure. My eyes squinted to see the road and my hands were locked on the steering wheel in a death grip. About three hours from Grand Lake Stream, with a stiff back, a sore neck, and my eyes screaming for a break, I decided to stop at the next fast food place or gas station for a pit stop and a coffee break. I was traveling east on "Rural Route 9" – and rural it was! It might have been a very scenic drive with great mountain views if the torrential rains would have let up so that I could see more than my windshield wipers.

Because I originally didn't plan on driving, I didn't print out the directions from the lodge's website – which I later realized was a big mistake. I relied instead on my usually trusty GPS machine. I drove on for another hour on Route 9 without seeing so much as a hotdog stand when finally the cheerful "lady" inside my GPS unit said, "Left turn ahead." What a welcome relief – an intersection ahead, civilization, perhaps gas and coffee, I thought. The next command the nice lady gave me was, "Left turn in 400 yards." It was raining hard and I could not make out the intersection, and then she said, "Left turn in 200 yards." Still no intersection – then to my shock she said, "Left turn here." "Here" was a single-lane dirt logging road heading directly into a dense forest in the middle of nowhere – with no signage. While I

Grand Lake Stream is one of Maine's best landlocked salmon fisheries. Photo by King Montgomery.

had never been to Grand Lake Stream, I knew that many of the sporting camps were remote – accessible only by logging roads, boat, or float plane – I thought there should at least have been a sign. I nervously and cautiously crept down the road. After about a half mile there was a fork in the road and a sign indicating Grand Lake Stream was 24 miles to the right which was also what my GPS was saying – so I was on the right road, or at least a road that would eventually – hopefully – take me to Grand Lake Stream.

That sign was the last vestige of civilization I would see for the next two hours or so – but it was far from the last confusing fork in the road I would encounter that evening. If everything worked out right, I would get to camp just before dark and in time for dinner with my group. My biggest fear, other than getting lost, was getting a flat tire. This was a fate that had ruined a fishing trip earlier that spring on a long, lonely dirt road in the Pocono Mountains of Pennsylvania. So my tack was slow and steady – slow enough to avoid most potholes. During the drive I encountered no other *Homo sapiens* – only two curious moose who wandered out onto the road to see who was foolish enough to drive down this road in a little Subaru Forester. The road was maintained by a logging company that proudly posted signs every few miles stating, "Logging trucks have the right of way." Like they really needed to remind me to keep my Subaru out of the way of an oncoming logging truck!

After negotiating several more forks in the road while continually praying that the GPS would provide me with safe passage, I discovered my GPS was not my nemesis, when I noticed my tire air pressure light had come on. My GPS was showing seven long miles still to go. How bad was my tire? How far could I make it before it went flat? How long would it take me to walk to the lodge? How dark would it be when I arrived? Not liking any of my answers – without getting out of the car to check the tire, as I felt every second counted – I did my best Mario Andretti imitation and started driving as fast as the road would let me, the whole time looking at the miles remaining on my GPS, watching each tenth of a mile tick off – painfully slowly, but thinking that each tenth of a mile I drove would be one less I would have to walk. I love the backwoods of Maine, but that evening I was sure missing cell phone coverage, gas stations, and paved, well-lit roads with signage. With two miles to go I began to breathe a little easier as I knew I could walk to Grand Lake Stream and arrive just before dark – although without a change of clothes, supplies, and my fishing equipment. As I got to the one-mile mark, my optimism really kicked in – my glass went from half empty to half full. I was certain that the village of Grand Lake Stream would have a gas station and I could get air for what was left of my tire. A moment later, little Miss GPS said, "You have reached your destination." I left the dirt road, crossed the single-lane bridge over Grand Lake Stream, and turned right into the Pine Tree general store and gas station. I frantically looked for an air pump, but to no avail. I jumped out of the car and took a quick look at my tire, which was all but resting on the rim. I ran into the store, which had a line of anglers at the cash register waiting to pay for their takeout meals. Not wanting to be rude, I waited a few seconds but then blurted out, "I am sorry to interrupt, but my tire is almost flat – where is your air pump?"

"We don't have one," the clerk replied. "There's one at the fire station. When I am done with these customers, I'll draw you a map to get you there."

"Thank you," I replied, "but I don't have time for a bleeping map." (I didn't really say bleeping, but god I wanted to). "Is Weatherby's nearby?"

"Yes" the clerk replied, "two hundred yards up the hill and across the street."

"Thank you," I blurted out as I ran out the door and jumped into the car. As I turned the car around, I could feel the tire folding under the rim. I drove slowly up the hill and made a wide, slow turn into Weatherby's. I drove slowly past the main lodge where dozens of anglers and guides were walking along the driveway toward the lodge for dinner. I frantically looked for my friend's car and our cabin, but to no avail. In a panic to get my car and belongings in front of our cabin, I parked in the middle of the driveway – I didn't think the tire could make one more turn. I ran back to the lodge and interrupted discussions of the day's fishing. "Does anyone work here," I blurted out. As luck would have it, Frank Lepore, the lodge manager, was in the group. I hurriedly explained my predicament and he took over. "You're in the Upper Birth Cabin – let's get your car over there right now." Lepore, sensing I was in Stress City, said, "Relax, you're on vacation, go have a drink on me, your friends are fishing but will be back in about half an hour for dinner. Tomorrow is Sunday. You enjoy your fishing, and Monday I'll have your tire repaired or replaced." And he did. Monday, while I was catching landlocked salmon, lodge owner Jeff McEvoy removed my tire, found the leak, plugged it and took the tire to the firehouse to fill it up before placing it back on my car. I am from New Jersey, and you would be hard-pressed to find that kind of service in my neck of the woods – no pun intended. At Weatherby's it's the standard that they set.

Grand Lake Stream starts at the sluice gates of the dam on West Grand Lake and flows three-and-a-half miles down to Big Lake. Both lakes harbor landlocked salmon, lake trout, brook trout, and smallmouth bass. Anglers on Grand Lake Stream come there primarily for the salmon, although an occasional brook trout, lakers, and smallmouth are caught in the stream.

The most popular spot on the river is Dam Pool, also called Town Pool, just below the sluice gates on West Grand Lake. There is plenty of room in the pool on both sides of the river and on both sides of the island at the tail-out. Below the island, the stream turns into runs and riffles for several

Hub City

GRAND LAKE STREAM
Population: 109

ACCOMMODATIONS

Weatherby's, 3 Water Street / 207-796-5558 / 207-926-5598 / www.weatherbys.com
Leen's Lodge / 1-800-995-3367 / www.leenslodge.com
Indian Rock Camps / 207-796-2822 / www.indianrockcamps.com
Canal Side Camps / 207-796-2796 / www.canalside.cabins.com

FOOD AND SUPPLIES

The Pine Tree Store, 3 Water Street / 207-796-5027
Princeton Food Mart, Variety, 123 Main Street, Princeton / 207-796-2244 / www.mainefoodmarts.com

FLY SHOPS, GUIDES, AND SPORTING GOODS

The tiny hamlet of Grand Lake Stream has more camps and guides than anywhere in Maine. The Grand Lake Stream Guides Association's website has a complete listing of all guides in Grand Lake Stream / www.grandlakestreamguides.com
Weatherby's, 3 Water Street / 207-796-5558 / 207-926-5598 / www.weatherbys.com
The Pine Tree Store, 3 Water Street / 207-796-5027
Eddie's Flies and Tackle, 303 Broadway, Bangor / 207-947-1648

MEDICAL

Eastern Maine Medical Center (EMMC), 489 State Street, Bangor / 207-973-7000 / www.emmc.org

AIRPORT

Bangor International Airport, Geoffrey Boulevard / www.flybangor.com / Grand lake Stream is two hours from the Bangor Airport.

FOR MORE INFORMATION

Grand Lake Area Chamber of Commerce, 3 Water Street / www.grandlakestream.org

hundred yards to the bridge in town. "In town" consists of one retail outlet, the Pine Tree Store, a well-stocked general store and gas station (with no air pump), and about a dozen "fish camps".

Salmon move in and out of the two lakes, and quite frequently they stack up like cordwood in Dam Pool. Stable releases and crystal clear water give anglers the opportunity to sight-fish for large landlocked salmon. For the most part wading is easy, but I always carry a wading staff.

There is good access off Water Street, which follows the stream from the dam on West Grand Lake downstream to Big Lake. Plan to arrive on the water early to get prime fishing locations, especially for the pools in town: Dam Pool, Pine Tree Pool (behind the store), and Hatchery Pool behind the state hatchery. (Note: many of the anglers are staying at camps under the American Plan, which means they go back for dinner at prime fishing time. On more than one occasion I had the Dam Pool to myself during dinner time.) As the season progresses, the fish move upstream toward the dam. Fishing usually slows by mid-July through August because as the water warms, the salmon return to the cooler water in the deep lakes. Mid-September through the season closure on October 20 can provide excellent fishing, as the cooler weather brings the salmon back into the river on their spawning runs.

The season "officially" opens on April 1 and runs until October 20. But for all practical purposes, the salmon season begins in early May after the ice leaves the lakes and the landlocks follow their favorite forage fish, which is smelt, on their spawning runs into Grand Lake Stream. Not long after the smelt run, white suckers move into GLS to spawn and another wave of salmon follow, targeting the sucker spawn. The first reliable mayfly hatches are the Hendricksons around the middle to the end of May followed by March browns and sulphurs. Late May and June bring heavy caddis hatches followed by stoneflies and terrestrials.

I have the most success fishing nymphs. I would not be caught on this stream without a good supply of small, bright green caddis pupa. Popular streamers include Gray Ghost, Black Ghost, Nine-Three, and the Barnes Special in sizes 6-10. Small caddis dries work well when the fish are looking up. During the fall spawning run, the fish are more interested in spawning than eating – during the fall, small seems to be the ticket. Size 20 caddis pupa and size 20 Blue-winged Olives attract the most attention. Spring fishing is usually more reliable than fall, although if you time it right you can have exceptional fall days.

An angler fights a landlocked salmon. Photo by King Montgomery.

Stream Facts

Seasons/Regulations

Grand Lake Stream is flyfishing only, with a daily limit of one salmon of 14 inches or greater from April 1 to September 30. Then it is catch-and-release until the season closes on October 20. While the season opens April 1 (and runs until October 20), fishing doesn't really begin until early May when the ice leaves the lakes.

Fish

The target species are landlocked salmon. Maine Division of Inland Fisheries biologist, Greg Burr, rates Grand Lake Stream as one of the top landlocked salmon streams in the state of Maine. The others he mentioned were the West Branch of the Penobscot, the Roach, the East Outlet of Moosehead Lake, and the Rapid River. The landlocked salmon run 16 to 20 inches, and fish up to 24 inches are not uncommon. There is tremendous smallmouth bass fishing in the lakes.

River Characteristics

The river bottom for the most part is gravel, so for much of the stream (but not all) wading is relatively easy. The water from the dam is crystal clear, giving you the opportunity to sight-fish for large, landlocked salmon.

What the Experts Say

Jeff McEvoy, owner of Weatherby's, on the movement of salmon:

"Beginning mid-September, the salmon move from West Grand Lake downstream to Grand Lake Stream to spawn. Fish that drop into the river will spawn in late October/November and then drop downstream to Big Lake. Some will overwinter in the stream. Drawn by high flows and the spring smelt run, the salmon will move back upstream from Big Lake, filling the lower pools first - gradually moving up to the dam at West Grand. Fish will stay in the stream as long as conditions are suitable. If water temps stay cool, fish will hold and feed on insects. If it warms up, many of the fish will move to West Grand Lake for the summer."

History

Grand Lake Stream was fished by the likes of Stan "The Man" Musial, Joe Brooks, Curt Gowdy, A. J. McClane, Ted Williams, and Generals Jimmy Doolittle and Matthew Ridgway.

Tackle

A 9-foot, 5-weight outfit is perfect for this stream with a floating fly line. For streamer fishing, I prefer a 9-foot, 6-weight outfit with a sink tip line.

Directions to Weatherby's in Grand Lake Stream

From I-95/Maine Turnpike continue north past Bangor to Exit 217 in Lincoln. Take Route 6 east to Route 1 in Topsfield. Take Route 1 south (about 15 minutes). At the sign, turn right on the Grand Lake Stream Road. Go 10.5 miles to the camp on right, before you cross Grand Lake Stream. The Dam Pool and most of the stream is just a short walk from Weatherby's, which overlooks the section from the bridge in town upstream to the dam. There is good access to the pools below the town from Water Street. Weatherby's has an excellent map showing the trails and pools on Grand Lake Stream.

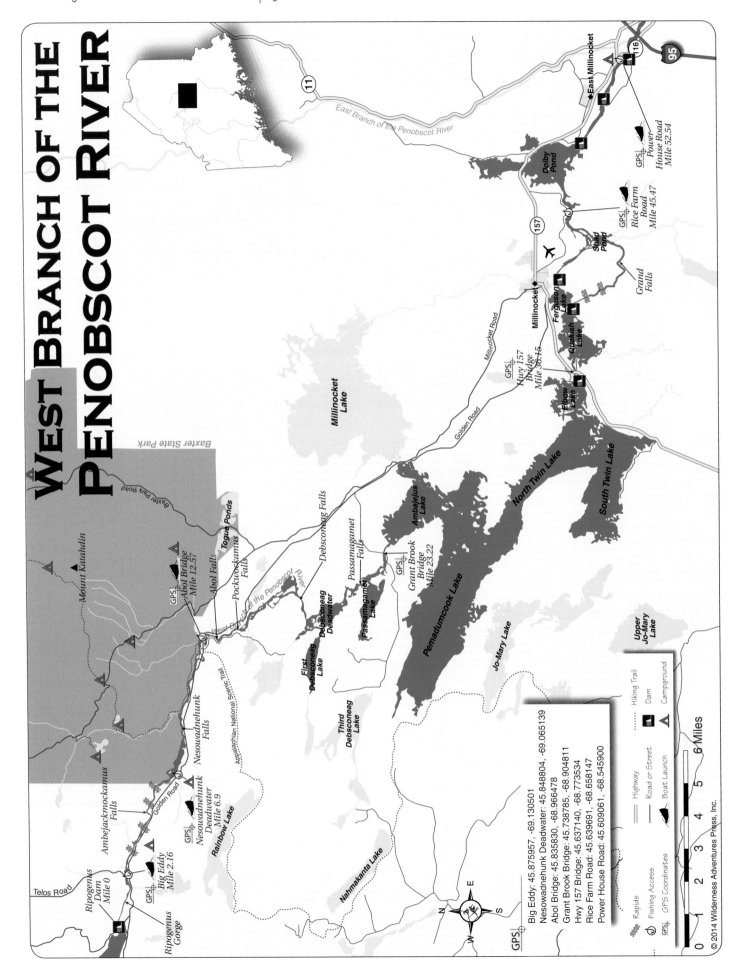

WEST BRANCH OF THE PENOBSCOT RIVER

© 2014 Wilderness Adventures Press, Inc.

GPS

Big Eddy: 45.875957, -69.130501
Nesowadnehunk Deadwater: 45.848804, -69.065139
Abol Bridge: 45.835830, -68.966478
Grant Brook Bridge: 45.738785, -68.904811
Hwy 157 Bridge: 45.637140, -68.773534
Rice Farm Road: 45.639691, -68.658147
Power House Road: 45.609061, -68.545900

Rapids
Fishing Access
GPS   GPS Coordinates

Highway
Road or Street
Boat Launch

Hiking Trail
Dam
Campground

0   1   2   3   4   5   6 Miles

West Branch of the Penobscot River (Five Stars)

With Mount Katahdin looming as the backdrop, the West Branch flows through Baxter State Park. It has to be the most scenic river and valley in Maine. Probably the greatest gift ever given to the state of Maine is Baxter State Park. Visionary Governor Percival Baxter purchased 201,000 acres of wilderness lands in central Maine and donated them to the state in 1931 on the condition that they remain "forever wild." The park offers plenty of camping opportunities for anglers who don't mind roughing it – Baxter has no paved roads, no amenities, and you must bring your own water. However the ponds and streams in the park offer some of the best brook trout fishing in the United States.

From Ripogenus Dam, the West Branch flows – or should I say roars its way - towards Millinocket. This is a deep, loud river, in many places more suited for whitewater rafting and kayaking than the tranquil pursuit of flyfishing. What draws anglers back time and again is the world-class flyfishing. The West Branch is considered to be one of the best landlocked salmon rivers in the United States, as well as a great brook trout fishery. There is good fishing from Ripogenus Dam downstream some 35 miles to Millinocket. From the dam to Abol Bridge is the best known and most heavily fished section of the river. Golden Road runs along the south shore of much of this stretch, providing easy access. The road was built and is maintained by logging interests – be alert for logging trucks (and moose) when you drive it.

The West Branch averages about 200 feet in width and offers some of the state's best dry-fly fishing. You need to be very careful where you wade, as many of the pools are over one's head – the locals refer to these as "hat floaters". There are wadeable sections – you should do some scouting or hire a guide before attempting to wade the West Branch.

The best way to reach and fish the most productive water is to fish from inflatable rafts customized for flyfishing. The best water to float varies with the seasonal movement of the fish and the forage, and the natural progression of hatches makes each trip unique. While you can bring your own raft or rent one, I strongly recommend you hire a guide for a float until you have learned the river. The biggest pool on the river, and perhaps in all of Maine, is Big Eddy. You could spend the better part of an entire day in a boat fishing Big Eddy and not cast to the same fish twice.

The season officially opens on April 1, but flyfishing doesn't get going until the smelt run, which starts right after ice-out. This usually is between May 1 and May 15, depending on the severity of the winter. Early season flyfishing is unpredictable – feast or famine – but early season streamer fishing can produce some of the biggest landlocked salmon of the season. The smelt run can last as long as three weeks – one of the longest and heaviest smelt runs in the state. Mayfly hatches start in late May and continue through June. Caddis hatches are common all season long and they can be of epic proportions. This river is a caddis factory, and a pair of green or olive soft hackle wet flies is usually all I'll need to get into action during a caddis hatch. Stonefly hatches also occur throughout the season, and they bring some of the river's biggest fish to the surface. When stoneflies are hatching, a big Gray Wulff or Stimulator will usually bring solid strikes.

I highly recommend a trip to the West Branch of the Penobscot to sample this world-class landlocked salmon fishery and to fish in the company of bald eagles, loons, and moose; all in the shadow of Mount Katahdin, Maine's highest mountain and the northern finish line for "through hikers" on the Appalachian Trail.

Big Eddy, shown here, is perhaps the biggest pool in Maine.

STREAM FACTS

Seasons/Regulations

The season opens on April 1, but doesn't get rolling until the smelt run shortly after ice-out in early to mid-May. The West Branch of the Penobscot River from Ripogenus Dam downstream to Telos Road Bridge is flyfishing-only from April 1 until September 30 with a one-fish limit – the fish has to be a minimum of 26 inches. From the Telos Road bridge downstream to Debsconeag Falls is artificial-lures-only from April 1 until August 15 with a one-fish limit. From August 16 until September 30 it is flyfishing-only with a one-fish limit – the fish must be at least 18 inches.

Spring

The good fishing starts with the annual spring smelt run. Streamers work well early in the season. Late May and early June start the first decent hatches of blue-winged olives and Hendricksons. I consider mid-May through mid-June prime time to tackle landlocked salmon on the West Branch.

Summer

The river is well-known for its epic caddis hatches, which last all summer and carry well into fall. Be sure to include caddis pupae and larvae in your fly box – green is particularly effective. During the caddis hatches, soft hackle wet flies are very effective. For dry flies, it is hard to go wrong with Elk Hair Caddis and Henryville Specials. Stonefly hatches occur throughout the season, and can often bring some of the river's biggest fish to the surface. Coldwater releases keep the West Branch fishable all summer, but the best landlocked salmon fishing is late spring and early fall.

Fall

Early fall can be good with terrestrials and streamers as well as occasional small dry-fly imitations of blue-winged olives, which are the most reliable fall mayflies on the West Branch.

Fish

The West Branch of the Penobscot is world famous for its landlocked salmon. With salmon averaging two pounds and four- to five-pounders occasionally caught, it certainly is one of the best landlocked salmon rivers in the United States. It also has a robust native brook trout population.

River Characteristics

The West Branch is a big, wide river with heavy flows – some sections are impossible to wade, but there are areas that are wadeable with care.

Tackle

I use a 9-foot, 5-weight outfit for nymphing and dry fly fishing. I use a 9-foot, 6-weight outfit to throw streamers on 150- to 200-grain sink tip lines.

Directions/Access

Golden Road runs along the south bank of the West Branch and provides easy access. A few good spots include where the Telos Road crosses the stream, and the area around Abol Bridge and Pray's Campground in the middle of Big Eddy. Big Eddy is the most famous and largest pool on the river and perhaps even in Maine. The town of Millinocket offers the shortest drive to fishable water on the West Branch. From Millinocket, follow signs for Baxter State Park to the sign for Big Moose Inn and Golden Road. The first spot you come to is Abol bridge (Abol Campground & Store), a good spot to start fishing.

Power canoes work well to boat upstream on the West Branch of the Penobscot River.

Hub Cities

MILLINOCKET

Population 4,506

ACCOMMODATIONS

Big Moose Inn, Cabins & Campground, Baxter State
  Park Road / 207-723-8391 / www.bigmoosecabins.com

Katahdin Inn & Suites, 740 Central Street / 207-723-4555
  / www.katahdininnandsuites.com

Katahdin Cabins, 169 Medway Road / 207-723-6305 /
  www.katahdincabins.com

Mountain View Drifter Lodge & Outfitters, Brownville
  Road / 207-723-5535 / www.mountainviewdrifter.com

Pray's Cabins & Country Store, 101 Morgan Lane /
  207-723-8880 / www.campstore.com

CAMPGROUNDS AND RV PARKS

Baxter State Park, 64 Balsam Drive / 207-723-5140 /
  www.baxterstateparkauthority.com

Abol Bridge Campground & Store, mile 18.5, Golden
  Road / www.abolcampground.com

RESTAURANTS

**Fredericka's Restaurant at Big Moose Inn, Cabins &
  Campground,** Baxter State Park Road / 207-723-8391 /
  www.bigmoosecabins.com

Appalachian Trail Cafe, 210 Penobscot Ave. /
  207-723-6720 / www.appalachiantraillodge.com

**New England Outdoor Center – River Drivers
  Restaurant,** 30 Twin Pines Road / 207-723-8475 /
  www.neoc.com

FLY SHOPS, GUIDES AND SPORTING GOODS

**Rick Theriault guides out of Mountain View Drifter
  Lodge & Outfitters,** Brownville Road / 207-723-5535 /
  www.mountainviewdrifter.com

AIRPORTS

Bangor International Airport, Geoffrey Boulevard /
  www.flybangor.com / Bangor International Airport is
  one hour and fifteen minutes from Millinocket.

MEDICAL

Millinocket Regional Hospital, 200 Somerset Street /
  207-723-5161

FOR MORE INFORMATION

Katahdin Area Chamber of Commerce, 1029 Central
  Street / 207-732-4443

Maine Chamber of Commerce / www.visitmaine.com /
  www.mainetourism.com

KOKADJO

Population "Not Many"

When I fish the West Branch of the Penobscot, I use the
tiny hamlet of Kokadjo as my base camp. I stay at Kokadjo
Camps. They have beautiful, modern cabins overlooking
First Roach Pond – the headwaters of the Roach River,
which is a tremendous landlocked salmon and brook
trout fishery. While small, the Roach is a major spawning
river for brook trout and landlocked salmon coming out
of Moosehead Lake. The headline on the camp's website
is "Where the Pavement Ends and the Moose Outnumber
the People". Kokadjo is about one hour and fifteen minutes
from the West Branch and twenty-five minutes from
Greenville. Kokadjo Camp is owned and operated by Fred
and Marie Candeloro. In addition to the cabins, the camp
has a restaurant, trading post, and gas station. When I asked
Fred and Marie about the official "Welcome to Kokadjo"
sign which reads, "Population Not Many," their explanation
went something like this: The sign once said "Population
3" (Fred, Marie, and a local guide). Then the guide got
married and they repainted the sign to read "Population 4."
Later the woman's elderly father moved in and the sign was
repainted again to say "Population 5." A few years later the
father passed away and it was again time to repaint the sign
– this time they changed it to "Population Not Many."

ACCOMMODATIONS

Kokadjo Camps, 3424 Lily Bay Road / 207-695-3993/
  www.kokadjo.com / Marie@Kokadjo.com

Northern Pride Lodge, on First Roach Pond /
  207-695-2890 / www.northernpridelodge.com

GREENVILLE

Population 1,646

ACCOMMODATIONS

Leisure Lake Resort, Motel and Restaurant /
800-726-2302 / www.leisurelakeresort.com

Moosehead Hills Cabins, 418 Lily Bay Road /
207-695-2514 / info@mooseheadhills.com

Wilson Pond Camps / 877-695-2860 / www.
wilsonpondcamps.com

CAMPGROUNDS

Lily Bay State Park, 13 Marie's Way / 207-695-2700

RESTAURANTS

The Black Frog Restaurant / 207-696-1100 /
www.theblackfrog.com / Lakefront dining on
Moosehead Lake. Good food, reasonable prices, casual
atmosphere and the funniest menu you will ever read.

Flatlanders Pub, Moosehead Lake, Pritham Ave. /
207-695-3373 / Causal dinning, great sandwiches and
the best lobster roll in the region.

Greenville Inn, 40 Norris Street / 207-695-2206 /
www.greenvilleinn.com

Rod-N-Reel Café, 44 Pritham Avenue / 207-695-0388 /
www.rodnreelcafe.com

GUIDES, FLY SHOPS, AND SPORTING GOODS

Maine Guide Fly Shop, 34 Moosehead Lake Road
/207-695-2266 / www.maineguideflyshop.com / Dan
Legere, owner and guide, is one of the few guides who
offers float trips on Ripogenus Gorge.

Penobscot Drift Boats, 364 Hudson Road, Glenburn
/ 207-947-5608 / www.penobscotdriftboats.com /
Ian Cameron also offers float trips on the Ripogenus
Gorge.

AIRPORTS

Bangor International Airport is two hours from
Greenville.

MEDICAL

Charles A. Dean Memorial Hospital, 15 Pritham Avenue
/ 207-695-5200 / www.cadean.org

FOR MORE INFORMATION

Moosehead Lake Chamber of Commerce /
www.mooseheadlake.org

Canoe fishermen on the West Branch of the Penobscot River.

Western Maine's Rangeley Lake Region

The Rangeley region has long been known as "the Land of the Giants" – giant brook trout – and while the number and size of the brook trout are down from their historic numbers of the late 1800s, brook trout of five pounds are taken every season. The village of Rangeley is named after James W. Rangeley, who purchased the township in the 1820s. The great fishing for giant brook trout around Rangeley remained pretty much a local secret until 1862, when a New York City businessman, George Shepard Page, returned from a trip to Rangeley with eight brook trout with a combined weight of 52 pounds – the largest weighed 8.75 pounds. Two years later he took home a 10-pound male and an 8.75-pound female brook trout. In 1867, Page returned with a friend – in ten days they landed 59 trout with a total weight of 293 pounds, an average of five pounds per trout. When the New York City papers got wind of Page's catches and published accounts of this great fishery, it wasn't long before Rangeley became known as "the Land of the Giants" and the brook trout capital of the world. As a result of this publicity, a new industry was born in the region: guiding and catering to fishermen. Large hotels and sporting camps were built as people flocked to the Rangeley Lakes Region to hunt and fish in and around the region's beautiful, pristine lakes and rivers. In the mid-1800s, getting to Rangeley required some effort – taking a train to the town of Phillips and then taking a stagecoach the last 15 miles to the town of Rangeley.

OVERHARVESTING

In the late 1890s, a direct rail line to Rangeley was built and the fishing boom went into full swing. Anglers flocked to the area's hotels and fish camps in great numbers. At that time it was common practice for anglers and guides to kill everything they caught. They would take their daily limit (which at the time was 50 pounds per person) back to the hotel or camps to show their mettle to the staff and the other guides and anglers. This large-scale harvesting of brook trout took a toll, and their numbers and size declined.

In the 1890s, landlocked salmon were introduced by the state to fill the void left by the decline of the giant brook trout. To this day the landlocked salmon are doing quite well, but their success was also at the expense of the brook trout. By the early 1900s, brook trout over five pounds were becoming rare. (Note: Prior to the salmon stockings, landlocked salmon were native to only four river basins in Maine: St. Croix, including West Grand Lake in Washington County; the Union, including Green Lake in Hancock County; the Penobscot, including Sebec Lake in Piscataquis County; and the Penobscot, including Sebago Lake in Cumberland County.) Today landlocked salmon provide good fisheries in 176 lakes and 44 rivers in Maine. Maine supports one of the largest sport fisheries for this species in the world.

DEMISE OF BLUEBACK TROUT

Another major factor in the decline of the "giants" was the disappearance of the "blueback trout" (*Salvelinus oquassa*), a small cousin of the brook trout. Historic records show that they inhabited Maine's lakes in staggering numbers – there were reports of schools of them being so thick you could practically walk across the water on their backs. They were reported to have disappeared in Maine by the early 1900s, although I have interviewed guides who claim they still exist in remote sections of the North Woods, and recently the state has been doing some limited experimental stocking of bluebacks .

Bluebacks spend most of their life in the deepest parts of coldwater lakes and were an important food source for the larger brook trout. The only time bluebacks left their deep water habitat was during their fall spawning runs, during which time they would fill the shallows and small tributaries in immense schools. During this time they were netted and even dynamited to feed lumber company crews. They were salted and smoked to tide the locals over the harsh Maine winters. With the decline of blueback trout, the state started stocking smelt to bolster the brook trout and salmon stocks. The salmon have done quite well foraging on the smelt. In the competition for food and spawning grounds, the brook trout lost out.

The town of Rangeley is located along the shores of Rangeley Lake – the surrounding North Woods area is 99 percent forested. Having spent a large part of my adult life within sight of the New York City skyline, it is always a pleasant change of scenery for me to visit the forests and lakes in the Rangeley region and a town without traffic lights, parking meters, honking cars, and rush-hour traffic. The Rangeley region still gives anglers a chance of landing a trophy brook trout. Three- and four-pound trout are not uncommon, and five-pounders are landed every year. Using Rangeley as your hub city, you can easily fish three trophy tailwaters: the Rapid River, the Upper Dam Pool, and the Magalloway River.

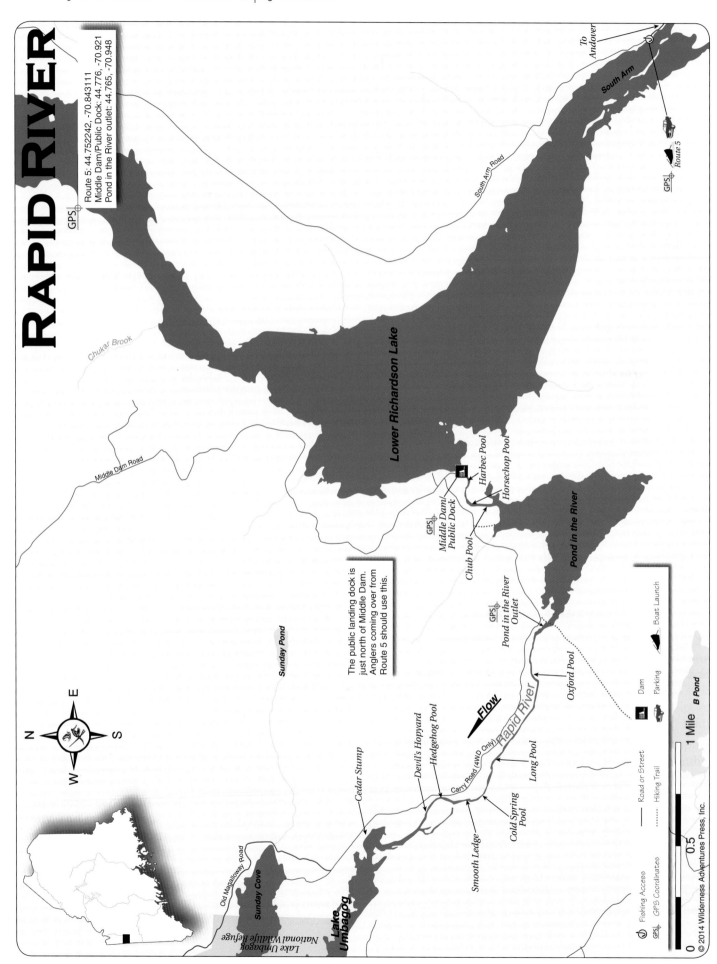

RAPID RIVER

Route 5: 44.752242, -70.843111
Middle Dam/Public Dock: 44.776, -70.921
Pond in the River outlet: 44.765, -70.948

Chukar Brook

Middle Dam Road

Lower Richardson Lake

South Arm Road

South Arm

To Andover

Route 5

Harbec Pool

Horsechop Pool

Middle Dam/
Public Dock

Chub Pool

Pond in the River

Pond in the River
Outlet

The public landing dock is
just north of Middle Dam.
Anglers coming over from
Route 5 should use this.

Sunday Pond

Oxford Pool

Rapid River

Flow

Long Pool

Carry Road (4WD Only)

Cold Spring
Pool

Smooth Ledge

Hedgehog Pool

Devil's Hopyard

Cedar Stump

Old Magalloway Road

Sunday Cove

Lake
Umbagog

Lake Umbagog
National Wildlife Refuge

B Pond

Dam

Parking

Boat Launch

Fishing Access

GPS Coordinates

Road or Street

Hiking Trail

0   0.5   1 Mile

© 2014 Wilderness Adventures Press, Inc.

RAPID RIVER (FOUR STARS)

The Rapid River provides the kind of fishing that serious trout and salmon anglers dream about – the Rapid is nothing short of spectacular. It is the most reliable and consistent trophy brook trout fishery in the lower 48 states. While five-pound brook trout have largely disappeared in the Northeast, the Rapid still produces them – not nearly in the numbers historically seen, but the Rapid still gives anglers a legitimate chance to land a true trophy brook trout. In the mid-1990s, the state of Maine implemented catch-and-release for brook trout on the Rapid and since then, the size of brook trout has increased and the number of five-pound fish caught every year keeps going up.

The Rapid River is situated in the heart of the Richardson Tract, which has over 22,000 acres of public lands in Maine's Western Mountains, and reaching the river can be problematic. Your options include boat, float plane, or a long drive over confusing logging roads which, if you don't get lost in the process, take you to a locked gate and a very long walk to the river.

On my first trip to the Rapid, I met two anglers from western Massachusetts, Rob Cramer and Mike Cole. They are Rapid River regulars and they knew the logging roads well. Every morning they would drive from their campsite to the last gate on the road to the Rapid and then ride mountain bikes to Middle Dam Pool. They were very helpful in giving me the lowdown on Rapid River, Upper Dam Pool, and the Deerfield River in western Massachusetts. In preparing for a return visit to the Rapid, I reached out to Cramer for directions to the Rapid via logging roads. After several failed attempts to write down directions through the maze of logging roads, Cramer in frustration emailed me, "You can't get there from here". The best way to access the Rapid River is by boat from the Andover boat launch on Lower Richardson Lake. It is about five miles by water to Middle Dam – anglers can tie up their boats at Middle Dam, which is the start of the Rapid River.

The Rapid is in fact a rapid river, falling some 1,100 feet in less than four miles from its source at Middle Dam on Lower Richardson Lake downstream to Umbagog Lake on the Maine/New Hampshire border. According to Maine's regional fisheries biologist David Boucher, anglers can expect to connect with native brook trout averaging around 14 inches with fish in the 18- to 24-inch range possible and landlocked salmon ranging from 12 to 20 inches.

Middle Dam pool fishing is excellent, and while it gets a lot of pressure, there is usually plenty of room. Fishing is done from the dam piers and by wading the back eddies from the banks of the river. The Rapid is about 50 to 70 feet wide except for the area known as the Pond-in-the-River. The right bank below the Middle Dam has a mile-long road which follows the river. A foot trail gives access on the left bank. About one mile below Middle Dam is the Pond-in-the-River, a 500-acre, deep pond which in addition to providing good fishing serves as a thermal refuge for the brook trout in summer, when the river temperatures can get into the 70s. The Pond is closed to fishing during this period.

Once on the Rapid most anglers use the old Carry Road, that follows the river on the north bank and provides access to the most popular pools. About 80 percent of fishing occurs from the Pond-in-the-River upstream to Middle Dam. Lower Dam Pool is about a mile walk downstream from Middle Dam and has some excellent dry-fly water.

Trophy brook trout are one of the reasons to fish the Rapid River, as Nate Dickinson learned.

STREAM FACTS

Season/Regulations

The Rapid is flyfishing-only and catch-and-release for brook trout. You are allowed to keep two landlocked salmon per day, with a 12-inch size limit. While the spring fishing is the most consistent, the fall fishing can be excellent. Prime time is mid-May into early July.

Fish

Since the establishment of catch-and-release regulations for brook trout, the number of five-pound brookies caught every year keeps going up. The Rapid is considered by many to be the best river in North America for trophy, three- to five-pound brook trout.

River Characteristics

Except for Pond-in-the-River, the Rapid is not wide, but it is deep and wild. Wading is difficult – I would never attempt to wade the Rapid without cleated wading boots and a staff.

What the Experts Say

Robert Duport, head guide at Lakewood Camps on the size of the brook trout in the Rapid River: "On any given day when the water is at its coldest, both early and late in the season, you have a shot at a four- to five-pound brook trout on the Rapid. They don't come easily but they are there."

Brett Damm, owner of Rangeley Region Sport Shop on the Rapid River hatches: "Caddis and stoneflies are the staples, and blue-winged olives are always around. Mid-June to mid-July the alderfly hatch is the best hatch in the region."

History

Lakewood Camps – located on Lower Richardson Lake about 0.25 miles from Middle Dam – dates back to 1853, making it the oldest continuously operated sporting camp in Maine. The camp consists of about a dozen rustic lakefront cabins and the main lodge on Lower Richardson Lake at which the owners, Whit and Maureen Carter, provide their guests with three solid home-cooked meals a day. Just below Lower Dam is Forest Lodge, where author Louise Dickinson Rich wrote "We Took to the Woods" and several other popular novels about early life along the Rapid River.

Tackle

I use a 9-foot, 5-weight outfit for nymphing and dry fly fishing and a 9-foot, 6-weight outfit to throw streamers on 150- to 200-grain sink tip lines.

Below the Pond, short trails off Carry Road provide access to another dozen pools.

Most of the fishing on the Rapid is wading. You can also rent a boat or hire a guide and fish the lower end of the Chub Pool and the Pond-in-the-River down to the Lower Dam. The favorite pools, starting with Middle Dam (which is a short walk from Lakewood Camps) and moving downstream are Harbec Pool, Horsechop Pool, Chub Pool, Pond-in-the-River, and Lower Dam.

Major hatches start in mid-May with blue-winged olives followed by Hendricksons and March browns. The best hatch of the season is the alderfly hatch in June into early July, which provides the best dry-fly fishing of the season. I have had my best results on the Rapid with streamers, small CDC Blue-winged Olive Emergers, and small green caddis larva and pupa, and I wouldn't go to the Rapid without a good supply of small Elk Hair Caddis.

Access

The best access is via a five-mile boat ride from Andover. When we fish the Rapid, we always stay at Lakewood Camps – it makes for a hassle-free trip. They pick you up at their dock in Andover and motor you over to their camp. Their American Plan provides three meals a day. It is a short walk to the river, which enables you to fish before breakfast and after dinner. The Rapid only earned a four-star rating due to access issues. If you stay at Lakewood Camps the access issues disappear and you can enjoy a five-star fishery.

Inset: Rick Steven fishing at Middle Dam on the Rapid River.
Jeff Poor with a Rapid River landlocked salmon. Photo by Nate Dickinson.

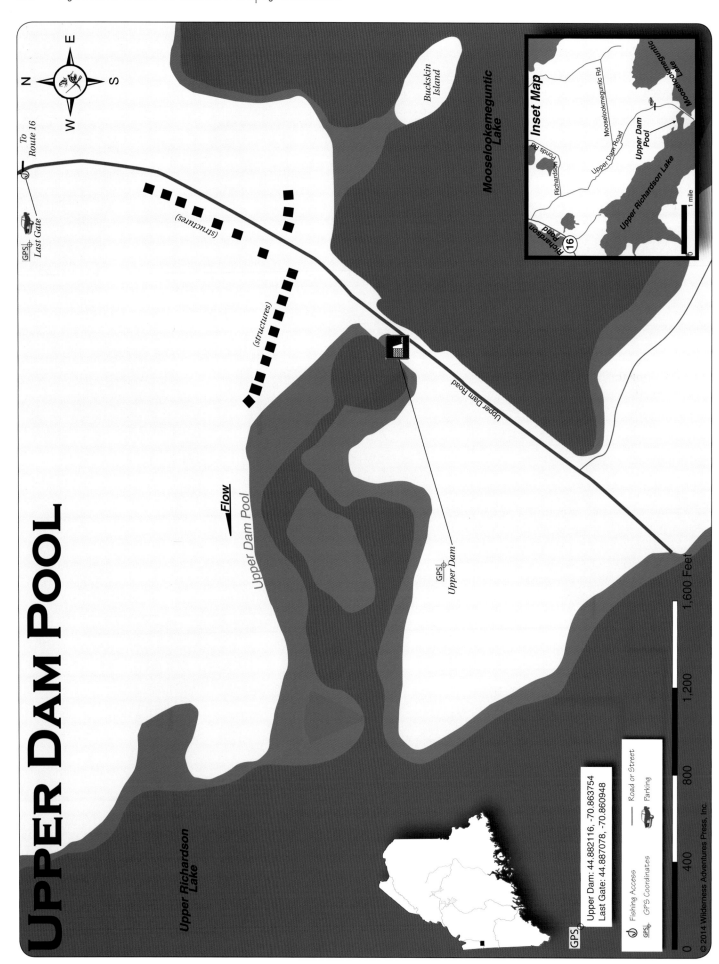

UPPER DAM POOL

Buckskin Island

Mooselookemeguntic Lake

To Route 16

Last Gate

(structures)

(structures)

Flow

Upper Dam Pool

Upper Dam Road

Upper Dam

Upper Richardson Lake

1,600 Feet

1,200

800

400

0

GPS

Upper Dam: 44.882116, -70.863754
Last Gate: 44.887078, -70.860948

Fishing Access
GPS Coordinates

Road or Street
Parking

Inset Map

Mooselookemeguntic Rd

Upper Dam Road

Richardson Ponds Rd

Upper Dam Pool

Upper Richardson Lake

Richardson Pond

Mooselookemeguntic Lake

16

1 mile

© 2014 Wilderness Adventures Press, Inc.

UPPER DAM POOL (FIVE STARS)

In the 1850s, the Upper Dam was built on the western end of Mooselookmeguntic Lake for log-driving purposes. Upper Dam Pool, which sits between Mooselookmeguntic and Upper Richardson Lakes in the Rangeley region, is famous not just for its world-class brook trout fishery but also for the world-renowned fly patterns that were developed there, the most famous of which is Carrie Stevens' Gray Ghost streamer. The giant brook trout over five pounds which once lurked there are largely a thing of the past, but it is still common to catch brook trout over 15 inches and salmon over 20 inches.

Upper Dam Pool is very large – 0.5 miles long and well over 100 yards across, delivering the water from Mooselookmeguntic Lake to Upper Richardson Lake. The pool has a very strong current down the middle with large back eddies on both sides. Most anglers fish streamers in the fast water down the middle of the pool, and dries or nymphs along the edges of the back eddies.

The fishery consists of wild salmon that drop down from Mooselookmeguntic Lake and hatchery salmon which move up from Upper Richardson. Most of the brook trout from both of the lakes are wild. Regulations consist of flyfishing-only with a limit of one salmon per day over 16 inches. It is no-kill on brook trout.

In June of 2013, Rick Steven and I had three, what can only be described as epic, days of fishing at Upper Dam Pool. The Rangeley region had a lot of rain the week before and the fish moved up from the lakes into the streams. After several good days of fishing on the Rapid River we decided to try the Upper Dam Pool. This was our first trip to Upper Dam and, while I had read everything I could find about the pool, I really didn't know what to expect.

The afternoon of our first day at Upper Dam, as we donned our waders in the parking area by the locked gate some 600 yards from Upper Dam Pool, two anglers coming back from fishing the pool said, "You better hurry up!"

"Good fishing?" I inquired.

"Good?" one of them said. "I have been coming here since 1985 and this is by far the best day I have had."

Rick later teased me that I forgot my back problems and knee replacement issues and practically sprinted to Upper Dam Pool. We had great success on streamers, dries, and nymphs – the best brookie day I have ever had. The next two days were carbon copies of the first day. As we were leaving on our last day, we stopped to talk to one of the cabin owners. I asked him if the fishing was always this good. He said, "You guys don't know how lucky you are – I have been fishing here for fifty years and this is the best week I have ever had!"

Back at the car we met another angler, Bruce Felmly, an attorney from New Hampshire, who was gearing up to fish the pool. He asked how we did, and all I could do was gush. I told him what the cabin occupant had said, and he asked if it was Paul Bean. I told him I didn't catch his name but he was in the first cabin. Felmly said, "Yes, that's Paul – he is fourth generation in that cabin and his grandfather was the dam keeper and knew Carrie Stevens." Felmly is a regular at Upper Dam, and said he had his best day ever on Columbus Day 2009. He went on to say the biggest fish are normally landed at the end of September into early October, when they come up from the lake to spawn. I gave him my card and asked if I could email him some questions about the fishery. A few days later he sent me a copy of an old email he had sent to four of his colleagues entitled "The Day" – Columbus Day 2009. Here is the email Felmly sent me:

Paul, Tom, Rufus, and David,
Since you are reasonably tolerant of my fishing tales, I thought you might enjoy the attached photos of Columbus Day evening and the best day I have ever had on brook trout. Over 20 years of fishing this water and lots of good fish, but nothing like this.

After our Boston meeting Susan and I went up to Rangeley on Sunday. I finished my various boat storage chores Monday afternoon and drove to Upper Dam. It is the outlet of one of the big lakes and is 500 yards of big moving water between two lakes. It is no-kill in October and big brookies and salmon come in to spawn, up from the lake, I had the place to myself, the wind was blowing 20 mph. When I left the water the air temp was 36 degrees. And the big fish were in and look-in' up.

I landed and released 10 fish in 2 hours, and never moved from my favorite perch at the tail of the pool. Long casts, short casts, left, right, I moved fish everywhere within 90 feet. I ended up taking nine brook trout, all over 14 inches. Three of the fish released were over 20 inches. The best was about 22-23 inches. Five or six ranged about 17-18 inches. And one smallish salmon about 15 inches. Three brookies on streamers, the rest took small parachute dries in the surface film.

Hereafter this will be known in my fishing journal as – 'The Day.'
Tight lines amigos,
Bruce

Above: The iconic Upper Dam Pool. Photo by Jeff Poor. Right: A large Upper Dam Pool brook trout. Photo by Bruce Felmly.

In the early days at Upper Dam, brook trout averaged five pounds and well-to-do anglers traveled to this remote section of the Maine wilderness by railroad to Bemis Station on the south end of Mooselookmeguntic Lake, and took a small steamer five miles to the dam. Bemis claimed to be the only log cabin train station in the nation. A well-maintained hotel and several cabins were built by the dam and flyfishing-only regulations were established.

There are few places that hold a more revered place in flyfishing history than the iconic, century-old Upper Dam. To anglers across Maine and the nation, Upper Dam is more than a fishing location, it's hallowed ground. Upper Dam Pool is often the first place fly fishers visit when they are in the Rangeley area. They come not just for the great landlocked salmon and brook trout in the pool, which connects Mooselookmeguntic and Upper Richardson Lake, but also to walk back in angling history and fish the waters where legendary anglers like Carrie

Stevens developed world-renowned fly patterns. She tied all of her flies hand-held without a vise, the most famous of which, as noted was her Gray Ghost streamer. Upper Dam Pool has a long history of providing excellent fly fishing for trophy brook trout and landlocked salmon, but it wasn't propelled to the national stage until July 1, 1924, when Stevens landed a 6-pound, 13-ounce brook trout. The fish was the first to be landed on her Gray Ghost – a fly which she developed only minutes before landing that great fish. The fish won Ms. Stevens second place in the 1924 *Field &*

Stream fishing contest. The publicity she received resulted in a flood of requests from fishermen across the nation to purchase her flies, so she found herself in the fly-tying business.

Directions/Access

From Rangeley, take Routes 4 North /16 West for five miles to where Route 16 splits off west toward Wilson Mills. Take Route 16 West for another 12.9 miles to the dirt road access to Upper Dam. The road to Upper Dam has three gates. The first is near Route 16 and is opened each spring as snow allows. The second is 1.2 miles from the dam and is open until June 30 to allow anglers closer access to Upper Dam. It is closed from June 30 through Labor Day. The final gate is closed year round, but the walk from the parking area at the gate to the dam is only 600 yards.

For years, NextEra Energy Maine Operating Services LLC owned and operated Upper Dam. In 2005, the company was notified by the Federal Energy Regulatory Commission that the dam was a "high hazard dam" and the commission requested that it be replaced. When I visited Upper Dam in the spring and fall of 2013, work was ongoing to replace the dam. When I returned home from the fall trip, I inquired of NextEra as to what steps they were planning to take to preserve in some reasonable facsimile the iconic, century-old historic dam house structure. They responded that they had sold all of their hydro assets to Brookfield Renewable Energy. I sent a similar inquiry to Brookfield and they responded that they were "obligated to remove all structures and replace them with new buildings. The new gatehouse is smaller than the existing one and will be a steel frame building, with siding and a roof that will match the character of the existing camps at upper dam." They also said, "The existing piers have to be removed." When I asked if they will be replicating the piers for folks to fish off, they responded, "That is the part we are still assessing."

STREAM FACTS

Seasons/Regulations

The season runs from April 1 until the end of September under flyfishing-only regulations, with a limit of one salmon per day over 16 inches. It is no-kill for brook trout. The month of October is no-kill for both salmon and brook trout.

Fish

The fishery consists of wild salmon that drop down from Mooselookmeguntic Lake and hatchery salmon which move up from Upper Richardson. Most of the brook trout from both of the lakes are wild.

River Characteristics

Upper Dam Pool is very large – 0.5 miles long and well over 100 yards across, delivering the water from Mooselookmeguntic Lake to Upper Richardson Lake. The pool has a very strong current down the middle with large back eddies on both sides. Most anglers fish streamers in the fast water down the middle of the pool and dries or nymphs along the edges of the back eddies.

History

Many of the traditional Maine streamers were developed here (including Carrie Stevens' Gray Ghost). Upper Dam was the hotbed for the development of hundreds of streamer patterns by dozens of tyers – most tied to imitate smelt, the primary forage fish at Upper Dam. In addition to Stevens' Gray Ghost, the Black Ghost was developed by a local guide and champion caster, Herbie Welsh. He once tossed a fly 124 feet in a competition. It is said that he taught Ted Williams to cast and guided President Hoover. Then there was Cornelia "Fly Rod" Crosby (1854-1946), one of the first women to guide in Maine. Fly Rod was an outdoor writer, expert fly caster, hunter, and promoter of Maine's sporting tradition. In 1895, she traveled to New York to promote Maine's North Woods recreational opportunities at the Sportsmen's Show at Madison Square Garden. Between the show and her numerous publications, Fly Rod was largely responsible for attracting thousands of "sports" to visit Maine. In 1897, the Maine legislature honored her by presenting her with the first Maine guiding license – license Number 1.

Tackle

I use a 9-foot, 5-weight outfit for nymphing and dry fly fishing and a 9-foot, 6-weight outfit to throw streamers on 150- to 200-grain sink tip lines.

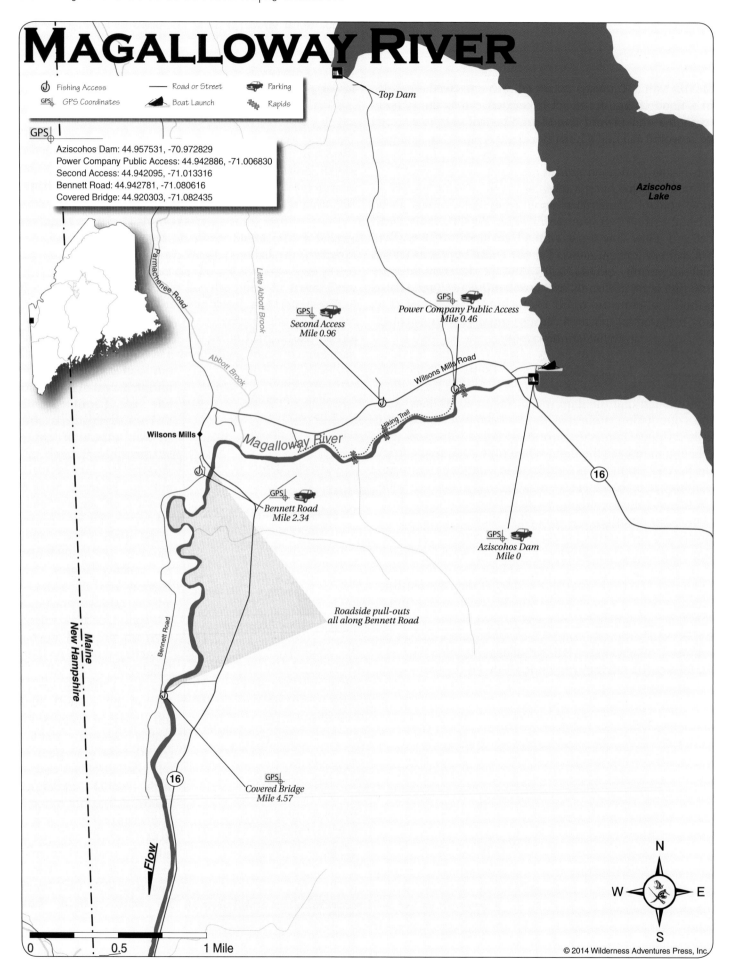

MAGALLOWAY RIVER

Fishing Access
GPS GPS Coordinates
Road or Street
Boat Launch
Parking
Rapids

GPS

Aziscohos Dam: 44.957531, -70.972829
Power Company Public Access: 44.942886, -71.006830
Second Access: 44.942095, -71.013316
Bennett Road: 44.942781, -71.080616
Covered Bridge: 44.920303, -71.082435

Top Dam

Aziscohos
Lake

Parmachenee Road

Little Abbott Brook

Abbott Brook

GPS
Power Company Public Access
Mile 0.46

GPS
Second Access
Mile 0.96

Wilsons Mills Road

Hiking Trail

Wilsons Mills

Magalloway River

16

GPS
Bennett Road
Mile 2.34

GPS
Aziscohos Dam
Mile 0

Bennett Road

Roadside pull-outs
all along Bennett Road

Maine
New Hampshire

16

GPS
Covered Bridge
Mile 4.57

Flow

N
W E
S

0   0.5   1 Mile

© 2014 Wilderness Adventures Press, Inc.

MAGALLOWAY RIVER (FIVE STARS)

The Magalloway flows through a remote section of northwestern Maine near the northern New Hampshire border. In 1910 when the Aziscohos Dam at Wilson Mills was completed, creating Aziscohos Lake, the Lower Magalloway was not a true tailwater river, as the water flowed over the top of the dam. At that time, Aziscohos Dam – a masterpiece of early concrete dam construction was the largest dam in the world. What is even more impressive is what the dam builders had to overcome. The site was 40 miles from the nearest railroad station in Colebrook, New Hampshire, and the only way massive amounts of cement and steel could be transported was by horse-drawn wagons. They moved thousands of tons of materials over narrow, muddy roads and they had to navigate through the tremendously steep Dixville Notch. In one instance, a piece of steel weighing five tons took a team of 20 horses three weeks to transport due to an unexpected thaw resulting in deep mud along the route.

In the 1980s, a tube was installed in the bottom of the dam for the purpose of creating electricity, and the Magalloway became a true tailwater fishery. The whitewater gushing from the hydroelectric tube keeps the Magalloway ice cold all season – late summer fishing can be excellent, even when other rivers in the region are experiencing the dog days of summer. Today, the lower Magalloway tailwater has a good population of native brookies and landlocked salmon. Route 16 parallels the tailwater section downstream to the bridge in Wilson Mills. (Note: Wilson Mills has no retail stores, so make certain you have plenty of gas and supplies before venturing into this remote section of western Maine.)

The releases can be extreme, making wading very difficult, especially for the first two miles below the dam – studded wading boots and a staff are a must. From Route 16 below the dam there is easy access from the parking area and trail which starts by the power station. The trail follows the stream and is fairly easy to walk. A few miles downriver in Wilson Mills, Route 16 crosses the river and provides access to a much tamer section of river. There is parking by the bridge and Bennett Road, a dirt road off to the right, provides access to several beautiful runs and pools downstream from the bridge.

The Magalloway was a sleepy little river until word spread that President Dwight Eisenhower had traveled to the Magalloway in June of 1955 to sample its trophy brook trout and landlocked salmon fishery. I have seen pictures of the president fishing at Little Boy Falls above Lake Aziscohos, where legend has it that a little boy was kidnapped by two trappers. According to the legend, Chief Metalluck of the Abenaki Tribe rescued the boy near the falls and returned him to his parents. After Eisenhower's visit, the Magalloway started to attract more anglers and, despite its remoteness it can draw a crowd, especially on weekends.

Maine is one of the best places in the country to see moose. Photo by Wes Lavin.

DIRECTIONS/ACCESS

From Rangeley, take Routes 4 North /16 West for five miles to where Route 16 splits off and goes west toward Wilson Mills. Take Route 16 West for approximately 18.7 miles (5.8 miles past Upper Dam Road). After crossing the Magalloway just below the dam, continue a short distance to the power company lot on the left. A trail starts from the parking area and follows the river for several miles downstream. The next access point is about 0.5 miles down Route 16. There is a trail to the river on the left just before Mountain View Road. The next access is 1.3 miles past Mountain View Road – take Bennett Road on the right just before the bridge in Wilson Mills. This section of river runs through a meadow and features several good runs and pools.

STREAM FACTS

Season/Regulations

Flyfishing-only from April 1 until September 30, although for all practical purposes the fishing is not productive until mid-May. You may keep one fish from April 1until August 15 – then it is catch-and-release until the season ends on September 30.

Fish

The Magalloway has nice-sized brookies and landlocked salmon.

River Characteristics

The first couple of miles below the dam consist of fast pocket water and a few plunge pools. Below the Route 16 bridge at Wilson Mills there are several beautiful pools and runs.

What the Experts Say

Brett Damm, owner of the Rangeley Region Sport Shop, on the size of brook trout on the Magalloway River: "Brook trout average between 12 and 16 inches, but there are 20-inch trout in every hole. While not every angler can or will catch four-pound trout, they will be fishing over them."

History

Built in 1910, the Aziscohos Dam, a masterpiece of early concrete dam construction, was the largest dam in the world at that time.

Tackle

A 9-foot, 5-weight outfit is perfect for this river.

The Magalloway River Gorge (as seen from the Route 16 Bridge just below the dam): treacherous to wade – rewarding to fish.

Hub City

RANGELEY

Population 1,166

If you go to Rangeley and I hope you do – a must stop is the Rangeley Region Sports Shop. They have been servicing anglers for almost 70 years – they offer the best products and unmatched service. Their motto: "We wish to continue the tradition of serving sportsmen to make fishing the historic waters of the Rangeley Lakes area a memorial experience."

ACCOMMODATIONS

Lakewood Camps, Andover / 207-243-2959 / 207-243-2959 winter / www.lakewoodcamps.com

Loon Lodge Inn, 16 Pickford Road / 207-864-5665 / www.loonlodgeme.com

Rangeley Inn & Motor Lodge, 2443 Main Street / 800-666-3687 / www.rangeleyinn.com

Saddleback Inn, 2303 Main Street / 207-864-3434 / www.rangeleyrentals.com / They have cabins in every price range.

Mollyocket Motel, 1132 South Main Street, Route 26, Woodstock / 888-569-8611 / www.mollyocketmotel.com / Very nice motel, clean rooms and good restaurant with great food at reasonable prices. When traveling to the Rapid, we stay the night before at the Mollyocket Motel. It is only 20 miles from Andover, where Lakewood Camps picks us up.

CAMPGROUNDS

Rangeley Lake State Park / 207-864-2003
Black Brook Cove Campground / 207-486-3828

RESTAURANTS

Red Onion Restaurant, 2511 Main Street / 207-864-5022 / rangeleyredonion.com

Sarge's Sports Pub & Grub, 2454 Main Street / 207-864-5616

Loon Lodge Inn, 16 Pickford Road / 207-864-5665 / www.loonlodgeme.com

Swig N Smelt Pub, 976 Saddleback Road / 207-864-5671

GUIDES/FLY SHOPS/SPORTING GOODS

Rangeley Region Sports Shop, 2529 Main Street / 207-864-5615 / www.rangeleysportsshop.com

Robert Duport (guide), Kingfield / 207-235-2573

Sun Valley Sports, 129 Sunday River Road, Bethel / 207-824 -7553 / www.sunvalleysports.com

Rapid River Fly Fishing / Andover / 207-650-3890

Kris Thompson, Pond in the River Guide Service 207-864-9140 / www.rangeleyflyfishing.com

AIRPORT

Bangor International Airport, Geoffrey Boulevard / www.flybangor.com / Bangor is less than three hours from Rangeley and Andover.

MEDICAL

Rangeley Region Health Center, 25 Dallas Hill Road / 207-864-3303 / www.rangeleyhealth.org

FOR MORE INFORMATION

Rangeley Chamber of Commerce / 207-864-5364 / www.rangeleymaine.com

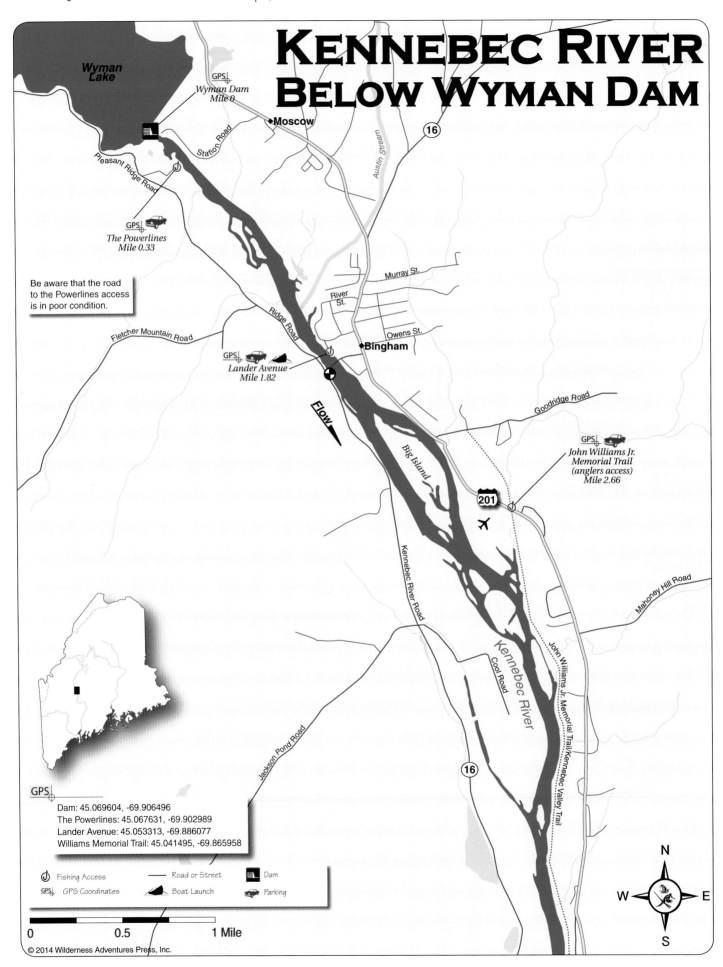

KENNEBEC RIVER
BELOW WYMAN DAM

Wyman Lake

GPS
Wyman Dam
Mile 0

◆Moscow

Station Road

16

Austin Stream

Pleasant Ridge Road

GPS
The Powerlines
Mile 0.33

Be aware that the road
to the Powerlines access
is in poor condition.

Fletcher Mountain Road

Murray St.

River St.

Ridge Road

Owens St.

GPS
Lander Avenue
Mile 1.82

◆Bingham

Flow

Goodridge Road

GPS
John Williams Jr.
Memorial Trail
(anglers access)
Mile 2.66

Big Island

201

Kennebec River Road

Kennebec River

Cool Road

Mahoney Hill Road

John Williams Jr. Memorial Trail/Kennebec Valley Trail

Jackson Pond Road

16

GPS
Dam: 45.069604, -69.906496
The Powerlines: 45.067631, -69.902989
Lander Avenue: 45.053313, -69.886077
Williams Memorial Trail: 45.041495, -69.865958

Fishing Access   Road or Street   Dam
GPS GPS Coordinates   Boat Launch   Parking

0   0.5   1 Mile

N
W   E
S

© 2014 Wilderness Adventures Press, Inc.

KENNEBEC RIVER (FIVE STARS)

The Kennebec River is one of the longest rivers in Maine, flowing some 120 miles from Moosehead Lake in central Maine to the tidal waters at Popham Beach on the coast. The two branches (East and West Outlets) of the Kennebec flow out of Moosehead Lake to Indian Pond. The Kennebec River then flows down to the Harris Station Dam. This is a very popular whitewater rafting destination.

Below the dam the river flows through Kennebec Gorge, where access is very limited. Along the way its flow is altered by nine dams, and below most of these dams there is good fishing. Some consider the Kennebec the finest and most diverse coldwater fishery in all of New England. On the Kennebec you have the opportunity to fish for native brook trout, landlocked salmon, wild rainbows, and a tremendous brown trout fishery. While the brown trout fishery relies largely on stocked fish, the fishes' growth rate is phenomenal, and because of the coldwater releases the browns hold over well.

For my money, the best fishing on the river is the section below Wyman Dam in Bingham (Wyman Lake and Dam are in Moscow, but the water I fish is in Bingham). Water releases from Wyman Dam make this section of river the most attractive and productive fishery on the river – it has a tremendous population of wild rainbow trout, as well as native brook trout and landlocked salmon. In addition to the native brook trout and landlocked salmon, what keeps anglers coming back is the wild rainbow trout fishery – the best in New England.

This section of the Kennebec is a caddis factory, but it also supports good Hendricksons, quill Gordons, March browns, and blue-winged olives. The blue-winged olives can be found April through September. The olive hatches are most concentrated on cloudy days. The best fishing of the year occurs during the alderfly hatch in July.

The Kennebec River below Wyman Dam in the Upper Kennebec Valley is one of the best wild trout rivers in the East. Wyman is a massive bottom-release dam providing cold water throughout the summer, which makes this section of the river one of the best season-long tailwaters in Maine. The best fishing occurs in the upper two miles, from the dam downstream to the mouth of Austin Stream – this is the prime spawning area for the rainbows. During my first trip to the Kennebec in Bingham, I had the good fortune of fishing with Todd Towle, who owns Kingfisher River Guides. Towle came highly recommended by Robert Duport, who guides on the Rapid River. When I booked Towle, I asked him just how good the Bingham fishery was. His instant response, "It is flat out the best wild rainbow fishery in New England – bar none." It didn't take Towle long to back up his statement. On our first morning with him my fishing partner, Joe Darcy, took a beautiful 20-inch-plus wild rainbow on a size 20 Zebra Midge. Towle knows the river, the hatches, and how to outsmart the river's big wild rainbows.

DIRECTIONS/ACCESS

Directions to Kennebec in Bingham: Take I-95 to Exit 133 and follow Route 201 north for 38 miles to Bingham. Route 201 closely follows the river through Bingham and provides easy access. Just downriver of Northern Country Rivers Outfitters on Route 201 is the John Williams, Jr. Memorial Trail, a rails-to-trails project which gives excellent access to the river.

The Kennebec River is the best rainbow trout fishery in New England. Photo courtesy Joe Darcy.

STREAM FACTS

Season/Regulations

The season on the Kennebec River from Moosehead Lake to the Atlantic Ocean runs from April 1 until the end of October. The Kennebec River below Wyman Dam in Moscow is regulated as artificial-lures-only with a daily harvest limit of one fish. Landlocked salmon and rainbow trout must be 16 inches, brook trout 12 inches.

Fish

The best wild rainbow fishery in New England and good fishing for native brook trout and landlocked salmon.

River Characteristics

The river has many long, easily wadeable pools at low water. Wyman Dam Power Plant controls the flows; it releases in bursts rather than constant flows, and during releases the water rises quickly. The river is usually low in the morning and again in the evening.

What the Experts Say

Todd Towle, of Kingfisher River Guides, guided me to my first trip to the Kennebec River. When I asked him just how good the Bingham fishery is – his instant response was, "It is flat out the best wild rainbow fishery in New England – bar none."

Tackle

A 9-foot, 4-weight is perfect for fishing dry flies and small nymphs on the Kennebec.

The Kennebec River below Wyman Dam. Below: Wyman Dam.

On Maine's lodging roads, the trucks and moose have the right of way. Photo courtesy Joe Darcy.

Hub City

BINGHAM

Population 992

ACCOMMODATIONS

Gateway Recreation and Lodging, Route 21 / 800-440-0053 / www.gateway-rec.com

North Country Cabins / 800-348-8871 / www.northcountryrivers.com

Pine Grove Lodge, 823 Ridge Road, Pleasant Ridge / 207-672-4011 / www.pinegrovelodge.com

CAMPGROUNDS AND RV PARKS

Evergreens Campground, Ferry Street, Route 201A, Solon / 207-643-2324 / www.evergreenscampground.com

RESTAURANTS

Thompson's Restaurant, 348 Main Street / 207-672-3820 / All the food is homemade – a favorite eatery of the locals.

Kennebec River Pub, 1771 Route 21 / 207-663-4446

Jimmy's Shop N Save, full service grocery store on Route 201 in Bingham

FLY SHOPS AND GUIDING SERVICES

Kingfisher River Guides – Todd Towle / Kingfield / 207-265-5823 / kingfisherguides@tds.net

Kennebec River Outfitters, 469 Lakewood Road, Madison / 207-474-2500 / www.kennebecriveroutfitters.com

AIRPORTS

Bangor International Airport, Geoffrey Boulevard / www.flybangor.com / Bangor International Airport is one and a half hours away.

MEDICAL

Bingham Area Health Center, 237 Main Street / 207-672-4187 / www.healthchch.org

FOR MORE INFORMATION

Upper Kennebec Valley Chamber of Commerce / 207-672-4100 / www.upperkennebecvalleychamber.com

New Hampshire

New Hampshire Facts

Area: 9,351 square miles – 46th largest in U.S.
Population: 1,318,114
State Fish: Brook trout

Trout Fishing License

Purchase online at fishnh.com
Stocking reports: fishnh.com
Annual resident fee: $35
Non-resident annual fee: $53
Non-resident one-day fee: $15
Non-resident three-day fee: $28
Non-resident seven-day fee: $35

State Records

Landlocked salmon, 18 pounds, 8 ounces by Mr. P.H. Killelea / August 30, 1914 / Pleasant Lake, New London

Landlocked salmon, 18 pounds, 8 ounces by Mrs. Letty M. Clark / August 31, 1942 / Pleasant Lake, New London

Brook trout, 9 pounds by Val Woodruff / May 8, 1911 / Pleasant Lake, New London

Brown trout, 16 pounds, 6 ounces by Ken Reed Jr. / July 4, 1975 / Connecticut River, Pittsburg

Rainbow trout, 15 pounds, 7 ounces by Lance King / September 16, 1996 / Pemigewasset River, Bristol

New Hampshire's weather (as described to me by one of the residents): "We get nine months of winter followed by three months of poor sledding." White Mountain National Forest, with 48 peaks over 4,000 feet, dominates much of northern New Hampshire's landscape. The weather in the national forest can change in an instant. In his book *The Worst Weather on Earth: A History of Mt. Washington Observatory*, William Putnam states: "There may be worse weather, from time to time at some forbidding place on Planet Earth, but it has yet to be reliably recorded." Bill Bryson, in his laugh-out-loud funny book, *A Walk in the Woods*, credits Mt. Washington for having the lowest wind chill ever recorded with a 100 mph wind speed and a temperature of minus 47 degrees F, unmatched even in Antarctica. The take-home message is, never venture out into the North Woods without foul weather gear and an extra fleece jacket. The positive side is that New Hampshire has over 12,000 miles of rivers and streams and over 1,000 lakes and ponds, so in the Granite State you're never far from great fishing.

On my first trip to northern New Hampshire, we traveled up Route 3 from Vermont and then along the New Hampshire/Quebec border. Once in New Hampshire, every few miles we were greeted with signs warning about moose/car collisions. Please take those signs very seriously – I did, and it may have saved my life. It certainly saved our trip, as well as the front end of my new Honda Pilot.

After checking into our cabin at Lopstick Lodge in Pittsburg, we headed to a pub frequented by the locals, the Buck Rub on Main Street in downtown Pittsburg, for dinner. New Hampshire is rugged and so are its people. The parking lot at the pub was packed with pickup trucks, most had gun racks, and of course New Hampshire's license plates proudly display the state's slogan, "Live Free or Die". Joe Darcy, my fishing partner, and I had earlier questioned whether we needed to shower and change out of our fishing clothes for dinner. Upon entering the Buck Rub we noted that all the men and most of the women were dressed in jeans, flannel shirts, and baseball caps – we fit in nicely. We feasted on large, greasy burgers smothered with onions and mushrooms and buried under enormous mounds of sweet potato fries – not the healthiest meal, but we loved every morsel – fishing trips are a good excuse to break your diet.

After dinner Darcy and I started our five-mile ride back to the lodge. The folks there had advised us not to drive over 40 miles per hour if we wanted to have a chance of avoiding a collision with a moose. Even though we were not in a high moose area, I heeded that advice – and thank God I did! As we rounded a curve on a dark stretch of Route 3, a moose jumped out of nowhere into the beam of my headlights. I jammed on the brakes as hard as I could and swerved to avoid the moose. Darcy and I braced for the inevitable collision, but somehow we missed the moose, which couldn't have been more than a car's length away when we stopped. I still remember the moose looking at us with a confused look on its face as if to say, "What the hell was that all about". One of the selling points my car salesman touted was Honda's "brake assist" feature. In the promotional brochure it states, "Break assist is a component of the anti-lock braking system, which helps apply full braking force in emergency situations". I can attest that it works!

We had booked Greg Ingis to guide us for our two days of float trips on the upper Connecticut and the Androscoggin Rivers. Ingis knows the rivers, the hatches, and the fish. He handled the boat exceptionally well, and he cooks up a mean (in a good way) shore lunch. But what I remember most was Ingis entertaining us with one North Woods story after another. One was so fascinating and

A New Hampshire fall brookie. Photo courtesy Greg Ingis.

unusual – it was about the Indian Stream Republic. Darcy and I had never heard of the republic, so when I got home I ordered the book, *Indian Stream Republic* by Daniel Doan. Doan meticulously describes a little-known group of American pioneers who formed their own government in an effort to keep their lands free from the border disputes between the United States and Canada. The Treaty of Paris ending the American Revolution set the United States boundary with Canada at "the northwestern-most head of the Connecticut River." The Connecticut River has three headwater streams feeding into it in this area, so there was bound to be confusion and squabbles over who owned the land in this remote corner of the United States.

The settlers in this region led strenuous lives trying to tame a rugged piece of the North Woods – they spent their days clearing forests, building cabins, planting crops, and engaging in subsistence hunting. But when both the United States and Canada wanted to tax them, New Hampshire's "Live Free or Die" spirit came alive, and in 1832 they declared themselves the independent Indian Stream Republic. They established their own constitution, legislature, laws, courts, and their own 41-man militia.

In 1835, conflict broke out after Canada arrested a leader of the Indian Stream Republic. In retaliation, a pro-Canadian resident was arrested in New Hampshire. Events escalated, and New Hampshire's governor, William Badger, ordered the New Hampshire militia to occupy the Indian Stream Republic. In 1836, Canada gave up their claim and the citizens of the Indian Stream Republic accepted New Hampshire's authority. In November of 1840, New Hampshire passed legislation incorporating all 200,000 acres of the Indian Stream Republic into the Township of Pittsburg. As a result, Pittsburg has more area than any other township in the lower 48 states. (It also boasts a population of more moose than people.)

Lopstick Lodge and Cabins are a good base camp for fishing the upper Connecticut River in Pittsburg. "Lopstick" is a Canadian logging term – a fir tree is denuded of all its lower branches, leaving just a small "Christmas tree" at the top. It therefore is a lopped stick. That is how they marked the corners of the wood lots. After reviewing the lodge's history and finding out that one of the prior owners retired after winning the Tri-State Lottery, I figured the Lopstick had good karma, and judging from the success of our trip, I would say it did. The cabins are clean, comfortable, and well-maintained with great views of First Connecticut Lake. The lodge, which is Orvis-endorsed, has a great selection of flies and tackle and has excellent guides. Lopstick is conveniently located just 1.1 miles from the famous Trophy Trout tailwater section on the upper Connecticut River below First Connecticut Lake. This is in the heart of moose country, and "Moose Alley" starts on Route 3 just north of the lodge in Pittsburg.

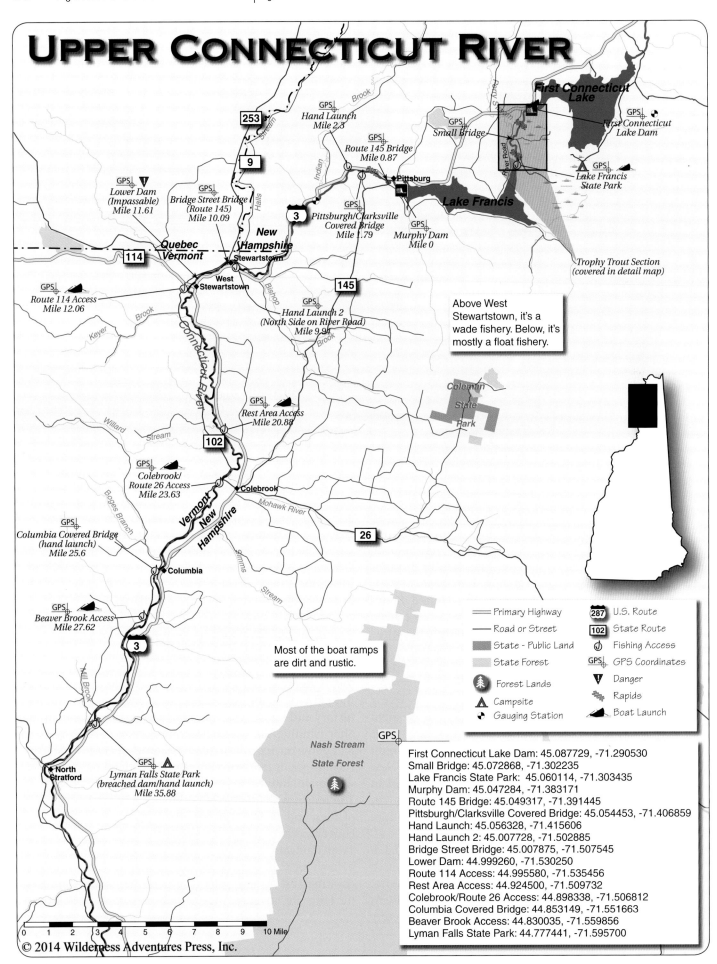

UPPER CONNECTICUT RIVER

First Connecticut Lake

First Connecticut Lake Dam

253
9

Hand Launch
Mile 2.3

Small Bridge

GPS

GPS
Route 145 Bridge
Mile 0.87

River Road

GPS
Lake Francis
State Park

3
Pittsburg

Lower Dam
(Impassable)
Mile 11.61

GPS
Bridge Street Bridge
(Route 145)
Mile 10.09

New
Hampshire

GPS
Pittsburgh/Clarksville
Covered Bridge
Mile 1.79

Lake Francis

114

Quebec
Vermont

Stewartstown

GPS
Murphy Dam
Mile 0

GPS
Route 114 Access
Mile 12.06

West
Stewartstown

145

Trophy Trout Section
(covered in detail map)

GPS
Hand Launch 2
(North Side on River Road)
Mile 9.94

Above West
Stewartstown, it's a
wade fishery. Below, it's
mostly a float fishery.

Coleman
State
Park

GPS
Rest Area Access
Mile 20.88

102

GPS
Colebrook/
Route 26 Access
Mile 23.63

Colebrook

Mohawk River

GPS
Columbia Covered Bridge
(hand launch)
Mile 25.6

Vermont
New
Hampshire

26

Columbia

GPS
Beaver Brook Access
Mile 27.62

3

Most of the boat ramps
are dirt and rustic.

Primary Highway	287 U.S. Route
Road or Street	102 State Route
State - Public Land	Fishing Access
State Forest	GPS GPS Coordinates
Forest Lands	Danger
Campsite	Rapids
Gauging Station	Boat Launch

GPS

Nash Stream
State Forest

GPS
Lyman Falls State Park
(breached dam/hand launch)
Mile 35.88

North
Stratford

First Connecticut Lake Dam: 45.087729, -71.290530
Small Bridge: 45.072868, -71.302235
Lake Francis State Park: 45.060114, -71.303435
Murphy Dam: 45.047284, -71.383171
Route 145 Bridge: 45.049317, -71.391445
Pittsburgh/Clarksville Covered Bridge: 45.054453, -71.406859
Hand Launch: 45.056328, -71.415606
Hand Launch 2: 45.007728, -71.502885
Bridge Street Bridge: 45.007875, -71.507545
Lower Dam: 44.999260, -71.530250
Route 114 Access: 44.995580, -71.535456
Rest Area Access: 44.924500, -71.509732
Colebrook/Route 26 Access: 44.898338, -71.506812
Columbia Covered Bridge: 44.853149, -71.551663
Beaver Brook Access: 44.830035, -71.559856
Lyman Falls State Park: 44.777441, -71.595700

0 1 2 3 4 5 6 7 8 9 10 Mile

© 2014 Wilderness Adventures Press, Inc.

UPPER CONNECTICUT RIVER (FOUR STARS)

The headwaters of the mighty Connecticut River start as a mere trickle near the Canadian border in Pittsburg, New Hampshire. It then flows through Fourth Connecticut Lake and continues on through Third, Second, and First Connecticut Lakes. The famous Trophy Trout section begins at the base of the dam on First Connecticut Lake and goes downstream 2.5 miles to Lake Francis. Below Murphy Dam on Lake Francis is a second and larger tailwater section providing coldwater trout habitat for some 30 miles downstream. These two tailwaters in Pittsburg have it all: scenic beauty and a great spring, summer, and fall fishery. Anglers can tangle with three species of trout and landlocked salmon and enjoy close encounters with moose (hopefully not while driving), bear, bald eagle, and river otter.

The Trophy Trout section below First Connecticut Lake is all wade fishing. From the lake downstream to the confluence with Perry Stream, which is a productive native brook trout tributary, the Connecticut River is mostly riffles and runs. From Perry Stream downstream to Lake Francis there are more pools and dry fly water. Salmon run up the river from Lake Francis in the spring after ice–out, following the spawning run of smelt, but most of the anglers who fish the trophy stretch are there for the brook trout.

Below Lake Francis the water stays cool all summer and there is plenty of dry fly water. The most prolific hatches include Hendricksons, Cahills, sulphurs, blue-winged olives, and assorted caddis. Inglis says that, day in and day out, blue-winged olives are the bread and butter hatch – they begin in June and continue until the end of the season. Below Lake Francis there are some landlocked salmon but most fishing is for trout, both wild and stocked, including some monster browns. As you move downstream from Lake Francis, the river flows through meadows and farmland – the bottom is largely gravel and the wading is fairly easy. The river widens farther down and the pools become quite deep. For this reason, most anglers prefer to float-fish the lower section. This section harbors some very big brown trout. In fact, the state record brown trout - weighing 16 pounds, 6 ounces - was caught in the upper Connecticut, and more recently a 15-pound, 8-ounce brown was taken below Murphy Dam. On the first day of my most recent trip we floated the river below Murphy Dam and were treated to all three species of trout, both wild and stocked. We did not land a landlocked salmon, although they are present.

A trophy-stretch brown. Photo by Greg Ingis.

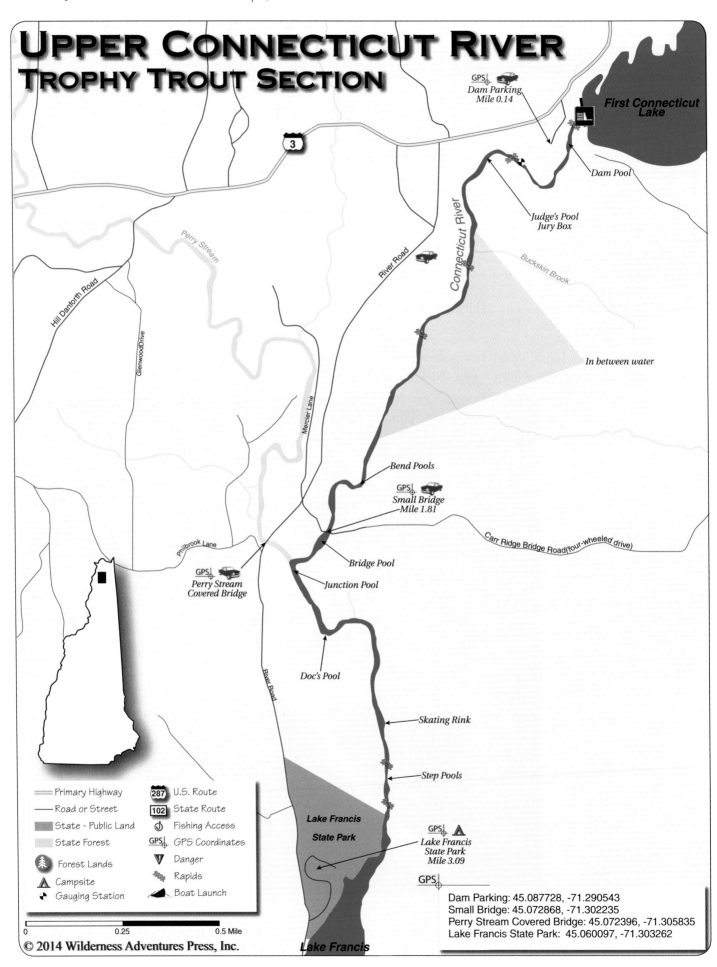

UPPER CONNECTICUT RIVER
TROPHY TROUT SECTION

First Connecticut Lake

GPS Dam Parking Mile 0.14

Dam Pool

Judge's Pool Jury Box

Connecticut River

Buckskin Brook

River Road

Perry Stream

Hill Danforth Road

GlenwoodDrive

In between water

Mercier Lane

Bend Pools

GPS Small Bridge Mile 1.81

Carr Ridge Bridge Road(four-wheeled drive)

Philbrook Lane

GPS Perry Stream Covered Bridge

Bridge Pool

Junction Pool

River Road

Doc's Pool

Skating Rink

Step Pools

Lake Francis State Park

GPS Lake Francis State Park Mile 3.09

GPS

Lake Francis

Primary Highway	287 U.S. Route
Road or Street	102 State Route
State - Public Land	Fishing Access
State Forest	GPS GPS Coordinates
Forest Lands	Danger
Campsite	Rapids
Gauging Station	Boat Launch

0   0.25   0.5 Mile

© 2014 Wilderness Adventures Press, Inc.

Dam Parking: 45.087728, -71.290543
Small Bridge: 45.072868, -71.302235
Perry Stream Covered Bridge: 45.072396, -71.305835
Lake Francis State Park: 45.060097, -71.303262

DIRECTIONS/ACCESS

Access to the Trophy Trout Stretch

There is ample parking right below the dam on First Connecticut Lake at the start of the Trophy Trout section. From the first parking area to the left off Route 3, take the dirt road to the right of the parking area for 200 yards. This leads to an additional parking area and a trail to the stream. The next section is accessed from River Road, a well-maintained dirt road off Route 3 which leads to the Lake Francis Campground. A mile down River Road toward the campground, about 200 yards before you reach the covered bridge over Perry Stream, there is a dirt road on the left which takes you within 100 yards to a small bridge over the Connecticut River, with parking and good access. There is a trail which runs from the covered bridge downstream along the river to the Lake Francis Campground. You can access the trail from the covered bridge or behind the visitor center at the campground.

Access to Tailwater below Lake Francis

Below the Murphy Dam on Lake Francis is the second tailwater section of the Connecticut River. Route 3, which follows the river, provides excellent access. The cool water from the dam provides quality trout water for some 30 miles downstream. Most of this section is very wadeable.

STREAM FACTS

Seasons/Regulations

The season runs from January 1 through October 15 for trout. The salmon season ends September 30. If you catch a salmon while fishing for trout after September 30, you must release it. Fishing typically begins to heat up after ice-out, which is usually during the first week in May and which triggers the smelt's spring spawning run up out of the lake into the river, with the landlocked salmon in close pursuit.

Trophy Trout Regulations

The Trophy Trout section starts below the tailwater dam on First Connecticut Lake and runs downstream to Lake Francis. This section is fly-fishing-only with a daily limit of two brook trout of at least 12 inches and two salmon of at least 15 inches.

Regulations below Murphy Dam

The New Hampshire general regulations apply below Murphy Dam all the way to the Vermont border. For brook, brown, and rainbow trout the daily limit is five fish or five pounds, whichever is reached first. There is no length limit. For trout, the season runs from January 1 to October 15. For landlocked salmon, the season runs from April 1 to September 30. There is a daily limit of two salmon of at least 15 inches.

Fish

The river has rainbow, brown, native brook trout, and landlocked salmon. The tailwater below Murphy Dam has some monster brown trout. This is where the state record 16-pound, 6-ounce brown was taken.

Tackle

A 9-foot, 5-weight rod is ideal for most fishing conditions, but if you're targeting big browns in the deep pools below Murphy Dam, I would suggest throwing big streamers on a 6-weight rod using a sink-tip line.

The dam on First Connecticut Lake – the start of the Trophy Trout Stretch.

Hub City

PITTSBURG

Population 869

Pittsburg offers numerous lodging options, including traditional North Woods sporting camps, country inns, cabins, motels, and campgrounds. If you are a camper it's hard to beat Lake Francis State Park, which has streamside campsites at the lower end of the trophy stretch as well as lakeside sites on Lake Francis.

ACCOMMODATIONS

Cabins at Lopstick, 45 Stewart Young Road / 800-538-6659 / www.lopstick.com

Tall Timber Lodge, 609 Beach Road / 800-835-6343 / www.talltimber.com

Snowfield Cabins, 25 Kingfield Road / 603-538-7008 / www.snowfieldcabins.com

Mountain View Cabins & Campground, 2728 North Main Street / 603-538-6305 / www.moutainviewcabinsandcampground.com

North Woods Country Lodge and Cabins / www.northcountrylodgeandcabins.com

The Partridge Cabins & Lodge, 3 Partridge Road / 800-538-6380

Spruce Cone Cabins and Campground, 2067 North Main Street / 800-538-6361/ www.spruceconecabins.com

Lakeside Cabins & Lodge / 603-538-6935

Mountain View Cabins & Campground, 2787 North Main Street / 603-538-6305

Ramblewood Cabins & Campground, 59 Ramblewood Road / 877-726-2539 / www.ramblewoodcabins.com

CAMPGROUNDS

Lake Francis State Park, 439 River Road / 877-647-2757 / www.nhstateparks.org

RESTAURANTS

Young's General Store, Route 3 / 603-538-6616 / Pizza, deli, meats, groceries, gas, and liquor store

Murphy's Steakhouse at the Bear Tree Inn, 3329 Route 3 / 603-538-9995 / www.atbeartree.com

Back Lake Tavern at the North Woods Country Lodge and Cabins / 603-538-6521 / www.northcountrylodgeandcabins.com

Dube's Pittstop, Route 3 in downtown Pittsburg / 603-538-9944 / Best breakfast in the North Woods; all pies, cakes, and breads are baked fresh on the premises daily.

Indian Stream Steakhouse, 1041 S. Main Street, 603-538-9996

Buck Rub Pub, 2253 N. Main Street / 603-538-6935 / www.buckrubpub.com

HOSPITALS

Upper Connecticut Valley Hospital, Corliss Lane, Colebrook / 603-237-4971 / www.ucvh.org

FLY SHOPS/GUIDES

Cabins at Lopstick, 45 Stewart Young Road / 800-538-6659 / www.lopstick.com

North Country Fly Shop, Chuck DeGray, 9 Mountain Ash Drive / 603-538-1151

Osprey Fishing Adventures, Ken Hastings, Colebrook / 603-922-3800 / www.ospreyfishingadventures.com

MASSACHUSETTS

MASSACHUSETTS FACTS

Area: 10,550 Square Miles – 44th largest in the U.S.
Population: 6,587,536
State Fish: Cod

TROUT FISHING LICENSE

Annual Resident: $27.50*
Annual Non-Resident: $37.50*
Non-Resident 3-day: $23.50*
*Plus Wildlands Conservation Stamp

STATE RECORDS

Brook Trout, 10 pounds, 0 ounces by Peter Harand / 2008 / Ashfield Lake

Brown Trout, 19 pounds, 10 ounces by Dana Deblois / 1966 / Wachusett Reservoir

Rainbow Trout, 13-pounds, 13 ounces by Jeffery Greco / 1999 / Wachusett Reservoir

When I think of Massachusetts, I think of its great sports teams like the Celtics, Red Sox, and the Bruins. And when I think of Massachusetts' world-class fishery – historically, I always thought of its coastal fishery. For over three decades, I made annual pilgrimages to ply the waters off the Cape and the islands – Martha's Vineyard and Nantucket – with the long rod. Even though I spent 30 years of my life in New Jersey, I landed my first fly-rod striped bass, bluefish, and bluefin tuna in Massachusetts. While I had always heard of Massachusetts' world-class sweet water fishery, it wasn't until recently that I had the opportunity to explore it. When I was working full time with limited vacation time, it was hard for me to tear myself away from a chance at a Massachusetts saltwater inshore grand slam: a striped bass, bluefish, bonito, and false albacore in one day. In planning for my retirement and this book, I knew that I could keep my love affair with Massachusetts's coastal fishing and still have time to test the trout waters of the bay state. While only one Massachusetts tailwater made the cut for inclusion in this book, it made it with flying colors – easily earning my five star ranking. How could it not? The Deerfield River from Fife Brook Dam down to the Mohawk Campground flows though the picturesque Berkshire Mountains of northwestern Massachusetts. It has a good supply of high-quality cold water, and it is rich in aquatic insect biomass and abundant stream-bred, stocked, and holdover trout. This 8.5 mile portion also has two catch-and-release sections. It's no wonder that the bay state anglers consider the Deerfield the state's premier blue-ribbon trout stream.

Aaron Jasper with a 24-inch brown taken at dusk on a dry fly in Massachusetts. Photo courtesy Chris Johnson.

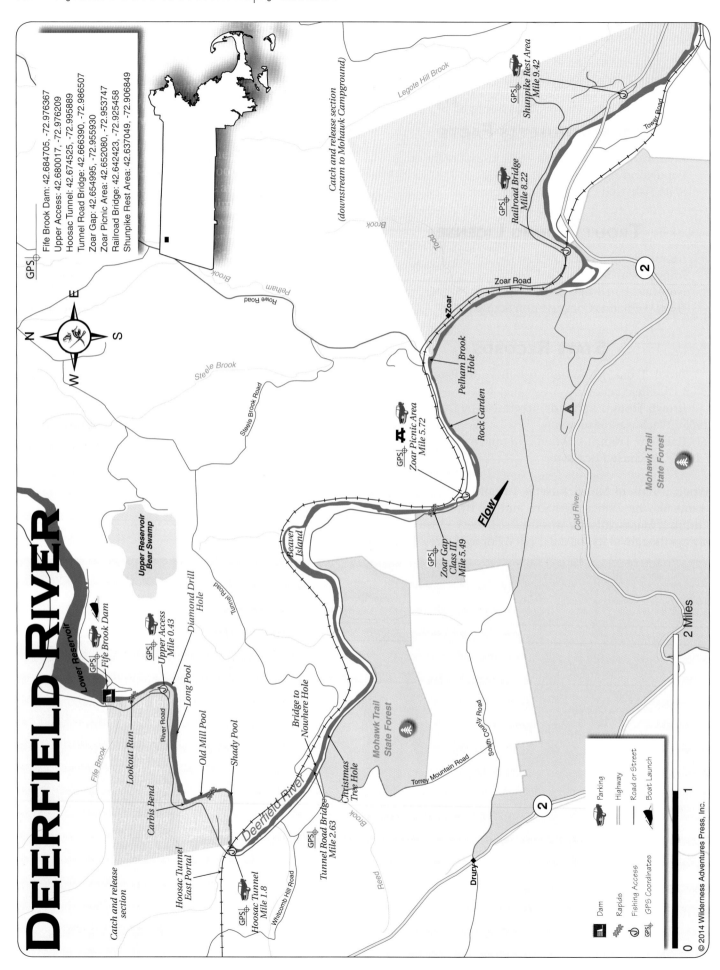

DEERFIELD RIVER

© 2014 Wilderness Adventures Press, Inc.

GPS
Fife Brook Dam: 42.684705, -72.976367
Upper Access: 42.680017, -72.976209
Hoosac Tunnel: 42.674525, -72.995889
Tunnel Road Bridge: 42.666390, -72.986507
Zoar Gap: 42.654995, -72.955930
Zoar Picnic Area: 42.652080, -72.953747
Railroad Bridge: 42.642423, -72.925458
Shunpike Rest Area: 42.637049, -72.906849

Catch and release section

Catch and release section (downstream to Mohawk Campground)

Upper Reservoir Bear Swamp

Lower Reservoir

Fife Brook Dam

Fife Brook

Steele Brook

Steele Brook Road

Rowe Road

Pelham Brook

Lookout Run

Carbis Bend

Old Mill Pool

Shady Pool

Long Pool

Diamond Drill Hole

Upper Access Mile 0.43

River Road

Tunnel Road

Hoosac Tunnel East Portal

Whitcomb Hill Road

Hoosac Tunnel Mile 1.8

Deerfield River

Bridge to Nowhere Hole

Christmas Tree Hole

Tunnel Road Bridge Mile 2.63

Reed Brook

Beaver Island

Mohawk Trail State Forest

Torrey Mountain Road

South County Road

Drury

Zoar Gap Class III Mile 5.49

Zoar Picnic Area Mile 5.72

Rock Garden

Zoar

Pelham Brook Hole

Zoar Road

Cold River

Mohawk Trail State Forest

Todd Brook

Railroad Bridge Mile 8.22

Legote Hill Brook

Shunpike Rest Area Mile 9.42

Tower Road

Flow

Map Legend

Dam
Rapids
Fishing Access
GPS GPS Coordinates

Parking
Highway
Road or Street
Boat Launch

0   1   2 Miles

DEERFIELD RIVER (FIVE STARS)

The Deerfield River gets its start in the Mount Snow region of southwestern Vermont and flows through the rugged and picturesque Berkshire Hills in northwest Massachusetts for some 76 miles to the Connecticut River. A total of ten hydroelectric dams have been built on the Deerfield River. The last one to be built on the Deerfield was Fife Brook Dam in the early 1970s. It is the releases from Fife Brook Dam that provide some of the best trout fishing in New England.

In 1997, the Federal Energy Regulatory Commission entered into an agreement with New England Power Company as part of the relicensing for the operation of the company's dams. The agreement included increased minimum flows and a coordinated water release schedule to improve the river's recreational use. This agreement also included the company's donation of conservation easements of some 18,000 acres of land along the river, thereby protecting the land from development pressures and guaranteeing public access. As with all tailwater dams, you should know the release schedules, and know also that they don't have to follow their schedule. At times, the flows from Fife Brook Dam can raise the river level over two feet in a matter of minutes – a rafters and kayakers dream – a fly fisher's nightmare. Power generation releases are usually from 9:00am to 2:00pm. Most nights the flows drop to 125cfs, and then mid-morning rise to 800 or 1,000cfs. The power company is required to keep conservation flows in the summer to protect the trout.

The best water on the river is from Fife Brook Dam 8.5 miles downstream to the Route 2 bridge by the Mohawk Campground. This section has high-quality water, a good biomass of insect life, and it supports the highest concentrations of wild browns in the river. There is some rainbow trout reproduction – the state stocks this section in both spring and fall with brown and rainbow trout. From Fife Brook to Mohawk Campground, there are two separate catch-and-release sections. The first runs from Fife Brook Dam downstream to Hoosac (railroad) Tunnel. The second catch-and-release section runs from Pelham Brook downstream to the Mohawk Campground and the Route 2 bridge. The river has a nice mix of rapids and riffles, as well as some long deep pools as it flows through a narrow gorge. The two catch-and-release sections offer excellent dry-fly fishing – some of the best in the East.

The Deerfield River is an excellent rainbow trout fishery. Photo by Bryan Lynch.

While wade fishing is possible during low water – it is very difficult during high water – great care should be taken. The best way to fish the river is from a raft outfitted for fly fishing. I strongly recommend using a guide, as you will have to navigate class III and class IV rapids. In addition, some put-in and take-out locations used by the locals guides require a winch to get the rafts in or out of the river. If you don't plan to float the river, concentrate your wade fishing during low flow conditions – when the levels drop to 125cfs you can wade most of the river from Fife Dam downstream to Route 2. Low water usually produces excellent dry fly fishing.

DIRECTIONS/ACCESS

The Deerfield is easily accessed from Route 2, the Mohawk Trail – the first officially dedicated scenic road in New England. The trail transverses some 50,000 acres of state parks and forests – some of the most beautiful landscapes in New England. From Shelburne Falls, you can access the Deerfield River off of Route 2 which follows the river up to the lower catch-and-release section at the Route 2 bridge by the Mohawk Campground. Just before the Route 2 bridge at the campground, Zoar Road comes in on the right. Zoar Road eventually turns into River Road and they provide access to 8.5 miles of quality trout water and the two catch-and-release sections on the Deerfield.

Fall fishing on the Deerfield can be rewarding through more than the fishing. Photo by Bryan Lynch.

STREAM FACTS

Seasons/Regulations

Excellent year-round trout fishery, the Deerfield has no closed season. In winter the action slows, but some big browns are taken every winter on streamers.

Fish

The river below Fife Brook Dam has wild browns and rainbows and the Deerfield is heavily stocked by the state from April through October. There is a good holdover rate and trout in the 15- to 16-inch range are common, with fish up to 24 inches not uncommon and fish from 24 to 30 inches are caught every season.

Hatches

The best hatches of the season start in the spring with the blue quills, blue-winged olives, and Hendricksons, followed by March browns, light Cahills, and sulphurs. Golden stoneflies and yellow Sallies hatch sporadically spring and summer. As with most tailwaters, midges are a must – larva, pupa, and adult patterns are all important on the Deerfield. The most reliable mayfly hatches on the Deerfield are the blue-winged-olives and sulphurs.

River Characteristics

Deerfield is mostly deep runs, riffles, and long, slow pools. There are many sections that you can wade fish during low water. The river is floatable year round but due to fluctuating water levels, getting caught in low water periods can severely damage a traditional wood or fiberglass drift boat. The full-time guides on the Deerfield float with large inflatable rafts. Some areas are almost impossible to put in and take out. On our most recent float trip, Tom Harrison of Harrison Anglers had to winch-in and winch-out our raft from high above the river.

What the Experts Say

From *A Guides Perspective*, By Chris Jackson:

The Deerfield River in western Massachusetts should be on the "bucket list" of any serious angler in the Northeast, with plenty of stocked rainbows and a robust population of wild brown, rainbow, and indigenous Eastern brook trout to target. The wild browns in particular grow to impressive sizes and are self-sustaining in spite of lack of any recognition or management plan by the state. Hatches on the river seldom achieve the blizzard-like proportions of those to the west in the Catskills, but they are consistent. A prudent angler should bring all of the standard mayfly patterns but put extra emphasis on caddis imitations – probably the most important insect for Deerfield anglers – from size 14 on down to size 20. Large attractor patterns like the Bugmeister, the Stimulator, and the Chubby Chernobyl will raise fish when the water is up, and those looking to connect with a wild brown over 20 inches should throw big streamers that imitate sculpin, dace, or small trout. A word of caution as well, the Deerfield is subject to daily hydro-peaking and at high water is better suited for fishing from a drift boat or with a two-handed rod. For both safety and productive wade fishing, go to H2oline.com (Waterline) for release information, and time your fishing for before or after the water release at Fife Brook Dam.

Flows

Releases from Fife Brook Dam can add two feet to the water level in a matter of minutes. When wading, study your surroundings carefully so that you can tell if the water starts to rise. If it does, leave the river immediately. Normally you can fish the area below the dam early in the day before the releases start, and then drive downstream to the lower catch-and-release area and get another hour or so of fishing before the releases reach you. For up-to-date release schedules call 888-356-3663 or go on line at www.h2online.com.

History

In 1997, a relicensing agreement included a coordinated water release schedule to improve the river's recreational use and the trout fishery really responded.

Tackle

For winter and early spring fishing, I'll use a 9-foot, 6-weight outfit rigged with a sink-tip line to drag big streamers through the deeper holes. Often the biggest trout of the season are caught this way. For most of the season a 9-foot, 4-weight is the ideal outfit. Chris Jackson, the owner of Fly Fish the Deerfield River, feels the key to success on the river is long leaders – up to 16-feet - especially when fishing dry flies in low water conditions. With a long leader, you don't "line" the fish and you will get longer drag free floats.

Hub Cities

CHARLEMONT
Population 1,266

ACCOMMODATIONS

Red Rose Motel, 1701 Mohawk Trail, / 413-625-2666 / www.redrosemotel.com

Dancing Bear Guest House, 22 Mechanic Street / 413-625-9281 / www.dancingbearguesthouse.com

The Oxbow Resort, Route 2 www.oxbowresortmotel.com / 413-625-6011

Cavalier Cottage Bed & Breakfast, 236 East Oxbow Road / 413-625-2262 / www.cavaliercottage.com

CAMPGROUNDS AND RV PARKS

Country Aire Campground, 1753 Mohawk Trail / 413-339-6600 / www.countryairecampground.com

Mohawk Park Family Campground & Pub, Mohawk Trail, / 413-339-4470

FLY SHOPS/GUIDES

Chris Jackson, Fly Fish the Deerfield Outfitters, Ashfield / 413-625-6283 / www.flyfishthedeerfield.com

Brian Lynch, Pheasant Tail Tours, Colrain / 413-834-7301 / www.pheasanttailtours.com

RENTAL/REPAIR

Balise Chevrolet, Buick, GMC, 440 Hall of Fame Avenue, Springfield / 413-342-5079

MEDICAL

North Adams Regional Hospital, 71 Hospital Avenue, North Adams / 413-664-5000

SHELBURNE FALLS
Population 1,893

RESTAURANTS

West End Pub, 16 State Street / 413-625-6216 / www.westendpubinfo.com / Casual dining – where the locals dine.

Fox Town Dinner, 25 Bridge Street / 413-625-6606

The Bakers Oven Bistro & Bar, 24 Bridge Street / 413-489-3110 / bakersovenbistro.com

CAR REPAIR

Davenports' Service Station, 269 Mohawk Trail / 413-625-9544

FLY SHOPS/GUIDES

Harrison Anglers, PO Box 2012, Buckland / 413-222-6720 / info@harrisonanglers.com

FOR MORE INFORMATION

Shelburne Falls Village Information Center, 75 Bridge Street / 413-625-2544

GREENFIELD
Population 17,456

ACCOMMODATIONS

West Winds Inn, 151 Smead Hill / 413-774-4025

Brandt House, 29 Highland Avenue / / 800-235-3329 / www.brandthouse.com

RESTAURANTS

The Hope and Olive, 44 Hope Street / 413-774-3150 / www.hopeandolive.com

Main Street Bar & Grille, 94 Main Street / 413-774-6388 / www.mainstreetbargrille.com

Pete's Seafood Restaurant, 54 School Street / 413-772-2153

CAR RENTAL/REPAIR

Enterprise-Rent-A-Car, 136 River Street / 413-774-5092

AIRPORTS

Bradley International Airport, Hartford CT / 56 miles from Greenfield

MEDICAL

Baystate Franklin Medical Center, 164 High Street / 413-773-0211

CONNECTICUT

CONNECTICUT FACTS

State Abbreviation: CT
Area: 5,544 square miles – 48th largest
Elevation –Highest Point: Mt. Frissell at 2,380 feet
Capital: Hartford
Largest City: Bridgeport
Population: 3,580,709
State Nickname: The Constitution State
State Motto: *Qui transtulit sustinet,* He who transplanted still sustains
State Song: Yankee Doodle
Name for Residents: Nutmegger
State Flower: Mountain laurel
State Animal: Sperm whale
State Tree: White oak
State Fish: American shad
State Bird: American robin

TROUT FISHING LICENSES

Annual resident fee: $28.00
Annual non-resident fee: $55.00
Non-resident 3-day fee: $22.00

STATE RECORDS

Brook trout, 9 pounds, 3 ounces by Dave Andes / 1998 / Blackwell Brook
Brown trout, 16 pound, 14 ounces by Samuel Wright / 1986 / East Twin Lake
Rainbow trout, 14 pounds, 10 ounces by Michael Ludlow / 1998 / Mansfield Hollow Lake

For over three decades, I made frequent trips to the Connecticut coast to ply the waters off Penfield Reef in Long Island Sound for striped bass and bluefish. Penfield was only 70 miles from my home in northern New Jersey, and I would frequently go up after work for a few hours if the tides were right. While I was well aware of the blue ribbon trout streams in Connecticut's Berkshires, they were just a little far off for an evening of fishing. In planning for my retirement and this book, I knew I would have plenty of time to explore Connecticut's tailwaters without compromising my time in the salt. Connecticut's world-class tailwaters did not disappoint – I hope you will give them a try.

From 1988 to 1995, the Connecticut Fisheries Division of their Department of Energy & Environmental Protection (DDEP) conducted a comprehensive statewide survey of the state's streams, gathering site-specific data on trout populations, habitat, water quality, and angler effort and catch. They found that more than 4,000 of their 6,587 miles of flowing water contained wild reproducing trout. Following the surveys, streams were classified based on their trout populations. They rank their Wild Trout Management Areas (WTMA) in three classes:

Class 1 are streams with abundant wild trout, and these streams are not stocked. They are open year round for catch-and-release only, with barbless single-hook artificial lures and flies only.

Class 2 are streams with wild trout and some stocked fry and fingerling trout. They are managed under general regulations, with a maximum harvest of two trout which must be at least 12 inches long.

Class 3 are streams which harbor some wild trout and stocked with catchable-size trout and require a 9-inch minimum size.

Trout Management Areas (TMA) which are capable of sustaining trout populations through the summer months, are managed for catch-and-release throughout the year. TMAs which provide good habitat only during the cooler months are managed for catch-and-release through fall and winter, but then are open to harvest in the spring to allow anglers to catch and keep fish which would otherwise die during the summer. To give anglers the opportunity to catch large trout, the state created Trophy Trout areas which receive increased numbers of larger hatchery trout.

While there are numerous excellent freestone streams in the state, when anglers think of trout fishing in Connecticut they usually think of its two blue ribbon trout streams, the Housatonic and the West Branch of the Farmington, which are both tailwaters and nationally recognized as high-quality trout fisheries. Veteran fishing guide Rob Nicholas, who has been guiding on both the Housatonic and Farmington Rivers for over 20 years, puts the quality of these two very different rivers this way: "There is always good fishing regardless of weather patterns and time of year, on one or both of these great dry fly rivers. The Housatonic is often best fished from a drift boat when the flows exceed 600cfs and the Farmington is a very manageable river for wading. The two rivers are only 40 minutes apart, making it possible to fish both in one day."

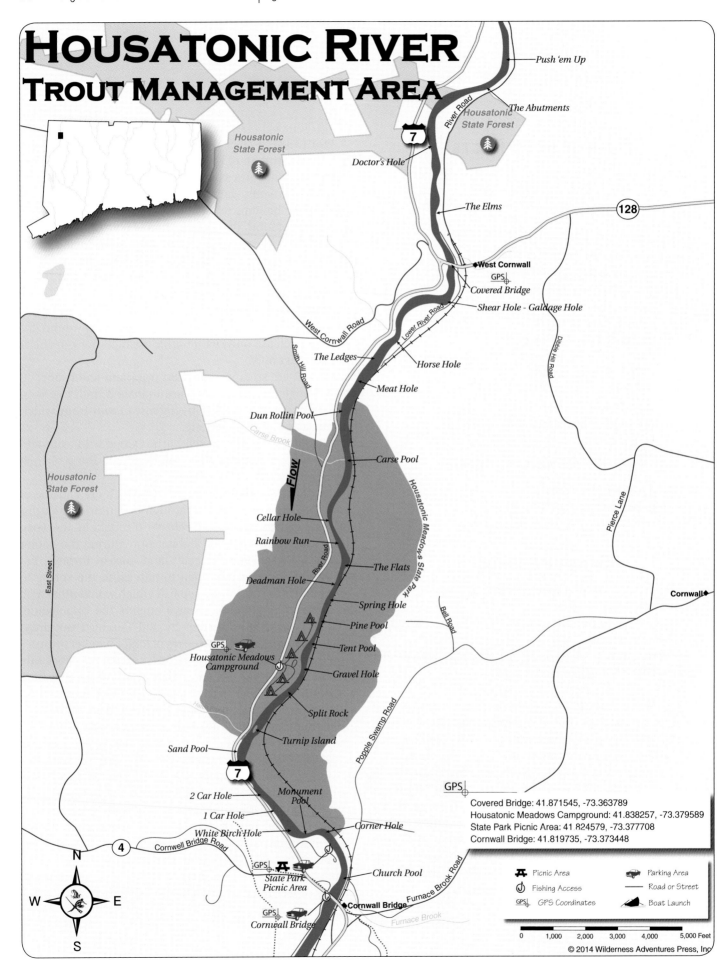

HOUSATONIC RIVER
TROUT MANAGEMENT AREA

Push 'em Up

The Abutments

Housatonic State Forest

Housatonic State Forest

Doctor's Hole

River Road

7

128

The Elms

West Cornwall

GPS

Covered Bridge

Shear Hole - Galdage Hole

West Cornwall Road

Lower River Road

Dibble Hill Road

The Ledges

Smith Hill Road

Horse Hole

Meat Hole

Dun Rollin Pool

Carse Brook

Carse Pool

Housatonic State Forest

Flow

Cellar Hole

Housatonic Meadows State Park

Rainbow Run

Pierce Lane

East Street

The Flats

Deadman Hole

River Road

Cornwall

Spring Hole

Bell Road

Pine Pool

GPS

Tent Pool

Housatonic Meadows Campground

Gravel Hole

Split Rock

Popple Swamp Road

Turnip Island

Sand Pool

7

GPS

2 Car Hole

Monument Pool

Covered Bridge: 41.871545, -73.363789
Housatonic Meadows Campground: 41.838257, -73.379589
State Park Picnic Area: 41.824579, -73.377708
Cornwall Bridge: 41.819735, -73.373448

1 Car Hole

Corner Hole

White Birch Hole

4

Cornwell Bridge Road

GPS

Church Pool

Furnace Brook Road

State Park Picnic Area

N

W E

S

GPS

Cornwall Bridge

Furnace Brook

Picnic Area

Fishing Access

GPS GPS Coordinates

Parking Area

Road or Street

Boat Launch

0   1,000   2,000   3,000   4,000   5,000 Feet

© 2014 Wilderness Adventures Press, Inc

HOUSATONIC RIVER (FOUR STARS)

The Housatonic – or the "Housy" as its regulars respectfully call it—is certainly one of the East Coast's premier trout streams, and it offers some of New England's most breathtaking scenery, especially in the fall. "Housatonic" is an Indian name meaning "river beyond the mountains". The Housatonic begins in the Berkshires of Massachusetts and flows south into Litchfield County in the northwestern corner of Connecticut, where it has become a popular destination trout fishery. Eventually it flows into Long Island Sound and the mouth of the Housatonic; where it enters the sound is a very popular striped bass destination.

While the Housy flows for some 130 miles and provides opportunities to catch a wide variety of fish, the jewel in the river is the 10.4-mile Trout Management Area located within the towns of Salisbury, Canaan, Sharon, and Cornwall. The TMA starts at the bridge at Routes 7 and 112 and runs downriver 10 miles to Cornwall Bridge. The state posts areas around coldwater tributaries as trout refuges that are off limits to fishing during the summer months. For the most part, the Housy depends on annual trout stockings, and a large percentage of these fish hold over. In addition, the state stocks par trout which grow in the river and look and act like wild trout.

DIRECTIONS/ACCESS

The Trout Management Area starts in the town of Cornwall Bridge and runs about 10.4 miles upstream to the Push 'em Up Pool north of the covered bridge in West Cornwall. From Cornwall Bridge, take Route 4 west across the river and turn right on Route 7 North. Route 7 provides numerous access opportunities to fish, from Cornwall Bridge upstream to the covered bridge in West Cornwall. From the covered bridge you can access additional waters in a beautifully wooded section of the river known as The Elms.

Church Pool

After crossing the Cornwall Bridge, turn right onto Route 7 north and take the first right off Route 7, which takes you 300 yards to the Church Pool, with ample parking next to the church.

Housatonic Meadows State Park

Continuing north on Route 7, it's a short distance to the entrance to the Housatonic Meadows State Park and some of the best pools on the river. As you enter the park you will see the popular Monument Pool. I like to continue downstream along the park road to the end, which provides access to a beautiful stretch of river.

Housatonic Meadows State Campground

A short distance north of the state park on Route 7 you can access the river in Housatonic Meadows State Campground. The campground provides good access, but it receives a fair amount of fishing pressure. From the campground upstream to the covered bridge in West Cornwall, there are several roadside pull-offs.

Covered Bridge

At West Cornwall, I find better access by crossing the river on Route 128 to the east side via the covered bridge. From there you can access a short section of nice water downstream of the bridge by turning right onto Lower River Road and taking the first dirt road on the right to the state parking area, where there is excellent access to the river, just below the covered bridge.

A beautiful Housatonic River rainbow caught by Torrey Collins. Photo by Dave Skok.

The Elms

There are several miles of water upstream of the bridge known as The Elms. This section doesn't get the pressure that the river gets from the covered bridge in West Cornwall downstream to Cornwall Bridge. The Elms can be reached by taking the second left in West Cornwall onto Old River Road. After crossing the railroad tracks twice, the road narrows and turns to gravel, but it is easily negotiated in any vehicle. There are numerous pull-offs and trails down to the river.

Stream Facts

Seasons/Regulations

The Housatonic Trout Management Area is open to year-round, catch-and-release fishing except the areas within 100 feet of the mouth of coldwater tributaries which provide thermal refuges for the trout in the summer. These areas are closed to fishing from July 1 to August 31. The refuges are well posted, as is the fly-fishing-only section, which starts at Cornwall Bridge and runs 3.5 miles upstream. The prime fishing is from late April to mid-June and again in the fall. Fall can be magical on the Housy – the waters begin to cool, angling pressure is low, the state heavily stocks the river in the fall, and the blue-winged olive hatch brings the season's best fish to the surface. Plus the Housatonic Valley hardwoods put on a spectacular display of brilliant colors, making your day on the water just that much more rewarding.

Fish

The Housatonic relies on the liberal annual stocking of trout by the state in both spring and fall. A good number of these fish hold over to the next season.

River Characteristics

The Housatonic River reminds me of some of the bigger western waters and, in fact, several guides offer float trips on the river. Most of the TMA is made up of long, deep pools separated by short runs and riffles. Wading can be difficult, especially during periods of high water; cleated wading shoes and a wading belt and staff are a must.

What the Experts Say

Veteran guide and store manager of Housatonic River Outfitters, Torrey Collins, describes the Housatonic River this way: "The Housy looks and feels much like a western river. Not only is she quite beautiful, but also plenty big enough to float a drift boat or raft down her. The cobbled bottom and fertility (she flows through a lot of limestone geology) create a fishery with heavy hatches, an abundance of bigger bugs, crustaceans, and some large holdover trout. The skilled nympher can find good fishing under most conditions – they have the most constant results and catch many of the larger trout. Hendricksons are the first hatch of the season that really gets the trout fired up, including the big ones – the evening spinner falls typically produce bigger fish on dries than the afternoon hatch.

What's in a Name?

"Housatonic" is an Indian name meaning "river beyond the mountains".

Hatches

For many eastern anglers, the Hendrickson (*Ephemerella subvaria*) hatch is a signal that spring trout fishing season is in full swing. The Housy is known for its tremendous mayfly hatches, and its Hendrickson hatches and spinner falls are among the best in the East. The Farmington also has excellent Hendrickson hatches, but the spinner fall is usually better on the Housy. If time allows, I try to fish the Hendrickson hatch on the West Branch of the Farmington during the day and drive the 30 miles to the Housy in the evening to catch the spinner fall. Mid-May into June, you can expect March browns and light Cahills. I have also witnessed both brown and green drakes and trico hatches in the "Horse Hole". The Housatonic also has very prolific fall blue-winged olive hatches both *Baetis* (size18) and *Acentrella turbida* (sizes 24 to 28), which can bring some of the season's biggest fish to the surface. As in so many of our eastern tailwaters, midge patterns work year round.

Tackle

For the Housatonic River, I carry two outfits: a 9-foot, 4-weight with a floating line for most of my dry fly and nymph fishing and a 9-foot, 6-weight with a sink tip for fishing streamers in some of the deeper pools and runs.

River Flows

For information call Northeast Utilities (888-417-4833).

Photo by Mandy Sanasie.

Photo by Rob Nicholas.

The Housatonic River feels and fishes a lot like a big western river, according to Housatonic River Outfitters owner Torrey Collins.

Photo by Rob Nicholas.

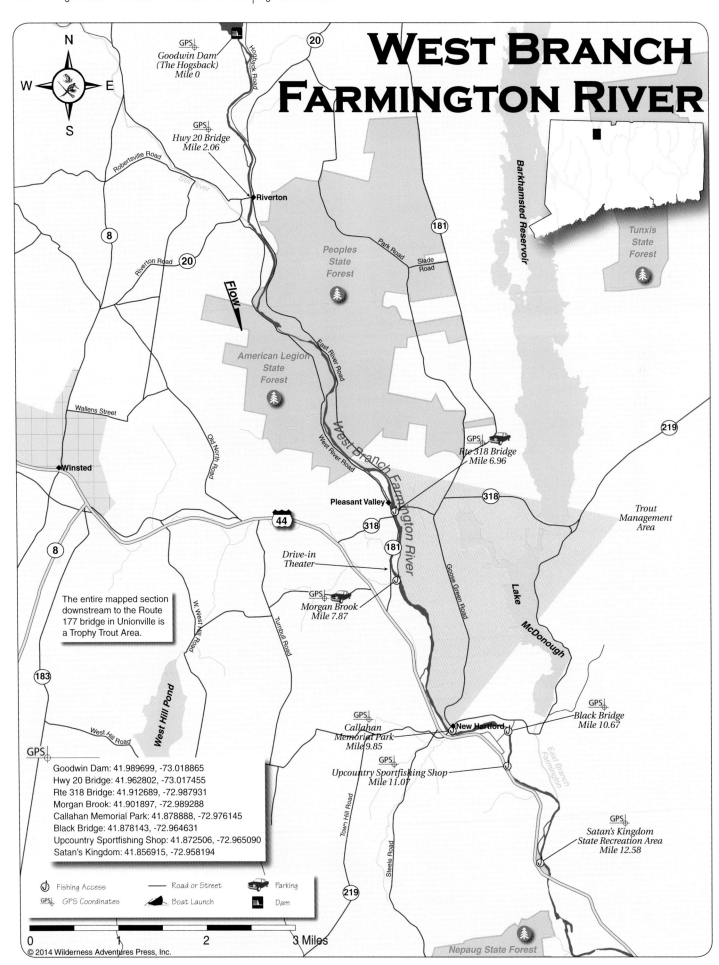

WEST BRANCH FARMINGTON RIVER

Goodwin Dam
(The Hogsback)
Mile 0

GPS
Hwy 20 Bridge
Mile 2.06

Riverton

Barkhamsted Reservoir

Tunxis State Forest

Peoples State Forest

Park Road

Slade Road

American Legion State Forest

East River Road

West Branch Farmington River

West River Road

GPS
Rte 318 Bridge
Mile 6.96

Pleasant Valley

Trout Management Area

Drive-in Theater

GPS
Morgan Brook
Mile 7.87

Goose Green Road

Lake McDonough

The entire mapped section downstream to the Route 177 bridge in Unionville is a Trophy Trout Area.

West Hill Pond

GPS
Callahan Memorial Park
Mile 9.85

New Hartford

GPS
Black Bridge
Mile 10.67

East Branch Farmington

GPS
Upcountry Sportfishing Shop
Mile 11.07

GPS
Goodwin Dam: 41.989699, -73.018865
Hwy 20 Bridge: 41.962802, -73.017455
Rte 318 Bridge: 41.912689, -72.987931
Morgan Brook: 41.901897, -72.989288
Callahan Memorial Park: 41.878888, -72.976145
Black Bridge: 41.878143, -72.964631
Upcountry Sportfishing Shop: 41.872506, -72.965090
Satan's Kingdom: 41.856915, -72.958194

GPS
Satan's Kingdom
State Recreation Area
Mile 12.58

Winsted

Robertsville Road

Riverton Road

Wallens Street

Old North Road

W. West Hill Road

Turnbull Road

West Hill Road

Town Hill Road

Steele Road

Hogback Road

Still River

FLOW

Fishing Access
GPS GPS Coordinates
Road or Street
Boat Launch
Parking
Dam

0   1   2   3 Miles

© 2014 Wilderness Adventures Press, Inc.

Nepaug State Forest

WEST BRANCH OF THE FARMINGTON RIVER (FIVE STARS)

When most anglers talk about fly fishing the Farmington River, they are referring to the West Branch of the Farmington in the area from Riverton downstream to New Hartford. The Farmington River is the largest trout fishery (in terms of stocking) in Connecticut, with approximately 46,000 fish stocked annually. The coldwater releases from Colebrook and Goodwin Dams (also referred to as West Branch and Hogback Dams) are located just upstream of the town of Riverton. These releases provide a high-quality, year-round trout fishery; in fact, because of the high-quality coldwater releases, the Farmington is the only river in the state which receives summer trout stockings. The section below Goodwin Dam downstream for about 2.5 miles to the Still River is a beautiful piece of crystal clear water flowing through a heavily forested area. However, the trout population here is not as dense as farther downstream, as most of the river's nutrients settle out in the reservoirs, reducing the diversity and abundance of aquatic insects directly below the reservoir.

The Still River enters the Farmington below Riverton and adds much-needed nutrients to the relatively sterile water released by the dam. From the confluence with the Still River downstream, the population of aquatic insects is abundant and the trout growth is exceptional. Below Route 219 downstream to Collinsville, the river is still influenced by the tailwater releases, and it remains a tremendous trout fishery. Excellent access is provided off Route 44. Below Collinsville, the river begins to change into a warmwater fishery.

There is another Trout Management Area on the mainstem of the Farmington River which starts at the Collinsville Dam and extends downriver four miles to the Route 4 bridge. Fishing here is catch-and-release from September 1 to the third Saturday in April (opening day in Connecticut). From opening day through the end of August the creel limit is two fish per day, 12 inches or greater.

DIRECTIONS/ACCESS

Satan's Kingdom

From the hub city of Farmington, take Route 10 north to Route 44 and go west for about 15 miles to the bridge over the mainstem of the Farmington River as it enters Satan's Kingdom. I find the best fishing from Satan's Kingdom upstream to the West Branch and the entire West Branch all the way to Hogback Road just below the dam.

Satan's Kingdom is easily reached by taking Route 44 west until you cross the river at Satan's Kingdom. You will see a large public lot on the right. Fish the pool from the lot and on upstream. (Note: This is where most of the whitewater rafting starts, which is one of the reasons I fish from here upstream).

The UpCountry Sportfishing shop is just a few miles west of Satan's Kingdom on Route 44 in Pine Meadow. They have up-to-the minute information and there is access to the river behind the store.

Black Bridge Pool

From the UpCountry Sportfishing shop in the Pine Meadow Section of New Hartford, take Route 44 for 0.4 miles and turn right at the post office onto to Wickett Street. Take the next right onto Ten Street, then the next left one block to New Milford Elementary School. Turn right onto Black Bridge Road and park on either side of the bridge.

The 219 Bridge Pool in New Hartford

Another 0.5 mile up Route 44 is the Route 219 Bridge Pool. This pool marks the lower end of the Trout Management Area. Take Route 219 north across the bridge and turn right into Callahan Memorial Park, which provides excellent access to the popular Wall section of the river.

Morgan Brook, Drive-In, and Church Pools

These can be accessed by taking Route 44 west of Route 219 for 1.5 miles to Route 181 in Barkhamsted. Turn right onto Route 181 North and you will have several pull-offs at Morgan Brook, across from the drive-in theater, and finally across from the Church is a very large and popular pool which runs from the Route 318 bridge downstream past the Church. Access is from pull-offs along Route 181 across from the Church. There is also a parking area on the east side of the Route 318 bridge and along a dirt road which runs downstream from the parking area on the east side of the bridge.

The state forests on both sides of the river upstream of the Route 318 bridge have the look and feel of the deep woods of Maine. Here you can fish in a wilderness-like setting with access to over a dozen popular, well-known and named pools. This section has been designated as Wild and Scenic by the National Park Service, the only Wild and Scenic river in Connecticut. From the Route 318 bridge in Pleasant Valley you have access to both sides of the river via East and West River Roads. East River Road is accessed from the east side of the Route 318 bridge by making the first left after crossing the bridge. The road closely follows the river upstream for about four miles to the Route 20 bridge in Riverton. A short way up River Road you will enter the Peoples Forest, which provides two large recreation areas along the river with easy access and plenty of parking.

The famous Church Pool on the West Branch of the Farmington, with Route 318 Bridge in background.

The first is Mathies Grove and a little farther upstream is Whittemore Recreation Area. Above Whittemore there are numerous pull-offs with easy access to the river. One of the most beautiful sections is along Hogback Road, which comes in on the left side of Route 20 upstream of Riverton. Hogback Road gives you access to the first 1.5 miles of the West Branch of the Farmington below the Goodwin Dam and the West Branch Reservoir. Here you will be fishing gentle riffles and beautiful pools in some of the most scenic settings. From the west side of the Route 318 bridge you can take West River Road along the river through the American Legion State Forest.

STREAM FACTS

Seasons/Regulations

The Farmington River from Goodwin Dam on the West Branch downstream to the Route 177 bridge in Unionville is designated as a Trophy Trout area by the DEEP. The daily limit is two fish of at least 12 inches, except for the Trout Management Area on the West Branch. The TMA begins at the power lines which cross the river in the Mathias Grove section of the Peoples State Forest about a mile above Route 318, and it extends downstream 3.5 miles to the Route 219 bridge in New Hartford. The TMA is managed as catch-and-release year round with no tackle restrictions, except that only barbless hooks may be used.

Fish

The state heavily stocks the river, which also has wild trout and a good holdover population. DEEP surveys indicate that over 35 percent of the fish in the TMA section are wild or holdover trout. Trout in excess of 20 inches are not uncommon.

River Characteristics

The Trout Management area on the West Branch of the Farmington River is the most heavily fished section of any stream in Connecticut, with annual angler effort up to 12,960 hours per mile, so the trout get well-educated early in the year. Long leaders and light tippets are required for successful dry fly fishing. This section of the West Branch has many large, deep pools loaded with wild, holdover, and freshly-stocked trout. Pools like Church, Boneyard, and Greenwoods harbor large trout and can have rising trout 365 days a year.

What the Experts Say

Veteran fishing guide Rob Nicholas, who has been guiding on both the Housatonic and Farmington Rivers for over 20 years, puts the quality of these two very different rivers this way: "There is always good fishing regardless of weather patterns and time of year, on one or both of these great dry fly rivers. The Housatonic is often best fished from a drift boat when the flows exceed 600cfs and the Farmington is a very manageable river for wading. The two rivers are only 40 minutes apart making it possible to fish both in one day."

Hatches

The West Branch of the Farmington River has tremendous aquatic insect biomass and diversity. Heaviest hatches include early black stoneflies, blue quills, and Hendricksons in the early spring. Late spring brings March browns, and heavy sulphur hatches both *invaria* and *dorothea*, followed by *isonychias*, which continue through October. August has a heavy trico hatch, and most afternoons from mid-October until the end of November, the West Branch has a reliable hatch of small (#24-28) blue-winged olives (*Acentrella turbida*). Over the duration of this hatch the fish get super-selective – locals in the area are known to fish a small Blue-winged Olive wet fly right in the surface film. As in many of our tailwaters, midges work year round.

Tackle

I prefer to fish the Farmington with a 9-foot, 4-weight outfit.

Hub Cities

CORNWALL

Population 1,399

ACCOMMODATIONS

The Cornwall Inn, 270 Kent Road, South, Cornwall Bridge / 860-672-6884 / www.cornwallinn.com

CAMPGROUNDS

Housatonic Meadows Campground, on the river in Cornwall / 860-672-6772

RESTAURANTS

Wandering Moose Café, 421 Sharon Goshen Turnpike, West Cornwall / 860-672-0178 / www.themoosecafe.com

GUIDES/FLY SHOPS

Rob Nicholas / Housatonic Anglers, 26 Bolton Hill Road / 860-672-4457 / www.housatonicanglers.com

Housatonic River Outfitters, Inc. 24 Kent Road, Cornwall Bridge / 860-672-1010 www.dryflies.com

Housatonic Meadows Fly Shop, 13 Route 7, Cornwall Bridge / 860-672-6064 / www.flyfishct.com

Aaron Jasper's Fly Fishing Evolution Guide Service / www.flyfishingevolution.com

Housatonic Fly Fishermen's Assn. /Anglers www.HFFA.net / They have published a very comprehensive guide, *Fishing the Housatonic River Trout Management Area*. The guide has excellent maps and hatch chart.

FOR MORE INFORMATION

Litchfield Hills Travel Information / 800-663-1273 / www.litchfieldhills.com

FARMINGTON

Population 25,529

ACCOMMODATIONS

The Farmington Inn, 827 Farmington Avenue / 860-677-2821 / www.farmingtoninn.com

The Simsbury Inn, 397 Hopmeadow Street, Simsbury / www.simsburyinn.com

CAMPGROUNDS

American Legion State Forest / Austin Hawes Campground, West River Road, Pleasant Valley / 860-424-3474 / seasonal / Located on the banks of the West Branch of the Farmington River.

RESTAURANTS

Piccolo Arancio, 819 Farmington Avenue Farmington CT / 860-674-1224 / www.piccoloarancio.com

Log House Restaurant, 110 New Hartford Road, Route 44, Barkhamsted / 860-379-8937 / www.theloghouserestaurant.com

Portobello's Ristorante & Pizzeria, 107 Main Street, Route 44, New Hartford / 860-693-2598

GUIDES, FLY SHOPS AND SPORTING GOODS

Up Country Sportfishing, 352 Main Street, Route 44, New Hartford / 860-379-1952 / www.farmingtonriver.com

The Complete Angler, 172 Heights Road, Darien / 203-655-9400 / www.compleat-angler.com

The Valley Angler, 56 Padanaram Road, Danbury / 203-792-8324

North Cove Outfitters, 75 Main Street, Old Saybrook / 860-388-6585 / www.northcove.com

Orvis Darien, 432 Post Road, Darien / 203-662-0844 / www.orvis.com/darien

Connecticut Outfitters, 554 Wethersfield Avenue, Hartford / 860-296-0110 / www.CT-OUTFITTERS.com

Farmington River Anglers Association / www.fraa.org / They have published a wonderful guide, *A Guide to Fishing the Farmington River*. It is loaded with information, hatch chart and a great map.

AIRPORTS

Bradley International Airport, Schoephoester Road, Windsor Locks / 860-292-2000 www.bradelyairport.com

MEDICAL

Middlesex Hospital, 28 Crescent Streets, Middletown / 860-224-4493

FOR MORE INFORMATION

Farmington Chamber of Commerce, 200 Main Street, Bristol / 860-676-8490 / www.farmingtonchamber.com

Mid-Atlantic States

Today mid-Atlantic anglers are blessed with a plethora of flyfishing destinations. There are thousands of miles of native brook trout streams in the Catskill, Pocono, and western Maryland mountains. The East hosts the world-renowned limestone streams of central Pennsylvania and the fabled waters of New York State's "Charmed Circle", the birthplace of American dry-fly fishing. The region's anglers also have the option of floating some of the East's great tailwater rivers like the Delaware, Lehigh, Youghiogheny, and the North Branch of the Potomac. Float one of these great tailwaters

and between the fish and the surroundings, you will swear you are on one of the West's great tailwater rivers.

Prior to the Civil War, northwestern New Jersey, Pennsylvania's Pocono Mountains, New York's Catskills, and the mountains of western Maryland were covered with old-growth forests, predominantly hemlocks. These trees shaded the region's trout streams, which kept their waters cool and stabilized their river banks, minimizing erosion and siltation. This habitat supported a healthy population of native brook trout (*Salvelinus fontinalis*) which are actually a member of the char family and are the only truly native

One of the many trout streams in the Mid-Atlantic States. Photo courtesy Joshua Bergan.

trout of the region. Brook trout need cooler water and are more sensitive to pollution than the non-native brown and rainbow trout.

During the Civil War the demand for leather goods exploded. The region's forests were clear-cut and hemlock bark, which is rich in tannin, was stripped from the trees and used to cure the leather. This forest devastation caused the waters to warm and destabilized the stream banks. The rivers became silt-laden, impairing brook trout spawning.

By the late 1800s, native brook trout were all but wiped out in the region's major rivers, surviving only in the headwater brooks and tributaries. As fishing for native brook trout declined, brown trout from Germany and rainbow trout from the West Coast were introduced to supply fish for anglers to pursue. These non-native trout, especially the brown trout, thrived in their new environment, and today the mid-Atlantic region boasts a healthy wild and stocked trout fishery.

Nineteen mid-Atlantic tailwaters made the grade of four or five stars, qualifying them for inclusion in this book. Ten are in New York, five in Pennsylvania, and four in Maryland.

NEW YORK

NEW YORK FACTS

Area: 47,214 square miles
Population: 19,254,6
State Fish: Brook trout

STATE FISHING LICENSE FEES

www.newyorkfishinglicense.org
Annual Resident Fee: $29.00
Non-Resident Annual Fee: $70.00
Non-Resident 7-day Fee: $35.00

STATE RECORDS

Brook trout, 6 pounds, 0 ounces by Richard Beauchamp / May 16, 2013 / Silver Lake

Brown trout, 33 pounds, 2 ounces by Tony Brown / June 10, 1997 / Lake Ontario

Rainbow trout, 31 pounds, 3 ounces by R. Kennard / July 19, 1994 / Indian Lake

New York City's quest for high-quality drinking water prompted the city's forefathers to acquire large land holdings in the Catskill and Croton watersheds, and to build elaborate reservoir and aqueduct systems to deliver the city's water supply. The first of these reservoirs was built on the Croton River in 1842. Today the city has a total of 19 water supply reservoirs, many of which have bottom-release tailwater dams. A total of 10 New York State rivers earned my four- or five-star rating. For the purpose of this book, I have divided the tailwaters of southeastern New York State into two sections: the Catskill and Croton watersheds.

Thanks to the foresight of the New York State Department of Environmental Conservation, which began acquiring streamside easements back in the 1930s, we now have public access to some of the best flyfishing waters in the East. The easements are for the most part permanent; giving anglers the right to walk along stream banks for fishing. Every East Coast fly fisher should experience Catskill waters, as much for their heritage as for the trout fishing. For me, a trip to the Catskills is as much spiritual as it is recreational.

Austin Francis, in his great work *Catskill Rivers*, aptly crowned the Catskills "The Birthplace of American Fly Fishing". Located about two hours northwest of Manhattan, the heart of the Catskills is steeped in angling history and tradition, and to this day is still a world-class fishing destination. If you draw a circle 30 miles wide around the village of Claryville, inside it are five of the country's most famous trout streams: the Beaverkill, Willowemoc, Esopus, Schoharie, and Neversink Rivers. Not far to the west lies the upper Delaware River system. The construction of dams on the East and West Branches of the Delaware has created a world-class tailwater trout fishery which extends down into the mainstem of the Delaware as far south as Callicoon, some 27 miles downstream from the junction of the East and West Branches.

When you wade the waters of these legendary trout streams, you are following in the footsteps of angling legends and pioneers such as Theodore Gordon, who developed American dry fly patterns and is hailed as the father of modern American angling; Edward Hewitt, who pioneered nymph fishing in North America; and George LaBranche, author of *The Dry Fly and Fast Water*. Each one plied the waters of "The Charmed Circle". In my early visits to the Catskills, I had the pleasure of meeting local Catskill fly-tying pioneers Elsie and Harry Darbee and Walt and Winnie Dette, who kept the Catskill tradition alive by tying and selling traditional Catskill patterns out of their homes on the banks of the Willowemoc Creek in Roscoe, New York. This tradition is still carried on today by the Dette's daughter, Mary Dette Clark and her grandson, Joe Fox.

TROUT REGULATIONS

SEASON

The New York State (NYS) trout season runs from April 1 to October 15.

A fishing license runs from October 1 to September 30 of the following year.

CREEL LIMIT

An angler may harvest up to five trout per day, with no minimum size.

SPECIAL REGULATIONS

The Catskill Watershed

The Neversink River has a five trout limit of 9 inches, except for the Unique Area, which is managed under Catch-and-Release-Artificial Lures Only regulations. The entire river below the Neversink Reservoir is open to fishing from April 1 until October 15.

The Mongaup River below the Rio Dam is Artificial Lures Only, with a limit of thee trout 12 inches or larger. The season runs from April 1 to October 15.

On the West Branch of the Delaware River from Cannonsville Dam downstream, anglers may harvest two trout per day over 12 inches except in the Catch-and-Release-Artificial Lures Only section, which runs from the Route 17 bridge in Deposit downstream for two miles. Fishing is open from April 1 to October 15 and then is closed from October 16 to March 31 to protect spawning trout.

The season on the Border Water section of the West Branch of the Delaware runs from the first Saturday after April 11 to October 15, with a limit of two trout at least 12 inches per day. From October 16 through the Friday preceding the first Saturday after April 11, fishing is Catch-and-Release-Artificial Lures Only.

The season on the Border Water section of the Upper Delaware River (between Pennsylvania and New York states) runs from the first Saturday after April 11 to October 15, with a one-trout limit of at least 14 inches per day. From October 16 through the Friday preceding the first Saturday after April 11, fishing is Catch-and-Release-Artificial Lures Only.

The season on the East Branch of the Delaware from the Pepacton Dam downstream to the Shinhopple bridge runs from April 1 to October 15, with a limit of two trout of at least 12 inches. Angling is prohibited from October 16 through March 31.

The season on East Branch of the Delaware from Shinhopple Bridge downstream to Hancock runs from April 1 to October 15, with a limit of two trout at least 12 inches. From October 16 through March 31 angling is Catch-and-Release Only.

On the Esopus Creek the season runs from April 1 to November 30 with a limit of five trout with no more than two longer than 12 inches.

The Croton Watershed

The East Branch of the Croton River from Diverting Reservoir to East Branch Reservoir is regulated as Artificial Lures Only. It is open to fishing year round, with a daily limit of one trout 14 inches or more.

The West Branch of the Croton River from the Croton Falls Reservoir to the East Branch of the Croton River is regulated as Catch-and-Release – Artificial Lures Only and is open to fishing from April 1 to September 30.

The West Branch of the Croton River from West Branch Reservoir to Croton Falls Reservoir has a limit of five trout of 9 inches from April 1 to September 30.

The Amawalk Outlet from Amawalk Reservoir to the Muscoot River is regulated as Artificial Lures Only and is open to fishing from April 1 to September 30, with a daily limit of three trout 12 inches or more.

New York is one of the best states in the nation for big brown trout. Photo courtesy Lee Hartman.

THE UPPER DELAWARE RIVER SYSTEM

Chris Santella's book, *Fifty Places to Fly Fish Before You Die*, highlights 50 of the world's greatest places to flyfish, and the Upper Delaware system made his cut. The Upper Delaware River system has the distinction of being the easternmost "western" trout river in the United States. The fishery began to develop in the 1960s with the construction of the Pepacton Reservoir on the East Branch and the Cannonsville Reservoir on the West Branch. Prior to the construction of the Cannonsville and Pepacton Dams and their subsequent coldwater releases, the Upper Delaware was an excellent smallmouth bass fishery. (The middle and lower sections of the Delaware River still provide excellent fishing for smallmouth bass and many other species of warmwater fish.) Coldwater releases from these dams converted the lower East and West Branches and the first 30 miles of the Upper Delaware River into a world-class wild trout fishery. The trout are wild, large, and highly selective.

While doing the research for my book, *Flyfisher's Guide to the Big Apple*, Wilderness Adventure Press, 2011, I had the pleasure of interviewing Lee Hartman, who started fishing the Upper Delaware in 1973. Lee began guiding in 1985 and owned the Indian Springs Flyfishing Camp right on the banks of the Delaware until he recently sold it. I have known Lee for over 30 years – he is an excellent fly fisherman and guide, and he hosts trips to spectacular world-wide flyfishing destinations. Lee was one of the early pioneers of the Upper Delaware River trout fishery and co-founded the Friends of the Upper Delaware River (FUDR) in 2002, hosting the founding meeting at his Indian Springs

Flyfishing Camp. FUDR is leading the fight to protect this world-class trout fishery as much for the fishing as for the local economies which depend on this resource for their livelihoods.

During the interview, Lee relayed a story of one of his early experiences trying to gain access to the Delaware in search of some of its legendary trout. Lee was focusing his efforts in the Lordville area. One day he drove into a farm owned by "Bunny" Gail. When Lee approached Mr. Gail and politely asked for permission to access the river from his property, Mr. Gail responded, "Yeah, you can fish it, it will cost you two bucks – but you ain't gonna catch nothin' but those bleeping, bleeping trout! Those dams ruined our catfish and bass fishin." Lee and I had a good laugh about this and I said, "Well, I guess one man's trash is another man's treasure." Lee found his treasure in the big, beautiful trout of the Upper Delaware and he has spent the last 30 years of his life sharing his treasure with others.

Angler Brian Crowden with a 26-inch brown trout from the West Branch of the Delaware. Photo by Kevin Cabelman.

Because of the protections provided by the federal Clean Water Act enacted in 1972, the pollution block has eased and the water quality in the Philadelphia section of the Delaware River has improved dramatically. In the last three decades, the runs of anadromous fish have improved to a point that we now have an excellent American shad and striped bass fishery. Shad are quite common during their spring spawning runs along the entire length of the Delaware River and up the East Branch to its junction with the Beaverkill. Anglers are now targeting striped bass in the lower river, and I personally know of one large striper taken out of the East/West Branches' Junction Pool and several smaller ones which have been taken on the West Branch near Balls Eddy.

The Mainstem of the Delaware is the longest undammed river in the East, flowing some 321 miles from Hancock to the mouth of the Delaware Bay. The Upper Delaware River flows through a remote section of Pennsylvania's "Endless Mountains" to the west and the Catskills Mountains to the east. The first 102 miles of the Mainstem of the Delaware are protected by its federally-designated Wild and Scenic status and managed under the supervision of the National Park Service (NPS).

When you combine the East and West Branches below their dams with the Mainstem, the Delaware River system provides almost 80 miles of a quality tailwater fishery. Finding trout in this vast area can be extremely difficult, especially when they are not actively surface feeding. The West Branch below the Cannonsville Dam and the Mainstem of the Delaware are the only major Catskill streams which aren't stocked. However, they are loaded with big wild trout. While blind-casting nymphs and streamers can be productive, most anglers relish the chance to catch the Delaware's large, selective wild trout on a dry fly. The Delaware doesn't give up its trout easily however. In fact, many anglers consider it one of the toughest rivers in the world to have success on – that's why experienced anglers keep returning to test their skills.

The Delaware River system harbors some of the largest, strongest, stream-bred brown and rainbow trout in the East. Starting in mid-June, the water from the Beaverkill warms the lower East Branch and Mainstem. Trout then start to migrate up the East or West Branches to the coldwater refuges provided by the releases from the bottom of the two reservoirs.

Al Caucci reports that the Delaware and its two branches have almost all of the East's significant hatches. Caucci has authored numerous flyfishing articles and several books, including his milestone work, *Hatches*. Al also developed the "Comparadun" fly series, was a co-founder with Hartman of the Friends of the Upper Delaware, and is the former owner of the Delaware River Club. Al was also one of the early pioneers of this great fishery starting in the early 1960s and over the years, he has discovered about 30 "super" hatches of mayflies in the system. The hatches start in April with blue-winged olives, blue quills, and quill Gordons. In late April, you can expect great Hendrickson hatches which can last well into May, especially on the West Branch. Late April and early May also bring several good caddis hatches, especially the apple caddis with a light green body. While most anglers will tell you that their favorite hatches on the Delaware System are the green and brown drakes, Lee Hartman's favorite Delaware River hatch is the March brown. Unlike the green and brown drake hatches which can last only for a week or so, the March brown hatch starts around mid-May and lasts for several weeks. The hatch is very sporadic, lasting all day – in small numbers. March browns are big mayflies, so they need more time than their smaller relatives to dry out their wings and leave the water. Lee reports that once the trout get keyed into March browns, they become less selective as they have fewer naturals to target. Towards the end of May the system gets good numbers of large sulphurs and green and brown drakes in the afternoons and evenings.

"Second Season"

Most of the region's trout waters begin to warm as summer approaches, but the Delaware's coldwater releases open up the Delaware's "Second Season", a term coined by Al Caucci. During this time of the year, fishing pressure in the system starts to diminish, but not the hatches or the fishing. Starting in June the Delaware system has prolific sulphur hatches in sizes 16 to 20, with excellent spinner falls at dusk. This hatch is virtually a daily occurrence all summer and well into September. In late June through July, look for tan caddis, blue quills, light Cahills, and slate drakes. Small blue-winged olives can be the most reliable hatch all summer long, lasting well into the fall. Summer mornings can also give you good action on trico spinners in sizes 24 to 28, providing you with the challenge of joining the 20/20 club with a big, wild Delaware trout – a 20-inch trout on a size 20 fly! It's a goal I have yet to achieve in the Delaware River system. On days when flying ants hit the water, flying ant patterns in sizes 16 to 24 in black and reddish brown can usually bring up the most selective trout and provide anglers with nonstop summer action.

Most of the Delaware guides do not use the traditional "Catskill-style" hackled dry flies, preferring instead to fish low-riding Comparaduns, CDC Duns, or Parachute Hackle patterns.

ECONOMIC BENEFITS

The coldwater releases from Cannonsville and Pepacton Reservoirs not only provide excellent trout fishing, but they provide an important boost to the local economy. The communities along the river are highly dependent on tourism, especially anglers. In 1996, Trout Unlimited funded a study of "The Economic Impact of Trout Fishing on the Delaware River Tailwaters in New York". The study found that trout fishing in the upper Delaware system generates 17.7 million dollars in direct expenditures in local business revenues and generates 29.98 million dollars in local economic activity annually. The study also reported that improved water release strategies on the Delaware River would increase angler visits and economic benefits to the local communities along the river in terms of jobs, wages, and local tax revenues.

The reservoir releases have converted the Delaware from a warmwater fishery to a world-class tailwater trout fishery. This will continue, provided the releases are kept at the correct volume. New York City has the responsibility for managing the releases, although the Delaware River Basin Commission (DRBC) which has representatives from New York, Pennsylvania, and New Jersey must approve the city's release management plan. Most anglers and guides on the river will tell you that the DRBC and New York City has at best a mixed history of managing the coldwater releases. When the releases are constant the fishery thrives, and when the releases are sporadic the fishery declines.

FUTURE OF THE UPPER DELAWARE RIVER FISHERY

As I mentioned previously, Lee Hartman invited several of the Upper Delaware flyfishing pioneers, including Al Caucci, to the founding meeting of the Friends of the Upper Delaware River in 2002. Lee feels that the Delaware River System, despite the ebb and flow of the release pattern is still a "quality fishery" producing some of the largest trout east of the Mississippi River. But he also feels that if the releases were more consistent, not only would we have the quality of stream-bred trout, but the quantity of wild trout would increase dramatically.

The Friends of the Upper Delaware River is an active advocacy group working to protect the Delaware ecosystem and they deserve your support.

Early-morning is a great time to prospect for the big ones. Photo by Steve Ohman.

Left: An angler plies an upper mainstem riffle. Photo courtesy Darren Rist. Below: Anpother dandy rainbow from the Upper Delaware. Photo courtesy Aaron Jasper.

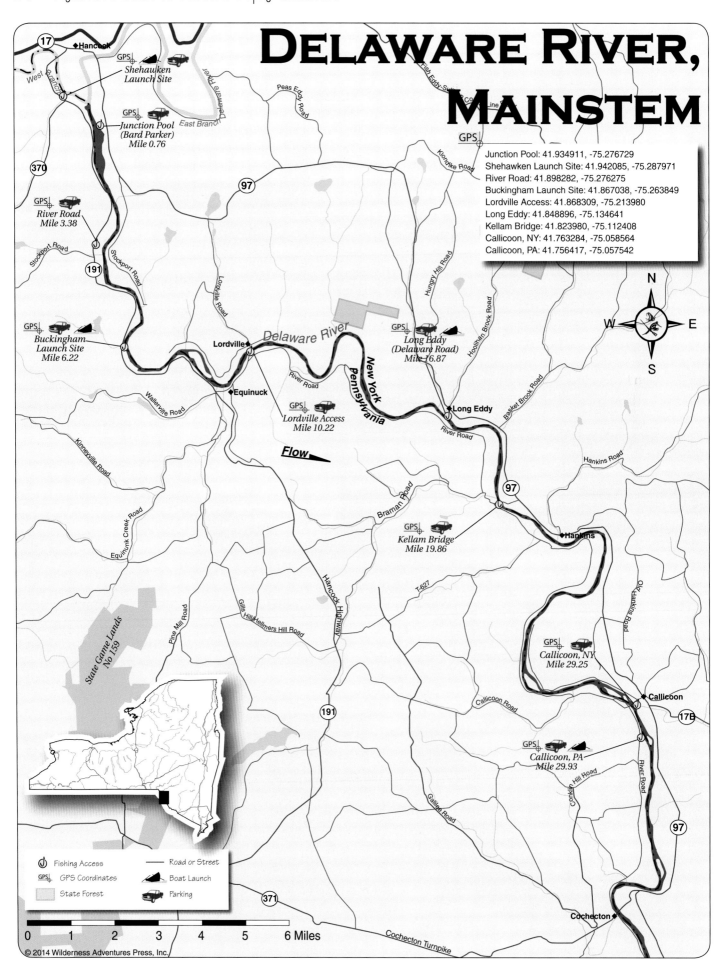

DELAWARE RIVER, MAINSTEM

GPS

Junction Pool: 41.934911, -75.276729
Shehawken Launch Site: 41.942085, -75.287971
River Road: 41.898282, -75.276275
Buckingham Launch Site: 41.867038, -75.263849
Lordville Access: 41.868309, -75.213980
Long Eddy: 41.848896, -75.134641
Kellam Bridge: 41.823980, -75.112408
Callicoon, NY: 41.763284, -75.058564
Callicoon, PA: 41.756417, -75.057542

Shehawken Launch Site

Junction Pool
(Bard Parker)
Mile 0.76

River Road
Mile 3.38

Buckingham
Launch Site
Mile 6.22

Lordville

Delaware River

Long Eddy
(Delaware Road)
Mile 16.87

Long Eddy

Equinuck

Lordville Access
Mile 10.22

Flow

New York
Pennsylvania

Kellam Bridge
Mile 19.86

Hankins

Callicoon, NY
Mile 29.25

Callicoon

Callicoon, PA
Mile 29.93

Cochecton

State Game Lands
No 159

Legend:
Fishing Access
GPS Coordinates
State Forest
Road or Street
Boat Launch
Parking

0 1 2 3 4 5 6 Miles

© 2014 Wilderness Adventures Press, Inc.

MAINSTEM OF THE UPPER DELAWARE RIVER (FIVE STARS)

The Delaware River system gives you the opportunity to fish for some of the biggest wild trout east of the Mississippi River. The Mainstem trout average 16 to 18 inches and 20-inch trout are common. Rainbows used to outnumber browns in the Mainstem, but most of the guides I interviewed feel that browns now outnumber the rainbows by as much as five to one. Rainbows only live for about four years, and while 16- to 18-inch bows are common, rainbows over 20 inches are rare. Browns live twice as long, and 20- to 24-inch browns are fairly common. Several guides I interviewed reported landing brown trout in the 26- to 28-inch range, and brown trout over 30 inches have been documented on the Mainstem.

I recently floated the Big D from the Buckingham boat launch on the Pennsylvania side of the Delaware downstream to Long Eddy, New York – a float of about 10 or 11 miles. We had hoped to catch the Big D's famous Hendrickson hatch, which in most seasons you can follow upstream for up to a month, from late April through May. My lifelong friend and mentor, Ed Jaworowski, had arranged our float trip with veteran Delaware River guide, Chuck Swartz. Chuck has fished the river for over three decades and has an intimate knowledge of every pool and run. His stories about the river, its ecological history, inhabitants, and trout captivated and entertained us all day. Chuck was great to fish with; knowledgeable, patient, with a positive attitude and good with the boat. In addition to the river's bounty of trout and shad we were also entertained by aerial displays by migrating spring warblers, waterfowl, and circling bald eagles.

When I asked Chuck how today's fishing compares to "the good old days," he gave Ed and me the "Cliff Notes" version of the history of trout fishing on the Delaware River.

Legend has it that the seeds of this fishery were planted when a train carrying milk cans filled with California's McCloud River rainbow trout destined for private club waters broke down along the Delaware in the late 1800s. Fortunately for the trout, the train's conductor was Dan Cahill, a flyfisherman and fly tier of Light Cahill fame. In an effort to save the precious cargo, Cahill and his crew took the milk cans loaded with the rainbow trout fingerlings and dumped them into Callicoon Creek just above its junction with the Delaware River. The Dan Cahill story has never been substantiated – it is believed to be a myth repeated by many writers including yours truly. Ed Van Put, with the New York State Department of Environmental Conservation, reports the state was doing experimental stockings of rainbow trout as long as 130 years ago. Today the Callicoon and its two branches (North and East) harbor wild rainbows and browns, and it is one of the many Delaware tributaries where wild rainbows return each spring to spawn.

The reservoir releases have converted the Delaware from a warmwater fishery to a world-class tailwater trout fishery. This will continue, provided the releases are kept at the correct volume. New York City has the responsibility for managing the releases, although the Delaware River Basin Commission (DRBC) which has representatives from New York, Pennsylvania, and New Jersey, must approve the city's release management plan. Most anglers and guides on the river will tell you that the DRBC and New York City has at best a mixed history of managing the coldwater releases.

Sixteen- to 18-inch wild rainbows are common in the mainstem of the Upper Delaware River. Photo by Lee Hartman.

When the releases are constant the fishery thrives, and when the releases are sporadic the fishery declines. To find fish in this river, a thermometer can be your most important tool – you want to fish water temperatures in the 52- to 68-degree range. The Mainstem "trout zone" runs some 27 miles, from Hancock to Callicoon. The first five to six miles are easier to wade than the bigger water downstream.

After the rainbows spawn in the tributaries in early spring they migrate back to the Mainstem and branches, usually by early May. When they return it is common to see pods of rainbows cruising as they sip insects off the surface in the river's long, flat pools. Our float with Chuck Swartz occurred on a bright sunny day – the water was low, clear, and in the slower pools the driftboat spooked fish as far away as 70 feet, making the fishing incredibly challenging. Ed proved to be up to the challenge and landed one of the two trout that took his dry fly – a beautiful 18-inch rainbow taken on a perfectly presented 70-foot cast with a long, drag-free float.

On that trip we rounded a bend in the river, just upstream from a beautiful long glide pool above the Equinunk Creek. As we got closer to the pool we could see a ton of rising fish – the most action we would see on the float. Chuck anchored the driftboat in a side channel and Ed and I got out and started wading toward the rising fish. As we got into position to cast, we had our only contentious boat encounter of the day. An aluminum jonboat propelled by an outboard motor flew right up the middle of the pool. The operator, seeing the rising fish, motored directly into them and proceeded to anchor not 50 feet in front of us. Needless to say this put the trout down. We elected to move on rather than stay and fight.

The most effective way to fish the Upper Delaware is by floating it. A float trip enables you to cover much more water, as a fair amount of the river is inaccessible by car or is on posted land. The Delaware does have plenty of good shore access points on both the Pennsylvania and New York sides of the river. There are several good books which give detailed directions to most of the good shore access points. Below I have listed a few of my favorite shore access spots.

SHORE ACCESS

Junction Pool (Bard Parker)

The first shore access point on the Mainstem is the world-renowned Junction Pool, where the East and West Branches join, forming the start of the Mainstem. There are two ways to access the Junction Pool. From Hancock, New York take Route 97 south and cross over the East Branch of the Delaware. Take the first right, which is Maple Street, and then take the first left onto La Barre Street. Continue on La Barre for one mile to the Hancock water pollution control facility. Access to the river is via a gravel road on the left. It is well-marked by the DEC, and the parking lot can hold over a dozen cars. The second option is from the Shehawken launch site on the Pennsylvania side of the West Branch which is just 0.9 miles downstream from the Route 191 bridge in Hancock. This access is on the lower West Branch – from the launch you can walk downstream 0.5 miles from Shehawken to the Junction Pool.

River Road, Stockport, Pennsylvania

River Road is a short section of a public dirt road off Route 191 which gives you access to the river. The road is heavily posted on both sides but it does provide public access to the river. To access River Road, take Route 191 south for 3.7 miles from the bridge in Hancock. Look for the small street sign marking River Road. Park along Route 191 and take the short walk down River Road to the Delaware. This is not an official launch site, but I have seen driftboats use it.

Buckingham, Pennsylvania Launch Site

The Buckingham launch site is well-maintained by the Pennsylvania Boat & Fish Commission and is a popular driftboat launch and take-out site. The launch is on Route 191, seven miles south of the Hancock Bridge.

Lordville, New York

From the town of Equinunk, Pennsylvania, take Lordville Road for about a mile south to the bridge at Lordville, cross over into New York, and there is parking and wading access next to the bridge. From Hancock, New York take Route 97 south for about five miles to Lordville Road, make a right, and continue to the bridge. There is no launch site at Lordville.

STREAM FACTS

Season/Regulations

The season on the Delaware River runs from the first Saturday after April 11 to October 15, with a one-trout limit of 14 inches or larger per day. From October 16 through the Friday preceding the first Saturday after April 11, fishing is catch-and-release.

History

The upper Delaware River system has the distinction of being the easternmost "western" trout river in the United States. The fishery began to develop in the 1960s with the construction of the Pepacton Reservoir on the East Branch of the Delaware and the Cannonsville Reservoir on the West Branch. Coldwater releases from these newly created dams converted the lower East and West Branches and the first 27 miles of the Mainstem of the Delaware River from a smallmouth bass fishery into a world-class wild trout fishery.

Fish

The Delaware River and its West Branch are the only two major Catskill trout streams which are not stocked. The Delaware River system gives you the opportunity to fish for some of the biggest wild trout east of the Mississippi River. Mainstem trout average 16 to 18 inches, and 20-inch trout are common. Rainbows only live for about four years, and while 16- to 18-inch bows are common, rainbows over 20 inches are rare. On the other hand, browns live twice as long as the rainbows, and 20- to 24-inch browns are fairly common. Several guides I interviewed reported landing browns in the 26- to 28-inch range, and brown trout of over 30 inches have been documented on the Mainstem of the Delaware.

River Characteristics

The Delaware River has the look and feel of a large western trout river. Its pools are among the largest in the East, ranging to as wide as 100 yards and as long as 300 yards. While you can have success on the Big D from shore, most anglers have better success floating the Mainstem.

What the Experts Say

Lee Hartman was one of the early pioneers of the Upper Delaware system and co-founded the Friends of the Upper Delaware. I asked Lee to describe his beloved Upper Delaware; below Lee shares some of his insight about this great river system:

There is one word that describes the Upper Delaware River. It is 'special'. The controlled flows from NYC's drinking water reservoirs fuel the river with cold water, creating a 75-mile coldwater eco-system. Below the fertile outflows are rainbow and brown trout, large and wild, feeding on a multitude of hatches throughout each season, becoming a fly angler's playground.

The river can best be described as a contradiction. Artificial but wild, intimidating in magnitude and yet delicately intimate. The jewel of the river is the rainbow trout; introduced into the river system in the late 1800's from California, adapted and survived man's encroachments for over 100 years. Those who visit the river immediately recognize the McCloud strain rainbow by its strength and acrobatic skills displayed at the end of their line.

The wild brown trout are not to be overlooked. Found mostly in the upper reaches of the river, these selective feeders commonly reach 20+ inches or more. Matching wits with this fish can be a challenging experience even for the most ardent angler.

At the heart of this valuable fishery are the sustainable reservoir releases and its spawning tributaries. The reservoirs act like giant filters creating cold clean water that sustains the aquatic life forms. No other major river system in the East enjoys the diversity of the hatches with a trout population, none of which has eaten a hatchery pellet.

Anglers who regularly fish the Delaware system often overlook or take for granted the engineered releases that created this unique fishery. If we are to protect its bounty for future generations then we all who fish its waters must keep a watchful eye on man's encroachments.

Flows

http://waterdata.gov/USA/UV USGS web site 01427207 Delaware River at Lordville

http://waterdata.gov/USA/UV USGS web site 01427510 Delaware River at Callicoon

Tackle

For early season streamer and nymph fishing, I'll use a 9-foot rod matched with a 6-weight line. Once the dry fly season gets underway, I'll switch to a 9-foot, 4- or 5-weight outfit.

WEST BRANCH DELAWARE RIVER

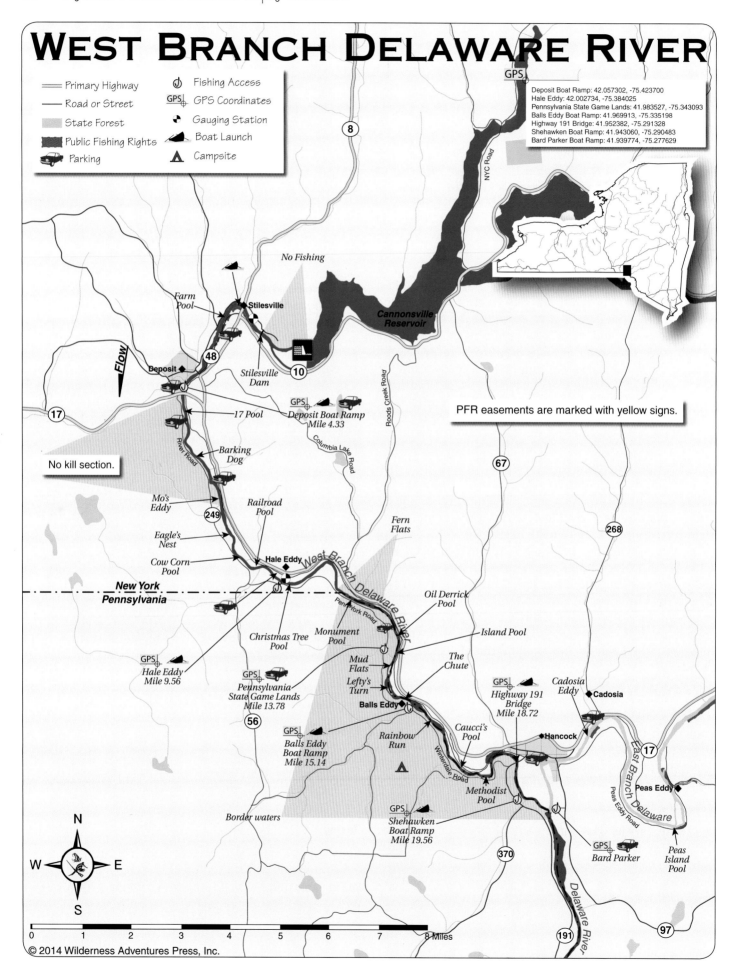

Primary Highway
Road or Street
State Forest
Public Fishing Rights
Parking
Fishing Access
GPS Coordinates
Gauging Station
Boat Launch
Campsite

Deposit Boat Ramp: 42.057302, -75.423700
Hale Eddy: 42.002734, -75.384025
Pennsylvania State Game Lands: 41.983527, -75.343093
Balls Eddy Boat Ramp: 41.969913, -75.335198
Highway 191 Bridge: 41.952382, -75.291328
Shehawken Boat Ramp: 41.943060, -75.290483
Bard Parker Boat Ramp: 41.939774, -75.277629

No Fishing

Farm Pool

Stilesville

Cannonsville Reservoir

Flow

Deposit

Stilesville Dam

PFR easements are marked with yellow signs.

17 Pool

Deposit Boat Ramp Mile 4.33

No kill section.

Barking Dog

Mo's Eddy

Railroad Pool

Fern Flats

Eagle's Nest

Cow Corn Pool

Hale Eddy

West Branch Delaware River

New York
Pennsylvania

Oil Derrick Pool

Penn York Road

Island Pool

Christmas Tree Pool

Monument Pool

Mud Flats

The Chute

Hale Eddy Mile 9.56

Lefty's Turn

Cadosia Eddy

Pennsylvania State Game Lands Mile 13.78

Highway 191 Bridge Mile 18.72

Cadosia

Balls Eddy

Caucci's Pool

Hancock

Balls Eddy Boat Ramp Mile 15.14

Rainbow Run

Peas Eddy

Winterdale Road

Border waters

Methodist Pool

East Branch Delaware

Shehawken Boat Ramp Mile 19.56

Bard Parker

Peas Island Pool

N
W E
S

0 1 2 3 4 5 6 7 8 Miles

© 2014 Wilderness Adventures Press, Inc.

WEST BRANCH OF THE DELAWARE RIVER (FIVE STARS)

The Cannonsville Dam on the West Branch was completed in the mid-1960s, and its coldwater releases changed the upper Delaware from a smallmouth bass fishery to a world-class wild trout fishery. In the December, 1994 issue of *Fly Fisherman Magazine*, John Randolph called the West Branch "The Big Horn of the East". From the Cannonsville Dam downstream to the village of Hancock, the West Branch offers over 15 miles of world-class dry-fly water. The upper West Branch reminds me of a western spring creek, while the lower section of the West Branch is wider, with more riffles, and it has the look of a large Eastern freestone stream.

The West Branch is a "match-the-hatch" dry fly fisherman's dream stream, from the early season *Baetis*, blue quill, and Hendrickson hatches to the drakes and sulphurs in June and the Cahills, tricos, olives, and slate drakes all summer long and well into the fall. The combination of big water, multiple hatches, long, slow pools, and heavy angling pressure make the West Branch trout some of the most difficult fish in the world to catch, but they are wild – they are beautiful – and they are big.

HOW GOOD IS THE WEST BRANCH?

Just how good is the West Branch? Well, on August 18 and 19 of 2003, the Pennsylvania Fish & Boat Commission (PFBC) sampled two sections of the West Branch. One section was at the PFBC's Balls Eddy launch site off Penn/York Road and the other was immediately downstream of the Hancock Bridge on Route 191. A total of 388 trout, both wild browns and rainbows, were captured in the 2,444 feet of river they sampled. Browns made up 85 percent of the sample and rainbows made up 15 percent. Trout of 14 inches or greater represented an astonishing 39 percent of the catch. The largest rainbow was 17 inches and the largest brown was 23 inches, but the crew saw a much larger

brown. This is even more amazing when you consider that this section of river is open to all methods of angling and that two fish per person per day may be harvested during the season.

The most popular section of river in the Delaware system is the no-kill stretch on the West Branch in Deposit. Since the no-kill stretch was established in 1998, not only has it become the most popular section, it is also the most productive. According to the New York State Department of Conservation (NYDEC), the two-mile stretch of the no-kill section starting at the Route 17 bridge and going downstream has about 1,000 trout per mile and has some of the largest trout in the West Branch. With fairly consistent water temperatures provided by the coldwater releases from Cannonsville, the summer months can provide excellent fishing. As the freestone streams in the region warm, many flyfishers begin to concentrate on the tailwater fisheries, where hatches are abundant and trout growth rates are phenomenal. Great summer hatches on the West Branch include olives, sulphurs, light Cahills, and slate drakes. The late season hatches of light Cahills and slate drakes can last for three or four months.

The West Branch runs cold even on 90-degree days. The river can be as cool as 50 degrees, so foggy summer mornings and evenings can be the rule. It's a good idea to wear long johns and bring a jacket even in summer. The upper seven miles of the West Branch are in New

The "Big Horn of the East" gives up trophies like this regularly. Photo by Aaron Jasper.

York State and the lower eight miles forms the boundary with Pennsylvania. The Pennsylvania water starts about one mile below the Hale Eddy Bridge. Both New York and Pennsylvania have a reciprocal fishing agreement, so you can fish both sides of the West and Mainstem with either state's license.

The West Branch downstream of Hale Eddy is known as the "Border Waters", where New York shares the river with Pennsylvania. The Pennsylvania State Game Lands contain several miles of prime trout water with good public access.

The West Branch provides trophy wild brown and rainbow fisheries from Cannonsville Reservoir downstream to the junction of the East Branch in Hancock. Regulations allow for two trout per day over 12 inches from opening day until October 15 (except for the no-kill section, which runs from the Route 17 overpass in Deposit downstream for two miles). The rest of the year it's closed to fishing to protect spawning trout.

I took my first trip to the West Branch at an invitation from Darren Rist, whom I had met while giving a program to his local Trout Unlimited club. When he learned I was writing a tri-state flyfishing guide, he offered to show me his home water, the West Branch. One beautiful fall morning, we met at his house on the river, just upstream from the Hale Eddy bridge. I inquired about the driftboat in his driveway and he informed me that he guides on the Delaware system as well as the Beaverkill and the Willowemoc. That morning he showed me several access points from Hale Eddy upstream to Deposit. At each location we were greeted by several rising trout, none of which had any interest in my Parachute Olive dry fly or terrestrials. After lunch, Darren gave me a West Branch 101 fishing lesson. The take-home message from his instructions was: long, fine leaders and drag-free floats. The fly should go over the fish before the leader and fly line. This is accomplished by a "reach cast," quartering downstream. Darren was a patient instructor, and using a 15-foot 6x leader with a size 18 Parachute Blue-winged Olive, I took my first West Branch trout – a wild brown of about 18 inches. I highly recommend booking a trip with Darren; he knows the rivers, their hatches, and the strategies and tactics to get you into fish.

Shore Access

Deposit

The first 1.5 miles of the West Branch from Cannonsville Dam downstream to Stilesville Dam is off limits to fishing. From the Stilesville Dam downstream to Hancock you have over 15 miles of excellent trout water. The area around Stilesville has some of the biggest fish in the West Branch, but it receives a fair amount of fishing pressure. The upper West Branch and the no-kill stretch can be reached by taking Route 17 west to Exit 84. From there take Routes 8 and 10 north for approximately 0.4 miles until you see the sign for the Deposit business district. Turn left and you will be on Pine Street, just before the Pine Street bridge over the West Branch. (Note: Deposit is 150 miles from NYC.) From here you have three options: Turn right onto Route 48 and go 1.2 miles to the DEC parking area on the left in Stilesville. Or turn left just before the Pine Street bridge (look for sign for the industrial park) and go 0.5 miles to the DEC parking area on the left. The Route 17 overpass and the start of the no-kill section is about 100 yards downstream from the lot. The lot is across the river from the Deposit sewage treatment plant, but this section of the river fishes very well, especially the run upstream from the plant. From here, you can continue a short distance downstream to the start of the no-kill section. This area is known as Norbord, after the factory located across the street from the river. While there is no DEC parking area, there is room for several cars to park along the river. A little farther downriver is another DEC parking area; it's a total of 0.8 miles from the first DEC lot. A third option is to cross the Pine Street bridge and park along either Pine Street or River Road, which comes in on the left by the bridge. Here you have good water and plenty of trout both above and below the bridge.

Hale Eddy

The section around the Hale Eddy bridge is another popular access point and the area above and below the bridge receives less pressure than the area around Deposit. Hale Eddy can be reached by taking Route 17 north of Roscoe for 32 miles and past Hancock for about six miles. Go past Lower Hale Eddy Road to the next left, which is Hale Eddy Road. Make a left onto Hale Eddy Road and go 150 yards to the railroad tracks and bridge. A DEC parking area is on the right just before the bridge. Boulders keep this access from being a driftboat launch site, but this section is excellent for wade fishing. There is a nice riffle to fish nymphs upstream of the bridge and a beautiful dry fly pool downstream of the bridge. You can cross the bridge and turn left for the Pennsylvania Game Lands and Balls Eddy, or turn right and head upstream towards Deposit. The Game Lands have two parking areas for walk-in access; the upper lot is farther from the water than the lower one. The length of the walks keeps the fishing pressure light in the Game Lands.

Hancock

There is good access to the lower West Branch in the town of Hancock, New York, with parking and access at the Route 191 bridge. There is parking on both the upstream and downstream sides of the bridge. The upstream side of the bridge, while not an "official" launch site, gives you drift boat access.

Balls Eddy

If you want to fish upstream of Hancock, cross the river on the Route 191 bridge into Pennsylvania and turn right on Winterdale Road, which follows the West Branch upstream. Most of the public water starts at the Balls Eddy launch site three miles above the Hancock Bridge on Winterdale Road. After traveling on Winterdale Road for three miles (note: you will have passed the Delaware River Club) it turns sharply to the left. Go straight onto Penn/York Road and follow the signs for a short distance to the Balls Eddy parking and launch area.

Pennsylvania State Game Lands

The next access upstream is in the Pennsylvania State Game Lands (SGL). As you leave Balls Eddy, turn right onto Penn/York Road (which becomes a dirt road) and go 1.3 miles to the lower SGL parking area on the right. To reach the upper SGL parking area, continue on Penn/York Road for another 0.5 miles to the lot on the right. Both of the SGL lots require a good walk to the river, which usually keeps the fishing pressure light. This is the last West Branch access area in Pennsylvania. If you continue upstream you will come to the Hale Eddy bridge (note: you will pass the West Branch Angler flyfishing resort on the way). Hale Eddy is 4.3 miles from Balls Eddy on Penn/York Road and a total of 7.3 miles from the Route 191 bridge in Hancock.

Shehawken

The Shehawken PABFC launch site is on Route 191 in Pennsylvania 0.9 miles downstream of the Hancock bridge. It is about 0.5 miles above the Junction Pool and it has nice runs both above and below the parking area. From Shehawken, you can fish downstream through several beautiful pools down to the Junction Pool about 0.5 miles downstream from the launch site.

STREAM FACTS

Season/Regulations

On the West Branch of the Delaware River from the Cannonsville Dam downstream, anglers may harvest two trout per day over 12 inches except in the Catch-and-Release – Artificial Lures Only (CRALO) section, which runs from the Route 17 bridge in Deposit downstream for two miles. Fishing is open from April 1 to October 15 and is closed the rest of the time to protect spawning trout.

Fish

The West Branch has more trout per mile than the East Branch or Mainstem. On August 18 and 19 of 2003, the Pennsylvania Fish and Boat Commission sampled two sections of the West Branch. One section was at the Balls Eddy launch site off Penn/York Road in Pennsylvania and the other was immediately downstream of the Hancock bridge on Route 191. A total of 388 trout, both wild browns and rainbows, were captured in the 2,444 feet of river they sampled. Browns made up 85 percent of the sample and rainbows made up the other 15 percent. Trout of 14 inches or greater represented an astonishing 39 percent of the catch. The largest rainbow was 17 inches and the largest brown was 23 inches, but the survey crew saw a much larger brown which they were unable to capture.

River Characteristics

The West Branch has been called the Big Horn of the East, which is quite a compliment for an eastern river. The upper part of the West Branch has the look and feel of a western spring creek, and as the river approaches Hancock it becomes wider, with more riffles, and it begins to take on the look of a large, eastern freestone stream.

I find I can wade the West Branch when the river drops below 1,000 cubic feet per second.

Flows

The Delaware River release hotline is 845-295-1006. It gives you up-to-the-minute online flow and temperature data.
http://waterdata.gov/USA/UV USGS web site 01425000 West Branch of the Delaware River at Stilesville
http://waterdata.gov/USA/UV USGS web site 0142650 West Branch of the Delaware River at Hale Eddy

Tackle

For early season streamer and nymph fishing, I'll use a 9-foot rod matched with a 6-weight line. Once the dry fly season gets underway, I'll switch to a 9-foot, 4- or 5-weight outfit.

Maps

Wilderness Adventures Press makes an 11x17 flyfishing map of the branches of the Delaware that include GPS for access points and public fishing rights locations.

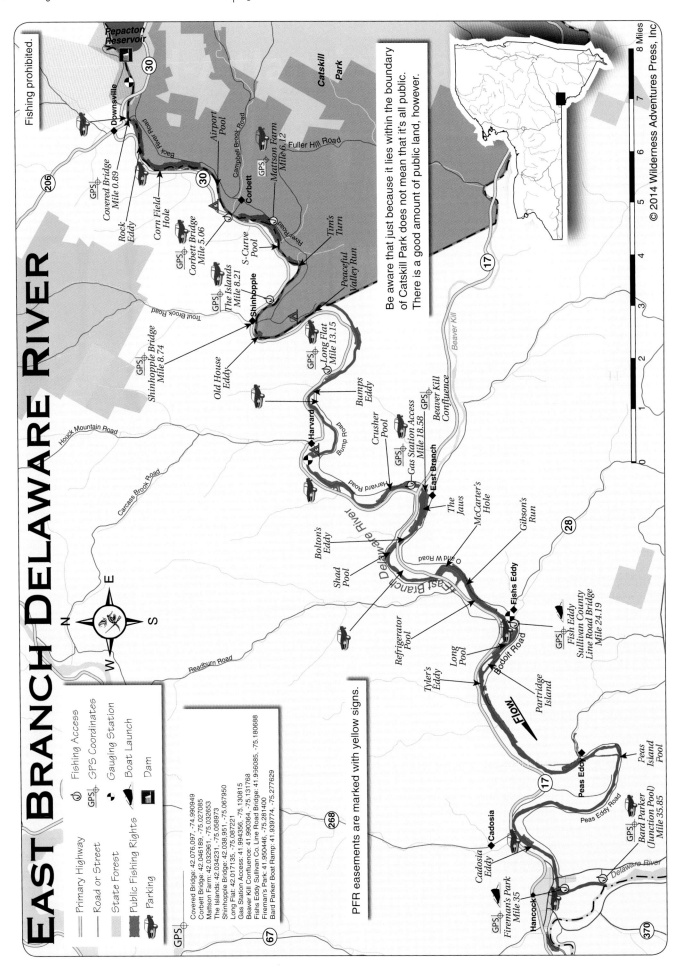

EAST BRANCH DELAWARE RIVER

Fishing prohibited.

Be aware that just because it lies within the boundary of Catskill Park does not mean that it's all public. There is a good amount of public land, however.

PFR easements are marked with yellow signs.

© 2014 Wilderness Adventures Press, Inc

8 Miles

GPS

Legend	
Primary Highway	
Road or Street	
State Forest	
Public Fishing Rights	
Parking	

- Fishing Access
- GPS Coordinates
- Gauging Station
- Boat Launch
- Dam

Covered Bridge: 42.076.097, -74.990949
Corbett Bridge: 42.046189, -75.027085
Mattson Farm: 42.032961, -75.032653
The Islands: 42.034231, -75.058973
Shinhopple Bridge: 42.038.951, -75.067950
Long Flat: 42.017135, -75.087221
Gas Station Access: 41.994356, -75.130815
Beaver Kill Confluence: 41.990364, -75.131768
Fishs Eddy Sullivan Co. Line Road Bridge: 41.956085, -75.180688
Fireman's Park: 41.950446, -75.281400
Bard Parker Boat Ramp: 41.939774, -75.277629

Pepacton Reservoir

Downsville

Back River Road

Covered Bridge Mile 0.89

Rock Eddy

Corn Field Hole

Corbett Bridge Mile 5.06

Campbell Brook Road

Corbett

Mattson Farm Mile 6.12

Fuller Hill Road

Airport Pool

S-Curve Pool

Tim's Turn

The Islands Mile 8.21

Shinhopple

Peaceful Valley Run

Shinhopple Bridge Mile 8.74

Trout Brook Road

Old House Eddy

Long Flat Mile 13.15

Catskill Park

Beaver Kill

Houck Mountain Road

Bumps Eddy

Harvard

Crusher Pool

Bump Road

Harvard Road

Gas Station Access Mile 18.58

Beaver Kill Confluence

East Branch

Bolton's Eddy

Shad Pool

The Jaws

McCarter's Hole

Gibson's Run

East Branch Delaware River

Carcass Brook Road

O and W Road

Refrigerator Pool

Fishs Eddy

Long Pool

Bodoit Road

Tyler's Eddy

Partridge Island

FLOW

Fish Eddy Sullivan County Line Road Bridge Mile 24.19

Readburn Road

Peas Eddy

Peas Island Pool

Peas Eddy Road

Cadosia Eddy

Cadosia

Bard Parker (Junction Pool) Mile 35.85

Fireman's Park Mile 35

Hancock

Delaware River

N E S W

EAST BRANCH OF THE DELAWARE RIVER (FIVE STARS)

The East Branch of the Delaware flows some 35 miles from Pepacton Reservoir to the town of Hancock, where it joins the West Branch, forming the Delaware River. About halfway down, the Beaverkill joins the East Branch, nearly doubling the size of the river. Releases from the reservoir near Downsville are usually at about 175 cubic feet per second (cfs), which keeps the upper East Branch down to the Beaverkill cold enough for trout year round. The upper East Branch, like the upper West Branch, is reminiscent of a western spring creek. It is dominated by browns with a few brook trout, especially near the mouths of its tributaries. It has great hatches all season long and is famous for its brown and green drake hatches, which might just be the best in the East. Its sulphur hatch is reliable most afternoons and evenings all summer and into the fall.

In addition to the solid population of wild browns, the state stocks the East Branch, much to the disappointment of its fly rod regulars. Its long, clear, slow pools make the East Branch very challenging – long leaders, light tippets, and delicate, accurate casts are a must. The upper East Branch has excellent public access, but on summer weekends it has a "canoe hatch", so fish it early mornings or evenings on weekends or during the week.

SHORE ACCESS TO THE UPPER EAST BRANCH

The Upper East Branch is accessed off Route 30 from the town of East Branch upstream to Downsville just below the Pepacton Reservoir. Take Route 17 (soon to be I-86) west 15 miles past Roscoe to Route 30 North which follows the East Branch for 15 miles upstream to Downsville and downstream 20 miles to Hancock.

Gas Station Access

The first good access on the upper East Branch is the DEC parking area on Route 30 about 0.3 miles upstream of Route 17, just past the first gas station.

Long Flat

The next DEC access area is five miles from Route 17. The state named this access area "Long Flat" but the locals call it "the cornfield". Speaking of cornfields, the upper East Branch flows through a picturesque, gentle valley which is filled with beautiful farmers' cornfields and vacationers' campgrounds.

Shinhopple

Continue north on Route 30 a total of 8.6 miles from Route 17 until you come to the former tackle shop owned by the late Al Carpenter at Shinhopple and the River Road bridge over the East Branch. The large, deep pool upstream of the bridge is difficult to wade, but the riffle below the bridge is great nymphing water and gets a shot of cold water from Trout Brook, which enters the river just below the bridge.

Wade access is available at many spots on the East Branch.

The Islands

The next DEC access is a total of 9.2 miles up Route 30 from Route 17. This is at a section of the river with islands. I prefer the water upstream of the islands and the parking area. If you continue another 0.3 miles from the DEC lot there is a pull-off which enables you to access the water above the islands.

Corbett Bridge

The Corbett bridge is on Route 30, 11.5 miles north of Route 17. Cross the bridge and park on the right side of the road.

Downsville Covered Bridge

Take Route 30 to Downsville turn right onto Routes 30 & 206 then right on Bridge Street to the covered bridge and Town Park on the right.

Mattson Farm

Continue on Routes 30/206 from Downsville towards Roscoe, to the next bridge over the East Branch and River Road. Turn right onto River Road for 4.2 miles to the DEC parking area. This access point is 2.5 miles upstream from the River Road bridge at Shinhopple.

THE LOWER EAST BRANCH

The lower East Branch runs from its junction with the Beaverkill downstream to the village of Hancock. This water is much bigger and faster, with more riffles and runs than the water above the junction with the Beaverkill. The lower East Branch is dominated by rainbow trout, with some browns mixed in. In summer, the waters from the Beaverkill can be in the high 70s and they warm the lower East Branch. When this happens most of the trout migrate either upstream towards the Pepacton Reservoir or downstream to the cool waters of the West Branch. During the summer, the thermal refuge on the East Branch runs from the reservoir downstream for about ten miles.

In recent years, anglers have seen an increase in the number of rainbow trout in the lower East Branch and lower Beaverkill. From the confluence with the Beaverkill to the junction with the West Branch, the lower East Branch takes on the character of a big freestone stream. The best fishing occurs from late April into early June and then again in the fall. The lower East Branch is paralleled by Route 30 from the town of East Branch down to Hancock.

While both branches have good fishing above their dams for both stocked and stream-bred trout, most flyfishers fish the tailwaters, since the hatches and therefore the fishing is more consistent, the fish are bigger, and the drive from Roscoe and New York City is shorter.

STREAM FACTS – THE EAST BRANCH OF THE DELAWARE

Season/Regulations

The season on the East Branch of the Delaware from the Pepacton Dam downstream to the Shinhopple Bridge runs from April 1 to October 15, with a two-trout limit of at least 12 inches. Angling is prohibited from October 16 through March 31.

From Shinhopple Bridge downstream to Hancock the season runs from April 1 to October 15, with a two-trout limit of at least 12 inches. From October 16 through March 31, angling is catch-and-release-only.

Fish

The East Branch has a healthy population of stream-bred trout, mostly browns, and they grow quite large feeding on the East Branch's prolific hatches. The lower East Branch has wild rainbows. Both sections are stocked by the state.

River Characteristics

The upper East Branch is characterized by long, clear, slow pools, making it a very challenging river to fly fish. The lower East Branch below its junction with the Beaverkill is much larger and faster, with more riffles and runs than the section above the Beaverkill.

Flows

http://waterdata.gov/USA/UV USGS web site 01417500 East Branch of the Delaware River at Harvard
http://waterdata.gov/USA/UV USGS web site 01421000 East Branch of the Delaware River at Fish's Eddy

Tackle

I like to fish the East Branch with a long, light-weight fly rod. If I am fishing the larger mayfly hatches, like the green and brown drakes, I'll use a 9-foot, 4-weight outfit. For smaller mayflies like sulphurs and olives, I prefer a 9-foot, 3-weight outfit.

DELAWARE RIVER SYSTEM HATCH CHART

Common Name (Scientific Name)	Hatch Period	Fly Patterns	Hook Sizes
Early Black Stonefly *Taeniopteryx nivalis*	March – early April	Black Elk Hair Caddis Dry	16-18
Early Brown Stonefly *Strophopteryx fasciata*	March – early April	Brown Bi-Visible Dry Stimulator Dry	14-16 14-16
Little Black Caddis *Chimarra atterrima*	Mid-April – mid-May	Black Elk Hair Caddis	16-18
Little Blue-winged Olive *Baetis tricaudatus* (formerly *Baetis vagans*)	Late February – mid-May Late August – early Nov.	Parachute Adams Parachute BWO	16-18 16-18
Blue Quill *Paraleptophlebia adoptiva* *Paraleptophlebia* spp.	Mid-April – early May June – September	Blue Quill Dry Blue Dun Dry Blue Quill Nymph	16-18 16-18 16-18
Quill Gordon *Epeorus pleuralis*	Mid-April – early May	Quill Gordon Dry Hare's Ear Wet	14 14
Hendrickson/Red Quill *Ephemerella subvaria*	Mid-April – early May	Hendrickson Dry Red Quill Dry	14 14
Black Quill *Leptophlebia cupida*	Mid-April – mid-May	Black Quill Dry	12-14
Tan Caddis *Hydropsyche* spp.	May – August	Elk Hair Caddis Dry Leonard Wright Caddis Dry	14-16 14-16
*March Brown *Maccaffertium vicarium* (formerly *Stenonema vicarium*)	Mid-May – early June	March Brown Dry Gray Fox Dry March Brown Wet	12 12-14 12
Blue-winged Olive *Drunella cornuta* (formerly *Ephemeralla cornuta*)	Late-May – mid-June	Blue-winged Olive Dry	14
Pale Evening Dun *Ephemerella invaria*	Early May – mid- June	Pale Evening Dun Dry Sulphur Spinner	14-16 14-16
Grannom *Brachycentrus fuliginosus*	Mid-April – mid-May	Brown Elk Hair Caddis Peacock Caddis Dry	12-14 12-14

(continued on next page)

The East Branch in Harvard. Photo courtesy Glen Zeeke.

Apple Green Caddis	Early May – mid-May	Tan/Green Elk Hair Caddis	14-16
Brachycentrus appalachia			
Great Brown Stonefly	Late May – June	Stimulator Dry	8-10
Acroneuria lycorias		Golden Stone Fly Nymph	8-10
Light Cahill	Mid-May – mid-June	Light Cahill Dry	12
Stenacron interpunctatum		Light Cahill Wet	12
(formerly *Stenonema canadense*)			
(formerly *Stenonema interpunctatum*)			
Sulphur	June – mid-July	Pale Evening Dun Dry	16-18
Ephemerella dorothea		Pale Evening Dun Spinner	16-18
Pink Lady	Late May – late-June	Pale Evening Dun Dry	14
Epeorus vitreus		Pale Evening Dun Spinner	14
Green Drake	Late May – mid-June	Green Drake Dry	8-10
Ephemera guttulata		Coffin Fly Spinner	8-10
Brown Drake	Late May – mid-June	Brown Wulff Dry	12-14
Ephemera simulans			
Slate Drake		Slate Drake Dry	10-12
Isonychia bicolor	Late May – June	Adams Dry	10-12
Isonychia sadleri & harperi	Mid-Sept. – October	Gray Wulff	10-12
		Leadwing Coachman Wet	10-12
Little Yellow Sally	June – mid-August	Yellow Elk Hair Caddis Dry	14-16
Isoperla bilineata		Stimulator Dry	14-16
Tiny Blue-winged Olive	June – mid-October	Parachute Adams	20-24
Acentrella turbida		Parachute BWO	20-24
(formerly Pseudocloeon)			
Blue-winged Olive	Late May – mid-July	Blue-winged Olive Dry	14-18
Attenella attenuata			
(formerly *Ephemerella attenuata*)			
Yellow Drake	Mid-June – mid-July	Yellow Drake Dry	10-12
Ephemera varia			
Golden Drake	Mid-June – July	Golden Drake Dry	8-10
Anthopotamus distinctus			
(formerly P*otamanthus distinctus*)			
Tricos	Mid-July – September	Trico Spinner Dry	22-26
Tricorythyodes allectus			
Tricorythyodes stygiatus			
White Fly	Late July – early Sept.	White Wulff Dry	12-14
Ephoron leukon			
October Caddis	Mid-Sept. – October	Orange Stimulator Dry	10
Pycnopsyche ssp.			
Midges	February – November	Griffith's Gnat	18-22
Chironomidae		Cream Midge Dry	18-24
		Zebra Midge Nymph	18-24
Flying Ants	September – October	Flying Ant Dry	16-20
Ants	May – October	Parachute Ant Dry	16-20
		Flying Ant Dry	16-20
		Black Wire Ant Wet	16-20
Beetles	May – October	Crowe Beetle	12
Grasshoppers	May – October	Dave's Hopper	10-12
Inchworms	May – October	Deer Hair Dry	12
Geometridae		Green Weenie Wet	12
Other Caterpillars	May – October	Woolly Worms	6-10

* *Stenonema fuscum* (Gray Fox) is now considered the same species as *Maccaffertium vicarium,* formerly *Stenonema vicarium*
    (March Brown)

Hub Cities

HANCOCK, POPULATION 1,031 / DEPOSIT, POPULATION 2,921

ACCOMMODATIONS

Delaware River Club, 1228 Winterdale Road, Starlight, Pennsylvania / 570-635-5880 / www.delawareriverclub.com / Lodging, fly shop and guiding

West Branch Angler, 150 Faulkner Road, Hancock / 000-201-2557 / www.westbranchangler.com / Lodging and guiding / Upscale log cabins on the river

Hancock House, 137 E. Front St., Hancock / 607-637-7100 / www.newhancockhouse.com

The Inn at Starlight Lake, 289 Starlight Lake Road, Starlight, Pa. / 570-798-2519 / www.innatstarlightlake.com

Wayne Aldridge's Lighthouse Lodge, 19 Latham Road, Deposit / 607-467-4215 / www.river-of-life.com

CAMPGROUNDS AND RV PARKS

Peaceful Valley Campsites, 486 Banker Road, Downsville / 607-363-2211 / www.peacefulvalley.com

Terry's Shinhopple Campground, 6275 Route 30, Downsville / 607-363-2536

Beaver Del Hotel & Campground, 8560 Route 17, East Branch / 607-363-7443 / www.beaverdel.com

RESTAURANTS

The River Run Restaurant, 150 Faulkner Road, Hancock / 800-201-2557 / www.westbankangler.com / Part of the West Bank Angler Resort

Hancock House, 137 E. Front St., Hancock / 607-637-7100 / www.newhancockhouse.co

The Inn at Starlight Lake, 289 Starlight Lake Road, Starlight, Pa. / 570-798-2519 / www.innatstarlightlake.com

FLY SHOPS AND GUIDES

Darren Rist, River Rapture Fly Fishing Guide Service, Hale Eddy / 973-300-5726 / dprist@earthlink.net

Delaware River Club, 1228 Winterdale Road, Starlight, PA / 570-635-5880 / www.delawareriverclub.com / Fly shop and guiding

West Bank Angler, 150 Faulkner Road, Hancock / 800-201-2557 / www.westbankangler.com / Fly shop and guiding

Old Souls, 63 Main St, Cold Spring / 845-809-5886 / www.oldsouls.com

Jerry Hadden's Guide Service / 570-853-4048 / www.jerryhadden.com

Rivers Outdoor Adventures, 22 Hughes St., New Ringgold, PA / 570-943-3151 / www.riversflyfishing.com

Border Water Outfitters, 159 E. Front St., Hancock / 607-637-4296 / www.borderwateroutfitters.com

Cross Current Guide Service / 914-475-6779 / www.crosscurrentguideservice.com

Aaron Jasper's Fly Fishing Evolution Guide Service / 201-913-8887 / www.flyfishingevolution.com / Aaron guides on the New York & Connecticut tailwaters.

Ben Turpin, 570-807-3027 / www.benturpin.com

AIRPORTS

Greater Binghamton Airport, 2534 Airport Road, Maine / 607-763-4471 / www.flybgm.com

MEDICAL

Margaretville Memorial Hospital, Route 28, Margaretville / 845-586-2631

Hancock Family Practice, 116 E. Front St. / 607-637-5711

FOR MORE INFORMATION

Hancock Area Chamber of Commerce, 158 E. Front St. / 607-637-4756 / www.hancockareachamber.com

Friends of the Upper Delaware River, 1148 5th Avenue, New York, NY / www.fudr.org

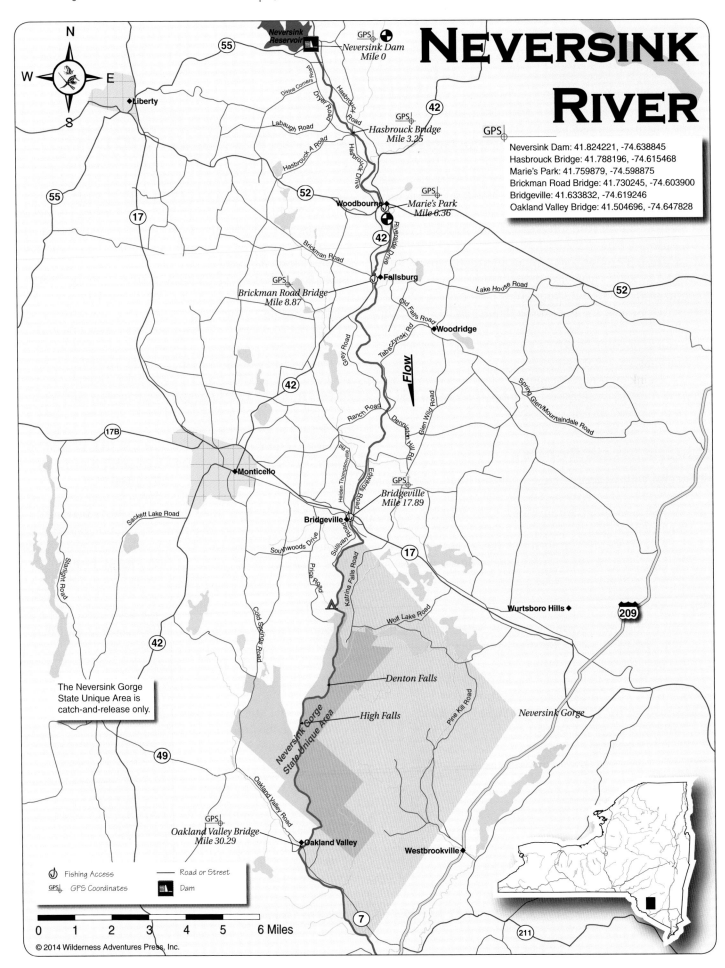

NEVERSINK RIVER

Neversink Dam: 41.824221, -74.638845
Hasbrouck Bridge: 41.788196, -74.615468
Marie's Park: 41.759879, -74.598875
Brickman Road Bridge: 41.730245, -74.603900
Bridgeville: 41.633832, -74.619246
Oakland Valley Bridge: 41.504696, -74.647828

Neversink Reservoir

Neversink Dam
Mile 0

Liberty

Hasbrouck Bridge
Mile 3.25

Woodbourne

Marie's Park
Mile 6.36

Fallsburg

Brickman Road Bridge
Mile 8.87

Woodridge

Flow

Monticello

Bridgeville
Mile 17.89

Bridgeville

Wurtsboro Hills

The Neversink Gorge
State Unique Area is
catch-and-release only.

Denton Falls

High Falls

Neversink Gorge

Neversink Gorge
State Unique Area

Oakland Valley Bridge
Mile 30.29

Oakland Valley

Westbrookville

Fishing Access

GPS Coordinates

Road or Street

Dam

0   1   2   3   4   5   6 Miles

© 2014 Wilderness Adventures Press, Inc.

NEVERSINK RIVER (FOUR STARS)

The Neversink River runs about 50 miles from its source on Slide Mountain to its junction with the Delaware River in Port Jervis. This is the southernmost river of the famous Catskill "Charmed Circle" streams and was a favorite of angling pioneers like Theodore Gordon, George LaBranche, and Edward Hewitt. I have divided the coverage of the Neversink Tailwater into two sections, from the dam down to Route 17 in Bridgeville and the Neversink Gorge downstream of Route 17 in Bridgeville.

NEVERSINK DAM TO BRIDGEVILLE (FOUR STARS)

In 1955, the state completed building the dam on the Neversink River, and for several years the fishing below the dam was poor due to inadequate water releases. We lost a good portion of the upper river when it was flooded to create the Neversink Reservoir, including Hewitt's property and the farm house where Theodore Gordon lived the last ten years of his life. But once the coldwater releases improved, we gained about 15 miles of a year-round tailwater fishery below the reservoir. Since 2004, the releases from the dam have been mandated at 115 cubic feet per second (cfs). With fairly stable releases, the water temperature rarely exceeds 70 degrees, providing an excellent tailwater fishery for almost 15 miles downstream.

The first seven miles below the reservoir contain a very good population of stream-bred brown trout in addition to a large number of stocked and holdover trout. This section has good hatches, and fishes well throughout the summer. Below the reservoir, the first access to public water is at Hasbrouck Bridge. According to NYDEC biologists, the Neversink's trout biomass compares favorably to that of the Beaverkill and Willowemoc. The state has done a terrific job in acquiring access easements and it has developed about a dozen parking areas along the Neversink River. Around the town of Bridgeville the cooling effect from the dam releases diminishes and the water warms in summer. The

Neversink tends to run low and clear, and even the stocked fish can become difficult to catch during these conditions. Because of the coldwater releases, the hatches run about a week behind those on the Beaverkill and Willowemoc.

DIRECTIONS/ACCESS

From Roscoe or Livingston Manor, take Route 17 East to Route 55 East. Cross the Neversink Reservoir Dam and take the first right onto Hasbrouck Road and continue for 2.2 miles to Clark A Road. Turn right on Clark A Road for 0.5 miles and turn right on Hasbrouck Road for 0.3 miles to the bridge. The public fishing starts at the bridge and runs downstream for many miles.

Hasbrouck Road

I like to cross the bridge and turn left on Hasbrouck Road. In the next mile there are two well-marked public fishing access parking areas.

Marie's Park

About 2.5 miles downstream of Hasbrouck Bridge you run into Route 42 in Woodbourne. Marie's Park is directly south east of the bridge. The water on the downstream side of the park is wide and shallow, with no holding water. Upstream of the bridge there is a boulder-strewn run with good flow and it always holds good numbers of trout.

The Neversink is an easily waded stream that holds good numbers of stocked and wild trout.

Fallsburg

If you head south on Route 42 you will find two more fishermen's parking areas around Fallsburg.

Brickman Road Bridge

Two miles below the town of Woodbourne Bridge is another bridge on Brickman Road. Turn left off of Route 42 south onto Brickman Road, cross the bridge and park on the right. Just upstream from the bridge is a beautiful waterfall and several deep pools. The large deep pool just below the bridge can be very productive, but you will need a hatch to bring the fish up from its depths. Over the last 30 years this section has only been posted a few times. My rule of thumb here is that if I see trout from the bridge, I assume it has been stocked and therefore open to the public.

Bridgeville

The state also provides public access to some nice water just south of Route 17 in Bridgeville. Take Exit 108 (Bridgeville Road) off of Route 17 and follow the signs for the Old Homestead Restaurant, which is just a short distance from the bridge over the Neversink. Park by the bridge and fish upstream or downstream.

From New York City and northern New Jersey you can access the Hasbrouck, Woodbourne, and Fallsburg sections of the Neversink by taking Route 17 north to the exit for Route 42 North, which provides good access to the river.

NEVERSINK GORGE (FOUR STARS)

Below Route 17 and Bridgeville, the Neversink flows through a steep, rugged gorge. In the gorge, a few small tributaries harbor native brook trout and add cool water to the Neversink. The state has designated this 7,000-acre preserve as the Neversink Gorge State Unique Area and has regulated it as Catch-and-Release – Artificial Lures Only. No stocking is done in the gorge. All the fish are wild, mostly browns, but brookies from the tributaries are not uncommon. It takes about a half hour to hike into the gorge and quite a bit longer to hike back out. Most of the gorge lacks trails and having a little mountain goat blood in you helps if you choose to fish it. When fishing a remote area, for safety reasons it's a good idea to have a partner, or at least let someone know where you are fishing and when you expect to return.

STREAM FACTS

Season/Regulations

The Neversink is open to fishing from April 1 until October 15 with a daily limit of five trout per day of 9 inches.

The Neversink Unique Area is regulated as catch-and-release – artificials only.

Fish

The coldwater releases and excellent habitat enable the Neversink to support a healthy population of stream-bred and holdover trout.

History

The Neversink is the southernmost of the famous Catskill "Charmed Circle" streams and it was a favorite of angling pioneers the likes of Theodore Gordon, Edward Hewitt, and George LaBranche.

River Characteristics

The river is easy to wade and most of the season it runs low and clear. It has an excellent population of wild and stocked trout and the state has developed numerous public access and parking areas.

River Flows

With the completion of the Neversink Reservoir in 1955 and mandated stable bottom releases, the Neversink has become a reliable year-round trout fishery. The tailwater trout fishery extends downstream some 15 miles below the reservoir.

http://waterdata.gov/USA/UV USGS web site 01436690 Neversink River at Bridgeville

Tackle

Because this is a tailwater fishery, the water is low and clear and spring creek tactics are necessary to take the Neversink's selective trout. I like to fish an 8-foot, 3-weight outfit with a long light leader.

Neversink Falls, located just upstream of the Old Falls Road Bridge in Fallsburg.

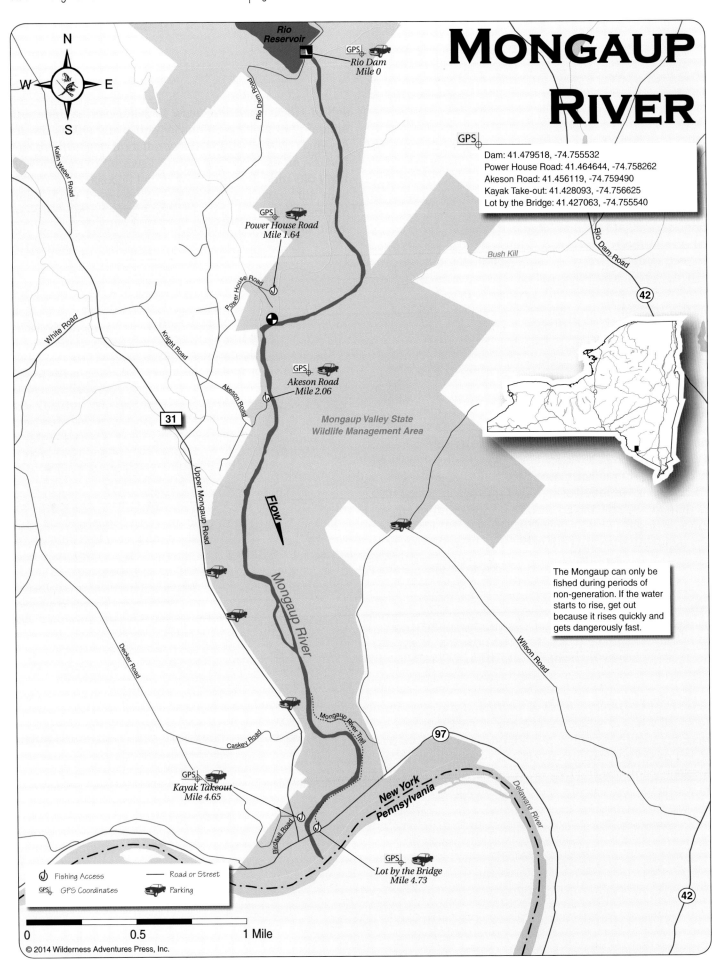

MONGAUP RIVER

Rio Dam
Mile 0

GPS
Dam: 41.479518, -74.755532
Power House Road: 41.464644, -74.758262
Akeson Road: 41.456119, -74.759490
Kayak Take-out: 41.428093, -74.756625
Lot by the Bridge: 41.427063, -74.755540

Rio Reservoir

Rio Dam Road

Bush Kill

42

Power House Road
Mile 1.64

Power House Road

White Road

Knight Road

Akeson Road

Akeson Road
Mile 2.06

Mongaup Valley State
Wildlife Management Area

31

Upper Mongaup Road

Flow

Mongaup River

The Mongaup can only be fished during periods of non-generation. If the water starts to rise, get out because it rises quickly and gets dangerously fast.

Decker Road

Wilson Road

Caskey Road

Mongaup River Trail

97

Kayak Takeout
Mile 4.65

Birdsall Road

New York
Pennsylvania

Delaware River

Lot by the Bridge
Mile 4.73

Fishing Access
GPS GPS Coordinates
Road or Street
Parking

42

0   0.5   1 Mile

© 2014 Wilderness Adventures Press, Inc.

MONGAUP RIVER (FOUR STARS)

The Mongaup River flows through three reservoirs before it joins the Delaware River above Port Jervis. New York State stocks the East, West, and Middle Branches of the Mongaup River, but for big trout the tailwater below the Rio Reservoir to the junction of the Delaware is the place to fish. This 3.5-mile section is not stocked, and at times it can be one of the better wild trout fisheries in the region. Most of the trout are browns, but occasional bows and brook trout are caught. It is managed under special regulations; fishing is artificials-only, with a daily limit of three trout over 12 inches. You can fish it from 8:00am to sunset between mid-April and mid-October.

The river can be difficult and at times dangerous to wade, especially when Alliance Electric Company turns on the turbines to generate power, which unleashes a wall of water rushing downstream; studded boots and a wading staff are a must. The lower Mongaup has a low angler catch rate, but it offers up some huge trout in a spectacular wilderness setting. Bill Dickson, a fishing partner of mine, used to drive over two hours from Philadelphia to the Mongaup just to get an evening's fishing in. To this day the Mongaup has given Bill his largest wild brown, brook, and rainbow trout in the East. His stream log reveals brown trout in excess of 20 inches and brook trout in the low teens. Some of the river's better hatches include sulphurs, Cahills, slate drakes, and a variety of caddis.

DIRECTIONS/ACCESS

From Port Jervis, take Route 97 North over the mountains at Hawks Nest for 6.4 miles to the Mongaup River just upstream from where it enters the Delaware. While most anglers park in the lot by the bridge, there are other good access points which allow you to fish waters which are less pressured. The first is a small parking lot on the right on Route 31 (Upper Mongaup Road) one tenth of a mile above Route 97. This is the takeout point for kayakers.

You can park in the lot and there is a trail which follows the stream for quite some distance upstream. The trail might be hard to spot, as a dirt mound has been placed in front of it to stop ATV use. There are two additional parking areas upstream off Route 31 (Mongaup Road). Take Mongaup Road for two miles and turn right on Knight Road for 0.4 miles to Rio Dam Road. Go one mile on Rio Dam Road to Akeson Road, turn right and go 0.4 miles to a parking area and riverside trail. Go back to Rio Dam Road, turn right and go one mile, and you will see a dirt road on the right which leads down to the stream just below the Rio hydroelectric facility. The dirt road is Power House Road, and it is 0.6 miles to the river. There is a parking area and a kiosk with a map showing the trail along the stream. (Actually there are two dirt roads on the right; take the one which forks to the left.) The last time I was there the road had two conflicting signs. One, posted by Alliance Energy which operates the facility, welcomes public access for fishing and kayakers. The other was from a homeowner association and it said, "Private Road No Entrance", but the road is a public access road.

The Mongaup River below Rio Reservoir.

Stream Facts

Seasons/Regulations

Fishing is artificials only, with a daily limit of three trout over 12 inches. You can fish from 8:00am to sunset between mid-April and mid-October. It is not stocked – all of its trout are wild and I strongly encourage you to release its trout.

Fish

The Mongaup has a low angler catch rate, but it does give up some huge trout. Bill Dickson, a fishing partner of mine use to drive over two hours from Philadelphia to the Mongaup just to get in an evening's fishing in. To this day, the Mongaup have given Bill his largest wild brown, brook and rainbow trout in the East.

River Characteristics

The river flows through a scenic, but rugged gorge. The banks are steep and the wading is difficult. But if you are careful you may be rewarded with a monster trout.

Flows

http://waterdata.gov/USA/UV USGS web site 01432900 Mongaup River at Mongaup Valley

Aaron Jasper and guide in the tri-state region (NY, NJ & PA) wisely advises his clients to fish the river only during periods when they are not generating power as the river is "dangerously quick in rising and velocity."

Tackle

The Mongaup River is mostly pocket water. I prefer to fish large weighted nymphs with a 9-foot 6-inch rod. In the fall big browns come up out of the Delaware River to spawn. This is the time to throw big streamers on a 6-weight rod using a sink-tip line.

The Mongaup River can be tough to wade, but the rewards can be worth the trouble.

NEVERSINK AND MONGAUP RIVER MAJOR HATCHES

Common Name *Scientific Name*	Hatch Period	Fly Patterns	Hook Sizes
Little Black Caddis *Chimarra atterrima*	Mid-April – mid-May	Black Elk Hair Caddis	16-18
Little Blue-winged Olive *Baetis tricaudatus* (formerly *Baetis vagans*)	Late Feb. – mid-May Late August – early Nov.	Parachute Adams Parachute BWO	16-18 16-18
Hendrickson/Red Quill *Ephemerella subvaria*	Late April – mid May	Hendrickson Dry Red Quill Dry	14 14
Tan Caddis *Hydropsyche spp.*	May – August	Elk Hair Caddis Dry Leonard Wright Caddis Dry	14-16 14-16
***March Brown** *Maccaffertium vicarium* (formerly *Stenonema vicarium*)	Mid-May – early June	March Brown Dry Gray Fox Dry March Brown Wet	12 12-14 12
Grannom *Brachycentrus fuliginosus*	May	Brown Elk Hair Caddis Peacock Caddis Dry	12-14 12-14
Apple Green Caddis *Brachycentrus appalachia*	May	Tan/Green Elk Hair Caddis	14-16
Light Cahill *Stenacron interpunctatum* (formerly *Stenonema canadense*) (formerly *Stenonema interpunctatum*)	Late-May – mid-June	Light Cahill Dry Light Cahill Wet	12 12
Sulphur *Ephemerella dorothea*	June – mid-July	Pale Evening Dun Dry Pale Evening Dun Spinner	16-18 16-18
Green Drake *Ephemera guttulata*	Late May – mid-June	Green Drake Dry Coffin Fly Spinner	8-10 8-10
Slate Drake *Isonychia bicolor* *Isonychia sadleri & harperi*	Late May – June Mid-Sept. – October	Slate Drake Dry Adams Dry Gray Wulff Leadwing Coachman Wet	10-12 10-12 10-12 10-12
Tiny Blue-winged Olive *Acentrella turbida* (formerly *Pseudocloeon*)	June – mid-October	Parachute Adams Parachute BWO	20-24 20-24
October Caddis *Pycnopsyche ssp.*	Mid-Sept. – October	Orange Stimulator Dry	10
Ants	May – October	Parachute Ant Dry Flying Ant Dry Black Wire Ant Wet	16-20 16-20 16-20
Inchworms *Geometridae*	May – October	Deer Hair Dry Green Weenie Wet	12 12
Other Caterpillars	May – October	Woolly Worms	6-10

* *Stenonema fuscum* (Gray Fox) is now considered the same species as *Maccaffertium vicarium*, formerly *Stenonema vicarium* (March Brown).

Hub Cities

ROSCOE
Population 541

ACCOMMODATIONS

Baxter House B & B, 2012 Old Route 17 / 607-290-4022 / www.Baxterhouse.net / Guide service and fly shop
Creek Side Cabins / 607-498-5873 / www.creeksidecabins.net
Lanza's Country Inn, 839 Shandelle Road / 845-439-5070 / www./ lanzascountryinn.com
Beaverkill Valley Inn, 7 Barnhart Road / 845-439-4844 / www.beaverkillvalleyinn.com / Inn overlooks the one mile of private water guests may fish.
Riverside Café & Lodge, Route 17 / 607-498-5305 / www.riversidecafeandlodge.com

CAMPGROUNDS AND RV PARKS

Roscoe Campsites, 2179 Old Route 17 / 607-498-5264 / www.roscoecampsite.com
Miller Hollow Campground, 26 Miller Hollow Road / 607-636-7492
Russell Brook Campsites, 731 Russell Brook Road / 607-498-5416 / www.russellbrook.com

RESTAURANTS

Raimondo's Restaurant & Pizzeria, Stewart Ave. / 607-498-4702 / Great Italian cuisine at affordable prices.
Roscoe Diner, Old Route 17 / 607-498-4405 / The most popular place to eat in the Catskills.
Buffalo Zach's Cafe, Old Route 17 / 607-498-4149 / www.buffalozachscafe.com

FLY SHOPS, GUIDES AND SPORTING GOODS

Darren Rist, River Rapture Fly Fishing Guide Service, Hale Eddy / 973-300 / dprist@earthlink.net
Baxter House, 2012 Old Route 17 / 607-498-5811 / www.baxterhouse.net
Catskill Flies, 6 Stewart Ave. / 607-498-6146 / www.catskillflies.com
The Little Store, 51 Stewart Ave. / 607-498-5553
Dette Trout Flies / 607-498-4991

The Beaverkill Angler, 59 Stewart Ave. / 607-498-5194 / www.beaverkillangler.com
Fir, Fin, and Feather Sports Shop, 109 DeBruce Road, Livingston Manor / 845-439-4476
Catskill Flyfishing Center & Museum, Old Route 17 between Livingston Manor and Roscoe / 845-439-4810

AIRPORTS

Sullivan County International Airport, 100 North Street, Monticello / 845-807-0272

MEDICAL

Catskill Regional Medical Center - Callicoon Campus, Route 97 South, Callicoon / 845-887-5530

FOR MORE INFORMATION

Roscoe/Rockland Chamber of Commerce / 607-498-5222 / www.roscoeny.com

MIDDLETOWN
Population 28,086

ACCOMMODATIONS

Courtyard by Marriott / 845-695-0606 / www.marriott.com
Holiday Inn / 877-863-4780 / www.holidayinn.com

CAMPGROUNDS AND RV PARKS

Oakland Valley Campgrounds, 399 Valley Road, Cuddebackville / 845-733-5494 / www.oaklandvalley.com
Spring Glen Campground, 108 Lewis Road, Spring Glen / 845-647-7075

RESTAURANTS

The Old Homestead Restaurant, 472 Bridgeville Road, Monticello / 845-794-8973 / www.theoldhomesteadny.com / Overlooks the Neversink River.

FLY SHOPS AND SPORTING GOODS

Modell's Sporting Goods, 470 Route 211 E. /
845-343-1808 / www.modells.com
Gander Mountain, 100 N Galleria Drive / 845-692-5600 /
www.gandermountain.com
Old Souls, 63 Main St, Cold Spring / 845-809-5886 /
www.oldsouls.com

AIRPORTS

Steward International Airport, Cochecton Turnpike,
Middletown, NY

MEDICAL

Horton Medical Center, 60 Prospect Ave. / 845-342-7350
Orange Regional Medical Center, 110 Crystal Run Road
/ 845-696-8731

PORT JERVIS

Population 8,845

FLY SHOPS, GUIDES AND SPORTING GOODS

Curt's Sporting Goods, Bait & Information, 390 Route
97, Sparrow Bush / 845-856-5024 / Curt is a real
fisherman and always has up-to-date information.
Pike County Outfitters / 570-296-9492 /
www.pikecountyoutiftters.net

*Roscoe, New York claims the
moniker Trout Town, U.S.A.*

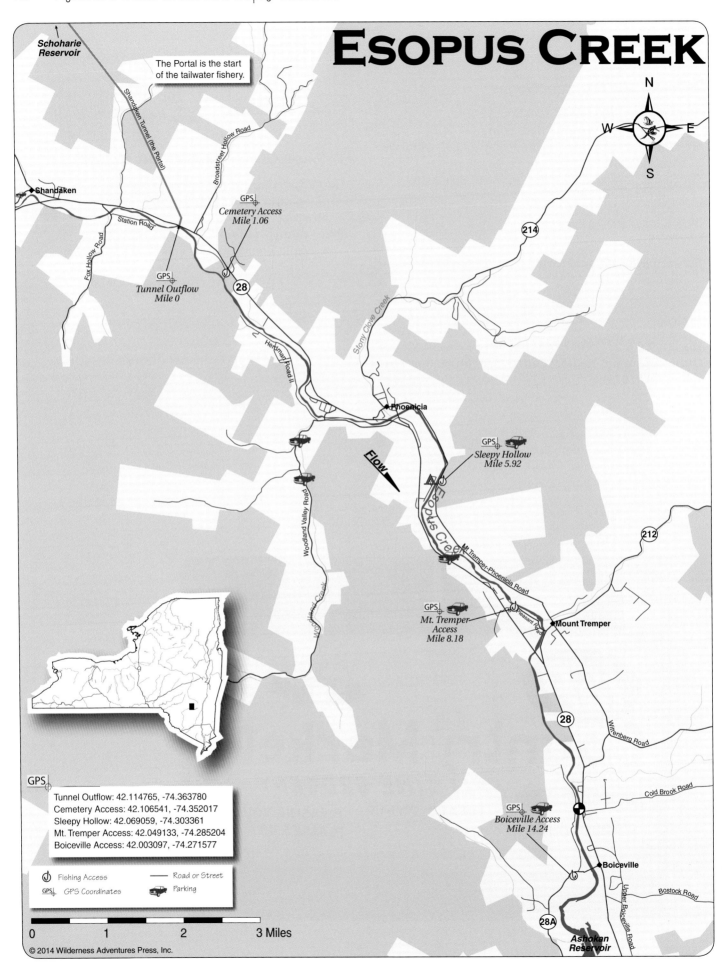

ESOPUS CREEK

Schoharie
Reservoir

The Portal is the start
of the tailwater fishery.

Shandaken

Shandaken Tunnel (the Portal)

Broadstreet Hollow Road

Station Road

Fox Hollow Road

GPS
Cemetery Access
Mile 1.06

GPS
Tunnel Outflow
Mile 0

28

214

Stony Clove Creek

Herdman Road II

Phoenicia

Flow

Esopus Creek

GPS
Sleepy Hollow
Mile 5.92

Woodland Valley Road

Woodland Creek

Mt. Tremper-Phoenicia Road

GPS
Mt. Tremper
Access
Mile 8.18

Pleasant Road

Mount Tremper

212

28

Wittenberg Road

Cold Brook Road

GPS
Boiceville Access
Mile 14.24

Boiceville

Bostock Road

Upper Boiceville Road

28A

Ashokan
Reservoir

GPS

Tunnel Outflow: 42.114765, -74.363780
Cemetery Access: 42.106541, -74.352017
Sleepy Hollow: 42.069059, -74.303361
Mt. Tremper Access: 42.049133, -74.285204
Boiceville Access: 42.003097, -74.271577

Fishing Access

GPS   GPS Coordinates

Road or Street

Parking

0   1   2   3 Miles

© 2014 Wilderness Adventures Press, Inc.

ESOPUS CREEK (FOUR STARS)

In terms of sheer numbers of trout, the Esopus is one the best wild rainbow streams in the East. "The Portal" is what the locals call the Shandaken Tunnel, bringing water some 18 miles from the reservoir on the Schoharie Creek through the mountains and into Esopus Creek, changing the character of the creek by adding substantial volumes of cold water and providing good fishing all summer in the 12-mile stretch from the Portal down to the Ashokan Reservoir. The stretch from the Portal down to the reservoir has an estimated fall wild trout population of over 100,000 fish, according to the New York State Department of Conservation (NYDEC). It has a higher percentage of wild trout than any other Catskill River except the West Branch and the Upper Delaware River, neither of which are stocked. Most of the Esopus rainbows are less than 11 inches, as the larger fish move down into the Ashokan Reservoir when they reach between one and two years of age. There is a late winter and early spring spawning run of rainbows which brings fish in the 16- to 22-inch range out of the reservoir and into the Esopus to spawn. Unfortunately this often happens before the opening day of trout season.

PORTAL TO BOICEVILLE (FIVE STARS)

The next valley north of the Esopus is home to the Schoharie Creek and its reservoir. In 1924 a large underground tunnel was built from the Schoharie Reservoir through the mountains south to the Esopus Creek at the village of Shandaken. Here the Schoharie's waters enter the Esopus at the Portal, forming the first large pool on the upper Esopus. The 12-mile section from the Portal (which is 3.5 miles west of the town of Phoenicia on Route 28) to Boiceville is called the "the Big Esopus." Route 28 provides easy access to the Esopus, as it parallels most of the lower or Big Esopus. Cold water from the Portal keeps the lower Esopus cool all summer.

During the summer this section of the river is very popular with "tubers". Plan to fish early and late in the day from Memorial Day through Labor Day, especially on weekends. The Big Esopus is comprised largely of fast riffles and pocket water, which provide great nymph and wet-fly fishing. This section is tough to wade, so I strongly recommend a wading staff and studded wading boots. While the DEC estimates that this section of the Esopus harbors about 100,000 wild rainbows, angler surveys indicate that very few wild rainbows are landed. To keep anglers and politicians happy, the state stocks the lower Esopus with over 25,000 brown trout annually. These stocked browns are larger and easier to catch than the wild rainbows. Spring angler surveys indicate that their catch is made up of 93 percent stocked browns. The best hatch of the year on the Esopus is without question the slate drakes, with some of the better fishing occurring during late August through early October. During this time, an *Isonychia* nymph or Leadwing Coachman wet fly are hard to beat.

While the Beaverkill, Willowemoc, and Neversink are classic dry fly waters, the Esopus' fast pocket water, smaller pools, and faster runs are built for traditional down-and-across wet fly fishing. Grab a box of your classic Catskill wet fly patterns and take a trip back into angling history on the Esopus.

DIRECTIONS/ACCESS

The easiest way to get to the Esopus is to take the New York State Thruway to Kingston and take Route 28 west for about 15 miles to Boiceville. Route 28 takes you around the north side of the Ashokan Reservoir and then parallels the Esopus Creek from Boiceville past Phoenicia to Big Indian. The lower 12 miles of the Esopus is closely paralleled by Route 28 and there are plenty of roadside pull-offs and DEC access areas.

In terms of sheer numbers of trout, the Esopus is one of the best rainbow fisheries in the East.

STREAM FACTS

Season/Regulations

New York State (NYS) general harvest regulations are five fish per day, with no size limit. The Esopus season runs from April 1 to November 30.

Fish

In terms of sheer numbers of trout, the Esopus is the best wild rainbow stream in the East. While the DEC estimates that the Esopus between the reservoir and the Portal harbors about 100,000 wild rainbows, angler surveys indicate that very few wild rainbows are landed. To keep anglers and politicians happy, the state stocks the lower Esopus with over 25,000 brown trout annually. There are native brook trout in its headwaters and stream-bred browns and rainbows throughout.

River Characteristics

The Esopus is comprised largely of fast riffles and pocket water, which provide great nymph and wet fly water. It is tough to wade, so I strongly recommend a wading staff and studded wading boots. The next valley north of the Esopus is home to the Schoharie Creek and its reservoir. In 1924, a large underground tunnel was built from the Schoharie Reservoir through the mountains south to the Esopus Creek at the village of Shandaken. Cold water from the tunnel keeps the lower Esopus cool all summer.

Flows

http://waterdata.gov/USA/UV USGS web site 01362500 Esopus Creek at Coldbrook

Tackle

Since I like to fish the Esopus with nymphs and wet flies, my rod choice is usually a 9-foot, 5-weight.

Hub City

PHOENICIA

Population 309

ACCOMMODATIONS

Catskill Rose Lodging & Dining, 5355 Route 212, Mount Temper / 845-688-7100 / catskillrose.com

CAMPGROUNDS AND RV PARKS

Woodland Valley Campground, 1319 Woodland Road / 845-688-7647

RESTAURANTS

Al's Restaurant & Lounge, 10 Main St. / 845-688-5880 / Al's has been in business for seventy years and has the best seafood in the Catskills. If you are in the area on a Monday night, the buffet is a must-try.

Brio's Pizzeria & Restaurant, 68 Main St. / 845-688-5370 / brios.com / The owner is from an old Italian family in Brooklyn, and with his twin wood-burning ovens he makes the best pizza in the Catskills. Don't overlook the rest of the menu, as I have never had a bad meal at Brio's, where the locals eat.

Bear Café, 295 Tinker St., Woodstock / 845-679-5555 / bearcafe.com

FLY SHOPS AND SPORTING GOODS

Catskill Forest Sports, State Route 28, Glenford / 845-657-8311 / www.catskillforestsports.com

Old Souls, 63 Main St, Cold Spring / 845-809-5886 / www.oldsouls.com

Water from Schoharie Reservoir floods into Esopus Creek via the Shandaken Tunnel.

THE TAILWATERS OF THE CROTON WATERSHED

The Croton watershed system in Westchester and Putnam Counties, which provides quality drinking water to New York City, also offers anglers excellent tailwater trout fishing, all within 50 miles of the city. These hemlock-lined streams linking the Croton Reservoir system provide year-round coldwater trout habitat for both wild and stocked trout. In addition to the tailwater fisheries, there are several good freestone streams in the watershed which provide good angling opportunities from April to June.

Most anglers I interviewed rated the top four tailwater sections in this watershed as the East Branch of the Croton River below the East Branch Reservoir, the West Branch of the Croton River below the West Branch Reservoir, and again below the Croton Falls Reservoir, and the Muscoot River below the Amawalk Outlet.

The East Branch of the Croton River below East Branch Reservoir.

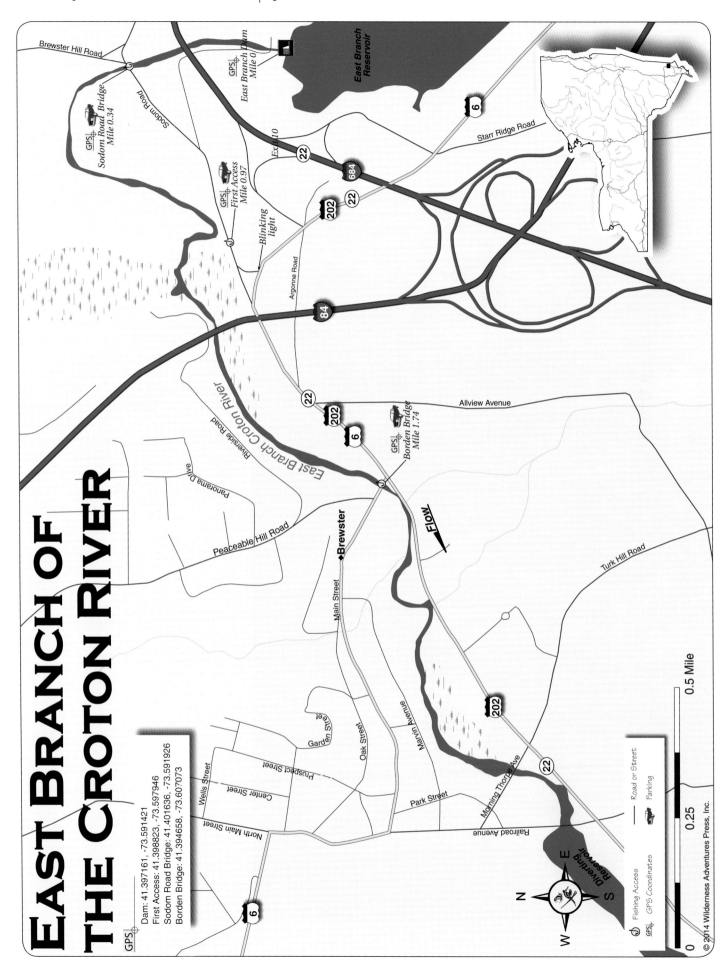

EAST BRANCH OF THE CROTON RIVER

GPS

Dam: 41.397161, -73.591421
First Access: 41.398823, -73.597946
Sodom Road Bridge: 41.401636, -73.591926
Borden Bridge: 41.394658, -73.607073

Brewster Hill Road

Sodom Road

GPS Sodom Road Bridge Mile 0.34

East Branch Dam Mile 0

GPS East Branch Dam Mile 0

East Branch Reservoir

Starr Ridge Road

6

Ext 10

22

684

202 22

Blinking light

GPS First Access Mile 0.97

Argonne Road

84

Riverside Road

East Branch Croton River

Panorama Drive

Peaceable Hill Road

22

202

6

GPS Borden Bridge Mile 1.74

Allview Avenue

Brewster

FLOW

Turk Hill Road

Main Street

202

22

Garden Street

Oak Street

Marvin Avenue

Prospect Street

Center Street

Wells Street

North Main Street

Park Street

Morning Thorpe Ave

Railroad Avenue

Diverting Reservoir

6

N
E
S
W

Road or Street

Parking

Fishing Access

GPS GPS Coordinates

0   0.25   0.5 Mile

© 2014 Wilderness Adventures Press, Inc.

EAST BRANCH OF THE CROTON RIVER (FOUR STARS)

Less than an hour north of NYC on the Saw Mill Parkway and Interstate 684 is the East Branch of the Croton River. The East Branch is the longest and most varied stream in the Croton system. The most popular section on the East Branch runs from East Branch (Sodom) Reservoir downstream 2.4 miles through Brewster to the Diverting Reservoir. This section is open to year-round fishing with artificial lures, with a daily limit of one trout 14 inches or larger. While most of the trout caught are freshly stocked, there are good numbers of holdover fish in the 14- to 16-inch range. This section has good public access, so it receives a lot of angling pressure. The bridge on Sodom Road provides easy access to the East Branch just below the East Branch Reservoir. This section starts with a power geyser locals call "The Bubble", as the water gushes from the bottom of the East Branch Dam. The Bubble keeps most of the East Branch cool throughout the summer. Just downstream from the Sodom Road bridge are two of the most popular pools in the watershed, the Bath Tub and the famous Phoebe Hole. It was in the Phoebe Hole that in July of 1983, angler Al Case hooked and landed a 10-pound, 13-ounce brown trout on a size 8 Grey Ghost streamer. Until recently, Al's trout held the IGFA four-pound tippet class world record.

Early season dry fly activity starts with midges and tiny blue-winged olives, however East Branch regulars report good success fishing small midges on light tippets year round. They also find streamers very productive when there is no insect activity, especially Muddlers and black Woolly Buggers. Hendrickson, sulphurs, and tricos, in addition to olives, are important hatches on the East Branch. As on every stream, trico fishing on the East Branch is a real challenge; long, delicate leaders are a must.

DIRECTIONS/ACCESS

From Interstate 684 take Exit 10 at Brewster. At the light at the bottom of the exit ramp, head northwest onto Routes 202, 22, and 6. After about 100 yards the routes fork at a blinking light. To reach the upper end of the artificials-only section, take the right fork onto Sodom Road. In less than 0.1 miles you have the first access point. Here the river is on your left and there is a pull-off on your right. My favorite stretch of river is upstream at the Sodom Road bridge. Continue a total of 0.2 miles after taking the right fork at the blinking light, stay left onto Sodom Road and go 0.2 miles to the bridge and a DEC-marked access point. This is just downstream from the East Branch Reservoir.

To reach the middle and lower sections, after taking the right at the exit light, take the left fork at the blinking light and follow Routes 202, 22, and 6 toward Brewster. In

Brewster, Routes 202 and 22 continue straight and Route 6 West turns right and crosses over the East Branch. There is parking and easy access to some nice water both above and below the Borden bridge. The lower 0.5 mile stretch of water before just upstream of the Diverting Reservoir can be accessed by continuing straight on Routes 202 and 22. There are several roadside pull-offs.

STREAM FACTS

Season/Regulations

The East Branch of the Croton River from the East Branch Reservoir downstream to the Diverting Reservoir is regulated as artificial lures only. It is open to fishing year round, with a daily limit of one trout 14 inches or more. A NYC Watershed Permit is required.

Fish

Most of the trout caught are stocked, but there are good numbers of holdover fish in the 14- to 16-inch range.

River Characteristics

This section starts with a powerful geyser locals call "The Bubble," gushing water from the bottom of the East Branch Dam. The Bubble keeps most of the East Branch cool all summer. Downstream the river flows through a series of gentle pools and riffles.

Flows

http://waterdata.gov/USA/UV USGS web site 01374505 East Branch Croton River at Brewster

Tackle

An 8- or 9-foot, 4- or 5-weight outfit would work well on the East Branch.

The East Branch of the Croton River below Sodom Road Bridge.

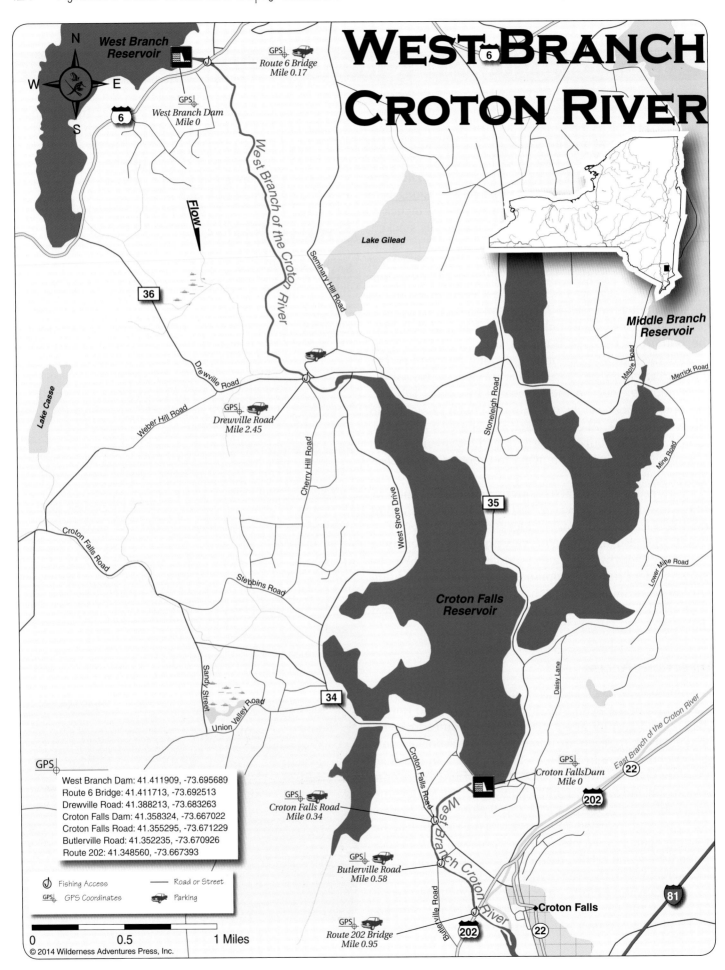

WEST BRANCH CROTON RIVER

West Branch Reservoir

N
W E
S

West Branch Dam
Mile 0

Route 6 Bridge
Mile 0.17

West Branch of the Croton River

FLOW

Lake Gilead

Middle Branch Reservoir

Drewville Road

Weber Hill Road

Seminary Hill Road

Lake Casse

Drewville Road
Mile 2.45

Cherry Hill Road

West Shore Drive

Stoneleigh Road

Maple Road

Merrick Road

Mine Road

Lower Mine Road

Croton Falls Road

Stebbins Road

Croton Falls Reservoir

Sandy Street

Union Valley Road

Daisy Lane

East Branch of the Croton River

Croton Falls Dam
Mile 0

GPS
West Branch Dam: 41.411909, -73.695689
Route 6 Bridge: 41.411713, -73.692513
Drewville Road: 41.388213, -73.683263
Croton Falls Dam: 41.358324, -73.667022
Croton Falls Road: 41.355295, -73.671229
Butlerville Road: 41.352235, -73.670926
Route 202: 41.348560, -73.667393

Croton Falls Road
Mile 0.34

West Branch Croton River

Butlerville Road
Mile 0.58

Butlerville Road

Croton Falls

Route 202 Bridge
Mile 0.95

Fishing Access
GPS Coordinates
Road or Street
Parking

0   0.5   1 Miles
© 2014 Wilderness Adventures Press, Inc.

WEST BRANCH OF THE CROTON RIVER, WEST BRANCH RESERVOIR OUTLET (FIVE STARS)

The West Branch of the Croton River flows through three NYC reservoirs before it meets the East Branch so therefore, there are three sections to fish. The first or upper section is known as Boyd's Corner Outlet. This section provides less than 0.5 miles of water; it is a put-and-take fishery and it did not make the cut of my favorite Croton Watershed streams.

The second section of the West Branch flows 2.3 miles from the West Branch Reservoir to the Croton Falls Reservoir. This section serves as the spawning and nursery water for the Croton Falls Reservoir wild browns and it is not stocked due to its excellent wild brown trout population. Unfortunately, despite the fact that the trout are wild, the regulations allow for a daily limit of five fish of 9 inches or more.

Despite its close proximity to the city, this section feels remote and wild. According to Croton Watershed Trout Unlimited, this stream is "arguably the prettiest in the Croton Watershed". This tailwater section flows cool all season, which runs from April 1 to September 30, when it closes to protect the spawning browns which migrate up from the Croton Falls Reservoir. This section of the West Branch is one of the most remote in the Croton system. It can only be accessed at its upper (Route 6) and lower (Drewville Road) limits. If you want excellent stream-bred brown trout fishing in total solitude, this is the stream for you.

As far as flies, this portion of the West Branch is known for its prolific caddis hatches, and locals report good success with green or olive caddis larva and pupa. It does have an excellent Hendrickson hatch, and the one mayfly not to be overlooked here is the sulphur (*Ephemerella dorothea*). From late May through June, the West Branch has a terrific sulphur hatch almost every evening. If you fish it, stay until dark to fish the spinner fall. Sulphurs are the most prolific mayflies throughout the watershed system.

DIRECTIONS/ACCESS

The upper access is off Route 6, located about two miles southwest of Carmel in Putnam County. From Brewster, take Route 6 West until you reach the "T" intersection with Routes 6 and 52 in Carmel. Turn left onto Route 6 for a short distance to where Route 6 crosses the West Branch just below the reservoir. There is parking on the right shoulder of the road. The downstream section can be reached off Drewville Road. Continue another 1.3 miles on Route 6 West and turn left on Route 36 (Drewville Road) for 1.5 miles to the bridge over the West Branch. You can park near the bridge or cross the bridge, turn left onto Seminary Hill Road, and go about 200 yards upstream to a small parking area on the left.

The West Branch of the Croton River below the West Branch Reservoir Outlet at Drewville Road.

STREAM FACTS

Season/Regulations

This section allows for a daily limit of five fish of 9 inches or more, and the season runs from April 1 to September 30.

Fish

This section serves as the spawning and nursery water for the Croton Falls Reservoir's wild browns. It is not stocked due to its excellent wild brown trout population.

River Characteristics

According to Croton Watershed Trout Unlimited, this stream is "arguably the prettiest in the Croton Watershed." This tailwater section flows cool all season, which runs from April 1 to September 30. It is the most remote in the Croton system, so if you want excellent stream-bred brown trout fishing in total solitude, this is the stream for you.

Flows

http://waterdata.gov/USA/UV USGS web site 0137462010 West Branch Croton River near Carmel

Tackle

An 8-foot, 4-weight outfit is perfect for this stream.

A huge Croton watershed brown trout.
Photo courtesy Aaron Jasper.

WEST BRANCH OF THE CROTON RIVER, CROTON FALLS RESERVOIR OUTLET (FIVE STARS)

(See map on page 124)

The West Branch at Croton Falls Outlet is another tailwater fishery which flows for one mile between Croton Falls Reservoir and the junction with the East Branch of the Croton River just upstream of the Muscoot Reservoir. This is the most popular stretch in the system and it is less than an hour from Manhattan. Not surprisingly the river can draw crowds, especially on weekends. It is managed under catch-and release – artificials-only regulations from April 1 until September 30. Due to the coldwater releases from Croton Falls Reservoir, it stays cool. It has a good population of wild browns and it is also stocked. Aaron Jasper, a flyfishing guide from North Jersey and a Croton watershed regular, told me that, "You can sight fish for giant browns in Croton Falls Outlet, both resident fish and lake-run fish." Aaron should know, as he landed a beautiful 28-inch brown trout and has lost even bigger fish in the Croton Watershed.

DIRECTIONS/ACCESS

From Main Street in Brewster, take Routes 202 West and 22 South. These follow the East Branch of the Croton River down to Diverting Reservoir and from the Diverting Reservoir down to its junction with the West Branch where they enter the Muscoot Reservoir. At about 3.8 miles west on Route 202 there are a few roadside pull-offs and access to the East Branch below Diverting Reservoir. This area has good pocket water for nymphing. After 4.2 miles, Route 202 West crosses the East Branch, and 0.1 miles past the bridge you come to the light at Route 34 (Croton Falls Road). Here you can turn right and access the West Branch. I prefer to continue another 0.2 miles to where Route 202 crosses the West Branch and fish the water upstream of the bridge. The next access is another 0.2 miles, where you turn right onto Butlerville Road. Go 0.1 miles, bear right at the stop sign, and continue a total of 0.4 miles to the bridge. At the bridge there is ample parking and easy access to a lovely wooded section of the stream. To access the upstream section just below the Croton Fall Reservoir, continue 100 yards from the bridge to the stop sign. Turn left onto Croton Falls Road for 0.1 miles to the DEC access area by the bridge.

STREAM FACTS

Seasons/Regulations

The stream is managed under catch-and-release – artificials-only regulations from April 1 until September 30.

Fish

Due to coldwater releases from the Croton Falls Reservoir, it stays cool. It has a good population of wild browns and it is also stocked.

River Characteristics

The river has the look of a small to mid-sized freestone stream and is easy to wade.

Flows

http://waterdata.gov/USA/UV USGS web site 01374701 West Branch Croton River near Croton Falls

Tackle

An 8-foot, 4- or 5-weight outfit would be perfect.

An angler fishing the West Branch of the Croton River below Croton Falls Reservoir Outlet.

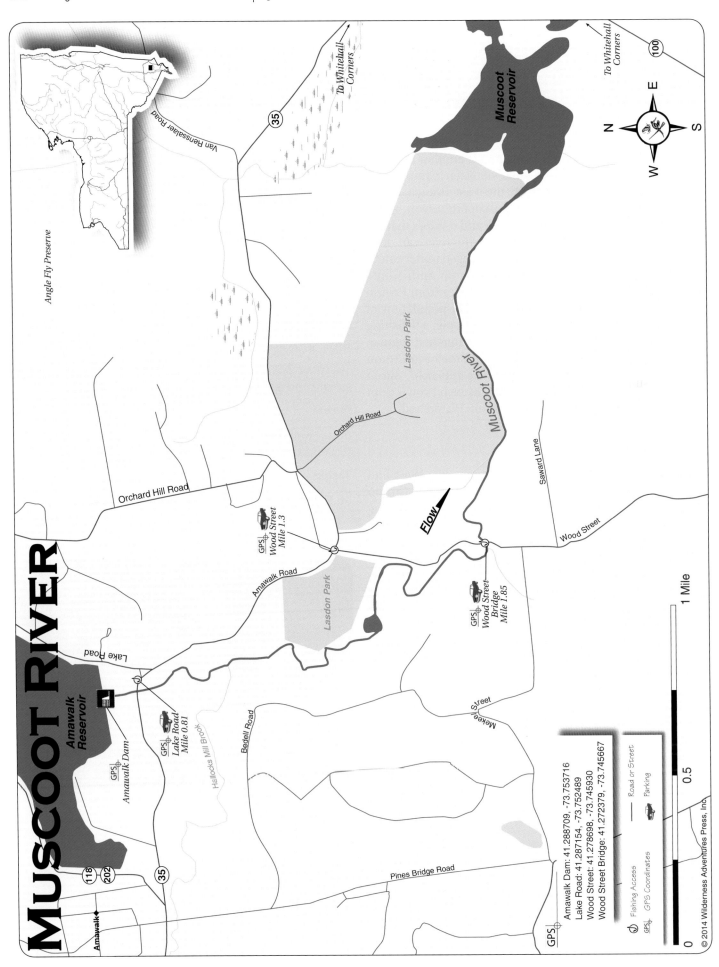

MUSCOOT RIVER

Amawalk Reservoir

Muscoot Reservoir

Angle Fly Preserve

Van Rensselaer Road

To Whitehall Corners

To Whitehall Corners

Lasdon Park

Muscoot River

Orchard Hill Road

Orchard Hill Road

Saward Lane

Flow

GPS Wood Street Mile 1.3

Amawalk Road

Lasdon Park

GPS Wood Street Bridge Mile 1.85

Wood Street

Lake Road

Amawalk Dam

GPS

GPS Lake Road Mile 0.81

Hallocks Mill Brook

Bedell Road

Meekee Street

Pines Bridge Road

Amawalk

118
202
35
35
100

Amawalk Dam: 41.288709, -73.753716
Lake Road: 41.287154, -73.752489
Wood Street: 41.278698, -73.745930
Wood Street Bridge: 41.272379, -73.745667

GPS

Fishing Access
GPS GPS Coordinates
Road or Street
Parking

0   0.5   1 Mile

© 2014 Wilderness Adventures Press, Inc.

N E S W

MUSCOOT RIVER (FIVE STARS)

The Muscoot River below the Amawalk Outlet is my favorite stream in the Croton system. It has both stocked and wild trout, flows through a beautifully wooded section, and receives less pressure than the East and West Branches of the Croton River. The Muscoot River flows 2.7 miles from the Amawalk Outlet to the Muscoot Reservoir. This upper section is stocked by the state, but the lower 1.9 miles from the old dam downstream to the Muscoot Reservoir has an excellent population of stream-bred brown trout. The season runs from April 1 to September 30. Fishing is limited to artificials only, with a daily limit of three trout 12 inches or more. Members of the Croton Watershed Chapter of Trout Unlimited report that the best hatch on the Muscoot River is the sulphur, which occurs from late May into early June. Although I have not had the opportunity to fish the sulphurs here, I plan to address that in the upcoming season. I have had numerous memorable evenings following sulphur hatches on other streams in the tri-state region. For most fly anglers, the green drake hatch defines their season, and while I love chasing drakes, particularly their spinner falls, no hatch gets me more excited than the sulphurs. I have seen seemingly barren pools come alive when the sulphurs do their thing, often after other anglers have left for dinner or because the mosquitoes were starting to attack. For sulphurs, you must stay to the end of daylight. Usually the last hour of light will bring the most fish to the surface during a sulphur hatch and the subsequent spinner fall.

I have had good success fishing all three stages of a sulphur's life cycle. Early in the evening I'll start by dead-drifting a sulphur nymph. A simple but effective pattern is a Pheasant Tail Nymph with a yellow abdomen. At the very beginning of the hatch, I'll swing a wet fly down and across and when fish start to rise, I'll go to a Sulphur Dun. As dusk turns toward dark, you normally you will be treated to a blizzard-like spinner fall, with every trout gorging themselves as if it was their "Last Supper". On most of the sulphur spinners I tie, I like to put a small orange ball of fur at the back of my spinner pattern representing the female's egg sack. For the wet fly, dun, and spinner, I'll use light gray polypropylene for the wings.

The Amawalk Outlet on the Muscoot River received a fresh breath of life when the DEC recommended, and New York City complied with, the installation of an oxygenating water fountain at the base of the outlet. Water in the bottom of a reservoir has very little oxygen, and a spouting plume of water mitigates the oxygen deficiencies in the water. Broken water absorbs more oxygen, and the fountain acts like a waterfall or riffle section of a stream.

DIRECTIONS/ACCESS

From the town of Croton Falls, take Route 202 West. After about five miles, Route 202 curves around the Amawalk Reservoir. At the light, make a left and take Routes 202 West and 118 South to Route 35 East. Turn left onto Route 35 East for 0.5 miles to the DEC sign and limited parking on Lake Road. Better access is another 0.7 miles east on Route 35 to Wood Street, which comes in on the right. Wood Street has road-side parking and access to a section of the Muscoot River with one beautiful pool and run after another. At 1.1 miles farther down, the river flows under Wood Street and there is a large DEC parking area. A more direct route from Route 684 would be to take the exit for Route 35. Take Route 35 West past Whitehall Corner to Wood Street on the left. If you see the reservoir, you passed Wood Street 1.1 miles back.

The Muscoot River below the Amawalk Outlet hosts both wild and stocked fish, and usually fewer anglers than other fisheries in the Croton System.

STREAM FACTS

Season/Regulations

The Muscoot River from the Amawalk Outlet downstream to the Amawalk Reservoir is regulated as artificial-lures-only and it is open to fishing from April 1 to September 30, with a daily limit of three trout 12 inches or more.

Fish

The upper section is stocked by the state, but the lower 1.9 miles from the old dam, downstream to the Muscoot Reservoir has an excellent population of stream-bred brown trout.

River Characteristics

While a tailwater fishery, it has the look of a mid-sized freestone trout stream. It flows through a beautifully wooded valley and it receives less pressure than the East and West Branches of the Croton Rivers.

Flows

http://waterdata.gov/USA/UV USGS web site 01374941 Muscoot River below Dam at Amawalk

Tackle

An 8- or 9-foot, 4- or 5-weight outfit works well on this stream.

Contact

A NYC Watershed Permit is required for all the streams in the Croton Watershed. One can be obtained free from the web site: www.nyc.gov/watershedrecreation.com

Hub City

MOUNT KISCO
Population 10,891

ACCOMMODATIONS

Holiday Inn, 1 Holiday Inn Drive, Mount Kisco / 914-241-2600 / www.mtkisco.com
Peekskill Motor Inn, 634 Main Street, Peekskill / 914-739-1500 / www.peekskill.com
Union Hotel, 59 Hudson Avenue, Peekskill / 914-737-9762

CAMPGROUNDS AND RV PARKS

Clarence Fahnestock State Park, 1498 Route 301, Carmel / 845-225-7207

RESTAURANTS

Flying Pig Café, 251 Lexington Ave. / 914-666-7445
Mardino's Italian Cuisine & Steakhouse, 473 Lexington Ave. / 914-666-2428
Henry's on the Hudson – Peekskill Motor Inn, 634 Main Street, Peekskill / 914-739-1500 / www.peekskill.com / Waterfront dining overlooking the Hudson River.

FLY SHOPS AND SPORTING GOODS

Old Souls, 63 Main St, Cold Spring / 845-809-5886 / www.oldsouls.com
Bedford Sportsman, 25 Adams Street, Bedford Hills / 845-666-8091 / www.bedfordsportsman.com
Urban Angler, 206 5th Avenue, New York, NY / 212-689-6400 / www.urbanangler.com

AIRPORTS

Westchester County Airport, 240 Airport Road, White Plains

MEDICAL

Northern Westchester Hospital, 400 East Main Street / 914-666-1200 / www.nwhc.net

FOR MORE INFORMATION

Chamber of Commerce – Mt. Kisco, 3 North Moger Street / 914-666-7525 / www.mtkisco.com

CROTON WATERSHED MAJOR HATCHES

Common Name *Scientific Name*	Hatch Period	Fly Patterns	Hook Sizes
Little Black Caddis *Chimarra atterrima*	Mid-April – mid-May	Black Elk Hair Caddis	16-18
Little Blue-winged Olive *Baetis tricaudatus* (formerly *Baetis vagans*)	April – mid-May	Parachute Adams Parachute BWO	16-18 16-18
Blue Quill *Paraleptophlebia adoptiva*	Mid-April – early May	Blue Quill Dry Blue Dun Dry Blue Quill Nymph	16-18 16-18 16-18
Quill Gordon *Epeorus pleuralis*	Mid-April – early May	Quill Gordon Dry Hare's Ear Wet	14 14
Hendrickson/Red Quill *Ephemerella subvaria*	Mid-April – early May	Hendrickson Dry Red Quill Dry	14 14
Tan Caddis *Hydropsyche* spp.	May – August	Elk Hair Caddis Dry Leonard Wright Caddis Dry	14-16 14-16
Blue-winged Olive *Drunella cornuta* (formerly *Ephemerella cornuta*)	Late May – mid-June	Blue-winged Olive Dry	14
Pale Evening Dun *Ephemerella invaria*	Early May – mid- June	Pale Evening Dun Dry Sulphur Spinner	14-16 14-16
Light Cahill *Stenacron interpunctatum* (formerly *Stenonema canadense*) (formerly *Stenonema interpunctat*)	Mid-May – mid-June	Light Cahill Dry Light Cahill Wet	12 12
Sulphur *Ephemerella dorothea*	June – mid-July	Pale Evening Dun Dry Pale Evening Dun Spinner	16-18 16-18
Slate Drake *Isonychia bicolor* *Isonychia sadleri & harperi*	Late May – June Mid-Sept. – October	Slate Drake Dry Adams Dry Gray Wulff Leadwing Coachman Wet	10-12 10-12 10-12 10-12
Tiny Blue-winged Olive *Acentrella turbida* (formerly *Pseudocloeon*)	June – mid-October	Parachute Adams Parachute BWO	20-24 20-24
Tricos *Tricorythyodes allectus* *Tricorythyodes stygiatus*	Mid-July – September	Trico Spinner Dry	22-26
Midges Chironomidae	February – November	Griffith's Gnat Dry Cream Midge Dry Zebra Midge Nymph	18-22 18-24 18-24
Flying Ants	September – October	Flying Ant Dry	16-20
Ants	May – October	Parachute Ant Dry Flying Ant Dry Black Wire Ant Wet	16-20 16-20 16-20
Beetles	May – October	Crow Beetle	12

PENNSYLVANIA

PENNSYLVANIA FACTS

Area: 46,055 square miles – 33rd largest state in the union

Population: 12,742,886 – 6th most densely populated state

State Fish: Brook trout

FISHING LICENSE FEES

www.pa.wildlifelicense.com

Resident Annual: $22.70 plus Trout Stamp ($9.70)

Non-Resident Annual: $52.70 plus Trout Stamp ($9.70)

Non-Resident Seven-day: $34.70 plus Trout Stamp ($9.70)

Non-Resident Three-day: $26.70 includes Trout Stamp

STATE RECORDS

Brook trout, 7 pound, 0 ounces by Vonada Ranck / 1996 / Fishing Creek

Brown trout, 19 pound, 10 ounces by Fazle Buljubasic / 2000 / Walnut Creek

Rainbow trout, 15 pound, 6 ounces by Dennis L. Clouse / 1986 / Jordan Creek

PENNSYLVANIA TAILWATERS

When I was living in Philadelphia, Pennsylvania in the 1970s and 1980s, Penn's Woods was my playground. Pennsylvania still boasts a robust wild trout fishery, thanks in large part to the vision and leadership of the late Ralph Abele. Dr. Abele was one of the first fish commissioners in the country to recognize the negative impact that stocking hatchery fish can have on wild trout populations.

Pennsylvania has more miles of trout water than any other state in the lower 48, and in 1983 Dr. Abele launched Operation Future, which called on the Pennsylvania Fish Commission to survey all 10,000-plus miles of the commonwealth's trout waters. Operation Future marked a major change in trout management philosophy, from recreation-based to resource-based management in which decisions were based on the potential impact on the fisheries resource.

The survey found that over half of the state's waters supported wild trout. Based on that data, Pennsylvania classified its better wild trout streams as Class A Wild Trout Waters and eliminated them from the stocking list. Class A waters are defined as "streams that support a population of naturally produced trout of sufficient size and abundance to support a long-term and rewarding sport fishery." Class A Wild Trout streams represent the best of Pennsylvania's naturally producing trout waters. Today Pennsylvania manages approximately 487 sections of stream, totaling 1,436 miles, as Class A Wild Trout Waters. The commission manages these stream sections solely for the perpetuation of the wild trout fishery, and no trout are stocked in these waters.

Many of these streams are within range of Mid-Atlantic anglers; including several that I can attest indeed fulfill the definition of Class A Wild Trout Waters. Some of these streams are also classified as Wilderness Trout Streams. To qualify for wilderness status, a stream section must be remote and have naturally-reproducing trout, which combined offer sport fishing opportunities for the recreational angler in a wilderness setting away from roads or vehicular access.

The Pennsylvania Fish Commission has also adopted several types of special-regulation trout waters which extend the trout season and return more fish to the water in order to improve the quality of our fishing experience. These regulations apply to several categories of streams which are open to year-round fishing, including "catch-and-release", which allows fishing with artificial lures or flies, "catch-and-release – flyfishing only" and "delayed harvest – artificials only". Not only do streams in these categories give you the opportunity to fish year round but, because of the restrictions on harvesting, there are more fish available for anglers.

Two recent joint studies by the Pennsylvania Fish and Boat Commission and Pennsylvania State University indicate that Pennsylvania trout anglers experience both a high catch and a high release rate. The spring trout landing survey indicated that the state's anglers averaged slightly over one trout per hour caught, with 63.1 percent of those fish released. According to the study, an amazing 92.7 percent of wild trout were released, a testament to anglers' respect for our fisheries. The state annually stocks about 3.5 million legal-size trout, and the commission estimates that there are over 600,000 legal-size wild trout in the waters of the state. In addition to providing more angling opportunities, the state recently extended the trout season in the southeast and south-central regions by opening the season two weeks before the traditional mid-April opener.

In addition to Pennsylvania's numerous freestone streams and world-class limestone spring creeks, the state also hosts some great tailwater rivers and, while they are excellent, there are plans to make them even better. At their July 2012 meeting, the Pennsylvania Fish and Boat Commission voted unanimously to pursue a policy of developing tailwaters. After the meeting the commission issued a statement which said: "Pennsylvania's large reservoirs provide opportunities to expand wild-trout populations in the tailwaters with careful manipulation of cold-water releases from those reservoirs. ... Therefore, the commissioners direct the executive director to actively seek and maximize opportunities available to protect, conserve and enhance, wherever possible, wild-trout populations in tailwaters below existing reservoirs."

PENNSYLVANIA TROUT REGULATIONS

OPENING DAY

Pennsylvania recently set an earlier opening day for the 18 southeastern counties. Trout streams there warm faster than streams in other parts of the state, and the fish commission wanted to give anglers in this region a longer season. In 2014 the southeast regional opening day was March 29, and the traditional April 12 date applied to the rest of the state. It is always recommended that you check the regulations in the pamphlet you receive with your fishing license.

GENERAL REGULATIONS

Minimum Size: 7 inches
Fishing Hours: 24 hours a day after the 8:00am opening
Creel Limits:
Regular season (opening day through Labor Day): five fish (combined species of trout)
Extended season (After Labor Day to February 28): three fish (combined species of trout)
Fishing is closed from March 1 until opening day to allow for stocking.
Five Pennsylvania tailwaters made the four- or five-star rating and are included in this chapter. Three are big, brawling rivers – the Lehigh, Lackawaxen, and the Youghiogheny – and two are more intimate – the Pohopoco and Clark's Creeks. They are the two smallest tailwaters in the book, but they are little gems.

The Upper Lehigh Valley and the beginning of the tailwater fishery.

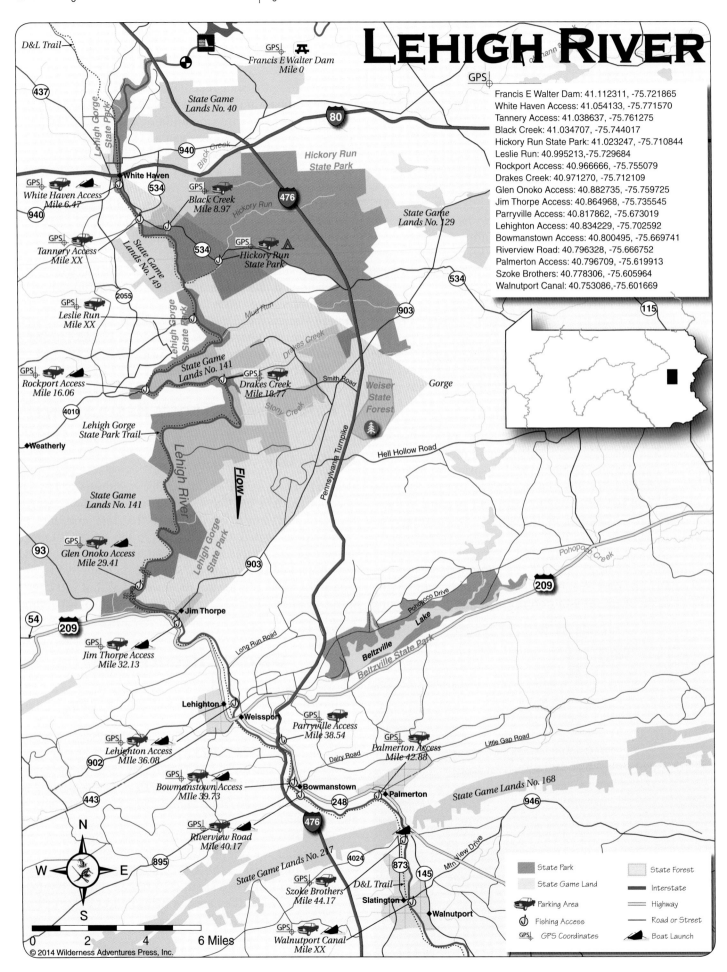

LEHIGH RIVER

D&L Trail

Francis E Walter Dam
Mile 0

GPS

Francis E Walter Dam: 41.112311, -75.721865
White Haven Access: 41.054133, -75.771570
Tannery Access: 41.038637, -75.761275
Black Creek: 41.034707, -75.744017
Hickory Run State Park: 41.023247, -75.710844
Leslie Run: 40.995213, -75.729684
Rockport Access: 40.966666, -75.755079
Drakes Creek: 40.971270, -75.712109
Glen Onoko Access: 40.882735, -75.759725
Jim Thorpe Access: 40.864968, -75.735545
Parryville Access: 40.817862, -75.673019
Lehighton Access: 40.834229, -75.702592
Bowmanstown Access: 40.800495, -75.669741
Riverview Road: 40.796328, -75.666752
Palmerton Access: 40.796709, -75.619913
Szoke Brothers: 40.778306, -75.605964
Walnutport Canal: 40.753086,-75.601669

State Game Lands No. 40

Hickory Run State Park

State Game Lands No. 129

White Haven Access
Mile 6.47

White Haven

Black Creek
Mile 8.97

State Game Lands No. 149

Tannery Access
Mile XX

Hickory Run State Park

Leslie Run
Mile XX

Lehigh Gorge State Park

State Game Lands No. 141

Drakes Creek
Mile 18.77

Smith Road

Weiser State Forest

Gorge

Rockport Access
Mile 16.06

Lehigh Gorge State Park Trail

Weatherly

State Game Lands No. 141

Lehigh River

Flow

Hell Hollow Road

Pennsylvania Turnpike

Pohopoco Creek

Glen Onoko Access
Mile 29.41

Jim Thorpe

Lake

Pohopoco Drive

Beltzville

Beltzville State Park

Jim Thorpe Access
Mile 32.13

Long Run Road

Lehighton

Weissport

Parryville Access
Mile 38.54

Palmerton Access
Mile 42.88

Little Gap Road

Lehighton Access
Mile 36.08

Dairy Road

Bowmanstown Access
Mile 39.73

Bowmanstown

Palmerton

State Game Lands No. 168

Riverview Road
Mile 40.17

State Game Lands No. 217

D&L Trail

Szoke Brothers
Mile 44.17

Slatington

Walnutport

Walnutport Canal
Mile XX

■ State Park		State Forest
State Game Land		Interstate
Parking Area		Highway
Fishing Access		Road or Street
GPS GPS Coordinates		Boat Launch

N
W E
S

0   2   4   6 Miles

© 2014 Wilderness Adventures Press, Inc.

LEHIGH RIVER (FOUR STARS)

The Lehigh River is the largest tributary of the Delaware River, running over 100 miles from its source near Gouldsboro in Wayne County downstream to Easton, where it joins the Delaware River in Northampton County. Today, the Lehigh River has the potential to give anglers access to some 70 miles of prime trout waters, but it wasn't always like that. Like many of our larger rivers, the Lehigh suffered from various pollutants, including acid leaking from coal mines. In addition to being polluted, historically the Lehigh has been too warm in summer to sustain a healthy trout population.

I recently read an article in a Pocono newspaper entitled "Lehigh River, from Worst to First". It depicted the decline of the river and the current efforts to restore its water quality, which has improved so much that the commissioner of Pennsylvania's Department of Conservation and Natural Resources (DCNR), Michael Di Berardinis, named the Lehigh as the commonwealth's River of the Year for 2007. At the press conference announcing his decision the commissioner stated, "The river is alive and thriving, with water quality better now than it has been in the last 150 years." Di Berardinis continued, "There are scores of partners working to preserve, protect, and enhance this great Pennsylvania natural resource, and its resurgence has pumped new life into the communities along the river."

The Lehigh River, as well as its numerous Class A wild trout tributaries, is one of Pennsylvania's best kept trout fishing secrets. I have had a cabin in the Upper Lehigh watershed for over 25 years and, while I have spent over two decades exploring the Lehigh's tributaries, like Mud and Hickory Runs, Black, Pohopoco and Tobyhanna Creeks, it was only recently that I began to enjoy the resurgence of the Lehigh River, and recognize its enormous recreation and economic potential. The coldwater releases from the Francis E. Walter Dam, if managed for trout, and with the aid of the numerous coldwater tributaries, create the ability to keep the Lehigh

River's water temperature below 68 degrees down through the Lehigh Gorge and beyond all summer long. Below the gorge, a second tailwater fishery is created by the bottom releases from the Beltsville Dam, which sends another shot of cold water into the Lehigh by way of Pohopoco Creek, extending the trout fishery all the way down to Walnutport in Northampton County, some 50 miles below the Walter Dam. Combine this with the Lehigh's roughly 20 miles of trout water above the Walter Dam, and you've got about 70 miles of quality trout water. If you add on the dozen or so wild trout streams that feed the Lehigh, you could spend a lifetime in the watershed and never fish the same stretch of water twice. In addition to the numerous Class A tributaries feeding the Lehigh with trout, there is also a tremendous stocking effort by the Lehigh River Stocking Association (LRSA) and increased stockings by the Pennsylvania Fish Commission; the Lehigh is becoming a "regional destination" trout river. According to the Lehigh River Coldwater Fisheries Alliance, "If managed properly the Lehigh could develop into a world-class fishing destination potentially generating up to $30 million annually for the local economy."

I have divided the Lehigh River into three sections: the upper tailwater below the dam, the gorge, and the lower river below the gorge.

The author nymphing just below Francis E. Walter Dam. With a good release plan, the Lehigh has the potential to become a world-class tailwater fishery. Photo courtesy Ed Jaworowski.

UPPER TAILWATER (FOUR STARS)

The upper tailwater is an excellent fishery as it flows from the Francis E. Walter Dam through river banks lined with hemlocks and rhododendron. This section benefits from the coldwater releases from the dam until around the middle of July. Dean Druckenmiller, the current president of the Lehigh Coldwater Fishery Alliance (LCFA) reported to me that after mid-July, releases coming from the dam are generally above 68 degrees, which is not very conducive for trout. I'll fish the upper tailwater from April until the water temperatures start to climb towards 68 degrees and then I'll switch over and fish the many Class A tributaries.

The section is easily accessed from the dirt road which follows the stream below the dam. It has most of the region's major hatches with the exception of green drake. The hatches are usually quite prolific, starting with the little black stone in early April and the little black caddis at the end of April. These are followed by good numbers of Hendricksons and grannom caddis. From mid-May through June is prime time on this section of the river, with multiple hatches of March browns, sulphurs, blue-winged olives, light Cahills, and slate drakes. If the water stays cool enough, you could have dry fly activity all summer long with small blue-winged olives, slate drakes, and light Cahills.

DIRECTIONS/ACCESS

From the intersection of Routes 115 and 940, take Route 940 west and, just past the Evening Hatch Fly Shop, turn right onto the road for the dam. Continue for three miles, crossing over the dam breast to the stop sign. Go straight for 0.4 miles to the picnic grove on the left. Take the dirt road at the back of the picnic area, which takes you 1.5 miles down to the river about a mile below the dam.

THE GORGE ****

Just south of White Haven the river runs through a remote and spectacularly rugged and scenic gorge. Much of the land on both sides of the gorge has been acquired by the state as part of Lehigh Gorge State Park. When you combine the surrounding state parks, state forests, and state game lands, the total lands in public ownership are over 110,000 acres. Over 30 miles of abandoned railroad bed that parallels the river on its west bank through the gorge has been converted into a multi-use trail. It provides excellent access to wilderness sections of the river for hikers, bikers, whitewater rafters, and anglers alike. Ample parking and access is available at three main locations: White Haven in the upper gorge and Rockport at mid-gorge, both of which

are located on the west side of the river; and on the east side at the lower end of the gorge just above Jim Thorpe at Glen Onoko. Every year, numerous trout over 20 inches are landed by spin and fly anglers alike in the gorge, with 14- to 18-inch fish being fairly common. The gorge also has an abundance of insect life, harboring all the hatches mentioned above in the upper tailwater section. Wading the gorge is possible but difficult (you will want studded boots, a wading staff, and it is a good idea to fish with a partner). I suggest you consider a guided float trip for your first Lehigh River experience. Not only will you enjoy the spectacular scenery and some excellent fishing, but you will also discover some productive wading and access areas and gain a healthy respect for this rugged landscape. I guarantee that the remote and rugged nature of the gorge rivals the scenery of any flyfishing destination in North America. At this writing only two guiding services have a state permit to float the gorge – they are listed in the back of the chapter. In the summer at the current release levels the Francis E. Walter Dam is not having a positive impact on the temperatures down through the gorge, which must rely on the cooling effects of the coldwater tributary streams for the trout's survival. In the section on directions below I have listed a dozen access points to the gorge.

Ready to float the Lehigh Gorge at Glen Onoko.

LOWER WATER (FOUR STARS)

As coldwater tributaries enter the river it grows in size, and by the time it has left the gorge and flows through the town of Jim Thorpe the Lehigh takes on the look of a large western river. From Jim Thorpe downstream to Northampton there are about 30 miles of quality trout water. Although there are several good access points where you can wade-fish (which I will cover in the section on directions), many anglers prefer to fish this section by driftboat. There are a number of guides and fly shops which will arrange a float trip for you. (See listings in the back of this chapter.) From Jim Thorpe downstream to Northampton the river can be divided into four different float trips of about five miles each: Jim Thorpe to Lehighton, Lehighton to Bowmanstown, Bowmanstown to Palmerton, and Palmerton to Walnutport. This section of the Lehigh is only about one hour from Manhattan and Philadelphia. For decades, the Pennsylvania Fish Commission has stocked the upper Lehigh above the Walter Dam and the first six miles below the dam downstream to Sandy Run. Starting in 2007, the fish commission increased its stocking of juvenile trout to 50,000 fish (30,000 browns and 20,000 rainbows.) And they expanded their stocking from Sandy Run in Luzerne County downstream to Palmerton in Carbon County. In addition, the Lehigh River

Stocking Association (LRSA) annually stocks about 5,000 legal trout up to 28 inches (before the recent economic downturn impacted LRSA membership, they used to stock 15,000 adult trout and about 40,000 to 50,000 fingerlings). Since its founding in 1990, the LRSA has stocked over 300,000 fish from Bear Creek downstream to Northampton. The Lehigh has many excellent coldwater tributaries with almost 50 miles of them being classified as Class A wild trout waters. If the Lehigh is running too high to safely wade, I strongly recommend fishing the Pohopoco, which is a tailwater fishery below the Beltsville Dam. The Pohopoco also has 10 miles of Class A wild brown trout water above the dam. Other first-class feeder streams include Hayes Creek, Hickory Run, Mud Run, Stony Creek, and Bear Creek, all great little trout streams in their own right.

WHAT DOES THE FUTURE HOLD FOR THE LEHIGH?

While the fishing immediately below the Walter Dam is terrific, with proper flow management the Lehigh could become a truly world-class trout fishery from the dam 50 miles down to Walnutport, rivaling that of the Upper Delaware River system. In August of 2007, the temperature of the water being released from the Walter Dam was 68 degrees, close to the maximum level most trout can tolerate

for extended periods of time. At that same time, the water coming out of the Beltsville Dam was a cool 53 degrees. The Beltsville Dam was designed with temperature controls for trout habitat, and it can discharge from a variety of elevations and therefore temperature zones. The Walter Dam was designed for flood control and is managed by the Army Corps of Engineers for flood protection, and for that reason they only fill the reservoir partway, so its waters don't get as cold as Beltsville. Currently, the Corps keeps the water behind the dam at an average depth of 50 feet, well below its capacity of 200 feet. At 50 feet, the water gets too warm to maintain the water downstream below 70 degrees, which is the maximum to which trout should be exposed. Management of FEW water releases should not be as complicated as those in the Delaware River system. The Lehigh is not used for water supply, only flood control, and there is only one agency, the Army Corps of Engineers, which has jurisdiction over the dam releases. Also unlike the Delaware, the Lehigh flows through only one state. The LRSA monitors the water about 0.5 miles above Jim Thorpe, and in the summer of 2007, which was a warm year, the river temperature regularly went above 70 degrees Fahrenheit, and on August 3, 2007, it came close to 80 degrees, a lethal temperature for trout. Fortunately the Lehigh River has many coldwater tributaries in which the trout can seek refuge.

In 2004, the Army Corps moved the road across the reservoir from the inside wall to the top of the dam, giving it the opportunity to store significantly more and therefore colder water. The Corps has commissioned a new study to see if the additional capacity would enable the discharges to be below 68 degrees all summer. The preliminary drafts have identified that they need to conserve more of the cold water in the reservoir and to do that they will need to construct a new discharge tower with selective levels for withdrawals.

If these recommendations are implemented, they would be a tremendous boost to the fishery, not to mention the local economy. In 1996, a study funded by the American Sportfishing Association and Trout Unlimited titled "The Economic Impact of Trout Fishing on the Delaware River Tailwaters in New York" found that trout fishing in the tailwaters of the Delaware River system yielded $17.7 million in direct expenditures for local businesses and generated $29.98 million in local economic activity.

ANGLER'S VOICES ARE NEEDED

In my recent interview with Lehigh River guide, Joe DeMarkis, he stated, "The Lehigh River is finally being recognized for its value as a fishing resource that continues to sustain itself, even with all the difficulties with its competing interests. I urge anglers to fish the Lehigh River. It is very accessible yet still offers remoteness, along with opportunities for hooking large trout throughout the watershed. The fishery needs the voice of anglers now!" If you want to be part of developing the next "world class" trout fishery, please support the Lehigh Coldwater Fishery Alliance. Their mission is to obtain a consistent release of coldwater (55 degrees F) from the Francis E Walter Reservoir through better utilization of Walter's storage capacity and discharge options, in an effort to improve overall flows, protect habitat, and enhance the Lehigh River's wild trout fishery. I have put their contact information at the end of this chapter.

Before fishing the Lehigh below the Walter Dam, it is a good idea to check flows on the United States Geological Survey (USGS) site at www.pa.waterdata.usgs.gov. For wading below the dam, 350 cubic feet per second (cfs) is best. Farther downstream in Lehighton 750 - 800cfs or lower is ideal for wading.

DIRECTIONS AND ACCESS TO THE
GORGE AND LOWER RIVER

You literally could fill a book (and I hope someone will) describing access to this great fishery. Much of the access to the river is publicly owned and there is very little posting on private property along the river. Below, I share a few of my favorite access points in the gorge and the lower river to get you started.

WEST SIDE OF THE LEHIGH

White Haven

White Haven provides access to the northern part of the gorge and the 30 miles of trail which run from White Haven downstream to Jim Thorpe on the west side of the river. The trail follows an abandoned railroad bed and is heavily used by hikers, bikers, and anglers. Take I-80 West to Exit 274. At the bottom of the ramp, turn left onto Route 534 and go west for 0.3 miles to Route 940 West. Turn left onto Route 940 West and drive 1.3 miles. Cross the river and turn left into the White Haven Shopping Center. Go through the shopping center parking lot and bear left to the entrance to Lehigh Gorge State Park. At the access point is the Pocono Whitewater Rafting and Bike Company which rents mountain bikes. Renting a bike is a good way to get to some of the more remote sections of the gorge.

Main Image: The bottom of the Gorge.
Inset: Lehigh River at the upper end of the gorge in White Haven.

Rockport

Rockport provides access to the mid-gorge section and can be reached off Lehigh Gorge Drive on the west side of the river. From the White Haven Shopping Center, follow Route 940 West for 1.3 miles to Lehigh Gorge Drive. Turn left onto Lehigh Gorge Drive and drive 5.0 miles to Rockport Road (look for the Flying Aces motorcycle club sign). Turn left onto Rockport Road and go 1.0 mile to the access point.

Jim Thorpe

Take I-476, (the northeast extension of the Pennsylvania Turnpike) to the Mahoning Valley exit. (This is north of I-78 and south of I-80). Take Route 209 South for 5.8 miles to the center of Jim Thorpe and Carbon County Court House parking lot just past the railroad station (Mauch Chunk Landing) on your right. Turn right into the large parking lot, and then turn left in the lot and go 300 yards to the gated dirt road and access point.

Lehighton

In Lehighton the best access is behind Dunbar's Bottling. From the northeast extension of the turnpike, take the Mahoning Valley exit. Take Route 209 South across the Lehigh River and continue on 209 South into Lehighton, to Dunbar's Bottling on the right. Take the dirt road behind Dunbar's (North Main Lane) to the river. While there is no official launch, many guides use this area to put in and take out their boats.

Bowmanstown

Bowmanstown has three good access points, one on the east side and two on the west side of the river. Take Route 248 below Parryville to Route 895 West. Turn right onto Route 895 and take the first right before the bridge. This is a dead-end street, with parking and walk-in access at the rafters' take-out location. To reach the first of the two access points on the west side of the river, continue west on Route 895 over the bridge and make the next two right-hand turns. This takes you to Marvin Gardens Park, which provides parking and good access to the river just above the bridge. The second access point on the west side of the river is the new park in Bowmanstown which provides several access points, good wading, and a boat launch. After crossing the river on the Route 895 bridge, make the first left onto Riverview Road, which has several roadside parking areas for anglers on the left. The park and boat launch are on the left 0.8 miles from Route 895.

Slatington

Behind the Szoke Brothers factory in Slatington there is a small parking area just outside the factory entrance and a narrow trail on the left which takes you to a beautiful and productive section of the river. Take Route 248 downstream of Palmerton to Route 873 South over the Lehigh. Once you cross the river, go 0.1 miles south to a large driveway and the entrance to the Szoke Brothers factory and parking. There is a boat ramp at the Route 873 Bridge.

EAST SIDE OF THE LEHIGH

Black Creek

The mouth of Black Creek where it flows into the Lehigh is just a short walk down the creek from the parking area on Route 534. Take I-80 West to Exit 274, the Hickory Run State Park exit. At the bottom of the exit ramp turn left onto Route 534 and drive east for 1.8 miles. Turn left at the stop, continuing on Route 534 East. One mile after the stop sign, Route 534 crosses Black Creek. Park on the left side of the road just past the bridge over the creek.

Hickory Run

To reach the mouth of Hickory Run where it flows into the Lehigh, take Route 534 east from Black Creek for 2.1 miles. You will cross Hickory Run and come to the park headquarters. This is a good place to pick up a map, and there is plenty of parking. Hickory Run flows 1.6 miles from Route 534 to the Lehigh River. A well-marked trail follows the creek to the river.

Drakes Creek

To reach the mouth of Drakes Creek where it flows into the Lehigh, take Interstate 80 West to Exit 284. Take Route 115 South for 1.8 miles to Route 903 South. Take Route 903 South for 8.2 miles to Smith Road. Take Smith Road for 0.7 miles to Drakes Creek Road. Then drive 2.3 miles on Drakes Creek Road to the state park lands. Here the road becomes a gravel road and follows the creek all the way to the river. Note: There is an active railroad bed at the mouths of Hayes, Hickory Run, and Drakes Creeks which gives you access to the waters above and below these streams.

Glen Onoko

Glen Onoko provides access to the rugged and scenic lower end of the gorge. Take the northeast extension of the Pennsylvania Turnpike to the Mahoning Valley exit. Take Route 209 South across the Lehigh River for 6.0 miles to Route 903. Take Route 903 North across the Lehigh and go 0.3 miles to the stop sign where Route 903 makes a sharp bend to the right. Go straight across the intersection to Coalport Road. Take Coalport Road 0.3 miles to the lower entrance to Lehigh Gorge State Park. Turn left into the park and go 1.6 miles to the access area. There is a great riffle section just upstream of the access area and several big beautiful pools at and below the access point. Just 100 yards downstream from the access point is a coldwater tributary which often has trout congregating at its mouth, especially in summer.

Parryville

Access in Parryville is at the mouth of the Pohopoco, whose water refreshes the Lehigh with a shot of the coldwater bottom releases from Beltsville Dam. From the Pennsylvania Turnpike's northeast extension, take the Mahoning Valley exit to Route 209 South to Route 248. Take Route 248 East for 1.6 miles to Canal Park on the right, next to the Rock Hill Concrete. Park in the Canal Park area. From here you can fish the Pohopoco downstream to where it enters the Lehigh, some 800 feet downstream from the turnpike bridge. The Pohopoco flows behind the Riverwalk Saloon which is across Route 248 from Canal Park. It then flows under Route 248 just 100 feet east of the park.

Palmerton

Access in Palmerton is by the old zinc smelting plant. Take Route 248 East from Bowmanstown to the exit for Palmerton. As you exit Route 248, before you come to the end of the ramp you will see a large dirt lot on the right which provides walk-in access.

A recent court settlement deemed the Lehigh River a navigable river, allowing anglers to wade anywhere on the river, provided they do not cross private property to access the river. While wading is legal, it is still treacherous, so studded sole boots and a wading staff are a must!

STREAM FACTS

Seasons/Regulations

The Lehigh River is regulated under the state's general regulations, which allow fishing by rod and reel from 8:00 am on the mid-April opening day until February 28. The harvest limit is five trout of 7 inches or better from opening day to Labor Day. The extended season runs from after Labor Day until February 28 with a harvest limit of three trout 7 inches or better. Fishing is closed from March 1 until opening day to allow for stocking.

Fish

The river has both stream-bred browns and native brook trout above the Francis E. Walter Dam as well as liberal stockings by the state. Below the dam, the state and the Lehigh River Stocking Association stock both adult and fingerling browns and rainbows. There are also stream-bred and holdover trout. In 2012, the largest rainbow reported to Fish Commission's Anglers Recognition Program – a 13-pound, 9-ounce fish – came from the Lehigh.

River Characteristics

Below the Francis E. Walter Dam, you have about 50 miles of a potentially world-class trout fishery. The river is heavily stocked and has a good holdover rate. Fish measuring in the high teens are common. This is a big, brawling river and wading is always difficult. You should consider hiring a guide for a float trip on your first visit.

What's in a Name?

Lehigh is derived from an Indian word which means "where there are forks".

River Flows

River flows are affected by the bottom releases from the Walter and Beltsville Dams, which are both controlled by the Army Corps of Engineers. Every other weekend during the summer, the releases from the Walter Dam are increased to support the whitewater rafting industry, which contributes a great deal of revenue to the communities in the Lehigh Valley. The problem with these releases is that they deplete the cold water in the reservoir by mid-July. Summer releases above 70 degrees are common. During mid- and late summer, the Lehigh River trout must rely on flows from the coldwater tributaries for survival. When the Lehigh is too high to safely wade, you still have over 50 miles of Class A wild trout tributaries to explore.

http://waterdata.gov/USA/UV USGS web 01447800 Lehigh River below Francis E. Walter Dam near White Haven

http://waterdata.gov/USA/UV USGS web 01449000 Lehigh River at Lehighton

http://waterdata.gov/USA/UV USGS web 01451000 Lehigh River at Walnutport

Tackle

When I float the Lehigh, I'll take two 9-foot rods, a 4- or 5-weight for dry fly fishing and a 6-weight for searching the water with streamers. When wading I'll usually fish a 9-foot, 5-weight rod.

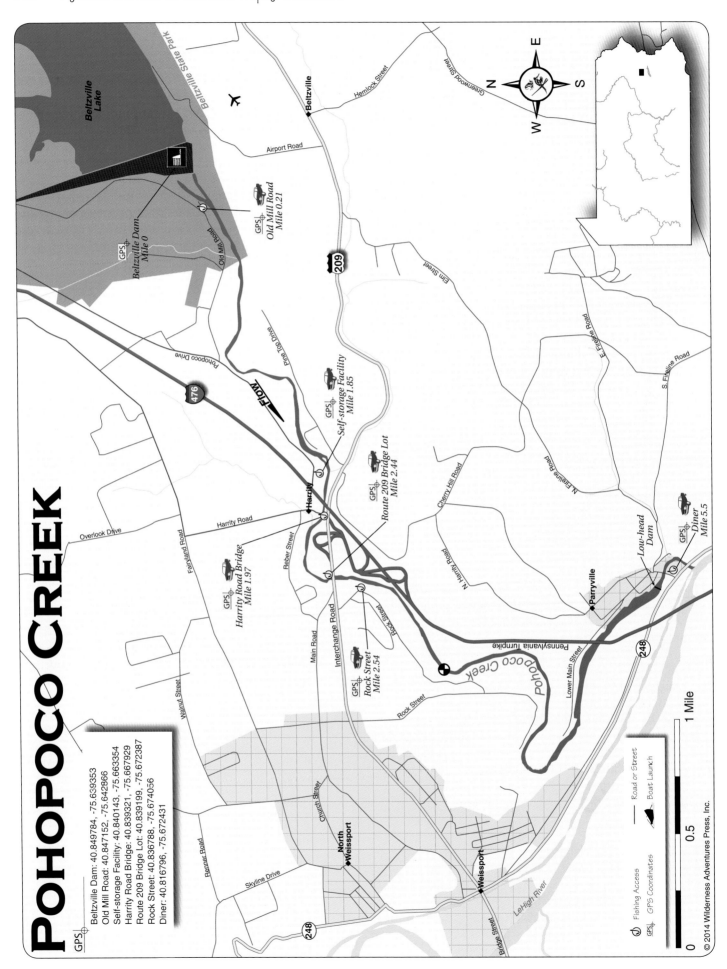

POHOPOCO CREEK

GPS

Beltzville Dam: 40.849784, -75.639353
Old Mill Road: 40.847152, -75.642866
Self-storage Facility: 40.840143, -75.663354
Harrity Road Bridge: 40.839321, -75.667929
Route 209 Bridge Lot: 40.839199, -75.672387
Rock Street: 40.836788, -75.674056
Diner: 40.816796, -75.672431

Beltzville Lake

Beltzville State Park

Beltzville Dam
Mile 0

GPS
Old Mill Road
Mile 0.21

GPS
Self-storage Facility
Mile 1.85

GPS
Route 209 Bridge Lot
Mile 2.44

GPS
Harrity Road Bridge
Mile 1.97

GPS
Rock Street
Mile 2.54

GPS
Diner
Mile 5.5

Low-head Dam

FLOW

Beltzville

Harrity

Parryville

North Weissport

Weissport

Pohopoco Creek

Pennsylvania Turnpike

LeHigh River

Airport Road

Hemlock Street

Greenwood Street

Elm Street

E Fireline Road

S Fireline Road

N Fireline Road

Cherry Hill Road

N Harrity Road

Pine Top Drive

Pohopoco Drive

Overlook Drive

Fairyland Road

Harrity Road

Reber Street

Main Road

Interchange Road

Rock Street

Rock Street

Walnut Street

Renner Road

Church Street

Skyline Drive

Bridge Street

Lower Main Street

Old Mill Road

209

476

248

248

N
E
S
W

Road or Street
Boat Launch

Fishing Access
GPS Coordinates

0   0.5   1 Mile

© 2014 Wilderness Adventures Press, Inc.

POHOPOCO CREEK (FOUR STARS)

Pohopoco Creek has two distinctly different sections, with stream-bred browns and native brookies above the Beltsville Dam. Below the dam you have a year-round tailwater fishery which harbors stocked, holdover, and wild trout. The tailwater section stays cool all summer and provides cool water downstream to the Lehigh. The waters in and around the junction of the Lehigh and the Pohopoco can yield some exceptional summer fishing all the way upstream to the outlet of Beltsville Dam. While this is mostly a caddis stream, it does have good sulphur and blue-winged olive hatches, and terrestrials are always a good bet. For years the state only stocked from the dam's outlet downstream 1.9 miles to the Pennsylvania Turnpike bridge. They recently added an additional section to the stocking list, from the turnpike downstream to the backwater of the Parryville Dam.

Recently, in late August after four days of heavy rains, with all of the region's freestone streams blown out, I fished the Pohopoco just below the Beltsville Dam and I had a ball. It was a Friday afternoon, and when I arrived streamside I couldn't believe my eyes. From the road I could see that the stream was clear and wadeable and there were dozens of trout dimpling the surface. I put on my hip boots and hurriedly walked down to the tail of the first pool. I tied on a size 16 Parachute Adams, only to have fish after fish refuse it. I carefully studied the water and found hundreds of size 20 black spent-wing flying ants in the surface film. I didn't have a flying ant pattern in my box (I certainly do now), so I tied on a size 20 McMurray Balsa Wood Ant. By now there must have been close to 50 trout rising in the pool I was fishing. There were so many fish working, and my ant was so hard to see, that often I would have a half dozen fish rise within inches of the drift line of my ant. There were so many naturals that I couldn't tell if they were on my fly or a natural ant next to it. I must have set up at least a dozen times without hooking a single fish. I switched to a size 20 Poly Wing Blue-winged Olive (BWO), and that was the ticket. I could see the poly wing, and to the fish apparently it looked close enough to a spent-wing flying ant. I took about a dozen fish, but then the trout wised up and again started to refuse my fly. After more than an hour of fishing without a strike, I decided to explore some other streams in the area, but before leaving I wanted to know if the earlier trout were refusing my ant or was I just striking at the wrong rise. I added about 18 inches of 6x tippet to my leader. Leaving the BWO as an indicator, I tied on a small ant to the tippet. I cast up and across and watched for the BWO to move, and sure enough I landed several trout on the ant using the BWO as a strike indicator. My score for the day was three nice-sized wild browns and about two dozen small 6- to 7-inch rainbows. I would later find out that the rainbows were from a recent stocking of surplus fish from the Fish Commission's hatchery.

Tailwater releases keep the Pohopoco cool all summer. On that late August day, the air was 85 degrees but the water was only 59 degrees in mid-afternoon. In addition to stocked trout, the lower Pohopoco has a good population of wild brown trout. In 2004, a mid-August survey by the state via electro fishing turned up 385 wild browns from 2 to 13 inches in a 625-yard section below the dam. Of the trout captured, 61 percent were 7 inches or better and only 57 trout were hatchery-raised trout.

An angler fishing the Pohopoco tailwater in late summer.

DIRECTIONS/ACCESS

From Stroudsburg, take Route 209 South for about 27 miles toward the northeast extension of the Pennsylvania Turnpike. Right before the turnpike entrance, you will see a sign for Beltzville Lake State Park. Take the right on Harrity Road over the bridge and turn right on Pohopoco Drive.

Self-storage facility

Shortly after the turn you will pass a self-storage facility. At the upper end of the parking lot for the self-storage facility is a sign for "Public Fishing Access".

Old Mill Road

Less than 0.7 miles up Pohopoco Drive, you can access a beautiful section of stream off Old Mill Road, which comes into Pohopoco Drive from the right. The first parking area is about 0.5 miles up Old Mill Road. You can fish up through nice pools and runs both up and downstream from here.

Harrity Road Bridge

Another good access area is the large gravel parking area just upstream from the Harrity Road bridge on the southbound side of Interchange Road (Route 209). This gives easy access to the runs above and below the bridge. Just south of the Harrity Road bridge on Route 209 is another parking area, just before Route 209 South crosses the Pohopoco. Make a sharp right hand turn into a dirt lot with signs indicating "Fishing Permitted, Walking In Only". A short walk up or downstream will give you access to some nice pools and runs.

Rock Street

Another access point is just below the Route 209 bridge. It has easy access, good parking, and a picnic area. Continue on Route 209 South over the stream and take the first road on your left which is Rock Street. The first left off Rock Street is a dirt road with "Fishing Permitted" signs and good access to the stream. To access this tailwater from the northeast extension of the Pennsylvania Turnpike, take the Mahoning Valley Exit and follow the directions above.

Access to the lower Pohopoco is from behind the diner on Route 248 where the stream enters the Lehigh. Upstream of the diner is a low head dam which has a deep plunge pool which usually harbors a good population of trout. This pool has excellent July midge fishing as trout move up from the Lehigh into the cooler water.

STREAM FACTS

Seasons/Regulations

The Pohopoco is regulated under the state's general regulations, which allow fishing by rod and reel from 8:00 am on the mid-April opening day until February 28. The harvest limit is five trout of 7 inches or better from opening day until Labor Day. The extended season runs from after Labor Day to February 28 and the harvest limit is three trout, 7 inches or better. Fishing is closed from March 1 until opening day to allow for stocking.

Fish

Above Beltsville Lake, the Pohopoco has 10.3 miles of Class A wild brown trout water. Below the lake it has good numbers of wild brown trout and it is stocked with both adult and fingerling brown and rainbow trout.

River Characteristics

Above the lake, it is a small freestone stream ranked Class A wild trout by the state. Below the Beltsville Lake Dam, it is a classic year-round tailwater fishery with both wild browns and stocked browns and rainbows.

What's in a Name?

Pohopoco is derived from an Indian word which means "at the creek between the hills".

Flows

http://waterdata.gov/USA/UV USGS web 01449800 Pohopoco Creek below Beltsville Dam near Parryville

Tackle

Below the dam it is a fairly good-sized stream and a 9-foot, 4-weight rod is perfect.

MAJOR HATCHES OF THE LEHIGH RIVER SYSTEM

Common Name *Scientific Name*	Hatch Period	Fly Patterns	Hook Sizes
Early Brown Stonefly	March – early April	Brown Bi-Visible Dry	14-16
Strophopteryx fasciata		Stimulator Dry	14-16
Early Black Stonefly	March – early April	Black Elk Hair Caddis Dry	16-18
Taeniopteryx nivalis			
Little Black Caddis	Mid-April – mid-May	Black Elk hair Caddis	16-18
Chimarra atterrima			
Blue-winged Olive	April – mid-May	Parachute Adams	18
Baetis tricaudulus	Mid-June – October	Parachute BWO	18
(formerly *Baetis vagans*)			
Blue Quill			
Paraleptophlebia adoptiva	April 15-30	Blue Quill Dry	16-18
Paraleptophlebia mollis	June – September	Blue Dun Dry	16-18
		Blue Quill Nymph	16-18
Quill Gordon	April 10 – May 5	Quill Gordon Dry	14
Epeorus pleuralis		Hare's Ear Wet	14
Hendrickson	April 10 – May 5	Hendrickson Dry	14
Ephemerella subvaria		Red Quill Dry	14
Tan Caddis	May – August	Elk Hair Caddis Dry	14-16
Hydropsyche recurvata		Leonard Wright Caddis Dry	14-16
***March Brown**	Mid-May – early June	March Brown Dry	12
Maccaffertium vicarium		Gray Fox Dry	12-14
(formerly *Stenonema vicarium*)		March Brown Wet	12
Grannom Caddis	Late-April – mid-May	Brown Elk Hair Caddis	12-14
Brachycentrus fuliginosus.		Peacock Caddis Dry	12-14
Apple Caddis	May	Tan/Green Elk Hair Caddis	14-16
Brachycentrus appalachia			
Light Cahill	Mid-May – mid-June	Light Cahill Dry	12
Stenacron interpunctatum		Light Cahill Wet	12
Sulphur	Mid-May – mid-June	Pale Evening Dun Dry	16-18
Ephemerella dorothea		Pale Evening Dun Spinner	16-18
Slate Drake		Slate Drake Dry	10-12
Isonychia bicolor	Late May – June	Adams Dry	10-12
Isonychia sadleri & harperi	Mid-Sept. – mid-Oct.	Gray Wulff	10-12
		Leadwing Coachman Wet	10-12
Ants	May – October	Parachute Ant Dry	16- 20
		Flying Ant Dry	16-20
		Black Wire Ant Wet	16-20
Inchworms	May – October	Deer Hair Dry	12
		Green Weenie Wet	12

* *Stenonema fuscum* (Gray Fox) is now considered the same species as *Maccaffertium vicarium,* formerly *Stenonema vicaruim* (March Brown)

Hub Cities

Jim Thorpe

Population 4,781

The town of Jim Thorpe is named after one of the great athletes of the twentieth century. Jim Thorpe was a Native American and a hero of the 1912 Olympics in Stockholm, Sweden, but until his death he had no connection with the town. He was born in Oklahoma in 1888 and as a young man attended the Carlisle Indian Academy near Harrisburg, but that is as close as he got to the town which now bears his name. He died a poor man, and his widow reached out to his native state of Oklahoma to see if they would develop a suitable memorial for him. Much to her sorrow, this was denied. She learned that two adjacent Pennsylvania towns (Mauch Chunk and East Mauch) along the banks of the Lehigh River were struggling for their economic survival and looking for a way to grow their economies. After some negotiations the two towns agreed to merge, adopt the name of Jim Thorpe, and they constructed a large mausoleum which bears his name and houses his remains. The town is experiencing an economic revival, and in fact, *Budget Travel* magazine in 2006 ranked Jim Thorpe as one of America's Top 10 Coolest Small Towns. Jim Thorpe provides good access to the bottom of the gorge and the lower river.

Accommodations

The Country Place Motel, 843 State Route 903 / 570-325-2214
Hotel Switzerland, 5 Hazard Square / 570-325-4563
Inn at Jim Thorpe, 24 Broadway / 570-325-2599 / www.innjt.com

Campgrounds and RV Parks

Jim Thorpe Camping Resort, Lentz Trail / 570-325-2644

Restaurants

Dom N Ali Steaks & Seafood Family Restaurant, 870 North St. / 570-325-8110 / www.domnali.com
The Emerald Restaurant & Molly Maguire's Pub at the Hotel Switzerland, 5 Hazard Square / 570-325-8995 / www.jimthorpdining.com

TB's 903, 874 State Route 903 / 570-325-0133
JT's All American Steak & Ale, 5 Hazard Square / 570-325-4563

Sporting Goods Stores

Four Seasons Sporting Goods, 29 Broadway / 570-325-4364

Airports

Carbon County Airport, 2321 Mahoning Drive, Lehighton / 570-386-5025
Wilkes-Barre/Scranton International / 570-602-2030

Medical

St. Luke's Urgent Care, 1104 North St. / 570-325-2400

For More Information

Jim Thorpe Chamber of Commerce, 2 Lehigh Ave. / 570-325-5810

White Haven

Population 1,097

White Haven provides good access to the top of the gorge and the tailwaters below the Francis A. Walter Dam.

Accommodations

Days Inn, Route 940 East / 570-443-0391
Holiday Inn Express, Route 940 / 866-270-5110
Mountain Laurel Resort, Route 940 / 570-443-8411 / www.mountainlaurelresort.com

Campgrounds and RV Parks

Lehigh Gorge Campground, 4585 St. / 570-443-9191 / www.lehighgorgecampground.com

Restaurants

Hanna's Ugly Mug, 217 Main St. / 570-443-7141 / Decent food, decent prices
White Haven Family Diner, 302 Main St. / 570-443-8797 / Famous for burgers
Antonio's Pizzeria & Restaurant, Main St. / 570-443-709

GUIDES AND SPORTING GOODS STORES

Joe DeMarkis' Rivers Outdoor Adventures, 22 Hughes Street, New Ringgold / 570-943-3151 / www.riversflyfishing.com / River Outdoor Adventures is one of two guiding services with a permit to float the gorge. They have rubbers rafts, which are required to fish the upper and middle gorge.

Fly Fish PA / 570-617-4390 /www.flyfishpa.net / Co-owned by Dean Druckenmiller (President LCFA) and Jake Markezin. They have the other permit to fish the gorge; they fish the lower gorge.

AIRPORTS

Carbon County Airport, 2321 Mahoning Drive, Lehighton / 570-386-5025

Wilkes-Barre/Scranton International / 570-602-2030

MEDICAL

St. Luke's Urgent Care, 1104 North St. / 570-325-2400

FOR MORE INFORMATION

White Haven Chamber of Commerce / www.whitehaven.org

BLAKESLEE

Population 3,794

Blakeslee provides good access to the river above the Francis Dam in the state game lands.

ACCOMMODATIONS

Blakeslee Inn and Restaurant, Route 940 / 570-646-1100 / www.blakesleeinn.com

Best Western, Route 115 / 800-772-7083 / 570-646-6000

RESTAURANT

Woody's Country House, 100 Route 15 / 570-646-1100 / www.woodyscountryhouse.com

Murphy's Loft Restaurant, Route 115 / 570-646-2813 / www.murphysloft.com

Robert Christians, Route 940, Pocono Lake / 570-646-0433 / www.robertchristians.com / Great burgers, dinner specials at affordable prices. This is where the locals dine.

FLY SHOPS AND SPORTING GOODS

The Evening Hatch, 5 Route 940 East, / 570-443-0772 / www.eveninghatch.com

A. A. Outfitters, Route 115 North / 800-443-8119 / www.aaoutfitters.com

AIRPORTS

Carbon County Airport, 2321 Mahoning Drive, Lehighton / 570-386-5025

Wilkes-Barre/Scranton International / 570-602-2030

MEDICAL

Hazleton General Hospital, 700 East Broad St., Hazelton / 570-501-4000

MORE INFORMATION

Pocono Mountain Vacation Bureau / 1-800-Poconos / www.poconos.com

Lehigh Coldwater Fishery Alliance, 22 Hughes Street, New Ringgold, PA 17960 / www.thelehighriver.org

Lehigh River Stocking Association, PO Box 54, Walnutport, PA, 18088 / www.lrsa.org

LACKAWAXEN RIVER

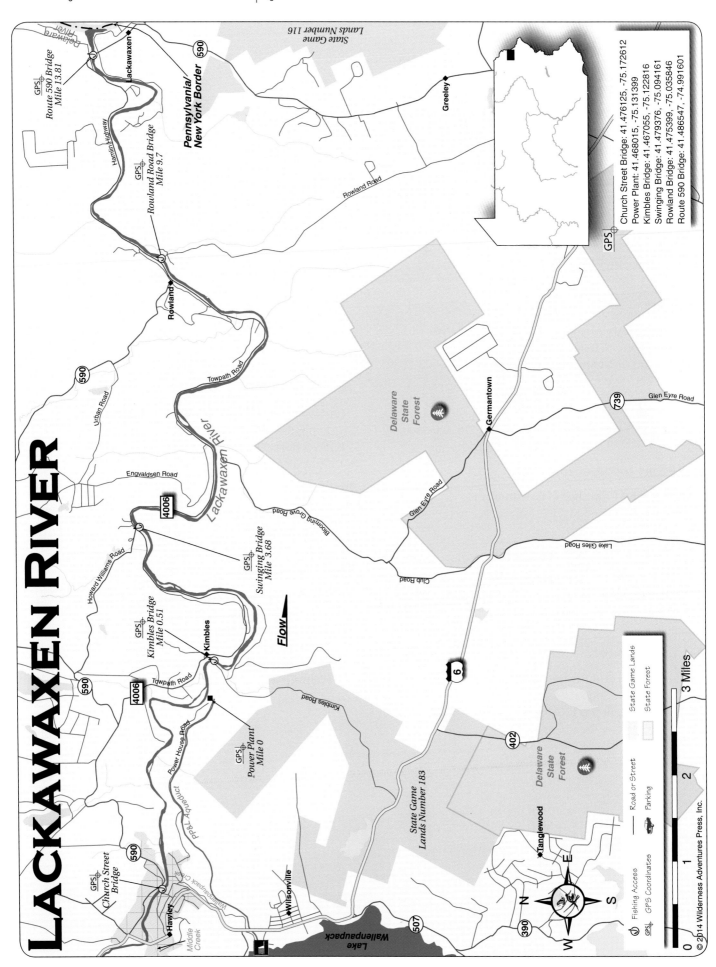

Church Street Bridge: 41.476125, -75.172612
Power Plant: 41.468015, -75.131399
Kimbles Bridge: 41.467055, -75.122816
Swinging Bridge: 41.479376, -75.094161
Rowland Bridge: 41.475399, -75.035846
Route 590 Bridge: 41.486547, -74.991601

© 2014 Wilderness Adventures Press, Inc.

LACKAWAXEN RIVER (FOUR STARS)

The Lackawaxen River is a big, brawling river which begins, according to the locals, at the junction of the West Branch of the Lackawaxen and Dyberry Creek in Honesdale, and flows some 30 miles to the Delaware River. The tailwater fishery begins at the outflow of Lake Wallenpaupack just south of Hawley. Pennsylvania Power and Light provides conservation coldwater releases piped in an aqueduct from Lake Wallenpaupack, keeping the river cool all summer long. The river fishes well from Kimbles downstream to the Delaware River. Route 590 provides easy access to most of the river. Between Kimbles and Rowland, Route 4006 provides excellent access to the river. This section of the Lackawaxen, "Lackey" to the locals, is big, beautiful, and challenging to fish and wade. It is stocked from 0.6 mile above Middle Creek downstream to the Delaware River both in spring and fall. Also in fall it gets a small spawning run of browns from the Delaware River.

One clear, crisp Sunday afternoon on Columbus Day weekend, I drove along the Lackey from Hawley to the Delaware River. It had been stocked only a few days before and I saw only three anglers all day. The Lackey flows through a densely forested valley which is especially gorgeous during fall foliage. It has a few riverfront vacation homes, but very little posting. Above Kimbles, Pennsylvania Power and Light (PP&L) releases water from Lake Wallenpaupack through an aqueduct to the Lackey in order to generate power. During the releases, the water rises rapidly, and if you are fishing during one of these releases, you must take care and get out of the river quickly. The Lackey has good diversity of hatches, with the Hendrickson being the heaviest and if you catch it at the right time, every fish in the river will be on them. During periods when no flies are emerging, I have had good success covering a lot of water with conehead Marabou Muddler streamers.

DIRECTIONS

From Hawley take Route 590 east to Route 4006, turn right on Route 4006 (Towpath Road) which takes you to the river at Kimbles, just downstream of the PP&L aqueduct. From Kimbles, Route 4006 follows the river downstream until it meets up with Route 590 along the lower river. While there is some posting, many of the landowners have posted their properties open for fishermen. The PP&L water-release hotline is 800-807-2474.

STREAM FACTS

Season/Regulations

The Lackawaxen River is regulated under the state's general regulations which allow fishing by rod and reel from 8:00am on the mid-April opening day until February 28. The harvest limit is five trout of 7 inches or better from the April opening day to September 7. The extended season runs from September 8 to February 28 and the harvest limit is three trout of 7 inches or better. Fishing is closed from March 1 until opening day to allow for stocking.

Fish

The river does have some holdover trout, and occasionally a few trout move up from the Delaware River, but for the most part you will be fishing for stocked trout. The Fish Commission stocks the Lackawaxen River several times in the spring and again in the fall.

River Characteristics

The Lackawaxen River, "Lackey" to the locals, not to be confused with the Lackawanna River in Lackawanna County, is a big, brawling river which flows some 30 miles from its source to the Delaware River. It has a good diversity of hatches with the Hendrickson being my favorite. The local chapter of Trout Unlimited has been very successful in getting landowners to post their properties "Open to Fishing".

What's in a Name?

Lackawaxen is derived from an Indian word which means "swift water".

River Flows

Above Kimbles, Pennsylvania Power and Light (PP&L) releases water from Lake Wallenpaupack through an aqueduct to the Lackey in order to generate power. During the releases the water rises rapidly, and you must take care and get out of the river quickly. The PP&L water release hotline is 800-807-2474.

http://waterdata.gov/USA/UV USGS web site 01432110 Lackawaxen River at Rowland

Tackle

This is big water, and for dry fly fishing I like a 9-foot 5-weight rod. When there is no surface activity, I'll fish a 6-weight and search the water with a white conehead Muddler Marabou.

The beautiful, brawling Lackawaxen River.

Hub Cities

HAWLEY POPULATION 1,216 / HONESDALE POPULATION 4,480

ACCOMMODATIONS

The Lodge at Woodlock, 109 River Birch Lane, Hawley / 570-685-8500 / www.thelodgeatwoodloch.com

The Settlers Inn, 4 Main Avenue, Hawley / 570-226-2993 / www.thesettlersinn.com

Cherry Ridge Campsites & Lodging, 147 Camp Road, Honesdale / 570-488-6654 / www.cherryridgecampsites.com

East Shore Lodging, 2487 Route 6, Hawley / 570-226-3293 / www.eastshorelodging.com

Gresham's Lake View Motel, Route 6, Hawley / 570-493-0943 / www.greshams.net

CAMPGROUNDS AND RV PARKS

Keen Lake Camping & Cottage Resort, 155 Keen Lake Road, Waymart / www.keenlake.com

Iron Point Recreation Area, Route 507, Greentown / 570-857-0880 / www.ironpoint.com

RESTAURANTS

The Settlers Inn, 4 Main Avenue, Hawley / 570-226-2993 / www.thesettlersinn.com / Beautiful restored country inn offering elegant dining.

MAJOR HATCHES FOR THE LACKAWAXEN RIVER

Common Name *Scientific Name*	Hatch Period	Fly Patterns	Hook Sizes
Blue-winged Olive	April – mid-May	Parachute Adams	18
Baetis tricaudatus	Mid-June – October	Parachute BWO	18
(formerly *Baetis vagans*)			
Blue Quill			
Paraleptophlebia adoptiva	April 15-30	Blue Quill Dry	16-18
Paraleptophlebia mollis	June – September	Blue Dun Dry	16-18
		Blue Quill Nymph	16-18
Quill Gordon	April 10 – May 5	Quill Gordon Dry	14
Epeorus pleuralis		Hare's Ear Wet	14
Hendrickson	April 10 – May 5	Hendrickson Dry	14
Ephemerella subvaria		Red Quill Dry	14
Tan Caddis	May – August	Elk Hair Caddis Dry	14-16
Hydropsyche recurvata		Leonard Wright Caddis Dry	14-16
*March Brown	Mid-May – early June	March Brown Dry	12
Maccaffertium vicarium		Gray Fox Dry	12-14
(formerly *Stenonema vicarium*)		March Brown Wet	12
Grannom Caddis	Late-April – mid-May	Brown Elk Hair Caddis	12-14
Brachycentrus fuliginosus.		Peacock Caddis Dry	12-14
Apple Caddis	May	Tan/Green Elk Hair Caddis	14-16
Brachycentrus appalachia			
Sulphur	Mid-May – mid-June	Pale Evening Dun Dry	16-18
Ephemerella dorothea		Pale Evening Dun Spinner	16-18
Slate Drake		Slate Drake Dry	10-12
Isonychia bicolor	Late May – June	Adams Dry	10-12
Isonychia sadleri & harperi	Mid-Sept. – mid-Oct.	Gray Wulff	10-12
		Leadwing Coachman Wet	10-12
Ants	May – October	Parachute Ant Dry	16- 20
		Flying Ant Dry	16-20
		Black Wire Ant Wet	16-20
Inchworms	May – October	Deer Hair Dry	12
		Green Weenie Wet	12

* *Stenonema fuscum* (Gray Fox) is now considered the same species as *Maccaffertium vicarium,* formerly *Stenonema vicaruim* (March Brown)

Boat House Restaurant, Route 507, Hawley /
   570-226-5027 / www.boathouse.com
Cora's 1850 Bistro, 108 Wellwood Avenue & Church
   Street, Hawley / 570-226-8878
Gresham's Chop House, Route 6, Hawley / 570-226-2990

FLY SHOPS AND SPORTING GOODS

Wallenpaupack Sports Shop, Route 6 Hawley /
   570-226-4797
Bright's Fly Shop, Route 590, Rowland / 570-685-7697 -
   for current river conditions and hatches. It is located
   right on the Lackawaxen River across the street from a
   local diner.
D & A Sports, 29 Roosevelt Highway, Waymart /
   570-281-3685

AIRPORTS

Wilkes-Barre/Scranton Airport, 100 Terminal Drive,
   Avoca / 1-877-2FLYAVP

MEDICAL

Wayne Memorial Hospital, 60 Park Street, Honesdale /
   570-253-8100 / wmh.org

FOR MORE INFORMATION

Hawley Chamber of Commerce, Route 6 Hawley /
   570-226-3191 / www.hawleywallenpaupackcc.com

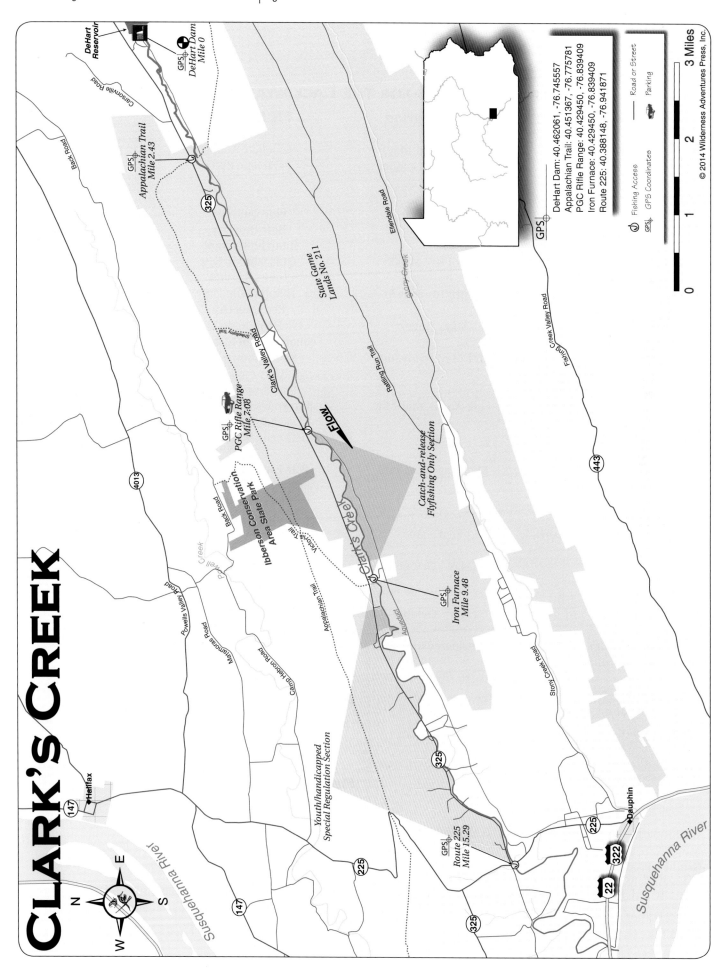

CLARK'S CREEK

DeHart Dam: 40.462061, -76.745557
Appalachian Trail: 40.451367, -76.775781
PGC Rifle Range: 40.429450, -76.839409
Iron Furnace: 40.429450, -76.839409
Route 225: 40.388148, -76.941871

Road or Street

Fishing Access

GPS Coordinates

Parking

© 2014 Wilderness Adventures Press, Inc.

0   1   2   3 Miles

DeHart Reservoir

GPS
DeHart Dam
Mile 0

Carsonville Road

Back Road

GPS
Appalachian Trail
Mile 2.43

325

Ellendale Road

Stony Creek

State Game
Lands No. 211

Shutmire Trail

Clark's Valley Road

Rattling Run Trail

Fish Dam Road

Creek Valley Road

GPS
PGC Rifle Range
Mile 7.08

FLOW

*Catch-and-release
Flyfishing Only Section*

443

4013

Back Road

Powell Creek

*Ibberson Conservation
Area State Park*

Victoria Trail

Clark's Creek

Aqueduct

GPS
Iron Furnace
Mile 9.48

Appalachian Trail

Susquehanna River

Powells Valley Road

Matamoras Road

Camp Hebron Road

Halifax

147

147

N
E
S
W

*Youth/handicapped
Special Regulation Section*

225

Story Creek Road

225

325

GPS
Route 225
Mile 15.29

325

225

322

22

Dauphin

Susquehanna River

CLARK'S CREEK (FOUR STARS)

Clark's Creek begins in Tower City and flows some 30 miles to the Susquehanna River just north of Harrisburg. It flows through a beautiful, heavily forested valley appropriately known as Clark's Valley in the Blue Mountains, the easternmost range in the Pennsylvania Appalachians. The creek and the valley are named for the late William Clark, who was a local farmer and a one-time Treasurer of the United States.

Clark's harbors a few native brook trout and some stream-bred browns, and it is heavily stocked by the state and the Dauphin County Anglers organization, which operates a cooperative fish hatchery on the stream. It fishes well from late March through September. The first hatch of the season is the early brown stonefly hatch in late March through early April. The next important hatch on the stream is the Hendricksons in late April. May brings a decent March brown hatch. These are the most reliable hatches on Clark's Creek. I have also run into sulphurs and blue-winged olives, but never in good numbers. Recently while checking my stream logs I was reminded about the excellent terrestrial fishing I had on Clark's Creek.

Summer fishing on Clark's can be very challenging but rewarding. In summer, the water is usually low and clear and the trout have been educated by all the fishing pressure early in the spring. You can almost always take a few trout on a floating ant, but what drives the Clark's Creek trout into a frenzy are inchworms. They appear in good numbers on Clark's from late May into early September. Look for them hanging by their threads over the water. On breezy days, the wind rocks the inchworms back and forth over the stream, tantalizing the trout. On a recent outing to Clark's Creek, I saw a trout jump two feet out of the water to try to grab one of these tasty (I assume) morsels. I have had trout that earlier refused my ant imitation presented on long leaders, with 8x tippets, streak halfway across the stream to inhale my inchworm patterns. On one blown cast, my inchworm pattern got caught on a small branch about a foot over the water and a trout jumped up and grabbed my fly, freeing me from the snag and yes, I landed the fish! I have had excellent success with trout feeding on inchworms on many streams, but never as voraciously as they do on Clark's Creek. The two inchworm patterns I use are a Floating Cork Inchworm and, for sub-surface fishing, my go-to fly is a Green Weenie.

DIRECTIONS/ACCESS

Clark's Creek initially really flew under my radar screen, at least as a tailwater fishery. I had fished it over a dozen times when I lived in Philadelphia, but that was some thirty years ago. From Philadelphia, my route to Clark's Creek was to take Route 322 north from Harrisburg along the Susquehanna River and then a short stretch on Route 225, which crosses Clark's Creek near its junction with the river. The Route 225 bridge marks the lower end of the special regulation area set aside for children and handicapped anglers (managed by the Dauphin County Anglers & Conservationists organization). After crossing the river, turn right onto Route 325, which closely follows the creek upstream past the youth and handicapped special regulation section to the Catch-&-Release, Fly-Fishing-Only section which runs for 2.4 miles. It starts at the Pennsylvania Game Commission's rifle range parking area on Route 325 and runs downstream to the Pennsylvania Game Commission access road at the Iron Furnace.

What I didn't know when I fished Clark's Creek 30 years ago was that, five or six miles upstream from the fly-fishing-only section, was the reason that Clark's stays cool all summer: The DeHart Reservoir, which supplies water for Harrisburg. It is a bottom-release dam which provides a cool shot of water to the stream below. The Harrisburg Water Authority maintains a constant conservation discharge of 10cfs.

STREAM FACTS

Season/Regulations

The Catch-&-Release Fly-Fishing-Only section is open to year-round fishing.

Fish

Clark's is heavily stocked and harbors wild browns and a few native brookies.

River Characteristics

Clark's is only about 30 to 40 feet wide and runs clear and fairly slow in the flyfishing stretch, making for extremely challenging fishing. Long leaders and light tippets are a must.

River Flows

The Harrisburg Water Authority maintains a constant conservation discharge of 10 cfs.

Tackle

I fish Clark's Creek with an 8-foot, 3- or 4-weight line. Long leaders and light tippets are a must.

YOUGHIOGHENY RIVER

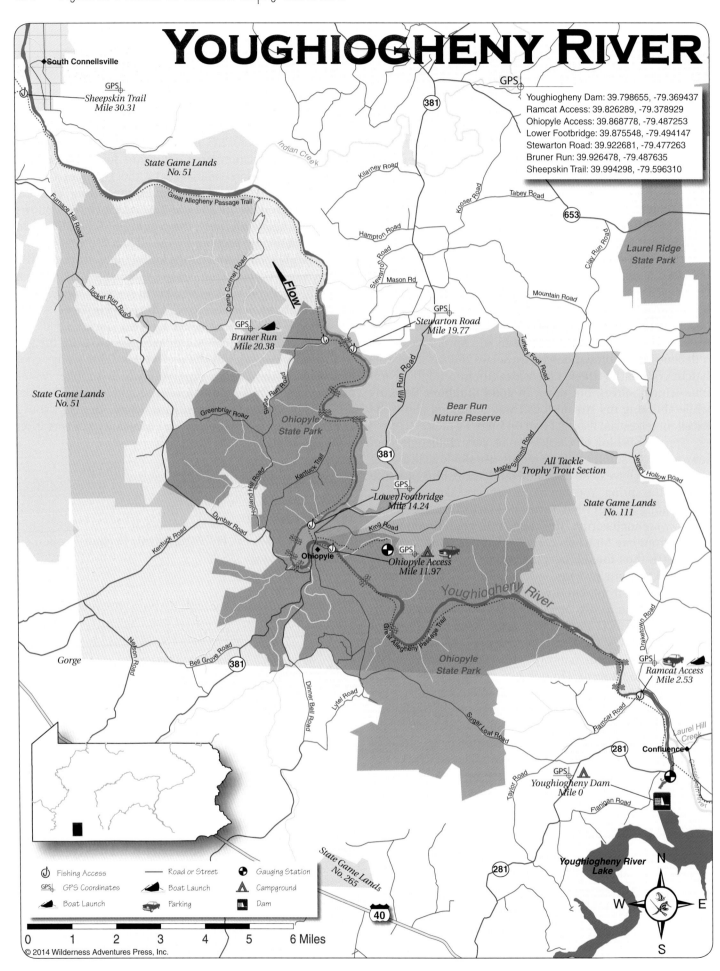

GPS

Youghiogheny Dam: 39.798655, -79.369437
Ramcat Access: 39.826289, -79.378929
Ohiopyle Access: 39.868778, -79.487253
Lower Footbridge: 39.875548, -79.494147
Stewarton Road: 39.922681, -79.477263
Bruner Run: 39.926478, -79.487635
Sheepskin Trail: 39.994298, -79.596310

South Connellsville

GPS
Sheepskin Trail
Mile 30.31

State Game Lands
No. 51

Indian Creek

381

Great Allegheny Passage Trail

Kilarney Road

Kooser Road

Tabey Road

653

Laurel Ridge
State Park

Furnace Hill Road

Camp Carmel Road

Flow

Hampton Road

Stewarton Road

Mason Rd

Mountain Road

Clay Run Road

Tucker Run Road

GPS
Bruner Run
Mile 20.38

GPS
Stewarton Road
Mile 19.77

Turkey Foot Road

State Game Lands
No. 51

Greenbriar Road

Sugar Run Road

Ohiopyle
State Park

Mill Run Road

Bear Run
Nature Reserve

All Tackle
Trophy Trout Section

Jersey Hollow Road

Kentuck Trail

381

State Game Lands
No. 111

Holland Hill Road

GPS
Lower Footbridge
Mile 14.24

Maple Summit Road

Dunbar Road

King Road

Kentuck Road

Ohiopyle

GPS
Ohiopyle Access
Mile 11.97

Youghiogheny River

Nelson Road

Great Allegheny Passage Trail

Drakentown Road

Gorge

Bell Grove Road

381

Ohiopyle
State Park

GPS
Ramcat Access
Mile 2.53

Dinner Bell Road

Lytel Road

Sugar Loaf Road

Ramcat Road

Laurel Hill Creek

281

Confluence

Taylor Road

GPS
Youghiogheny Dam
Mile 0

Flanigan Road

State Game Lands
No. 265

40

Youghiogheny River
Lake

281

Legend

Fishing Access
GPS Coordinates
Boat Launch
Road or Street
Boat Launch
Parking
Gauging Station
Campground
Dam

0 1 2 3 4 5 6 Miles

N
W E
S

© 2014 Wilderness Adventures Press, Inc.

YOUGHIOGHENY RIVER (FOUR STARS)

The Youghiogheny River (pronounced "yock-a-gainey") is a 134-mile long tributary of the Monongahela River. It flows north from the extreme western edge of Maryland toward Pittsburgh, Pennsylvania. The "Yough" (Yawk, as the locals pronounce it) is a big, rugged river. It can be divided into three distinct sections: the Upper Yough, the Middle Yough, and the Lower Yough.

The Upper Yough in western Maryland is an excellent tailwater fishery in its own right. Coldwater releases from the Deep Creek Lake hydroelectric station provide quality trout water and some great dry fly fishing for the six miles downstream of the dam. This section is covered in the chapter on Maryland.

There are two popular sections in Pennsylvania, the first of which is the tailwater section below the Youghiogheny Reservoir near the town of Confluence, known as the Middle Yough. It supports an excellent population of trout from the town of Confluence downstream to Ohiopyle, a distance of about 10 miles.

The section farther down from the reservoir below the town of Ohiopyle is referred to as the Lower Yough. This section is very dangerous to fish, but it does provide some of the best whitewater rafting in the East. The dam creating the Youghiogheny Reservoir was authorized by Congress as part of the Flood Control Act of 1938. In the early 1940s, the Army Corp of Engineers completed construction of the Yough dam with bottom-release capability. The dam provides well-oxygenated coldwater releases and sustains a trout fishery for many miles downstream. The river is typically about 200 feet across in this section and is difficult to wade. It is especially dangerous in high-water conditions.

Located at the southern reaches of the Laurel Ridge, Ohiopyle State Park encompasses approximately 20,500 acres of rugged natural beauty and serves as the southern gateway to the Laurel Highlands. Passing through the heart of the park are the rushing waters in the Youghiogheny River Gorge – a 1,500-foot-deep, heavily forested gorge which is the centerpiece of Ohiopyle State Park. The Yough provides some of the best whitewater boating in the eastern United States as well as spectacular scenery. Except for the center of the town of Ohiopyle, the entire 28-mile gorge is only accessible via the rails-to-trails project which follows the entire river from dam to the confluence with the Monongahela River. The trail is on the western side of the river and provides good walking access to the Trophy Trout section.

DIRECTION/ACCESS

From Somerset, it is about a 40-minute ride on Route 281 to the town of Confluence. Access to the Youghiogheny is provided by Route 281 in Confluence and from Route 381 in Ohiopyle. Route 2012 connects Routes 281 in Confluence and Route 381 in Ohiopyle. A bike trail follows the river from the Ramcat Access Area near Confluence downstream to a second access point in Ohiopyle.

Ed Jaworowski (left) Guide Harold Harsh (right) during lunch break on the Yough.

STREAM FACTS

Seasons/Regulations

The Youghiogheny from the dam downstream to confluence with the Casselman River is closed from April 1 until the season opener. The All Tackle Trophy Trout section runs from Ramcat Run downstream nine miles to the Route 381 bridge in Ohiopyle, about one-quarter mile above the Ohiopyle Falls. Trophy Trout regulations provide for year-round fishing, with no gear or bait restrictions. From opening day through Labor Day, you may harvest two trout 14 inches or greater. From the day after Labor Day until opening day no fish may be harvested.

Fish

The state frequently stocks legal-size trout in the first mile or so from the dam downstream to the Casselman River just below the town of Confluence. The state heavily stocks fingerling browns and rainbows throughout the Youghiogheny River Gorge and has been doing so since the 1970s. The majority of fish caught in the gorge are the result of these stockings, and these "river-raised" trout are beautifully colored and strong fighters.

River Characteristics

The river is big and brawling, so wading is difficult although not impossible. When the Yough is running high, the only place to safely wade is between the dam outflows downstream to Confluence. Below the town of Confluence, the Casselman and Laura Hill Rivers join the Yough, greatly increasing its volume. When the water levels are low, good wading access can be found just below the town of Confluence. Access is from the abandoned railroad bed, which is now a hiking and biking trail.

What the experts Say

"Yough River rainbows get to be huge. I've heard of them 25 inches and over near the falls at Ohiopyle", Pennsylvania Fish and Boat Commission biologist Rick Lorson said. "Good numbers, too. The Trophy Trout regulations are working." In 2012, two of Pennsylvania's top five trout recognized by the state's Angler Recognition Program were caught on the Youghiogheny, with the largest one being an 11-pound, 14-ounce rainbow. Lorson feels that 90 percent of the river's trout population is from fingerling stockings.

What's in a Name?

Youghiogheny is an Algonquin word for "a river flowing in a contrary direction", as it flows north out of western Maryland into southwestern Pennsylvania.

Flows

According to Ernie Pribanic of Laurel Highlands Guides, you should not wade the Yough below the Casselman River unless the flow is 1,500cfs or below.

USGS 03081000, Youghiogheny below Confluence, Pa. www.waterdata.usgs.gov

Hatches

Because of massive fingerling plantings, some anglers swear by two- to three-inch rainbow-trout pattern small crank baits for landing bigger fish. Fly anglers do well with big articulated streamers tied to resemble small trout. The main hatches are little black stoneflies followed by olive and tan caddis flies, quill Gordons, then March browns and sulphurs. I have seen a few green drakes in early June. The Yough has very reliable slate drake hatches which come off almost daily in July, and they continue to hatch through September. In the fall, look for blue-winged olives and the October caddis hatches.

Tackle

For a float trip, I would carry two outfits. A 9-foot, 5-weight is the perfect all-around rod on the river, but if you want to hook into one of the monsters the river hides well, throw big articulated streamers on a 7-weight outfit rigged with a sink tip or full-sink fly line.

Hub City

HARRISBURG

Population 49,673

ACCOMMODATION

Comfort Inn Riverfront, 525 South Front Street /
717-233-1611
Super 8, 4131 Executive Park Drive / 717-564-7790

RESTAURANTS

Santo's Pizza, 2019 Linglestown Road / 717-657-0810
Gabriella Italian Restaurant / 3907 Jonestown Road /
717-540-0040
Gilligans Bar & Grill, 987 Eisenhower Blvd. /
717-939-9575

FLY SHOPS/GUIDES

Clouser's Fly Shop, 101 Ulrich Street, Middletown /
717-944-6541 / www.clouserflyfishing.com
Rivers Outdoor Adventures, 22 Hughes Street, New
Ringgold / 570-691-5476
Yellow Breeches Outfitters / On the lake in Boiling
Springs / 717-258-6752

AIRPORTS

Harrisburg International Airport, 513 Airport Drive,
Middletown, Pa. 717-948-3900

MEDICAL

Harrisburg Medical Center, 100 Dr. Warren Tuttle Drive
/ 618-253-7671

FOR MORE INFORMATION

Harrisburg Chamber of Commerce, 1735 State Street /
717-238-9804

SOMERSET

Population 6,277

ACCOMMODATIONS

Holiday Inn Express, 132 Lewis Drive / 814-701-2762
Ohiopyle Vacation Rentals / 877-574-STAY /
www.ohiopylevacationrentals.com
Days Inn, Donegal / 724-593-7536
The Yough Tree House, 926 River Road, Confluence /
814-395-2001 / www.youghtreehouse.com

CAMPGROUNDS AND RV PARKS

Benner's Meadow Run Camping & Cabins, 315 Nelson
Road, Farmington / 724-329-4097 /
www.bennersmeadowrun.com
Paddler's Lane Camping, 255 Paddler's Lane,
Confluence / 814-964-0410
Hickory Hollow Campground, 176 Big Hickory Road,
Rockwood / 814-926-4636
Laurel Hill State Park, 1454 Laurel Hill Park Road /
814-445-7725
Ohiopyle State Park, 724-329-8591

RESTAURANTS

Crazy Alice's Café, 101 West Main Street / 814-443-6370 /
www.crazyalicescafe.com
Oakhurst Tea Room, 2409 Route 31 / 814-443-2897
/ Since 1977, Oakhurst has been serving an all-
you-can-eat Pennsylvania Dutch-Style Smorgasbord
lunch and dinner at very reasonable prices.
Caporella's Italian Restorante, 90 Pittsburg Street,
Uniontown / 724-438-8466 / www.caporellas.com
Ohiopyle Bakery & Sandwich Shoppe, 85 Main Street,
Ohiopyle / 724-329-BAKE

FLY SHOPS & GUIDES

Spring Creek Outfitters, 86 Big Frog Lane, Oakland, MD
/ 301-387-6587 / www.springcreekoutfitters.com
Wilderness Voyagers, Garrett Street, Ohiopyle /
800-272-4141
Laurel Highlands Guides / 742-433-7151 /
www.lauralhighlandsguideservice.com
White Water Adventures, 6 Negley Street, Ohiopyle /
800-992-7238 / www.wwaraft.com

AIRPORTS

Somerset County Airport, 159 Airport Lane /
814-443-2114 / www.somerset.pa.us/airport
Pittsburgh International Airport, 1000 Airport
Boulevard, Pittsburg / 412-472-3700 /
www.pitairport.com

MEDICAL

Somerset Hospital, 329 South Pleasant Avenue /
814-443-5000 / www.somersethospital.com

FOR MORE INFORMATION

Somerset Chamber of Commerce, 601 North Central
Avenue / 814-445-6431 / www.laurelhighlands.com

Maryland

Maryland Facts

Area: 12,407 square miles – 42nd largest state in the union

Population: 5,828,289 – 19th most populous

State Animal: No official state animal

State Fish: Rockfish (Striped Bass)

Trout Fishing License

www.dnr.state.md.us

Annual Resident: $20.50 plus a $5.00 Trout Stamp

Annual Non-Resident Fees are equal to a $30.50 minimum or reciprocal fee for state of residence, whichever is greater.

Non-Resident seven-day fee is equal to the fee charged a Maryland resident for a similar license by non-resident's home state, plus a $10.00 Trout Stamp.

Non-Resident three-day fees are equal to the fee charged a Maryland resident for a similar license by non-resident's home state, plus a $10.00 Trout Stamp.

State Records

Brook trout: 6 pounds, 2 ounces by Mike Fiorita, Jr. / April 10, 1999 / North Branch Potomac at Barnum

Brown trout: 18 pounds, 3 ounces by Gary Kuhn / August 3, 2001 / North Branch Potomac at Barnum

Rainbow trout:14 pounds, 3 ounces by Dave Schroyer / October 21, 1987 / Savage River Reservoir

Cutthroat trout: 7 pounds, 9 ounces by David G. Martin / May 20, 2000 / North Branch Potomac at Barnum

Maryland Tailwaters

Mid-Atlantic anglers often skip Maryland trout streams in favor of the better-known streams in neighboring Pennsylvania and the not-too-distant Catskill rivers in southern New York State. While Pennsylvania and New York streams are steeped in angling history and tradition – with noted angling legends like Vince Marinaro, Charlie Fox, and Ernie Schwiebert in Pennsylvania and Theodore Gordon, Art Flick, and the Dettes and Darbees in New York – Maryland boasts a few angling legends of its own, starting with the late Joe Brooks, one of the founders of the Brotherhood of the Jungle Cock, named after a bird whose feathers are treasured for tying the cheeks on many traditional streamer patterns. The Brotherhood, whose mission is to involve children in fly fishing, still exists today. Maryland is also the home state of "Lefty" Bernard Kreh, fly fishing's greatest teacher and biggest ambassador.

Maryland's blue ribbon tailwater rivers are a direct result of good fisheries management policies on the part of Maryland's Department of Natural Resources (DNR). Under the leadership of Dr. Bob Bachman, former director of Maryland's Freshwater Fisheries, in the mid-1980s the state stopped stocking trout in streams which could support natural reproduction. Under Bachman's visionary leadership, Maryland quickly became a leader in the region for wild trout management, especially tailwater trout. The state continues to work with landowners, the Army Corp of Engineers, mining companies, land trusts, and coldwater fisheries advocates like Trout Unlimited to improve habitat and water quality for the benefit of wild trout and recreational angling. In this chapter, we will explore four of Maryland's blue ribbon tailwaters: Big Gunpowder Falls, Savage, Youghiogheny, and the North Branch of the Potomac, as well as the regulations and management strategies the state is pursuing to ensure quality coldwater fisheries for future generations to enjoy.

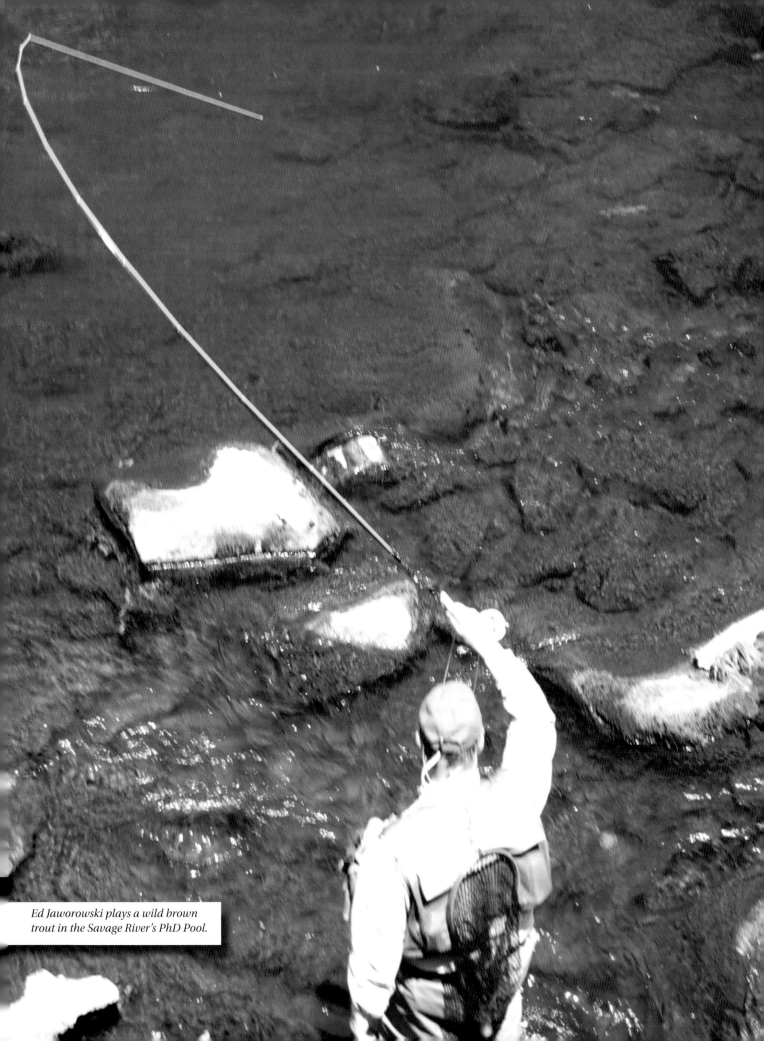

Ed Jaworowski plays a wild brown trout in the Savage River's PhD Pool.

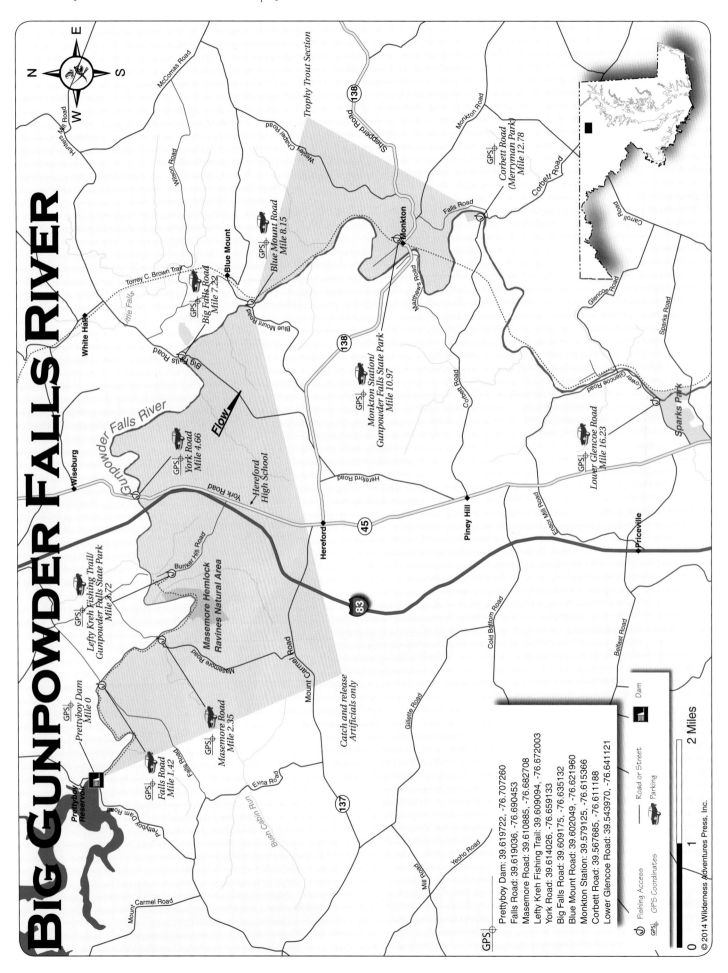

Big Gunpowder Falls River

Gunpowder Falls River

Prettyboy Reservoir

Prettyboy Dam Road

Mount Carmel Road

Bush Cabin Run

Wiseburg

White Hall

Little Falls

Torrey C. Brown Trail

Hunters Mill Road

McComas Road

Wilson Road

Big Falls Road

Falls Road

Blue Mount Road

Wesley Chapel Road

Sheppard Road

Trophy Trout Section

Monkton

Monkton Road

Corbett Road

Carroll Road

Glencoe Road

Sparks Road

Sparks Park

Lower Glencoe Road

Matthews Road

Falls Road

Hereford Road

Piney Hill

Hereford

York Road

Masemore Road

Bunker Hill Road

Masemore Hemlock Ravines Natural Area

Hereford High School

Flow

Evna Road

Gillette Road

Cold Bottom Road

Belfast Road

Mill Road

Yeoho Road

Edson Mill Road

Priceville

Catch and release
Artificials only

GPS | Prettyboy Dam Mile 0

GPS | Falls Road Mile 1.42

GPS | Masemore Road Mile 2.35

GPS | Lefty Kreh Fishing Trail/ Gunpowder Falls State Park Mile 3.72

GPS | York Road Mile 4.66

GPS | Big Falls Road Mile 7.22

GPS | Blue Mount Road Mile 8.15

GPS | Monkton Station/ Gunpowder Falls State Park Mile 10.97

GPS | Corbett Road (Merryman Park) Mile 12.78

GPS | Lower Glencoe Road Mile 16.23

Blue Mount

138

138

45

83

137

GPS

Prettyboy Dam: 39.619722, -76.707260
Falls Road: 39.619036, -76.690453
Masemore Road: 39.610885, -76.682708
Lefty Kreh Fishing Trail: 39.609094, -76.672003
York Road: 39.614026, -76.659133
Big Falls Road: 39.609175, -76.635132
Blue Mount Road: 39.602049, -76.621960
Monkton Station: 39.579125, -76.615366
Corbett Road: 39.567685, -76.611188
Lower Glencoe Road: 39.543970, -76.641121

Fishing Access

GPS | GPS Coordinates

Road or Street

Parking

Dam

0   1   2 Miles

© 2014 Wilderness Adventures Press, Inc.

BIG GUNPOWDER FALLS RIVER (FIVE STARS)

The Big Gunpowder Falls River is not big, averaging only about 40 to 50 feet in width. And although it does not have a falls, it does provide excellent trout fishing in a wilderness setting only an hour from the nation's capital. The river flows through the 20,000-acre Gunpowder State Park for more than 17 miles. It is one of the best tailwater rivers in the East. In fact in 2005, *Field and Stream* magazine ranked it as one of the top five tailwaters in the United States.

It hasn't always gotten such rave reviews – it was for many years a biological wasteland. Historically, releases from Prettyboy Reservoir were not conducive to protecting trout and aquatic life. The summer releases were so low that the river warmed to a point that trout could not survive, let alone reproduce. In 1986, Maryland Trout Unlimited negotiated a new flow-release policy with the city of Baltimore, which built and manages the reservoir for drinking water. It called for releases which would keep the water temperature in the 50s and low 60s even during summer's hottest days. Shortly after the new flow regimen was implemented, the state planted thousands of fertilized brown and rainbow trout eggs in the gravel below the dam and stocked thousands of fingerling and adult brown and rainbow trout throughout the tailwater. The first natural reproduction of stream-bred brown trout was documented in 1989. With the implementation of catch-and-release, artificial-lures-only regulations from the Prettyboy Dam downstream 7.2 miles to Blue Mount Road, the wild trout population took off. Today the water stays cold throughout the summer and the Gunpowder Falls River has become a truly "blue ribbon" trout stream. According to Dr. Bachman, "The Gunpowder River is one of the most prolific and dependable public wild trout fisheries in the East."

Oh, about the falls: many anglers – and a few outdoor writers – assume that the falls were flooded when the dam was built and the Prettyboy Reservoir was filled. While researching for this book, I reached out to Maryland's Department of Natural Resources outreach coordinator Keith Lockwood to learn the history of Big Gunpowder Falls. He replied, "Gunpowder Falls is not a waterfall but the actual name of the river. Falls is an archaic term that was used to describe a river or stream in the early days when the colony was settled." Other examples would include Jones Falls River and Gwynn's Falls River, both located near Baltimore.

When I asked my good friend and mentor, Ed Jaworowski, to join me on my first trip to the Gunpowder, he jumped at the opportunity, saying, "I'd love to, and I'll see if Lefty can join us." A few weeks earlier, Maryland's Governor Martin O'Malley had honored Lefty with the dedication of "The Lefty Kreh Fishing Trail" at Gunpowder Falls State Park, Lefty's home water. That afternoon, Ed emailed me that Lefty had invited us to stop by his house and chat about the Gunpowder River, and maybe take some photos on the river. A few mornings later, we arrived at Lefty's house. He greeted his long-time friend, Ed, and me with a big smile – more like a laugh and a warm handshake. Upon entering his living room, the first thing I noticed was a monster tarpon mounted over the couch. As I glanced around the room, every inch of wall space was adorned with beautiful art and photographs – all fishing-related. His living room

The Big Gunpowder Falls River was ranked as one of the top five tailwaters in the United States in 2005 by Field and Stream. Photo courtesy Ed Jaworowski.

Lefty Kreh fishing his home water.

would put any flyfisher's "man cave" to shame. I was in fly fishing's mission control room – the NASA of the flyfishing world.

After quite a few jokes and hilarious stories, Lefty leaned forward in his chair and started to tell us about the Gunpowder River. He explained that there are really three different sections of catch-and-release water on the river. The first begins at the dam at Prettyboy Reservoir and runs downstream to the power line below Falls Road. This section has a high gradient and runs through a mini-gorge with massive boulders, deep plunge pools, riffles, and runs. Large stands of hemlock and hardwoods shelter much of

this section from sunlight. In fact, between the cooling effects of the shade trees and the closeness to the coldwater dam releases, the water in this section can be 55-degrees or cooler even during the hottest days of summer, and sometimes it is cold enough to shut down a hatch and the fishing. Fishing here requires a bit of hiking and climbing – the wading is not easy, but the fishing and the setting are well worth the effort.

Lefty went on to explain that the second section, from the power line below Falls Road downstream to the cement bridge at York Road just below Interstate 83, is more of a traditional trout stream, with runs and riffles that, during

spawning habitat for browns, which thrive in this section of the river. Lefty feels that the larger browns are found in this section of the river. Ed and I would later discover that this section of the river is very popular for tubing, kayaking, and canoeing, so plan to fish it mid-week or early and late in the day during the warmer months.

From Blue Mount Road downstream 4.6 miles to Corbett Road, the Gunpowder is managed under Trophy Trout regulations which allow a harvest limit of two fish over 16 inches per day. There are no tackle restrictions under the Trophy Trout regulations.

Prior to our visit with Lefty, my goal was to get a quote or two from the legend, but this man is so giving and generous with his time and knowledge that by the end of the day, he had given me the lowdown on the river, tackle tips on everything from tippet rings to furled leaders, the names of the East's best tailwater guides and lodges, plus casting and photography lessons. All of this before seeing his dentist to fix a broken tooth and packing for a trip to Tennessee to fish the South Holston tailwater the next morning.

All trout in the catch-and-release section are stream-bred, the vast majority of them being browns with a few bows and brookies mixed in. The Gunpowder has an unbelievable biomass of wild trout, with estimates ranging from 3,500 to 5,000 trout per mile, rivaling even the best western rivers. Browns run about 8 to 14 inches, but there are bigger fish. With Washington only a little over an hour away and Baltimore less than an hour, the Gunpowder River gets a lot of fishing pressure. The trout are well-educated, and to be successful you will need long, light leaders, match-the-hatch flies, and a stealth approach.

The Gunpowder is open to year-round fishing, with water temperatures averaging from 50 to 60 degrees. Fishing can be good all winter, depending on air temperatures. Midges, streamers, and nymphs are your best bet in cold weather. The Gunpowder regulars will tell you that the river is a caddis factory. On days with no visible hatches, a green caddis pupa or emerger will often out-fish every other pattern. In spring, the river has good blue quill, quill Gordon, Hendrickson, and March brown hatches, but the best hatches on the river are the sulphurs. They start in mid-May with size 14-16 *Ephemerella invaria* down to a size 18 *Ephemerella dorothea* in June. Sulphur hatches start in the afternoon, and usually the day will end with a good spinner fall at dusk. In mid- to late summer, terrestrials become more prevalent and these are high on the menu for the trout. Ants and beetles are the perennial summer favorites for the Gunpowder regulars. (If you stay until dark, it's a good idea to leave a note on your dashboard notifying the park rangers.)

most flows, are easy to wade and fish, and there are several long, slow pools as well. This section has a much lower gradient than the gorge, and during low flows the fish can be very spooky. Access to this section has less shade and it is farther from the dam, so the water will be a little warmer but rarely gets up into the 60s even during the dog days of summer. This section can be accessed off Masemore, Bunker Hill, and York Roads.

The last stretch of catch-and-release water begins at York Road and runs downstream to Blue Mount Road. This section is slower moving, with some great pools and flats. Its largely gravel bottom provides easy wading and great

DIRECTIONS/ACCESS

Access is excellent with many road crossings, all of which have stream-side parking. There are foot paths on both sides of the river. From the north, take I -83 south to Exit 27 in Hereford. Turn right onto Mount Carmel Road for approximately 0.25 miles to Masemore Road. Turn right onto Masemore Road and follow it for 1.3 miles to the stream and parking area. This is the middle section of the catch-and-release water.

I prefer the water upstream of I-83, which crosses the river in Hereford just upstream of York Road. From the Baltimore Beltway (I-695), take I-83 north for 12.5 miles to Mt. Carmel Road. Turn right on Mt. Carmel Road to the traffic light. Turn left on York Road, go past the high school, and turn left on Bunker Hill Road. This will take you to the parking area. There are other parking areas: on Falls, Masemore, York, Big Falls, and Blue Mount Roads.

STREAM FACTS

Season/Regulations

Open to year-round fishing. Catch-and-release, artificial-lures-only from Prettyboy Reservoir downstream 7.2 miles to Blue Mount Road. From Blue Mount Road downstream 4.2 miles to Corbett Road, the Gunpowder is managed as Trophy Trout water, with a harvest limit of two fish over 16 inches per day. There are no tackle restrictions in the Trophy Trout section.

Fish

The catch-and-release section is not stocked – all fish are wild; mostly browns, but a few brookies and rainbows turn up once in a while.

River Characteristics

The upper section of the catch-and-release water below the dam flows through a mini-gorge. As you move downstream, you have a lower gradient with more pools and runs.

What the Experts Say

Dr. Bob Bachman, the former director of Maryland's Freshwater Fisheries says, "The Gunpowder River is one of the most prolific and dependable public wild trout fisheries in the East."

Micah Dammeyer, President of Knee Deep Fly Fishing, sums up the Gunpowder this way, "The Big Gunpowder Falls is a gem of a river located close to Baltimore and D.C. Great hatches, cold water, and plenty of river and green space to help you forget you are close to home make it my favorite. The Gunpowder's geographic location makes for a long fishing season, beginning with the emergence of stoneflies in March and ending with big caddis in the fall. Our sulfur hatch is the draw for lots of anglers in May, but the river entertains the locals with a great population of caddis that pop up all summer and the trico hatch will keep you up at night if you catch it at the right time.

"There's no place I'd rather spend an afternoon away from the city. Lots of others have the same idea but beating the crowd is merely a matter of walking five minutes down the trail. On a weeknight, even during a heavy spinner fall, you may find you're the only angler as far as you can see. My best tip for anglers who aren't hooking up: find a good log to sit on and watch what's going on for 15 minutes. Sometimes you have to get out of the water to see where the fish are holding and feeding."

What's in a Name?

Many anglers – and a few outdoor writers – assume that the falls (associated with the name Big Gunpowder Falls River) were flooded when the dam was built and the Prettyboy Reservoir was filled. While researching for this book, I reached out to Maryland's Department of Natural Resources outreach coordinator Keith Lockwood to learn the history of Big Gunpowder Falls. He replied, "Gunpowder Falls is not a waterfall but the actual name of the river. Falls is an archaic term that was used to describe a river or stream in the early days when the colony was settled." Other examples would include Jones Falls River and Gwynn's Falls River both located near Baltimore.

Flows

http://waterdata.gov/USA/UV USGS 01581920 Gunpowder Falls near Parkston, MD

Tackle

A 9-foot, 4-weight outfit is a good all-around choice. Long leaders with light tippets are your best bet.

Hub City

HUNT VALLEY

Population 20,776

ACCOMMODATIONS

Holiday Inn Express / 11200 York Valley Road /
877-859-5095

Courtyard by Marriott / 221 International Circle /
866-576-5620

Embassy Suites Hotel / 213 International Circle /
410-584-1400 / www.embassysuites.hilton.com/
HuntValley

RESTAURANTS

Hunt Valley Grill / Embassy Suites Hotel / 213
International Circle / 410-584-1400

Carrabba's Italian Grill / 130 Shawan Road /
410-785-9400

Boardwalk Burgers & Fries / 118BB Shawan Road /
410-329-9881

Barrett's Grill / 118 Shawan Road / 410-527-0999

FLY SHOPS/GUIDES

Knee Deep Fly Fishing, Micah Dammeyer, President &
Guide / 202-681-8765 / www.kneedeepff.com

Backwater Angler, Monkton / 410-357-9557 /
www.backwaterangler.com

Great Feathers Fly Shop, Sparks / 1-888-777-0838 /
www.greatfeathers.com

Trout & About Guide Service, Monkton / 410-472-0740 /
www.troutandabout.com

AIRPORTS

Baltimore-Washington International Airport / 7062
Friendship Road, Baltimore

MEDICAL

Greater Baltimore Medical Center, 9 Schilling Road /
410-771-9920 / www.gbmc.org/hunyvalley

FOR MORE INFORMATION

Hunt Valley Chamber of Commerce /
www.chamberofcommerce.com/huntvalley

WESTERN TAILWATERS

Go west, young man, go west – many East Coast anglers dream of going out west to the Rockies to fish some of the nation's best trout streams and possibly catch the fish of a lifetime. There is no question the West has some world-class streams – spring creeks, freestone, and tailwater rivers. I have fished the West about a dozen times and have treasured my time on the Big Horn, Yellowstone, Madison, Green, Henry's Fork, and the Snake Rivers. But I haven't enjoyed airport delays, lost gear, travel time, and the escalating costs of travel and lodging. All East Coast anglers have "western-type" destination options that will give the West's best rivers a run for the money and at a fraction of the cost. Western Maryland, for example, offers beautiful wilderness mountain escapes, great hatches, riverside cabins, campgrounds, and wild trout; all less than four hours from the nation's capital and the major cities of Philadelphia, Baltimore, and Pittsburgh.

My first trip to western Maryland was quite an eye-opener. While I knew the region's tailwaters held good numbers of wild trout, I was amazed at the wilderness settings I discovered. The region has vast mountain ranges protected by state-owned forests, plenty of wild trout and for the most part, relatively little fishing pressure. My friend, Ed Jaworowski, joined me on my first western Maryland trip. We used the town of Oakland as our base camp. Oakland has lots of options for accommodations and meals in every price range and it is reasonably close to all three of western Maryland's tailwaters.

We fished the upper Youghiogheny below Deep Creek Lake and the Savage River in Savage River State Forest and, while they are blue ribbon trout streams in their own right, the best part was our float trip down the North Branch of the Potomac with guide, Harold Harsh, of Spring Creek Outfitters in Oakland. This tailwater is big. It flows through a very remote section of the East Coast forming part of the boundary of Maryland and West Virginia. During our 10-hour float trip we did not see a house or another boat and saw only one wading angler. We floated the tailwater section below Jennings Randolph Lake and, while the number and diversity of trout we caught was impressive, the highlight of the float for me was being introduced to a large wilderness river loaded with insects and trout.

When our trip ended, we thanked Harsh and told him we would be back, and we have been back several times. Here, nestled in the forested mountains which mark the Maryland-West Virginia boundary are three blue ribbon tailwaters: the North Branch of the Potomac, the Savage – which is the first major tributary to the North Branch in Bloomington – and less than a half hour north of Bloomington, is the Upper Youghiogheny below Deep Creek Lake.

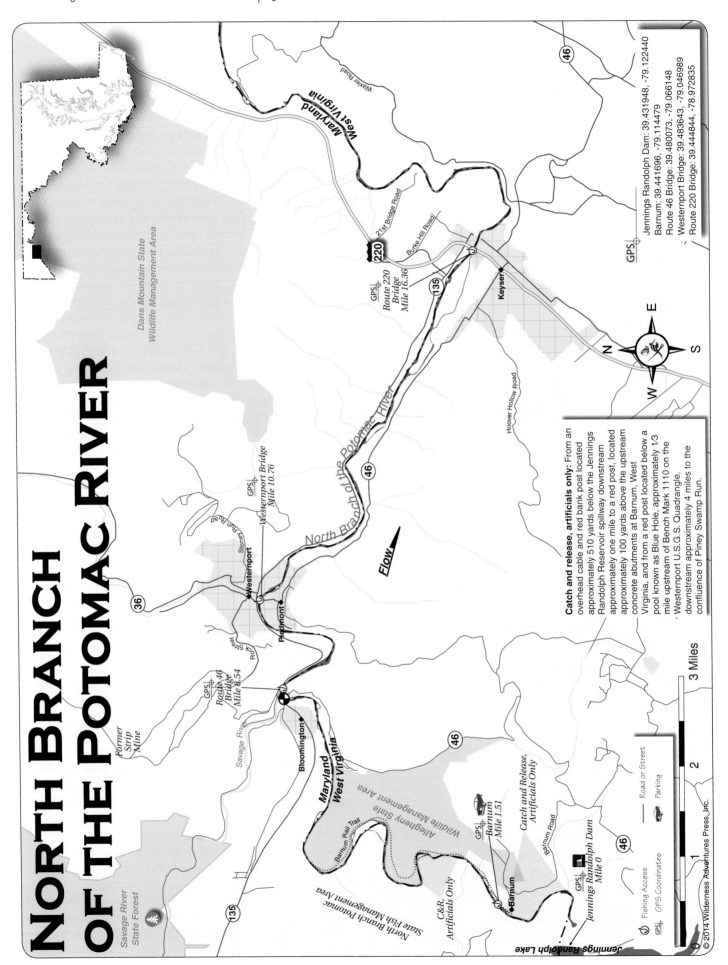

NORTH BRANCH OF THE POTOMAC RIVER

Savage River State Forest

Dans Mountain State Wildlife Management Area

Former Strip Mine

Maryland
West Virginia

Waxler Road

21st Bridge Road

Burke Hill Road

220
Route 220 Bridge
Mile 16.36

135

Keyser

Hoover Hollow Road

46

North Branch of the Potomac River

Flow

Westernport Bridge
Mile 10.76

Stoney Run Road

36

Westernport

Rock Street

Piedmont

Route 46 Bridge
Mile 8.54

Savage River

Bloomington

Maryland
West Virginia

Allegheny State
Wildlife Management Area

Barnum Rail Trail

Barnum
Mile 1.51

Catch and Release,
Artificials Only

Barnum Road

46

46

C&R,
Artificials Only

Barnum

135

North Branch Potomac
State Fish Management Area

Jennings Randolph Dam
Mile 0

Jennings Randolph Lake

Catch and release, artificials only: From an overhead cable and red bank post located approximately 510 yards below the Jennings Randolph Reservoir spillway downstream approximately one mile to a red post, located approximately 100 yards above the upstream concrete abutments at Barnum, West Virginia, and from a red post located below a pool known as Blue Hole, approximately 1/3 mile upstream of Bench Mark 1110 on the Westernport U.S.G.S. Quadrangle, downstream approximately 4 miles to the confluence of Piney Swamp Run.

N E S W

⌀ Fishing Access
GPS⌀ GPS Coordinates
— Road or Street
🅿 Parking

0   1   2   3 Miles

© 2014 Wilderness Adventures Press, Inc.

Jennings Randolph Dam: 39.431948, -79.122440
Barnum: 39.441696, -79.114479
Route 46 Bridge: 39.480073, -79.066148
Westernport Bridge: 39.483643, -79.046989
Route 220 Bridge: 39.444844, -78.972835

GPS⌀

NORTH BRANCH OF THE POTOMAC RIVER (FIVE STARS)

For nearly 100 years the North Branch of the Potomac was a dead, lifeless river – no fish, no insects, and no aquatic vegetation. The cause was acid mine drainage from coal mining operations. The turnaround on the river started with the 1970 Surface Mining Act, which required mining companies to eliminate acid runoff. The current owner of most of western Maryland's coal mines is the Mettiki Coal Company, which thankfully is an environmentally responsible corporate citizen that has pretty much eliminated acid runoff into the North Branch.

When Jennings Randolph Lake was built in 1982, it mitigated the acid water that flowed into it from the North Branch, and the outflow of the lake had an improved pH of 6.0. The state has also installed five limestone dosers upstream of the reservoir. These devices, developed in Sweden to combat acidity in some Swedish salmon rivers, look like small silos, and they automatically dump pre-determined amounts of limestone into the river. The water, which previously had a pH level of less than 4 (almost like vinegar) now runs over 7, slightly alkaline, and very conducive to aquatic life. The dam, owned and managed by the Army Corp of Engineers (ACE), has a release tower which allows for withdrawals of water from varying depths and temperatures. With an improved pH in the river, good water quality, and coldwater releases, the insect and trout life are really bouncing back in the North Branch.

The North Branch's two Trophy Trout sections offer spectacular scenery and the opportunity to catch five species of trout, which are either stream-bred or grew from fingerling stockings in the river. The North Branch is stocked annually with brown, cutthroat, and golden rainbows in legal sizes in the put-and-take sections. They no longer stock rainbows due to concerns over whirling disease, but there is a good population of wild rainbows. (Whirling disease is caused by a parasite which affects fingerling and fry trout and it has a mortality rate of up to 90 percent of infected populations.) In the upper-catch-and-release section just below Jennings Randolph Lake, the regional biologist for the Maryland Department of Natural Resources reports that they only stock fingerling trout – mostly browns – and from time to time, fingerling cutthroat trout which were last stocked in 2011. All trout in the lower catch-and-release are wild, except when some of the stocked adult trout from the put-and-take section migrate down into the no-kill section.

Brook trout are not stocked but reproduce naturally in the river. Harold Harsh told us that the river has yielded some very big fish. Wanting to know how big, I went on the Internet and found that the state record trout, a brown of 18 pounds, 3 ounces was taken out of the North Branch below Jennings Randolph Lake in the tiny hamlet of Barnum, West

Guide Harold Harsh with a nice brown trout on the North Branch of the Potomac.

Virginia. The lucky angler, Gary Kuhn, landed his trophy on August 3, 2001; besting the old brown trout record of 13 pounds, 7 ounces landed by Edward Martin on March 1, 2001, also on the North Branch at Barnum. Edward's father David Martin holds the current state record for cutthroat trout with a 7-pound, 9-ounce fish taken on May 20, 2000 on – where else? – the North Branch at Barnum. The state record brook trout of 6 pounds, 1 ounce was also landed in the North Branch tailwater below Randolph Dam. Are you noticing a trend here? While the North Branch does not hold the state record for rainbows (that belongs to the Savage River Reservoir, a 14-pound, 3-ounce fish), several 12-pound rainbows have been caught in the North Branch.

The river below the dam is up to 200 feet wide and has a challenging mixture of deep pools and boulder-strewn riffles and runs. Wading can be difficult depending on flows – a float trip is a good option for a first-time trip on the river. The North Branch source is a spring in Fairfax Stone, West Virginia. The river flows some 27 miles to Jennings Randolph Lake. Below the lake are over 20 miles of quality trout tailwater – one of the best stretches in the East. Most fly anglers concentrate on the eight-mile stretch from Barnum down to the confluence with the Savage River.

Bob Bachman, the retired Maryland Director of Fisheries and the person largely responsible for the restoration of the Gunpowder River, told me, "The North Branch has enormous potential; with good management it could well rival the fabled Madison in Montana." If the fishery continues to improve, we may soon be calling the Madison the North Branch of the West. Maryland and West Virginia have reciprocal agreements, so you can fish the North Branch with a license from either state. The river has whitewater releases on several weekends in spring, so check the schedule before you head to the river (call 301-962-7687 for the release schedule). Fishing is best with releases between 200 and 400 cubic feet per second.

There are two catch-and-release, artificial-lures-only sections below the dam. The first starts just above the parking area on Barnum Road and runs about one mile upstream. The second section begins at the Blue Hole about one mile downstream off Barnum Road. The approximately one-mile section between the two catch-and-release sections is regulated as open water, with no tackle restrictions and a five fish per day limit. The open water is stocked with adult trout including golden rainbows, some of which move into the catch-and-release sections of the river. Trails and abandoned railroad tracks parallel the river on the West Virginia side. Access at Barnum is at the ACE launch site and the put-in at the Blue Hole.

There are about 21 miles of water above the lake. The upper North Branch affords anglers an opportunity to fish for trout in a truly wild setting. Although some areas can be easily reached from roadways, much of the upper river is very remote and scenic and can only be reached by hiking in. For those anglers willing to walk, the reward is the opportunity to fish in solitude. The trout will be there, because the Maryland Department of Natural Resources' Fisheries Service stocks the remote areas from a tank truck that rides the railways (courtesy of the CSX Company through a cooperative agreement). About 14 miles are stocked under put-and-take regulations and about seven miles within the Potomac State Forest are managed under delayed-harvest regulations. Divided as it is by the Jennings Randolph Lake, the river differs greatly in character. Above the lake can best be described as wild and wooly. It's big, fast, and deep with steep, densely wooded hillsides. On the Maryland side of the river, movement upstream or down is hampered by a lack of trails and thick stands of mountain laurel. Best access is gained by crossing to the West Virginia side, where a railroad track parallels the river. You can walk upstream for eight miles before encountering another road. Those willing to walk can have large stretches of the river completely to themselves.

DIRECTIONS/ACCESS

From Oak-Mar Motel in Oakland, take Route 219 south 0.5 miles to Maryland Route 135 east, past the first blinker light. Turn right at the second blinker light and cross the bridge over the Savage River and make a right at the "T" intersection in Bloomington. Then take the next right onto West Virginia Route 46 which parallels the river (although it is out of sight) for seven miles to Jennings Randolph Lake. Before you reach the lake make a right turn onto Barnum Road, which takes you to the river at the put-and-take section, which is between the two catch-and-release sections.

STREAM FACTS

Regulations

There are two catch-and-release artificial-lures-only sections. The one-mile section between the catch-and-release sections is regulated as open water, with no tackle restrictions and a five fish per-day limit.

Fish

The trout in the special regulations sections are either stream-bred or grew from fingerling stockings. The open water is stocked with adult trout including browns, cutthroat, and golden rainbows. Fish over 10 pounds are caught every season on the North Branch. As noted, the current state record brown, cutthroat, and brook trout all came from the North Branch around Barnum, and it is one of the few places in the East where you can catch a "trout grand slam" in one day (brown, brook, rainbow, golden rainbow, and cutthroat trout).

River Characteristics

The river below the dam is up to 200 feet wide, and has a challenging mixture of deep pools and boulder-strewn riffles and runs.

What the Experts Say

Bob Bachman, the retired Maryland director of fisheries and the person largely responsible for the restoration of the Gunpowder River, told me, "The North Branch has enormous potential; with good management it could well rival the fabled Madison in Montana."

Flows

http://waterdata.gov/USA/UV USGS 01595800 North Branch Potomac River at Barnum

Tackle

I like a 9-foot rod matched with a 5-weight floating line and a reel with plenty of backing. On a float trip I'll add a 9-foot, 6-weight outfit, with a sink tip line for chucking streamers – again with plenty of backing.

Ready for a float trip on the North Branch.

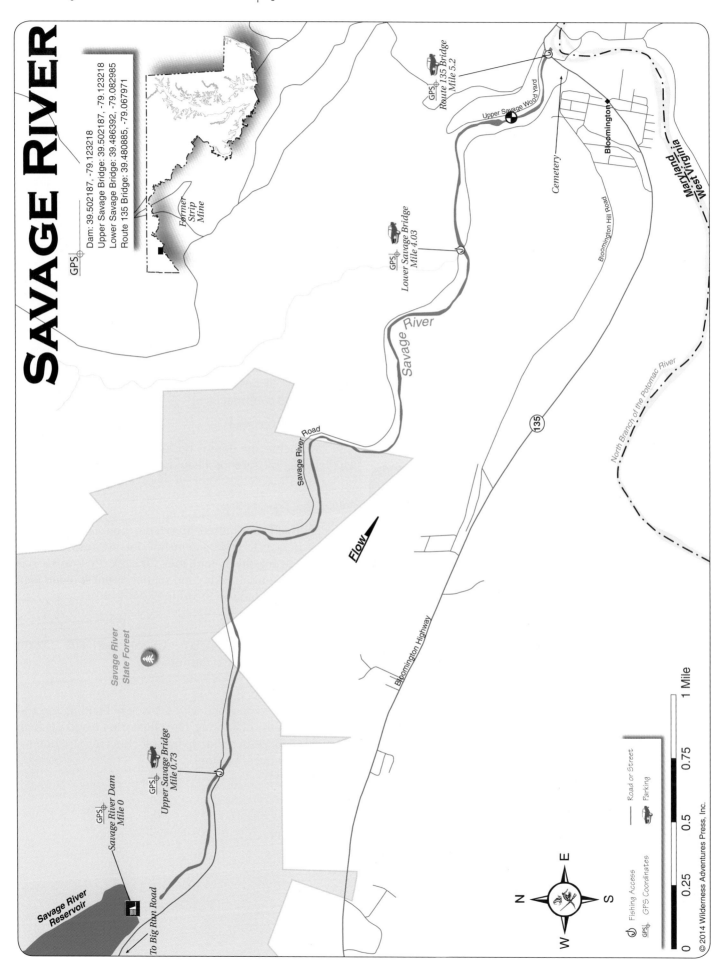

SAVAGE RIVER

GPS
Dam: 39.502187, -79.123218
Upper Savage Bridge: 39.502187, -79.123218
Lower Savage Bridge: 39.486392, -79.082985
Route 135 Bridge: 39.480885, -79.067971

Former Strip Mine

Route 135 Bridge
Mile 5.2

Upper Savage Wood Yard

Bloomington

Cemetery

Bloomington Hill Road

Maryland
West Virginia

Lower Savage Bridge
Mile 4.03

Savage River

North Branch of the Potomac River

135

Savage River Road

Flow

Savage River State Forest

Bloomington Highway

Savage River Dam
Mile 0

Upper Savage Bridge
Mile 0.73

Savage River Reservoir

To Big Run Road

N E S W

Fishing Access
GPS Coordinates

Road or Street
Parking

0   0.25   0.5   0.75   1 Mile

© 2014 Wilderness Adventures Press, Inc.

SAVAGE RIVER (FIVE STARS)

The Savage River tailwater starts at the outflow of the Savage River Reservoir and runs downstream to the confluence with the North Branch of the Potomac River in Bloomington, Maryland. It has a steep gradient with cabin-size boulders and strong runs and riffles. It flows through the 57,000-acre Savage River State Forest. The hillsides along the Savage are heavily forested with hardwoods and hemlock along with thick stands of rhododendron and mountain laurel. It has the look and feel of a rugged mountain freestone stream.

The Savage River Reservoir Dam was constructed in 1953 for flood control, and the water release from the bottom of thc dam is consistent at around 50-degrees, providing good year-round fishing except when winter snow cover prevents access. The river is only 50 to 60 feet wide with lots of pocket water and some deep pools. The river seems to be paved with greased, odd-sized rocks, and the wading ranges from difficult to treacherous. Cleated boots and a wading staff are a must. Some outdoor writers credit the river's name of "Savage" to its raging waters during times of high releases and, while that sounds reasonable, the river was actually named for an 18th century surveyor, John Savage. Flows of around 100cfs are good for fishing but tough for wading: 175cfs and up is too dangerous to wade and, as it drops below 75cfs, fishing becomes more difficult and you need to lengthen your leaders and lighten your tippets.

While much of the water is composed of riffles and runs, there are numerous deep pools with a few having flows slow enough to give the trout plenty of time to view your offering. The two most famous of these are the Ph. D pool at the upper bridge on Savage River Road and the 7x pool above the Garrett suspension foot bridge. As their names might imply, these pools and many others on the river will test your angling skills. In 1982, Maryland's DNR discovered natural reproduction of brook trout on the river below the dam. All stocking stopped in 1990, and now the stream is loaded with colorful native brook and stream-bred brown trout, plus a few rainbow and cutthroat trout which swim up from the North Branch of the Potomac.

The Savage River has two Trophy Trout sections which are contiguous. The first starts at the reservoir and runs downstream 1.25 miles to the Allegany Bridge. It is managed as fly-fishing-only. The section from the Allegany Bridge downstream for 2.75 miles to the junction with the North Branch of the Potomac is regulated as artificial-lures-only. Both sections allow two fish per day, brookies must be 12 inches and browns 18 inches to harvest, but most anglers release all fish.

The Army Corps of Engineers maintains the Savage River Dam for flood control and recreation. It is a destination for whitewater rafters on the infrequent occasion (usually only a few weekends a year) when sufficient water is released from the dam. Flows can vary depending on the release from the dam, so it's advisable to check the website or call (410-962-7687) to check the flow schedule before your trip.

The river's structure and its hatches will remind you of a typical eastern mountain freestone stream. The Savage has some of the best hatches in Maryland, both in terms of diversity and abundance. The river has all the major eastern hatches. Spring brings good hatches of the "early grays," quill Gordons, blue quills, and Hendricksons. In May and June you can expect March browns, gray fox (I know for my entomologist friends, they don't exist anymore but fish still love a Gray Fox dry fly) sulphurs, green drakes, and a great slate drake hatch. Summer fishing can be good with terrestrials, and fall fishing can be excellent with good *Baetis* hatches in sizes 18 to 22.

A native brook trout from the Savage River. Photo by Harold Harsh.

Ed Jaworowski with a wild brown trout taken in the Savage River's Ph. D Pool.

DIRECTIONS/ACCESS

From Interstate 68, take Exit 22 and turn left onto Chestnut Ridge Road. At the stop sign, turn left onto New Germany Road. After five miles turn left onto Big Run Road. At the end of the Big Run Road, turn right onto Savage River Road at the north end of the reservoir and go around to the tailwater.

I usually stay at the Oak-Mar Motel in Oakland; it's clean, comfortable, and reasonably priced. There are lots of meal options in town for any budget. From Oakland, it is about 21 miles to the junction pool of the Savage and North Branch Rivers. From Oakland, take Route 219 south 0.5 miles to Route 135 East. Go past the first blinker light, turn right at the second blinker light, and take it to Savage River Road into Bloomington. About four miles before you reach the Savage River, Route 135 East becomes a long, steep downhill. The sign for Savage River Road is hard to see, so if you cross a bridge and come to a "T" in the road, turn around and go back across the bridge (which is over the Savage River) and take the first right at the cemetery. There is good access, as Savage River Road runs along most of the stream and there are several places for anglers to pull off and park. There are also parking areas at the two suspension bridges and the two road bridges.

STREAM FACTS

Seasons/Regulations

The Savage River Trophy Trout area has two sections which are contiguous. The first is from the reservoir downstream 1.25 miles to the Allegany Bridge. It is managed as fly-fishing-only. From the Allegany Bridge downstream 2.75 miles to the North Branch of the Potomac is regulated as artificial-lures-only. Both sections allow two fish per day. Brookies must be 12 inches and browns 18 inches to harvest, but most anglers release all fish. Fish of these sizes are not uncommon.

Fish

All stocking stopped in 1990, and now the stream is loaded with some of the most colorful native brook and stream-bred brown trout you will find anywhere.

River Characteristics

The river is only 50 to 60 feet wide with lots of pocket water and some deep pools. Most sections of the river seem to be paved with greased, odd-sized rocks. Wading ranges from difficult to treacherous. Cleated boots and a wading staff are a must.

What is in a Name?

Some outdoor writers credit the river's name of "Savage" to its raging waters during times of high releases, and while that sounds reasonable, the river was actually named for an 18th century surveyor, John Savage.

River Flows

http://waterdata.gov/USA/UV USGS web 01597500 Savage River near Bloomington

Tackle

I like a 9-foot, 4-weight rod with a floating line.

The aforementioned Ph. D Pool. Photo by Ed Jaworowski.

YOUGHIOGHENY RIVER

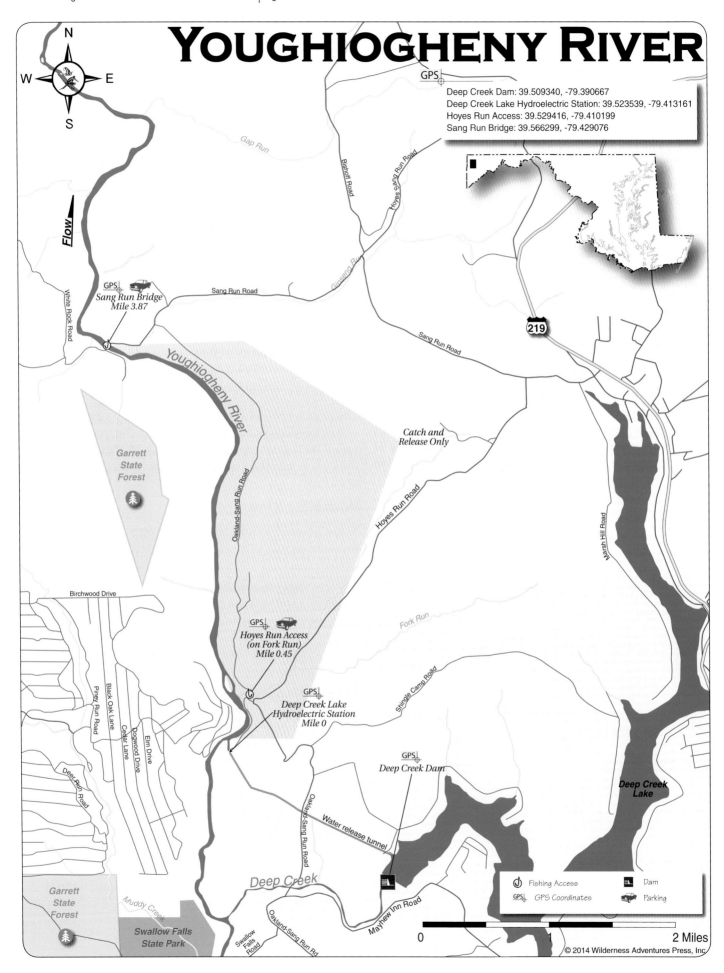

Deep Creek Dam: 39.509340, -79.390667
Deep Creek Lake Hydroelectric Station: 39.523539, -79.413161
Hoyes Run Access: 39.529416, -79.410199
Sang Run Bridge: 39.566299, -79.429076

Flow

Gap Run

Bishoff Road

Hoyes-Sang Run Road

Ginseng Run

Sang Run Road

219

Sang Run Road

White Rock Road

GPS
Sang Run Bridge
Mile 3.87

Youghiogheny River

Oakland-Sang Run Road

Garrett
State
Forest

Catch and
Release Only

Hoyes Run Road

Marsh Hill Road

Birchwood Drive

Fork Run

Piney Run Road

Black Oak Lane

Dogwood Drive

Cedar Lane

Elm Drive

GPS
Hoyes Run Access
(on Fork Run)
Mile 0.45

Shingle Camp Road

Deer Run Road

GPS
Deep Creek Lake
Hydroelectric Station
Mile 0

GPS
Deep Creek Dam

Deep Creek
Lake

Oakland-Sang Run Road

Water release tunnel

Deep Creek

Garrett
State
Forest

Muddy Creek

Swallow Falls
State Park

Swallow Falls Road

Oakland-Sang Run Rd

Mayhew Inn Road

Fishing Access

Dam

GPS   GPS Coordinates

Parking

0   1   2 Miles

YOUGHIOGHENY RIVER (FOUR STARS)

The Youghiogheny (pronounced "yock-a-gainey") River's four-mile catch-and-release, artificials-only section lies entirely within the Youghiogheny Wild and Scenic River Corridor. It is owned by the State of Maryland and managed by the Maryland Department of Natural Resources. The catch-and-release section runs from the Deep Creek Lake power plant downstream to the Sang Run Bridge. This section of the Youghiogheny in western Maryland is referred to as the Upper Yough.

The river flows north into Pennsylvania. There are two popular sections in Pennsylvania, the first of which is the tailwater section below the Youghiogheny Reservoir known as the Middle Yough section. It supports an excellent population of trout. The section farther down from the reservoir, below the town of Ohiopyle, is referred to as the Lower Yough, and it is an excellent smallmouth bass fishery.

In Maryland, the coldwater releases from the Deep Creek Lake hydroelectric station provide quality trout water and some great dry fly water for the six miles downstream of the dam.

While the Yough has most of the East's major mayfly hatches, the green drake hatch is the most popular. Anglers start targeting it around Memorial Day into the first two weeks of June. While the drakes get most of the publicity on the Yough, caddis – both dry and emergers – are the bread and butter flies of Yough regulars. If you're planning a trip, knowing the release schedule is critical to your success and safety. Releases are usually in the morning, but that can vary. Most days, the release only lasts a few hours. Depending on the release rate, it takes about two hours for the flow to reach the lower section down by Sang Run Road. So if the release starts at 10:00am, you can fish the lower section in the morning, take a lunch break, and possibly fish the upper section after the flows subside in the afternoon.

As I mentioned in the previous chapter, Native Americans named the river "Youghiogheny", which in our language translates to "a river that flows in a contrary direction" because,

as strange as it seems, the river flows from south to north. After the river flows out of Deep Creek, it flows north into Youghiogheny Lake on the Maryland/Pennsylvania border. The middle section of the river starts with the release from the Youghiogheny Lake dam just above the town of Confluence, Pennsylvania and runs downstream about 11 miles to Ohiopyle State Park. This section is covered in the Pennsylvania chapter.

Coldwater releases from the bottom layer of Deep Creek Lake and minimum flow maintenance by the power plant maintain coldwater habitat for trout during the critical summertime period. Daily discharges vary from under 100cfs to over 800cfs, causing river flow to rise abruptly during the releases. PennElec, which owns and manages the power plant, has an agreement with the state to provide minimum summer flows so that the trout can survive. While these flows do protect the trout, in the heat of summer the lower portions of the catch-and-release water can get into the 70s, and most trout move farther upstream toward the dam. This is where you should concentrate your summer fishing. The Yough is a relatively large river, averaging about 150 feet in width. The catch-and-release stretch of the river has a low to moderate gradient, shallow riffles, long runs, and some deep pools. The streambed consists of cobble, boulders, and some limestone bedrock.

The fishery is supported by annual stockings of fingerling brown and rainbow trout. The rainbows that are

A dandy tiger trout from the upper Youghiogheny River. Photo by Harold Harsh.

stocked are a warmwater strain, which enables them to tolerate higher temperatures than most other trout. These rainbows grow very well on the abundant aquatic insects found in the river. When the rainbows reach their adult stage, they have developed deep, heavy bodies and are very silvery in color. Brown trout grow to trophy size in the Yough, with some fish greater than 5 pounds caught every year. Currently, Maryland estimates that there are 1,300 adult trout per mile in the catch-and-release section of the Yough, of which they estimate over 150 trout per mile are greater than 12 inches long.

DIRECTIONS/ACCESS

From I-68, take Exit 14A and Route 219 South. Continue about 11 miles and turn right onto Sang Run Road. Proceed 0.3 miles and turn left onto Hoyes Run Road. Continue about 3 miles to the stop sign. Turn right onto Oakland-Sang Run Road and proceed 0.1 miles to the parking area on the left side of the road just across a small bridge. A sign illustrates the access trail along the river. To access the lower portion of the catch-and-release area at Sang Run, continue on Oakland-Sang Run Road for about 3.5 miles to the stop sign. Turn left onto Sang Run Road and proceed 0.1 miles to the parking area on the left.

STREAM FACTS

Seasons/Regulations

There is a four-mile catch-and-release, artificials-only section which runs from Deep Creek Lake power plant downstream to Sang Run Road and is open to fishing year-round.

Fish

The river is float-stocked every fall with a total of 20,000 fingerling trout – 10,000 browns and 10,000 rainbows.

River Characteristics

This catch-and-release stretch of the river has a low-to-moderate gradient, shallow riffles, long runs, and some deep pools.

What's in a Name?

As I mentioned in the previous chapter, Native Americans named the river "Youghiogheny", which in our language translates to "a river that flows in a contrary direction" because, as strange as it seems, the river flows from south to north.

River Flows

The state has an agreement with PennElec, which owns and manages the power plant, to maintain conservation flows in the summer months. For flow schedules, call 814-533-8911 or visit the website: http://waterdata.gov/USA/UV USGS 03076500 Youghiogheny at Friendsville, Maryland

Tackle

A 9-foot, 4-weight is a good all-around rod for this river.

WESTERN MARYLAND TAILWATERS MAJOR HATCHES

Common Name *Scientific Name*	Hatch Period	Fly Patterns	Hook Sizes
Early Black Stonefly *Taeniopteryx nivalis*	March – early April	Black Elk Hair Caddis Dry	16-18
Early Brown Stonefly *Strophopteryx fasciata*	March – early April	Brown Bi-Visible Dry Stimulator Dry	14-16 14-16
Quill Gordon *Epeorus pleuralis*	Mid-April – Early May	Quill Gordon Dry Hare's Ear Wet	14 14
Hendrickson/Red Quill *Ephemerella subvaria*	April 10 – May 5	Hendrickson Dry Red Quill Dry	14 14
Tan Caddis *Hydropsyche spp.*	May – August	Elk Hair Caddis Dry Leonard Wright Caddis Dry	14-16 14-16
*March Brown *Maccaffertium vicarium* (formerly *Stenonema vicarium*)	Mid-May – early June	March Brown Dry Gray Fox Dry March Brown Wet	12 12-14 12
Pale Evening Dun Ephemerella invaria	Early May – mid-June	Pale Evening Dun Dry Sulphur Spinner	14-16 14-16
Light Cahill *Stenacron interpunctatum* (formerly *Stenonema canadense*) (formerly *Stenonema interpunctatum*)	Mid-May – mid-June	Light Cahill Dry Light Cahill Wet	12 12
Sulphur *Ephemerella dorothea*	Mid-May – mid-June	Pale Evening Dun Dry Pale Evening Dun Spinner	16-18 16-18
Slate Drake *Isonychia bicolor* *Isonychia sadleri & harperi*	Late May – June Mid-Sept. – mid-Oct.	Slate Drake Dry Adams Dry Gray Wulff Leadwing Coachman Wet	10-12 10-12 10-12 10-12
Midges	February – November	Griffith's Gnat Cream Midge Dry	18-22 18-24
Flying Ants	September – October	Flying Ant Dry	16-20
Ants	May – October	Parachute Ant Dry Flying Ant Dry Black Wire Ant Wet	16- 20 16-20 16-20
Beetles	May – October	Crowe Beetle	12
Inchworms	May – October	Deer Hair Dry	12

* *Stenonema fuscum* (Gray Fox) is now considered the same species as *Maccaffertium vicarium,* formerly *Stenonema vicaruim* (March Brown)

Hub City

OAKLAND

Population 1,925

ACCOMMODATIONS

Oak-Mar Motel and Restaurant, 208 North Third Street / 301-334-3965

Streams & Dreams B & B, 8214 Oakland-Sang Run Road / 301-387-6881 / www.streams-and-dreams.net

Garrett Inn, 17848 Garrett Highway / 301-387-6696 / www.thegarrettinn.com

Savage River Outfitters rents cabins right on the river / 703-517-1040 / Swanton / www.savageriveroutfitters.com

CAMPGROUNDS AND RV PARKS

Deep Creek State Park has cabins and campsites / 888-432-2267 / www.reservations.dnr.state.md.us

Double G RV Park, 76 Double G Drive, McHenry / 301-387-5481 www.doublegrvpark.com / Open May 1 – October 31

RESTAURANTS

Cornish Manor Restaurant, 830 Memorial Drive / 301-334-6499

Brenda's Pizzeria, 2311 Garrett Highway / 301-387-1007

Black Bear Tavern & Restaurant, 99 Fort Drive, McHenry / 301-387-6800

FLY SHOPS, GUIDES, AND SPORTING GOODS

Savage River Outfitters / 703-517-1040 / Swanton / www.savageriveroutfitters.com

Spring Creek Outfitters, 86 Big Frog Lane / Harold Harsh / (H) 301-387-6587, (C)301-616-8123 / harold@springcreekoutfitter.com

Beaver Creek Fly Shop / Hagerstown / 301-393-9090 www.beavercreekflyshop.com

North Branch Angler, 6135 Oakland Sang Run Road 301-387-5314

AIRPORTS

Baltimore-Washington International Airport, 7062 Friendship Road, Baltimore

MEDICAL

Mountain Laurel Medical Center, 1027 Memorial Drive / 301-533-3330

FOR MORE INFORMATION

Garrett County Chamber of Commerce, 15 Visitors Center Drive, McHenry / www.garrett.chambermaster.com

Ed Jaworowski at the Lefty Kreh Fly Fishing Trail on Big Gunpowder Falls River.

Main Image: Beautiful fall day on Big Gunpowder Falls River.
Inset: Beautiful wild brown on Big Gunpowder Falls River. Photos courtesy of Micah Dammeyer, President of Knee Deep Fly Fishing.

Teo Whitlock of Altamont Anglers, holding the author's wild brown trout taken on a float trip on Tennessee's Watauga River. Photo courtesy Beau Beasley.

Air travel has always been problematic for me, what with flight delays and cancelations, missed connections, and lost bags. So as retirement approached, I decided I would do more driving than flying to world-class trout fishing destinations, since time away from work would no longer be an issue. I decided to write an East Coast trout guide book, *The 100 Best Trout Streams from Maine to Georgia*. I began doing research and came up with about 175 potential streams and rivers to include.

One of the areas I really wanted to explore was the Great Smoky Mountains National Park (GSMNP) in eastern Tennessee and western North Carolina. So my fishing partner, Joe Darcy, and I rented two cabins in Great Smoky Mountains National Park, one in Tennessee and one in North Carolina, so that we could absorb as much of the park as possible. Prior to leaving on the trip I got a call from Chuck Johnson, owner of Wilderness Adventure Press,

which had recently published my *Flyfisher's Guide to the Big Apple*. Chuck asked if I was working on another book, and I told him that I had begun doing the research for an East Coast trout guide covering the best waters from Maine to Georgia. Johnson asked me if it was going to include many tailwaters, and I told him that, yes, I was planning to explore about 70 tailwaters to potentially include in the book. He then told me that he was looking for an author to write an eastern trophy tailwater trout guide and asked if I would be interested. I of course jumped at the opportunity – nothing warms an outdoor writer's heart more than having a book contract before you start spending time and money doing research for the book.

Our trip to the GSMNP had already been planned and paid for before Johnson's call. We had done a great deal of research and had a list of about 15 streams and rivers we planned to fish. As it turned out, there were 11 freestone waters and only four tailwaters on our itinerary. We decided

to stay with the original plan and make future trips to target just tailwaters. It was Darcy's and my first trip to the park, and it lived up to everything we had heard about it. Every angler should visit the park, as much for its majestic mountains as the fishing. The park is home to the two tallest mountains in the East. Mt. Mitchell in North Carolina is 6,684 feet, making it the tallest in the East, and Clingmans Dome in Tennessee is a close second at 6,643 feet. If you ask the average person what the tallest mountain in the East is, they will likely tell you Mt. Washington (6,288 feet) in New Hampshire or Mt. Katahdin (5,267 feet) in Maine.

The Smoky Mountain Park's streams and rivers are teeming with wild trout – they no longer stock in the park, everything is wild. The streams were teeming with trout; browns were at the lower elevations and, as we moved upstream, rainbows started to dominate. Finally, near the headwaters, beautiful southern Appalachian native brook trout took over. The park has some of the most beautiful scenery and streams in the world. You could fish the park for a lifetime and never fish the same water twice.

But it was in the nearby tailwaters that we found our trophy trout. On this trip we fished the Hiwassee and the Clinch Rivers in Tennessee, and the Nantahala and Tuckasegee Rivers in North Carolina. They treated us well, no real trophies but lots of good-sized brown, rainbow, and brook trout, and it would not be long before we were back to fish the other trophy tailwaters of the Southeast.

Southern tailwaters really began to develop in the 1930s when, in order to meet the ever-expanding power requirements of the rural communities of the South, the Tennessee Valley Authority and the U.S. Army Corp of Engineers began to construct dams, mostly for electric power generation, but also for flood control and water supply, and they were good projects for job creation in a post-Great Depression economy.

VIRGINIA

VIRGINIA FACTS

Area: 42,774 square miles, 35th biggest in USA
Population: 8,096,604
State Fish: Brook trout

TROUT FISHING LICENSE

www.dgif.virginia.gov
Resident annual fee: $23.00 plus annual Stocked Trout Waters Fee of $23.00*
Non-resident annual fee: $47.00 plus annual Stocked Trout Waters Fee of $47.00*
Non-resident five-day fee: $21.00 plus Stocked Trout Waters Fee of $47.00*
*Only needed to fish designated stocked waters.

STATE RECORDS

Brook trout, 5 pounds, 10 ounces by Greg Orndorff / October 22, 1987 / Big Stony Creek
Brown trout, 18 pounds, 11 ounces by Bill Nease / 1979 / Smith River
Rainbow trout, 14 pounds, 7 ounces by Michael Lowe / June 28, 1993 / Greer's Pond

The Old Dominion state has almost 3,000 miles of trout streams, the vast majority of which contain naturally reproducing wild trout. Its high-elevation freestone streams in the Blue Ridge Mountains are noted for having some of the most productive native brook trout waters south of New England. While Virginia technically has four tailwater rivers, only two – the Jackson and the Smith – have reservoirs deep enough to provide water cold enough to sustain trout year round.

The author floating the Jackson River, while guide Blaine Chocklett from New Angle Fishing Company looks on . Photo courtesy Beau Beasley.

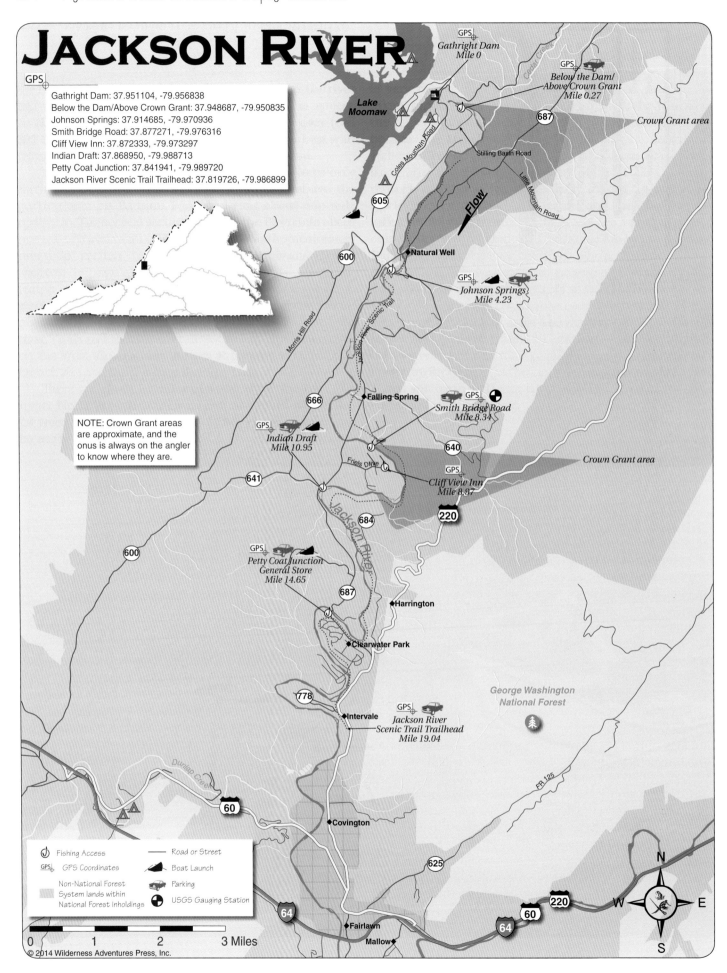

JACKSON RIVER

Gathright Dam: 37.951104, -79.956838
Below the Dam/Above Crown Grant: 37.948687, -79.950835
Johnson Springs: 37.914685, -79.970936
Smith Bridge Road: 37.877271, -79.976316
Cliff View Inn: 37.872333, -79.973297
Indian Draft: 37.868950, -79.988713
Petty Coat Junction: 37.841941, -79.989720
Jackson River Scenic Trail Trailhead: 37.819726, -79.986899

NOTE: Crown Grant areas are approximate, and the onus is always on the angler to know where they are.

Gathright Dam
Mile 0

Below the Dam/
Above Crown Grant
Mile 0.27

Crown Grant area

Lake Moomaw

Stilling Basin Road

Flow

Natural Well

Johnson Springs
Mile 4.23

Falling Spring

Smith Bridge Road
Mile 8.34

Indian Draft
Mile 10.95

Friels Drive

Cliff View Inn
Mile 8.97

Crown Grant area

Petty Coat Junction
General Store
Mile 14.65

Harrington

Clearwater Park

Intervale

Jackson River
Scenic Trail Trailhead
Mile 19.04

George Washington
National Forest

Covington

Fairlawn

Mallow

Fishing Access
GPS Coordinates
Non-National Forest
System lands within
National Forest inholdings

Road or Street
Boat Launch
Parking
USGS Gauging Station

0   1   2   3 Miles

© 2014 Wilderness Adventures Press, Inc.

JACKSON RIVER (FOUR STARS)

The Jackson River, which sits in the heart of the Allegheny Mountains of western Virginia, is one of the newest tailwater fisheries in the East and certainly one of the most contentious. Controversy has surrounded the Jackson from the time Congress approved construction of the Gathright Dam as part of the Flood Control Act of 1946. And today it represents one of the longest-running trout fishing controversies in the country. If the fishery wasn't so phenomenal, and if my good friend (and award-winning outdoor writer) Beau Beasley had not brought some clarity to the landowner/angler controversy with his great articles and talk, "Who Owns a River", I would not have considered including the Jackson in this book. But this is a river every angler should have the opportunity to fish, and the decisions on access to the river may have far-reaching consequences.

When the Army Corps of Engineers (ACE) received congressional approval to build a dam on the Jackson in 1946, they did not authorize funding for the venture. In fact, funding for the building of the dam was not approved until the 1960s. Meanwhile in the mid-1950s, the state of Virginia purchased over 18,000 acres of land along the Jackson and created the Gathright Wildlife Management Area. Many of the state's sportsmen's groups opposed the construction of the dam – they didn't want to lose a lot of the wildlife management area's land to the reservoir. In the end, the ACE won approval to go forward with the construction of the dam. As part of the mitigation agreement, the Corps installed a 260-foot mixing tower which has the ability to create proper oxygen and temperature levels for a world-class tailwater fishery below the dam.

Even before the dam was completed, downriver landowners worked to block the stocking of trout and the use of the river by the public. Based on the historical commercial use of the river, in 1978 the Corps of Engineers declared the Jackson River "navigable," thereby allowing the public to float the river. The landowners appealed the Corps' decision, which was upheld in 1984. Meanwhile the dam construction was completed, and by April of 1982 the lake was filled. Because of all the controversy surrounding access to the river, the Virginia Department of Inland Fisheries (VDGIF) did not stock the river until 1989, but stock it they did. In the first three seasons, the VDGIF released a total of over 300,000 adult brown and rainbow trout.

Despite the fact that the state was using public funds for stocking the Jackson, in 1991 landowners sued Chuck Kraft, Jr., a guide, and his clients for floating and fishing through their properties based on the colonial "Crown Grants" granting them ownership of the bottom of the river. The landowners contend that they have the rights to the riverbanks, the river bottom, and get this – the fish! While only a handful of landowners possess Crown Grants, many landowners post their properties and claim the exclusive right to "fishing and fowling".

Under United States law, most waterways are open to the public even if they run through private lands, so long as they have been used for commerce or navigation. But the landowners who filed suit against Kraft say they have exclusive rights over fishing and hunting based on the terms under which English kings granted the land to the original property holders in the mid-1700s. Crown Grants,

Tom Gilmore landing a rainbow trout on the Jackson River. Photo courtesy Beau Beasley.

while predating U. S. law, are recognized by Virginia and federal courts. The Virginia Supreme Court ruled that four landowners along a stretch of the Jackson River can bar fishing in their waters because of the grants, issued to previous landowners by Kings George II in 1750 and George III in 1769.

To date, the courts have ruled that the public can still float the Jackson in the posted sections. The state has long since stopped stocking the Jackson, but both the browns and the rainbows are naturally reproducing, and recently-conducted surveys indicate that the river has as strong a population of trout as it did when they were being stocked.

Even with a great deal of land off-limits to public fishing, the Jackson has enough public water to keep me coming back. Below I have given directions to five sections of the Jackson which are in George Washington National Forest and are open to public fishing. I have also added a sixth access point located on the Cliff View Inn property. It is a nice section of water and is open for fishing to the inn's guests. Most of the Jackson can be waded during low water. However, I think it's a good idea to float the river with a local guide on your first trip in order to get the lay of the land (or river, in this case).

DIRECTIONS/ACCESS

While there is a fair amount of private water, there is also plenty of public water. Below, I have given five public access points spread out from the Covington upstream some 18 miles to the Gathright Dam. All five of these public access points are located in George Washington National Forest. I list a sixth access point which is available to guests of the Cliff View Inn, which overlooks a beautiful section of the river.

Access from Covington, working our way upstream:

Petty Coat Junction General Store

From Covington, take Route 220 north to the first access point at Petty Coat Junction. Turn left on Route 687 and go 0.9 miles to the public access point, boat launch, and Petty Coat Junction General Store (they provide shuttle service for anglers who plan to float the river).

Indian Draft

After crossing the bridge at Petty Coat Junction, go 2.4 miles on Route 687 to the Indian Draft public access point (boat launch and parking).

Cliff View Inn access

Continue 0.2 miles on Route 687 to Friels Drive (Route 721) and turn right to get to the Cliff View Inn golf course and lodge. The inn has access to some great water, starting with the run behind the lodge. This section is only open to fishing for guests of the lodge.

Smith Bridge Road

From Friels Drive, the next access point is Smith Bridge Road (the bridge is closed). Go 1.1 miles on Route 687, turn right on Smith Bridge Road, go 0.7 miles to the end and turn right for parking and access. There is a lot of water below Smith Bridge which is not posted.

Johnson Springs Access Area

Continue 3.8 miles from the Smith Bridge access on Route 687, to Natural Well. Turn left at Natural Well Road and go over the bridge and in less than a mile, you will come to Johnson Springs, with access on the left. This is the first public access and put-in below the upper Crown Grant area.

Below the Dam and Above Crown Grant Area

From Johnson Springs, head south and turn right onto Route 666 (Morris Hills Road) and then right onto Route 605 (Coles Mountain Road) and follow signs for the visitor center. Just past the left turn for the visitor center, take the next right (Stilling Basin Road) for one mile, which will take you down to a nice stretch of water below the dam and above the first Crown Grant area.

Fellow author Beau Beasley wading the Jackson River.

Crown grants be damned – anglers will find fishing success. Photo Blaine Chocklett from New Angle Fishing Company.

STREAM FACTS

Seasons/Regulations

The 18-mile tailwater section of the Jackson from Moomaw Lake down to the town of Covington is open to year-round fishing under special regulations. Any type of bait or lure may be used, but only four trout per day may be kept and only one can be a brown trout over 20 inches. All rainbow trout between 12 and 16 inches and all brown trout less than 20 inches must be released.

Fish

The state no longer stocks the lower Jackson below Gathright Dam, but natural reproduction of both browns and rainbows has really taken off. Recent state-conducted surveys indicate that the number of fish in the river rival the number which were present when the state was stocking the Jackson. The river has produced fish up to 32 inches long, and 20- to 26-inch trout are frequently landed.

River Characteristics

The coldest water at the base of the Gathright Dam is mixed with warmer water closer to the surface of the lake to achieve a year-round temperature of 58 degrees – ideal for trout. The limestone riverbed nurtures nutrients and supplies a superior habitat and abundant aquatic life for the fish. The tailwater section is a mid-size stream averaging about 100 feet in width. It is characterized by long pool after long pool separated by mild riffles and pocket water. These long pools call for stealthy wading and accurate casting with long light leaders. Most of the river is easily waded.

What the Experts Say

Beau Beasley, award-winning outdoor writer and author of *Fly Fishing Virginia* and *Fly Fishing the Mid-Atlantic*, says, "The Jackson River is a four-season fishery if ever there was one – there's no bad time to go. That said, spring and fall are generally thought to be the best times to visit, but any bluebird day in the winter can result in rising fish along any stretch of the river."

What's in a Name?

The dam is named after Thomas Gathright, who owned the land that was flooded by the lake. The lake is named after Benjamin Moomaw, Jr. a wealthy Virginia businessman who was influential in gaining congressional approval for the project. He is known locally as "the Father of the Gathright Dam".

Flows

The water release schedule for the Gathright Dam is available by calling the Army Corps at 540-965-4117.

Hatches

The Jackson has excellent midge, blue-winged olive, Hendrickson, and sulphur hatches, but the mother lode of all hatches is the Mother's Day caddis hatch.

Tackle

A 9-foot, 4-weight outfit is ideal for the Jackson.

Tom Gilmore fishing the Jackson River, while guide Blaine Chocklett from New Angle Fishing Company mans the oars. Photo courtesy Beau Beasley.

Hub City

COVINGTON
Population 5,771

ACCOMMODATIONS

Cliff View Inn, 419 Friels Drive / 540-962-2200 / www.cliffviewgolf.com

Best Western Mountain View, 820 East Madison Street / 540-962-4951

Holiday Inn Express & Suites, 701 Carlyle Street / 540-962-1200

CAMPGROUNDS/RV PARKS

Buckhorne Country Store & Campground & RV Park, 3508 Douthat Road, Clifton Forge / 540-862-4502 / www.buckhorne.com

RESTAURANTS

Cucci Pizzeria, 562 East Main Street / 540-962-3964

D & J Family Restaurant, 904 South Monroe Avenue / 540-962-1874

Cat & Owl Steak & Seafood House, 110 Karnes Road / 540-862-5808

Jack Mason's Tavern, 400 East Ridgewood, Clifton Falls / 540-862-5624 / www.jackmasonstavern.com

FLY SHOPS/GUIDES

Blaine Chocklett, New Angle Fishing Co. / 540-354-1774 / www.newanglefishing.com

Anglers Lane, Graves Mill Shopping Center, Forest / 434-385-0200 / www.anglerslane.com

Orvis, 19 Campbell Avenue, Roanoke / 540-345-3635 / www.orvis.com/roanoke

Albemarle Angler, Barracks Road Shopping Center, 1129 Emmet Street, Charlottesville / 434-977-6882 / www.albemarleangler.com

AIRPORTS

Roanoke-Blacksburg Regional Airport, 5202 Aviation Drive N.W. / 434-9776882

MEDICAL

Valley Ridge Family Medicine, 2419 Valley Ridge Road / 540-863-8736

FOR MORE INFORMATION

Alleghany Highlands Chamber of Commerce, 241 West Main Street / 540-962-2178

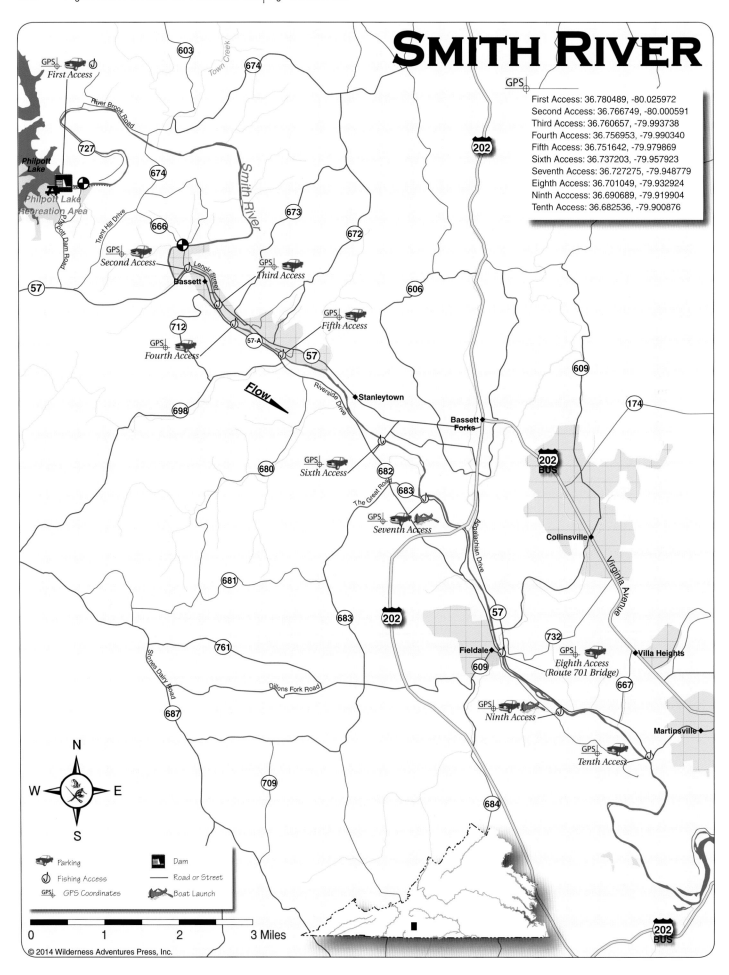

SMITH RIVER

SMITH RIVER (FOUR STARS)

The tailwater section of the Smith River below Philpott Lake once had the reputation of being the best trophy brown trout fishery east of the Mississippi. In 1974, the Virginia state record for brown trout was broken three times on the Smith, and at year's end the new record stood at 14 pounds, 6 ounces. That record stood until 1979, when Bill Nease set the new state record of 18 pounds, 11 ounces and less than two months later, Nease landed a 17-pound, 12-ounce fish. Both were landed in the tailwater section of the Smith River.

This quality tailwater fishery extends downriver some 20 miles from the dam, just above the town of Bassett to the town of Martinsville. There is excellent access as it flows through suburban and urban neighborhoods. The Smith is a mid-size river averaging about 100 feet wide in most sections. When they are not releasing water from the dam, the river consists of mostly shallow runs and slow-moving pools. It is easily waded when water is not being released, but it is impossible to wade when they are releasing water. Under normal conditions, wading must be done with great stealth, and long, light leaders are often required to entice a trout to take your offering. My favorite stretch of the Smith is the former three-mile trophy brown trout section which runs from Town Creek downstream to the Route 666 bridge in the town of Bassett. This section has the most streamside vegetation and shade trees, and a higher density of wild brown trout than the rest of the river.

DIRECTIONS/ACCESS

From Route 57 in Bassett, Virginia:

First Access

From Route 57 head north onto Philpott Dam Road. Turn right onto Dam Spillway Road and go 0.7 miles to the dam and power house. There is a large paved parking area at the base of the dam. At the downstream end of the parking area is the start of the Smith River Trail, which follows the river closely for about a half-mile downstream.

Second Access

From Philpott Dam Road, turn left onto Route 57 East, drive past Trent Hill Drive (Route 666) 1.8 miles to Trent Hill Drive (again). Turn left onto Trent Hill Drive and cross the bridge over the Smith. There is a parking area on your right at the intersection of Trent Hill Drive and Lenoir Street.

Third Access

Continue on Lenoir Street for half a mile to the second bridge. At the bridge, Lenoir Street turns into Route 57 East (Fairystone Park Highway). Continue for a short distance for street parking, a parking lot, and river access. This is in the heart of the town of Bassett.

Fourth Access

Cross back over the bridge and turn left onto Route 57-A East (Riverside Drive). Go 0.4 miles and turn left onto Route 673, which crosses the third bridge. There is parking on both sides of the bridge.

Fifth Access

Continue down Route 57-A East (Riverside Drive) 0.8 miles to Governor Stanley Highway on the left and the fourth bridge over the Smith River. Cross the bridge and there is parking on the left. On the upstream side of the bridge are several boulder-strewn pools which provide structure and good holding water for trout.

Sixth Access

Continue down Route 57-A (Riverside Drive) to Route 903 and the fifth bridge. There is parking before the bridge.

Smith River Outfitters guide Lisa "Cricket" Hall hooked up. Photo courtesy of Brian Williams of Smith River Outfitters.

Seventh Access

Continue down Route 57-A for 0.4 miles and turn left onto the Great Road. Continue on the Great Road for 0.5 miles to a parking area on the left and a canoe access point on the Smith River Trail. There is a nice run just down from the parking area.

Eight Access

Continue down Riverside Drive for three miles to the town of Fieldale, where Riverside Drive turns into River Road. Here is the sixth bridge, the Route 701 or Field Avenue bridge. Continue down River Road for 200 yards past the bridge and you will come to a trailhead parking area on the right. The Fieldale walking trail is across the street by the river and continues along the river for 0.9 miles to the next access area.

Ninth Access

For the next access, continue down River Road for 0.9 miles to parking area and canoe launch. This section has several long, slow, challenging pools. After this, River Road goes away from the river and after about a mile and a half, comes to a dead end.

Tenth Access

For the next access area, backtrack to the Route 701 bridge and after crossing the bridge, turn right on Route 57 East, which follows the river for two miles to the outskirts of Martinsville. This two-mile stretch of Route 57 has several pull-offs with easy access to the river.

A nice Smith River brown trout. Photo courtesy Brian Williams of Smith River Outfitters.

STREAM FACTS

Regulations

The Smith River from Philpott Dam downstream approximately 31 miles to the Route 636 bridge is managed for trophy brown trout. All brown trout between 10 and 24 inches must be released. There is a six-fish-per-day limit for brook and rainbow trout of at least 7 inches in length. Only one brown trout of at least 24 inches may be kept. There are no gear or bait restrictions.

Fish

The Smith holds a good head of wild browns, with many reaching trophy size. It is also heavily stocked with rainbows and brookies from October to May. With good numbers of trout and excellent access, the Smith gets its share of pressure. But it has 20 miles of coldwater trout fishing, and you can get away from the crowds if you do a little walking. This is especially true below the trophy stretch. According to the Virginia Fish and Wildlife Division, the Smith has one of the best catch rates in the state for wild brown trout at 1.5 fish per hour average for each angler.

Hatches

The Smith has a good diversity of hatches, with the super hatches being blue-winged olives, Hendrickson, March browns and sulphurs. As with almost all tailwaters, midges, larva, pupa, and adults produce action year round.

What the Experts Say

Brian Williams of Smith River Outfitters on the tailwater fishery, "The cold water creates a viable trout habitat, but the generation of hydro power causes such dramatic flow changes that the scouring of the bottom has contributed to the Smith being listed as impaired for macro invertebrates for a 25-mile section of stream. Even with the trials and tribulations the wild brownies have to contend with, it's still an amazing river, and when you find yourself waist deep in 45 degree water with sipping, popping, and outright ravenous feeding trout all around, you know why it's one of the best streams in the region.

"The wild brown population can be from 500 to 2,000 fish per mile depending on how far you go from the base of Philpott Dam. Closer to the dam, there are trout but they are small, ranging from 6 to10 inches. For the bigger bullies, head downstream where there are fewer fish but the baitfish that grow big browns are more plentiful, and you can expect to find fish in the 12 to18 inch range, with an occasional 20-plus incher. All year long the fishing can be excellent, but our favorite season is the fall. The browns are breeding and their colors are brilliant. The scenery is incredible with fall foliage more than making up for any missed rises."

Williams on the hatches, "There can be abundant blue-winged olives in May and June and we always look forward to the sulphurs which can hatch anywhere from April to June. You can expect to see midge hatches sporadically all year, and the trout will "sip" these little guys near the surface but good luck trying to fool them, even with a size 22. Fishing with a dry fly in sizes 10 to12 as an indicator fly and midge dropper sizes 16 to18 is our 'go-to' rig on the Smith for most of the season."

Flows

The Smith can be easily waded when no water is being released. Do not attempt to wade the river when they are generating power – it is too dangerous. For release schedules, call the Army Corps at 276-629-2432 for a taped power generation schedule for that day.

Smith River Outfitters guide Lisa "Cricket" Hall hooked up. Photo courtesy of Brian Williams of Smith River Outfitters.

Hub City

MARTINSVILLE

Population 13,733

ACCOMMODATIONS

Comfort Inn, 1895 Virginia Avenue / 276-666-6835
Econo Lodge Inn & Suites, 1755 Virginia Avenue /
276-632-5611
The Ketchie House Bed & Breakfast, 331 East Church
Street / 276-732-3491 / www.ketchiehouse.com

CAMPGROUNDS/RV PARKS

Indian Heritage RV Park & Campground, 184 Tensbury
Drive / 276-632-9500 / www.indianheritagervpark.com
/ Located on the banks of the Smith River.
Philpott Lake, 1058 Philpott Lake Dam Road,
Bassett / 276-629-2703 / Army Corps of Engineers
campgrounds.

RESTAURANTS

Hugo's Uptown Restaurant & Sports Bar, Jefferson
Plaza, 10 East Church Street / 276-632-3663 /
www.hugosuptown.net
Mtn' Jax Restaurant & Pub, 43-45 East Church Street /
276-403-4529
Rania's Italian Restaurant, 147 East Main Street /
276-638-4462 /www.raniasrestaurant.com

FLY SHOPS & GUIDES

Smith River Outfitters / 276-618-1457 /
www.smithriveroutfitters.com

AIRPORTS

Roanoke-Blacksburg Regional Airport, 5202 Aviation
Drive N.W. / 434-9776882

MEDICAL

Memorial Hospital of Martinsville & Henry County, 320
Hospital Drive / 276-666-7200 /
www.martinsvillehospital.com

FOR MORE INFORMATION

Martinsville/Henry County Chamber of Commerce /
276-632-6401 / www.martinsville.com

*Smith River Outfitters guide Lisa "Cricket" Hall
casting with a nice tight loop. Photo courtesy
Brian Williams of Smith River Outfitters.*

TENNESSEE

TENNESSEE STATE FACTS

State Abbreviation: TN
Area: 42,146 square miles, 36th biggest in the U.S.
Elevation – Highest Point: Clingmans Dome at 6,643 feet
Population: 6,403,353
State Fish: Largemouth bass

TROUT FISHING LICENSE

www1.tnwildlifelicense.com/start.php
Resident annual fee: $46.00
Non-resident annual fee: $81.00
Non-resident ten-day fee: $50.50
Non-resident three-day fee: $33.50
Non-resident one-day fee: $16.00

STATE RECORDS

Brook trout, 3 pounds, 14 ounces by Jerry Wills / August 15, 1973 Hiwassee River

Brown trout, 28 pounds, 12 ounces by Greg Ensor / August, 30, 1988 / Clinch River

Rainbow trout, 16 pounds, 15 ounces by Ronnie Rowland / September 6, 2002 / Ft. Patrick Henry Reservoir

When most anglers think of trout fishing in Tennessee, they most likely think about the great freestone trout streams in Great Smoky Mountains National Park, which eastern Tennessee shares with western North Carolina. Between the park and Cherokee National Forest, Tennessee has around 1,000 miles of wild trout water. Tennessee also hosts some world-class tailwater trout rivers, most of which are heavily stocked by Tennessee Wildlife Resources Agency (TWRA) with over one million trout per year, both fingerling and adult fish.

Angler satisfaction surveys by the TWRA reveal that trout anglers rank their fishing experiences on the state's tailwaters as good to excellent. When you look at the catch rates on Tennessee's tailwaters, it is easy to understand why. Recent surveys show that anglers' average catch rate per day for trout is 4.96 on the Hiwassee River, 5.2 on the Carney Fork, 5.88 on the South Holston, 7.22 on the Clinch, and a staggering 10.1 on the Watauga. To give you a comparison, I belonged to a private club on Pennsylvania's Brodhead Creek which has been keeping catch records for decades, and the highest average catch per day for any year was 2.3 trout– and most years the average was two or slightly below.

Let's take a look at the four Tennessee tailwaters that earned a score of four or five stars to be included in this book – the South Holston and Watauga in the northeast corner of the state, the Clinch just north of Knoxville, and the Hiwassee River in the southeast corner of the state.

A big rainbow from South Holston River. Photo courtesy Jon Hooper, G.M., South Holston River Lodge.

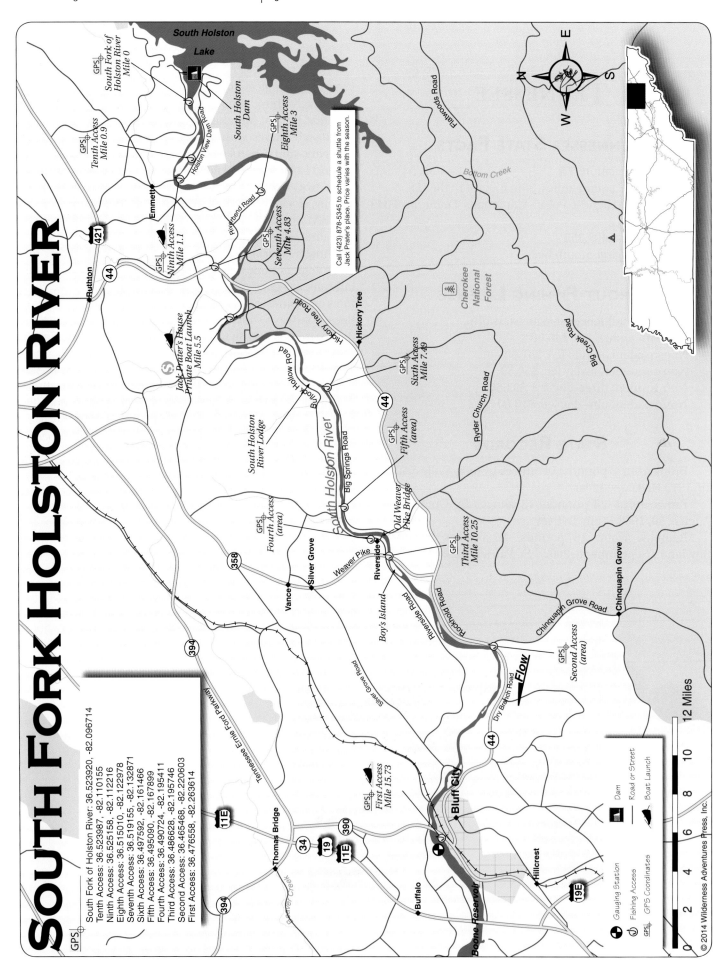

SOUTH FORK HOLSTON RIVER

South Holston Lake

South Fork of Holston River Mile 0

GPS | Tenth Access Mile 0.9

South Holston Dam

Holston View Dam Road

Emmett

421

44

Ruthton

GPS | Ninth Access Mile 1.1

Riverbend Road

GPS | Eighth Access Mile 3

GPS | Seventh Access Mile 4.83

Call (423) 878-5345 to schedule a shuttle from Jack Prater's place. Price varies with the season.

Fallwoods Road

Bottom Creek

Hickory Tree Road

Hickory Tree

Cherokee National Forest

Big Creek Road

$ Jack Prater's House Private Boat Launch Mile 5.5

South Holston River Lodge

Big Hollow Road

GPS | Sixth Access Mile 7.49

Ryder Church Road

44

GPS | Fifth Access (area)

Big Springs Road

South Holston River

Old Weaver Pike Bridge

GPS | Fourth Access (area)

358

Vance

Silver Grove

Weaver Pike

Riverside

Boy's Island

Riverside Road

Rockhold Road

GPS | Third Access Mile 10.25

Chinquapin Grove Road

Chinquapin Grove

394

Silver Grove Road

Flow

GPS | Second Access (area)

Dry Branch Road

44

Tennessee Ernie Ford Parkway

11E

Thomas Bridge

34

390

19

11E

GPS | First Access Mile 15.73

Bluff City

Hillcrest

19E

Beaver Creek

394

Buffalo

Boone Reservoir

GPS
South Fork of Holston River: 36.523920, -82.096714
Tenth Access: 36.523987, -82.110155
Ninth Access: 36.525158, -82.112216
Eighth Access: 36.515010, -82.122978
Seventh Access: 36.519155, -82.132871
Sixth Access: 36.497592, -82.161466
Fifth Access: 36.495090, -82.167899
Fourth Access: 36.490724, -82.195411
Third Access: 36.486628, -82.195746
Second Access: 36.465468, -82.220603
First Access: 36.476558, -82.263614

Gauging Station

Fishing Access

GPS | GPS Coordinates

Dam

Road or Street

Boat Launch

0 2 4 6 8 10 12 Miles

SOUTH FORK HOLSTON RIVER (FIVE STARS)

The tailwater on the South Fork Holston River was created in 1947 when the Tennessee Valley Authority (TVA) completed construction of the South Holston Dam, creating South Holston Lake which extends 24 miles up into the mountains of Virginia. Most of the South Holston watershed is forested, including portions in Cherokee National Forest in Tennessee and Jefferson National Forest in Virginia.

When the dam was first built, the water releases from the bottom of the deep reservoir were very low in dissolved oxygen levels. In 1991, the TVA built a weir in the river on both sides of Osceola Island to add oxygen to the river, and the insect life and trout population have really benefited from the oxygen-enriched cold water. In fact, today the South Fork of the Holston is Tennessee's premier tailwater. It has it all – good public access, great hatches, and an amazing biomass of trout which the TVA estimates at over 5,000 trout per mile.

The South Holston Dam has only one turbine, and it is a relatively small tailwater by Tennessee standards, averaging about 130 feet wide. The tailwater section runs 13.7 miles from the dam down to the mouth of Boone Reservoir. It takes about four hours for water to get from the dam all the way downstream to where it runs into the reservoir. You can wade fish up near the dam and then, when the water starts to rise, you can drive downriver and get in a few more hours of fishing. When the dam is not generating power you can wade most sections of the river – during periods of generation, floating the river is a much safer option.

Stocking of brown trout ceased in 2003 when it was determined that wild brown trout spawning was sufficient to maintain a fishable population. The wild trout in the tailwaters below the lake are as tough to fool as any tailwater or spring creek trout in the East. The tremendous amount of aquatic biomass makes for great hatches and big, fat, healthy – and selective – fish. Water levels and wade/float options vary greatly depending on generation schedules.

The river fishes well year round and you can find trout rising 365 days a year. Anglers come from all around the world to fish during the South Holston's legendary sulphur hatches. There are several species of sulphurs on the river; hatching begins in mid-April and can last into early November. These hatches are the most reliable and long-lasting hatches I am aware of anywhere in the United States. The South Fork of the Holston River is the best dry fly river I have ever had the pleasure to fish. But don't take my word for it. Angling legend Lefty Kreh says the South Holston "is perhaps the best trout fishing in the East." In addition to great sulphur hatches, you are likely to encounter blizzard-like blue-winged olives and midge hatches any time of the year.

My first trip to the South Holston was with my fellow outdoor writer and good friend, Beau Beasley. We were on a mission to photograph and "field test" Virginia's and Tennessee's top tailwaters for this book. After a few good days on the Jackson and Smith Rivers in Virginia, we were off to fish the South Holston and Watauga Rivers in Tennessee. Earlier in the season Ed Jaworowski and I had spent some time on the Gunpowder River in Maryland with Lefty. The Gunpowder is practically in Lefty's backyard, and it is a good little tailwater in its own right. Lefty told us that he was heading down to fish the tailwater section of the South Holston in a few days and he said, "Tom, you really should include the South Holston in your tailwater book." When I told him that I was planning to include it he responded, "When you go, you must stay at the South Holston River Lodge, they have great guides, food, lodging, and the lodge and its cabins overlook the river."

Beasley and I had met the folks from South Holston River Lodge earlier in the year at the Fly Fishing Show at Somerset, New Jersey. Jon Hooper, the lodge's general manager had invited us down to sample some of the river's tremendous dry fly fishing and we were glad to take him up on his invitation. We arrived late one evening in early May. Hooper was waiting for us with a cooler loaded with cold beer. After having a few drinks and getting the lowdown on the fishery from Jon, Beasley and I hit the sack. Hooper was going to stop by at 7:30am to pick us up for breakfast. About 7:15 the next morning, while having coffee on the deck, Beasley and I noticed a few dimples on the river. At first

Dave Doeren, with his big brown trout caught while wading the South Holston. Photo courtesy Teo Whitlock, Altamont Anglers.

there were just a few in the first pool below the lodge, but soon we started to see rises in the next pool upstream. By the time Hooper arrived there were dozens of fish rising in both pools. Hooper asked if we were ready to grab breakfast and when we showed him all the trout rising he took it in stride.

Beasley and I decided to skip breakfast and fish – we could eat breakfast 365 days a year but we didn't get the opportunity to fish over rising trout every morning. Hooper rigged us up with 15-foot 6x leaders and size 20 CDC Blue-winged Olive dries. In the next hour, Beasley and I landed about 15 wild trout in the 12- to 18-inch range and missed and broke off many more. In the afternoon we were treated to the South Holston's world-famous sulphur hatch, and we lost count of the number of trout we took on sulphur dries.

DIRECTIONS/ACCESS

From I-81 near Bristol, Tennessee, take Route 11 west towards Bristol to Route 421. Take Route 421 east to just past Ruthton. Turn right off of Route 421 onto Emmett Road. Take Emmett Road to where TVA Road forks to the left and follow TVA Road, which forms a loop that runs along both sides of the river. There are a number of different roads that cut away from and parallel the river, but unfortunately most of them are not on state maps. You need a DeLorme or other highly detailed map to really follow the river from this point downstream to Boone Lake. Wilderness Adventures Press has a large map of the South Holston that many fly shops carry, or you can get it direct from them at www.store.wildadvpress.com.

A "SoHo" brown landed by angler Angela Christian. Photo courtesy Jon Hooper, G.M. of the South Holston River Lodge.

Starting at Boone Lake and working upstream to the dam:

First Access

The Bluff City Highway bridge crosses the South Holston River at the mouth of Boone Lake. Bluff City has a public boat ramp at the mouth of lake; this is the lower take-out location. You could put in and row upstream or fish from shore. There are stripers at the mouth of Boone Lake.

Second Access

From the Bluff City Highway bridge working upstream to the dam, take Holston Drive 0.3 mile upstream to Main Street; turn left on Main, which turns into Route 44. Continue on Route 44 for 2.6 miles to the stop sign at Rockhold Road which is still Route 44. Most of the land on Rockhold Road is not posted and there are numerous roadside pull-offs.

Third Access

Continue 2.5 miles on Rockhold Road and turn left onto Old Weaver Pike (Price's Store is on the right at the intersection of Rockhold Road and Old Weaver Pike.) Continue 0.6 miles on Old Weaver Pike, cross the river on Old Weaver Pike Bridge, and turn left onto Riverside Drive. Drive 0.3 of a mile to the public access under Weaver Pike Bridge (not to be confused with Old Weaver Pike Bridge). This is the first public access point on the left side going upstream. (Note: The public access area under the bridge is not paved; you will need a 4-wheel drive vehicle to access the lot.)

Fourth Access

Another option is to turn right off of Old Weaver Pike Bridge onto Riverside Drive, which gives you roadside access to an additional mile of water.

Fifth Access

Big Springs Road runs upstream on the south side of the river from Old Weaver Pike Bridge for 2.5 miles to the Big Spring Turnaround. There are several pull-offs and access areas along Big Springs Road.

Sixth Access

The Big Spring Turnaround provides plenty of parking and access to some great dry fly water. From here you can walk and wade some beautiful water upstream.

Seventh Access

To reach the next access point, continue up Big Spring Road for another 0.5 mile and turn left onto Route 44 (Hickory Tree Road). Continue for 2.4 miles, crossing the Route 44 bridge over the river and go up the hill to the four-way stop sign. There is parking on the right, and you can walk back down the hill to the river.

Eighth Access

At the four-way stop sign, turn right onto River Bend Road and drive 0.7 miles to the River Bend Road cul-de-sac and parking area provided by TVA. There are two trails providing access to the stream.

Ninth Access

For the next access upstream, backtrack the 0.7 miles and turn right onto Piney Hill Road, go one mile to Emmett Road. Turn right onto Emmett Road and go 0.4 miles to Holston View Dam Road. (Note: South Holston is straight ahead on Emmett Road.) Turn right on Holston View Dam Road and go 0.2 of a mile to the bridge over the SoHo. There is a boat launch on each side of the bridge.

Tenth Access

Just 0.1 of a mile past the bridge is the Osecola Island Recreation Area. There is a good wading section below the Labyrinth Weir.

Eleventh Access

The next access is actually downstream from Osicola Island. Continue on Holston View Dam Road for 0.1 miles, turn right onto TVA Road South, and go 0.3 of a mile to public parking and access on the right. This is upstream from the Big Spring Turnaround.

Twelfth Access

You can also fish below the dam at low water. From TVA Road south, turn right onto Holston View Dam Road and continue for 0.9 miles to the base of the dam. There are several public parking lots and access points along the way.

STREAM FACTS

Seasons/Regulations

To protect the larger fish, the Tennessee Wildlife Resource Agency in 2000 implemented a 16- to 22-inch "slot limit". Under the rules, it is illegal to possess any trout in the 16- to-22-inch range. Only one trout of 22 inches may be harvested, while up to seven fish less than 16 inches may be kept. Since the implementation of the slot limit, the number of large fish has been increasing every year.

In 2004, TWRA stopped stocking brown trout in the river because of the self-supporting, spawning population. Wade fishing during spawning and egg incubation can have harmful effects due to harassment of spawning trout and trampling of redds. To protect spawning areas, the TWRA closes two sections of the river from November 1 through January 31. Since the implementation of the protected slot limit of 16- to 22-inches, wild brown trout over 20 inches have become common.

Fish

According to TWRA estimates, the river holds an astonishing 5,000 to 6,000 trout per mile. While there are some wild rainbows, some of the rainbows landed are a result of the annual stocking of adult and fingerlings rainbows in the lower river. According to TWRA surveys, the average catch rate per angler is an excellent 5.88 trout per day.

River Characteristics

The river flows through a valley with a mixture of hardwood forest and pastoral farms and meadows. The river bottom is largely rock ledges and cobble with a lot of grass and moss making the bottom very slippery in places. Studded boots and a wading staff are good insurance against a spill.

What the Experts Say

Angling legend Lefty Kreh says the South Holston "is perhaps the best trout fishing in the East".

Jon Hooper, general manager of South Holston River Lodge says this about the fishery, "It's a true western river style fishery, right here in the East. Trout can be found rising on the South Holston 12 months a year. If you have never been on the river during an epic summertime sulphur hatch, you are missing one of the best flyfishing experiences

The author casting, Jon Hooper, G.M. South Holston River Lodge, on the oars. Photo courtesy Beau Beasley .

of your life. These buttery mayflies come off like clockwork on the South Holston."

Flows

During periods of power generation, the flows are too high to be waded safely in most sections of the South Holston. Check the generation schedule, as you may be able to fish up near the dam before the releases start and then drive downriver and get in several more hours of fishing before the flows reach the lower section of river. You can get the dam release information online at the Tennessee Valley website (www.lakeinfo.tva.gov), or call the TVA hotline (1-800- 238-2264); the code for the South Holston is 01.

History

The South Holston tailwater was created in 1947 when the TVA completed construction of the dam on the South Fork. Turbine discharges from South Holston Dam historically experienced periods of low dissolved oxygen (DO) during summer and fall. In December of 1991, TVA built an aerating weir dam to boost DO levels and the health of the river increased dramatically.

Hatches

There are extensive hatches of several species of sulphurs from April into early November. You can run into blue-winged olives and midge hatches any day of the year.

Tackle

For most of the season a 9-foot, 4-weight with a floating fly line is the ideal outfit.

Hub City

BRISTOL
Population 26,702

ACCOMMODATIONS

South Holston River Lodge, 1509 Bullock Hollow Road / 423-878-3457 / www.SouthHolstonRiverLodge.com

Days Inn, 536 Volunteer Parkway / 423-968-2171

Hampton Inn, 3799 West State Street / 423-764-3600

CAMPGROUNDS AND RV PARKS

Cochran's Lakeview Campground, 821 Painter Creek Road / 423-878-8045 / Open year round

Farmer Bob Camping, 583 Whitetop Road, Bluff City / 423-538-8670

RESTAURANTS

Macado's, 714 State Street / 413-764-1100 / macados.net

Price's General Store, 3267 Rock Hold Road / 423-538-3337 / Where the locals go for breakfast and lunch.

Troutdale Bistro, 724 State Street /423-989-3663 / troutdalebistro.com

Carrabba's, 175 Market Street, Johnson City / 423-232-2858 / carrabbas.com

FLY SHOPS AND GUIDES

South Holston River Lodge, 1509 Bullock Hollow Road / 423-878-3457 / www.SouthHolstonRiverLodge.com

South Holston River Fly Shop, 608 Emmett Road / 423-878-2822 / www.southholstonriverflyshop.com / Rod & Matt Champion, Owners/Guides

Teo Whitlock Altamont Anglers, 30 Caledonia Road, Ashville, North Carolina / 828-252-9266 / www.altamontanglers

The Holston Angler, 40 Poplar Ridge Road, Piney Flats / 423-538-7412

Patrick Fulkrod, 1021 Commonwealth Avenue / 276-466-8988

AIRPORTS

Tri-Cities Regional Airport, 2525 Highway 75, Blountville / 423-325-6000 / www.triflight.com

MEDICAL

Holston Valley Medical Center, 130 Ravine Road, Kingsport / 423-224-4000

FOR MORE INFORMATION

Bristol Chamber of Commerce, 423-989-4850 / www.bristolchamber.org

A big brown trout from South Holston River angler David Galvin. Photo courtesy Jon Hooper, G.M. of the South Holston River Lodge.

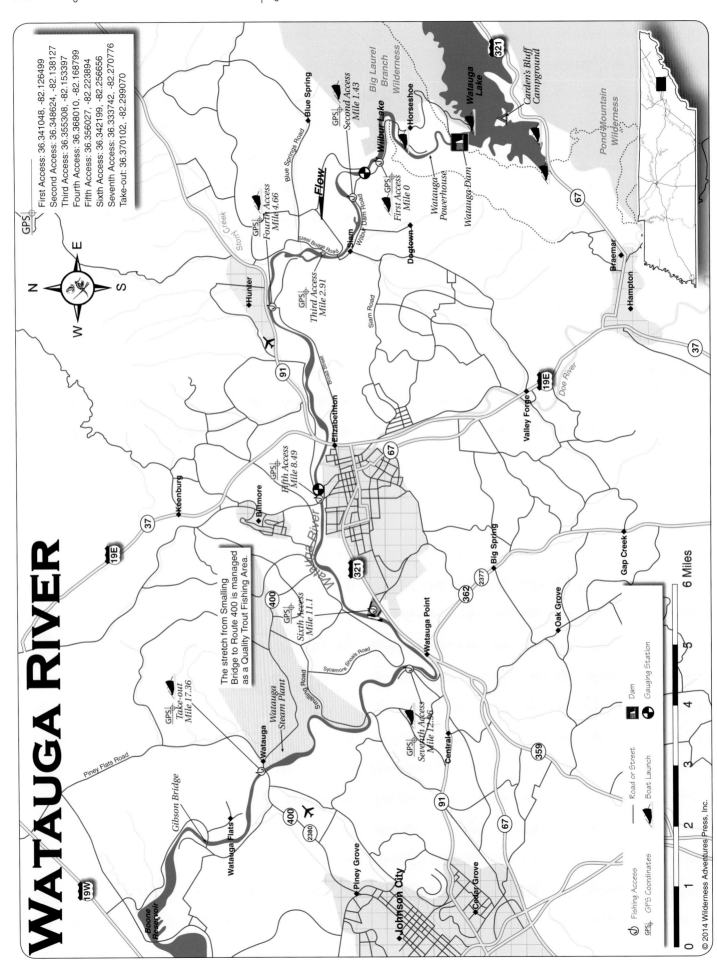

WATAUGA RIVER

First Access: 36.341048, -82.126499
Second Access: 36.348624, -82.138127
Third Access: 36.355308, -82.153397
Fourth Access: 36.368010, -82.168799
Fifth Access: 36.356027, -82.223894
Sixth Access: 36.342199, -82.256656
Seventh Access: 36.333742, -82.270776
Take-out: 36.370102, -82.299070

The stretch from Smalling Bridge to Route 400 is managed as a Quality Trout Fishing Area.

Blue Spring
Second Access Mile 1.43
Big Laurel Branch Wilderness
Watauga Lake
Carden's Bluff Campground
Pond Mountain Wilderness
Horseshoe
Wilbur Lake
Fourth Access Mile 4.66
First Access Mile 0
Watauga Powerhouse
Watauga Dam
Flow
Siam
Steel Bridge Road
Blue Springs Road
Stony Creek
Wilbur Dam Road
Dogtown
Third Access Mile 2.91
Hunter
Siam Road
Broad Street
Braemar
Hampton
Doe River
Valley Forge
Elizabethton
Fifth Access Mile 8.49
Keenburg
Biltmore
Big Spring
Gap Creek
Oak Grove
Sixth Access Mile 11.1
Watauga River
Watauga Steam Plant
Smalling Bridge Road
Sycamore Shoals Road
Watauga Point
Seventh Access Mile 12.96
Central
Piney Grove
Johnson City
Cedar Grove
Take-out 17.36
Watauga
Gibson Bridge
Watauga Flats
Piney Flats Road
Boone Reservoir

Fishing Access
GPS Coordinates
Road or Street
Boat Launch
Dam
Gauging Station

6 Miles
0 1 2 3 4 5

© 2014 Wilderness Adventures Press, Inc.

WATAUGA RIVER (FOUR STARS)

The Watauga River begins on Grandfather Mountain in western North Carolina and flows some 45 miles to Wilbur Dam in northeast Tennessee near Elizabethton. The tailwater section of the Watauga River begins at the outflow of the Wilbur Dam and runs 16.5 miles down to Boone Lake, the same lake that the South Holston River flows into. The Watauga is only about a 30-minute drive from the South Holston, so you can easily fish both rivers on the same trip. In fact, while I consider the South Holston to be the best trout river in the East, I wouldn't travel to northeast Tennessee without planning to fish both the South Holston and Watauga Rivers.

On our first trip to the Watauga, Beau Beasley and I floated the river with local guide Teo Whitlock. Jon Hooper, the general manager of South Holston River Lodge, had booked Whitlock for us, claiming he was the best guide on the river. It didn't take Beasley and me long to concur with Hooper's assessment. We met Whitlock at the Home Depot in Elizabethton. I must admit, seeing a pickup truck with a driftboat on a trailer in a Home Depot parking lot seemed a little bazaar, but Whitlock pointed out the Watauga flows right through downtown Elizabethton and folks are used to seeing driftboats in town. In fact, he said, some of the best sections to fish are in downtown Elizabethton.

Whitlock started the "float" by rowing quite a distance upstream from the launch site. He took us to a run, which because of the distance upstream from the launch site, gets very little pressure and was loaded with fish. Whitlock rigged us up with double nymphs and yarn strike indicators. Beasley and I missed our first few strikes, but soon we were into fish on a regular basis. Over lunch I mentioned to Whitlock that on the South Holston we never fished anything but dries, and so far on the Watauga we had fished only nymphs. Whitlock said that is pretty much the norm – the SoHo is more of a dry-fly stream and the Watauga is more of a nymph river. Whitlock guides on both rivers and feels the Watauga has more fish in the 16-to 23-inch range, but that the South Holston has more fish over 23 inches.

DIRECTIONS/ACCESS

Take I-181 to Johnson City and then Route 91/U.S. 321 to Elizabethton. Stay on Route 91 in Elizabethton.

First Access

I start my directions at Wilbur Dam about eight miles upstream from Elizabethton and work back downstream through town and below. From Elizabethton, take Route 91 North and follow signs for Wilbur Lake and Wilbur Dam. Below the dam is a TWRA public access point and boat launch off of Wilbur Dam Road.

Second Access

About one mile down from the dam launch site on Wilbur Dam Road are the Bee Cliff Cabins. They have a nice stretch of water which is available to their guests that runs from the cabins downstream past the Siam Steel Bridge.

Third Access

From the dam, continue downstream 2.2 miles to the Siam Steel Bridge. Cross the bridge and 0.25 mile down are stream access and a parking area on the left. There is a beautiful

Teo Whitlock and Dennis Killion with a Watauga brown. Photo courtesy Teo Whitlock, Altamont Anglers.

stretch of dry fly water from the parking area upstream to the bridge. (Note: Here Wilbur Dam Road becomes Steel Bridge Road and, farther downriver before you reach Route 91, it changes its name again to Blue Springs Road.)

Fourth Access

Four miles downstream from the dam, turn left off of Blue Springs Road onto Route 91. Go 0.9 miles and turn left on Broad Street. This will take you over Rev. Henry E. Colvard Memorial Bridge (some maps have this named Hunter Bridge). There is a TVA parking area and launch by the bridge. There is good holding water upstream of the bridge.

Fifth Access

Continue on Broad Street (Route 321 South) for about three miles, crossing the bridge over the Doe River. Continue for half a mile and turn right onto Route 400, crossing over the Watauga River on Sgt. Jefferson Bridge. Take the first left onto "Lovers Lane" and park under the bridge. This is a good section to nymph fish.

Sixth Access

Instead of making the right onto Route 400 South, you can continue straight on Route 321 South for 1.8 miles to Sycamore Shoals State Park.

Seventh Access

From Sycamore Shoals State Park go 1.5 miles, turn right onto Route 91, cross the bridge and make the first right onto Blevins Road. Go half a mile to the TWRA fishermen's access and boat launch. (Note: Trophy Trout Cabins are right there on the river: 423-330-2879.)

This is the boat launch for the Quality Trout Zone, which is downriver, starting at Smalling Bridge and running 2.6 miles downstream to the town of Watauga.

STREAM FACTS

Seasons/Regulations

The Quality Trout Zone starts at Smalling Bridge and runs 2.6 miles downstream to the Railroad Bridge in the town of Watauga. This section is managed for artificial-lures-only with a two-trout limit, with a minimum size of 14 inches.

Fish

All browns are wild; some "bows" are stocked, but the majority are wild.

What the Experts Say

Whitlock, who guides on both rivers, feels the Watauga has more fish in the 16-to 23-inch range, but that the South Holston has more fish over 23 inches.

River Characteristics

The Watauga has a steeper gradient than other Tennessee tailwaters; it has more of the look and feel of a freestone stream than a tailwater river.

What's in a Name?

Watauga is an Indian word meaning beautiful waters.

Flows

You can get the dam release information online at the TVA website (lakeinfo.tva.gov), or call the TVA hotline (1-800-238-2264); the code for the Watauga is 02.

History

Historically, dissolved oxygen (DO) concentrations in the discharge from Wilbur Dam were seasonally depressed. In 1991, hub baffles were installed in the dam to increase the amount of DO, and minimum flow standards were established. The aquatic life and trout responded well to these improvements. Then in February of 2000, there was a major fish kill on the Watauga River below Elizabethton. Toxic run-off resulting from a fire at North American Corporation killed nearly all the trout in the 10-mile section below Elizabethton. TWRA studies indicated that despite the nearly complete fish kill, the river's benthic community was not substantially impacted. Because adequate food supplies existed after the fish kill, in an effort to restore the fishery, the TWRA began an increased stocking effort, particularly of fingerling rainbow trout as well as adult rainbows and browns.

Teo Whitlock with a 24-inch Watauga brown trout, caught by Dr. John Ellis. Photo courtesy Teo Whitlock.

The author casting, Jon Hooper, G.M. South Holston River Lodge, on the oars. Photo courtesy Beau Beasley.

Hatches

The Watauga is known for great spring sulphur and caddis hatches, good fall blue-winged olive hatches, and year-round fishing with midges, which are a major part of the Watauga River's trout diet.

Tackle

For most of the season a 9-foot, 4-weight rod with a floating fly line is the ideal outfit.

Hub City

ELIZABETHTON

Population 14,204

ACCOMMODATIONS

Bee Cliff Cabins, 106 Bee Cliff & 406 Wilbur Dam Roads / 423-542-6033 / www.beecliffcabins.com
Trophy Trout Cabins on the river / 423-330-2879
Meredith Valley Cabins, 341 Sycamore Shoals Drive / 423-543-8603 / www.meredithvalleycabins.com
Doe River Inn, 217 Academy Street / 423-543-1444 / www.doeriverinn.com / B&B
Watauga River Lodge & Fishing Guide Service, 643 Smalling Road, Watauga / 828-260-5782 / www.wataugariverlodge.com

CAMPGROUNDS AND RV PARKS

Misty Waters, 246 Wilbur Dam Road / 423-543-1702 / Grocery store, RV sites
Cherokee National Forest, Low Gap, Forest Road 56 / 423-735-1500

RESTAURANTS

Dino's Restaurant, 420 E. Elk Avenue / 423-542-5541
The Captain's Table, 2340 Highway 321, Hampton / 423-725-2201
Nanny's Country Kitchen, 256 Highway 91 / 423-543-3336

FLY SHOPS AND GUIDES

Teo Whitlock Altamont Anglers, 30 Caledonia Road, Ashville, N.C. / 828-252-9266 / www.altamontanglers
Rivermen Outfitters, 819 Broad Street / 423-542-0063
East Tennessee Flyfishing, 111 Infinity Drive / 423-474-4588 / easttennesseeflyfishing@gmail.com
Silver Bow Anglers Flyfishing Guide Service, 107 Forest Avenue / 423-794-8977 / www.silverbowanglers.com
A&S Outfitters, 419 West Elk Avenue / 423-543-1552

AIRPORTS

Tri-Cities Regional Airport, 2525 Highway 75, Blountville /423-325-6000 / www.triflight.com

MEDICAL

Sycamore Shoals Hospital, 1501 W. Elk Avenue / 423-542-1300 / www.msha.com

FOR MORE INFORMATION

Elizabeth/Carter County Tourism Association / 423-547-3850 / www.tourelizabethtonchamber.com

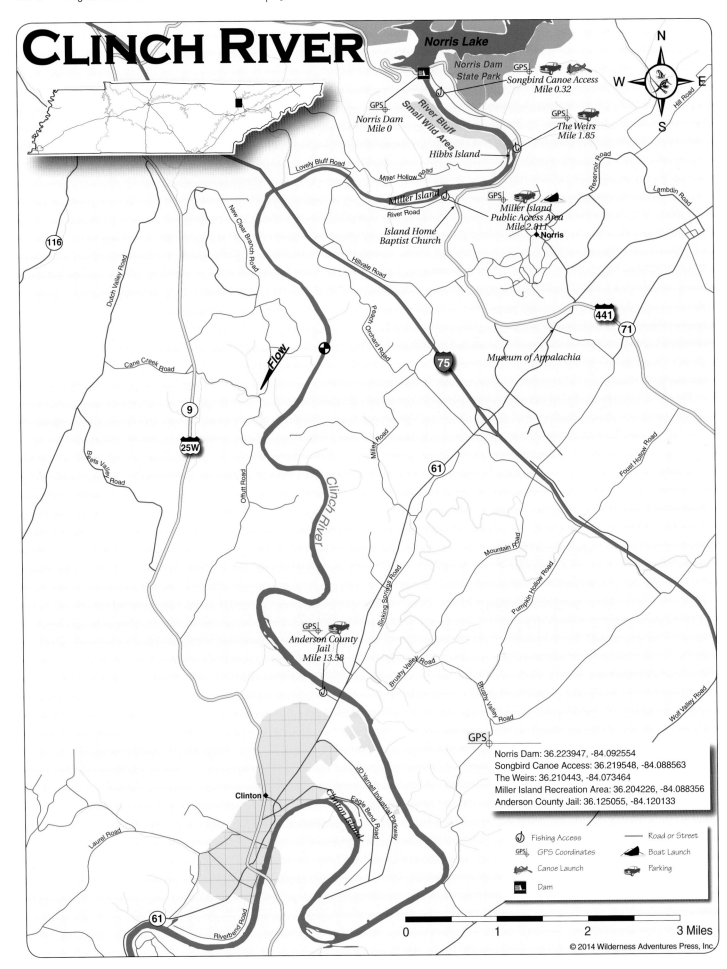

CLINCH RIVER

Norris Lake

Norris Dam
State Park

GPS
Songbird Canoe Access
Mile 0.32

GPS
Norris Dam
Mile 0

River Bluff
Small Wild Area

GPS
The Weirs
Mile 1.85

Hibbs Island

Lovely Bluff Road

Miller Hollow Road

Miller Island

River Road

GPS
Miller Island
Public Access Area
Mile 2.911

Island Home
Baptist Church

Reservoir Road

Lambdin Road

◆ Norris

116

New Clear Branch Road

Hillvale Road

441

71

Dutch Valley Road

Peach Orchard Road

75

Museum of Appalachia

Cane Creek Road

Flow

9

25W

Miller Road

Foust Hollow Road

61

Beets Valley Road

Offutt Road

Clinch River

Mountain Rd

Sinking Springs Road

Pumpkin Hollow Road

GPS
Anderson County
Jail
Mile 13.58

Brushy Valley Road

Brushy Valley
Road

Wolf Valley Road

GPS

Norris Dam: 36.223947, -84.092554
Songbird Canoe Access: 36.219548, -84.088563
The Weirs: 36.210443, -84.073464
Miller Island Recreation Area: 36.204226, -84.088356
Anderson County Jail: 36.125055, -84.120133

Laurel Road

Clinton ◆

JD Yarnell Industrial Parkway

Eagle Bend Road

Clinton Island

	Fishing Access	—	Road or Street
GPS	GPS Coordinates		Boat Launch
	Canoe Launch		Parking
	Dam		

61

Riverbend Road

0   1   2   3 Miles

© 2014 Wilderness Adventures Press, Inc.

CLINCH RIVER (FOUR STARS)

The Clinch is one of the best-known tailwater rivers in Tennessee. Located just 20 miles north of Knoxville near the town of Clinton, the Clinch gets a lot of fishing pressure – when possible, anglers should target the Clinch mid-week. It has a reputation for big trout which is well deserved. It currently holds the state record for the largest brown trout (28 pounds, 12ounces) and that was no fluke, as Tennessee Wildlife Resource Agency (TWRA) surveys have turned up several browns over 30 pounds.

The Clinch River tailwater was created in 1936 with the completion of the Norris Dam, the first TVA project to come online. As with many tailwaters, the Clinch had problems due to low dissolved oxygen and lack of minimum flows when the generators were not running. The TVA corrected these issues by installing a weir dam about two miles downstream from the Norris Dam at Hibbs Island. The outflow of the Norris Dam supports an excellent trout fishery for some 12 miles downstream. The dam has two generators and can only be waded when the turbines are not running. If you have the release schedule, you can move downstream when the release starts, as it takes about four and a half hours for water to get from the dam to the Route 61 bridge in Clinton.

The Clinch provides an excellent year-round fishery – it stays cool all summer, rarely getting above 60 degrees. The big hatch to catch is the sulphur hatch, which usually starts around mid-April if conditions are right and continues into summer. The Clinch is composed of a lot of shelf rock, which can make for some technical nymph fishing. It also has large flats that can hold rising cruisers. Long leaders and small flies are the most productive way to fish the Clinch. However, anglers willing to put the time in throwing large streamers can be rewarded with a true monster fish, especially in the fall and winter.

There is a small amount of natural reproduction in the tailwater, but recruitment to the fishery is minimal. TWRA's put-and-take and put-and-grow management plan is accomplished by heavy annual stocking. The prescribed annual stocking rates are 296,000 rainbow trout (260,000 fingerlings) and 120,000 adult brown trout. In an effort to produce large trout, the state recently implemented a protected length range (PLR) or slot limit for all trout. The daily creel limit remained at seven fish, of which one may exceed 20 inches and the rest must be less than 14 inches. There are no minimum size, gear, or bait restrictions. These regulations apply from the Norris Dam downstream to the Route 61 bridge in Clinton.

DIRECTIONS/ACCESS

From Interstate 75 approximately 20 miles north of Knoxville, take Exit 122 for Clinton/Norris and go north on Route 61. Turn left just past the Museum of Appalachia and follow the signs to Norris Dam. For the upper Clinch (my favorite section), go east on Highway 61 to Route 441. Take Route 441 north for about four miles until you see the Island Home Baptist Church on your right. Just past the church, River Road comes in on the left and gives you access to the Miller Island Public Access Area, a quarter of a mile from Highway 441. Here you can usually wade fish when water is not being released. If you continue on Highway 441 past River Road, Highway 441 parallels the river for about three miles until it crosses the dam. About one mile before the dam, there is access to the Weir Dams section with plenty of public parking. The next parking area past the Weir Dams on the left across from the Lenoir Museum is the Songbird Canoe access. The TVA owns all the land from the Miller Island access up to the dam and it is all open to public fishing. There is good fishing all along this stretch.

For the lower Clinch, go west on Route 61 from I-75 approximately six miles. Immediately after Highway 61 crosses the Clinch in Clinton, take the first road on the right. This will take you back to the Anderson County Sheriff's Office, Jail, and Emergency Medical Services. Park in the lot by the jail. You can fish right there or walk upstream along the river and fish for several miles.

Rainbows make up about 75 percent of the catch on the Clinch. Photo courtesy Michael "Rocky" Cox, Rocky Top Anglers.

STREAM FACTS

Season/Regulations

In 2011, the state implemented a new slot limit; fish in the 14- to 20-inch range may not be harvested. There is a seven-trout limit, of which one may exceed 20 inches and the rest must be less than 14 inches. The protected length range is in effect from the Norris Dam downstream to the Route 61 bridge in Clinton.

Fish

The Clinch relies on heavy stocking of both rainbow and brown trout. Bows make up about 75 percent of catches. Most fish are 11 to 12 inches, but fish of 14 to 16 are common. There are some very large browns in the river. TWRA angler surveys indicate very high catch rates of two trout per hour.

River Characteristics

The Clinch is big water, averaging about 250 feet in width. The bottom has a lot of shelf rock, which can make for some technical nymph fishing and difficult wading. It also has large flats that can produce excellent dry fly fishing especially during the sulphur hatch. The prime stretch for flyfishing for trout is the 13 miles from Norris Dam to the public access at the Route 61 bridge in Clinton. The Clinch is routinely referred to as "the Cinch" when it is fishing hot and conversely "the Grinch" when fishing is cold. With an average catch rate per day of 7.22 trout, the Clinch can't be a Grinch all that often.

What the Experts Say

Dane Law of Southeastern Anglers says, "Drifting the Clinch River is like floating a giant spring creek, with gin-clear water and a smooth glass surface. Catching its trophies can be a technical endeavor requiring delicate presentations and exact imitations."

Hatches

Vegetation provides good habitat for scuds, which are one of the most productive flies on the Clinch. Midge hatches occur daily on the Clinch, and a popular pattern is a Griffith's Gnat. Good sulphur hatches run from April through June. Chucking streamers is a lot of work, but often rewarded with big browns.

Flows

When they turn on the generators at Norris Dam, it takes about four and a half hours for the water to get from the dam to the Route 61 bridge at Clinton, so you can drive downriver and get in several more hours of fishing. When the generators are not running, there is good wading around Miller's Island and upstream of the Route 61 bridge. You can get the dam release information online at the TVA website (lakeinfo.tva.gov), or by calling the TVA hotline (1-800- 238-2264) and press code for the Clinch.

Tackle

For fall and winter fishing for big browns, I suggest a 9-foot, 6-weight outfit rigged with a sink tip line to drag big streamers through the deeper holes. The biggest trout of the season are often caught this way. For most of the season a 9-foot, 4-weight with a floating fly line is the ideal outfit.

Dense fog is common on the Clinch early in the morning. Photo courtesy Michael "Rocky" Cox, Rocky Top Anglers.

Hub City

CLINTON

Population 9,841

ACCOMMODATIONS

Holiday Inn Express, 111 Hillvale Road / 800-315-2621
Country Inn & Suites, 710 Park Place / 865-457-4311

CAMPGROUNDS AND RV PARKS

Norris Dam State Park, 125 Village Green Circle, Lake City / 865-426-7461 / www.norrisdamstate park.org / Cabins, campsites, and RV park
Clinton/Knoxville North KOA Camp and RV Park, 2423 Andersonville Highway / 800-562-8513

RESTAURANTS

Harrison's Grill & Bar, 110 Hillvale Road / 865-463-6368 / www.harrisonsgrill.com
Golden Girls Restaurant, 2211 N. Charles G. Seivers Blvd. / 865-457-3302
Riverview Grill, 1625 Oakridge Highway / 865-463-8550 / www.riverviewgrill.com

FLY SHOPS AND GUIDES

Southeastern Anglers, Reliance / 866-558-7688 / www.southeasternanglers.com
Ian Rutter, R&R Fly Fishers / 865448-0467 / randrflyfishing.com
Smoky Mountain Gillies, Knoxville / 865-577-4289 / www.smokymountaingillies.com
Holston River Flyfishing Guides, Knoxville / 865-558-7688 / www.holston-river-flyfishing-guides.com
Rocky Top Anglers / 865-388-9802 / www.rockytopanglers.com

AIRPORTS

Knoxville McGhee Tyson Airport, 2055 Alcoa Highway / 865-342-3000 / www.tys.org

MEDICAL

Fort Sanders Regional Medical Center, 1901 W. Clinch Avenue / 865-541-1111 / www.fsregional.com

FOR MORE INFORMATION

Anderson County Chamber of Commerce, 115 Welcome Ln / 800-524-3602 / www.andersoncountychamber.org

A rather large Clinch River brown trout. Photo courtesy Michael "Rocky" Cox, Rocky Top Anglers.

HIWASSEE RIVER

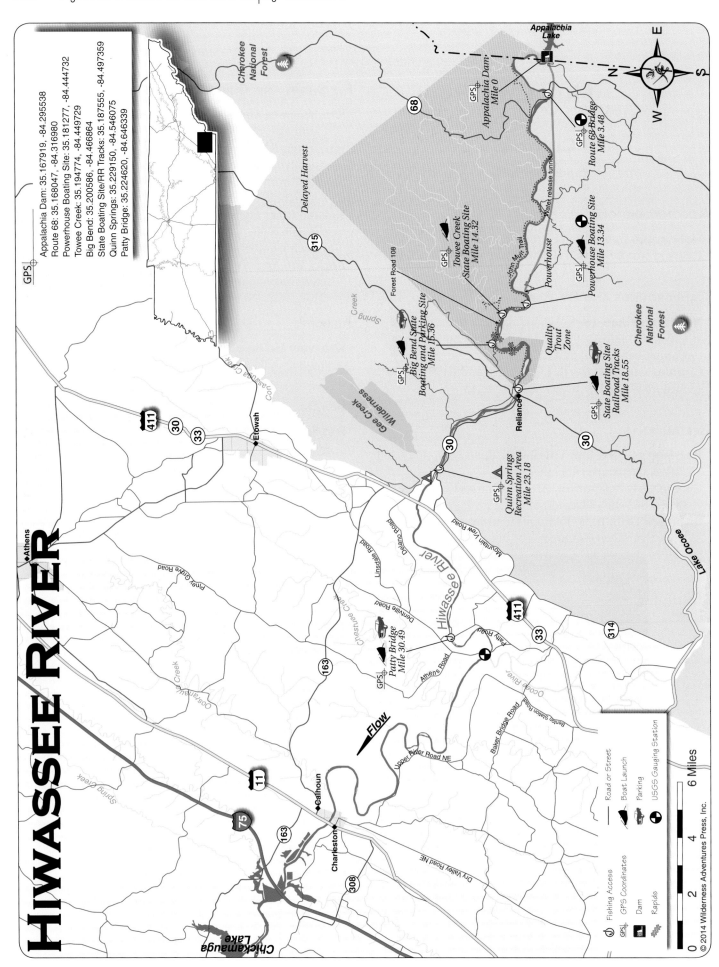

GPS

Appalachia Dam: 35.167919, -84.295538
Route 68: 35.168047, -84.316980
Powerhouse Boating Site: 35.181277, -84.444732
Towee Creek: 35.194774, -84.449729
Big Bend: 35.200586, -84.466864
State Boating Site/RR Tracks: 35.187555, -84.497359
Quinn Springs: 35.229150, -84.546075
Patty Bridge: 35.224620, -84.646339

Appalachia Lake

Appalachia Dam
Mile 0

Route 68 Bridge
Mile 3.48

Powerhouse Boating Site
Mile 13.34

Towee Creek
State Boating Site
Mile 14.32

Powerhouse

Water release tunnel

John Muir Trail

Quality Trout Zone

Big Bend State
Boating and Parking Site
Mile 15.36

Forest Road 108

Spring Creek

Gee Creek Wilderness

Delayed Harvest

Cherokee National Forest

Reliance

State Boating Site/
Railroad Tracks
Mile 18.55

Quinn Springs Recreation Area
Mile 23.18

Cherokee National Forest

Lake Ocoee

Hiwassee River

Patty Bridge
Mile 30.49

Athens Road

Mountain View Road

Delano Road

Lunsgate Road

Dentsville Road

Chestnut Creek

Upper River Road NE

Ocoee River

Benton Station Road

Baker Bridge Road

Dry Valley Road NE

Flow

Calhoun

Charleston

Chickamauga Lake

Spring Creek

Oostanaula Creek

Conasauga Creek

Piney Grove Road

Athens

Etowah

Legend:
- Fishing Access
- GPS Coordinates
- Dam
- Rapids
- Road or Street
- Boat Launch
- Parking
- USGS Gauging Station

0 2 4 6 Miles

68 315 411 30 33 11 75 163 308 314 411 33 30

HIWASSEE RIVER (FOUR STARS)

The Hiwassee River tailwater was created in 1941 when the Tennessee Valley Authority completed construction of the Appalachia Dam. The Hiwassee begins its 140-mile journey in northern Georgia, flows north into North Carolina, and then flows west into southeast Tennessee to its confluence with the Ocoee River. From the dam, the water travels via pipe some 12 miles downstream to the powerhouse.

Many of the TVA tailwaters flow through suburban and urban landscapes, and that is the case with the lower Hiwassee, but as you drive north from Route 411 along Kimsey Highway towards the tiny hamlet of Reliance, you begin to see the majestic forests of the Unicoi Mountains, which the Hiwassee River cuts through. Just north of Reliance, in Cherokee National Forest, the river flows through the beautiful Hiwassee Gorge. The scenery in the national forest is so spectacular that the river from the state line down to the Route 411 bridge was the first river in Tennessee to be designated as a State Scenic River. The trout management area runs from the powerhouse downstream to the Patty Bridge below the Route 411 bridge. Most of the good trout water lies in the section of river which flows through Cherokee National Forest.

DIRECTIONS

Take I-75 south from Knoxville and exit at Route 163. Take Route 163 East to just outside of Calhoun, where it junctions with U.S. 11. Turn south on U.S. 11 for about half a mile until you can again pick up Route 163 East. Continue on Route 163 to U.S. 411. Take U.S. 411 South until shortly after it crosses the Hiwassee River. Then take Route 30 East. You will now be following the Hiwassee River. There are access points along Route 30 until you get to the bridge that crosses the river at Reliance. Here you have two choices. If you continue on Route 30 East for about half a mile, Route 30 will sharply turn south away from the river. At that turn there is a gravel road to the left. Take the gravel road and shortly you will see a set of railroad tracks. Park and walk along the railroad tracks heading east. The tracks parallel the river through the Quality Trout Zone.

Your other option at the Reliance Bridge is to cross the river and take the first right. Follow the signs towards the powerhouse.

Good access from the bridge in Reliance to the powerhouse is provided by Forest Road 108 which follows the river on the north side. The only section where the road leaves the river is at Big Bend. Here you can access the river via the John Muir National Recreation Trail, which follows the river from Childers Creek to Big Bend parking lot.

Route 30 has access points all along the river until you get to the bridge at Reliance. There you can continue on Route 30 east for a quarter of a mile, when the road turns sharply south away from the river. At the turn there is a gravel road on the left – take the road a short distance to the railroad tracks. Park and walk east along the tracks; they parallel the river through the Quality Zone which is regulated as artificial-lures-only.

Dane Law with a nice Hiwassee brown. Photo courtesy Dane Law, Southeastern Anglers.

A Hiwassee River rainbow. Photo courtesy Dane Law, Southeastern Anglers.

STREAM FACTS

Seasons/Regulations

Open to fishing year round with general state regulations of seven fish per day of any size from April through September. Above Reliance, fishing is catch-and-release from October through March. In 1986, a Quality Trout Zone was established from the railroad bridge in Reliance upstream to the Big Bend parking area. In this section you are allowed to keep two trout of 14 inches or better during the regular season.

Fish

There is limited natural reproduction in the feeder streams. The state stocks over 100,000 rainbows and browns annually, and there is a good holdover rate – browns of 15 pounds and rainbows of up to 9 pounds have been landed. The stocking occurs year round, up to twice a month. According to TWRA surveys, angler catch rates exceed two fish per hour in the Quality Trout Zone.

River Characteristic

The Hiwassee has long, shallow bedrock pools, some as long as 300 yards and 100 yards wide. Great care must be taken while wading, as the bedrock forms ledges and drop-offs which can make for treacherous footing. In certain sections, the Hiwassee can be waded even with one generator running; and some wading is possible with two generators running.

What the Experts Say

Dane Law of Southeastern Anglers says, "The Hiwassee River is the jewel of southeastern tailwaters. It is much like a giant mountain stream flowing through the national forest with all of the major aquatic insect hatches, including its signature *Isonychia bicolor* hatch in summertime. This is dry fly driftboat fly fishing at its best."

Bob Borgwat who guides on both the Toccoa and the Hiwassee, says this about the seasons on the Hiwassee River, "As is usual on trout waters of the Southeast, the insect hatches of most interest to trout and trout fishermen begin in March and continue through summertime. Hiwassee River insect hatches are typically measured and observed with interest on the top seven miles of the river – from Appalachia Powerhouse, downstream to the Reliance railroad trestle. It is this tailwater stretch of the river that typically carries suitable temperature year round for both trout and insects and, as a result, remains fishable year round. Downstream from Reliance, the river often grows too warm to support trout from July through October."

Borgwat says this about the summer hatches, "Summertime heat begins to build on the river, and the sulphur mayflies keep the surface fishing active until the heat of July sets in. The largest individuals will be seen this month, before the even larger *Isonychia* mayfly emerges and provide what many anglers find to be the best dry fly fishing of the year. In the best years, *Isonychias* hatch heavy in July and persist through August."

Hatches

The Hiwassee is one of the few southern tailwaters that has a large diversity of mayfly, stonefly, and caddis hatches. The best hatches on the Hiwassee include Hendricksons, sulphurs, Cahills, and tons of caddis. *Isonychias* hatch throughout the summer and midges and small blue-winged olives hatch throughout the year. The Hiwassee is an excellent dry-fly stream.

What's in a Name?

Hiwassee is derived from the Cherokee word Ayuhwasi, meaning "savanna" or "large meadow."

Flows

You can get the dam release information online at the TVA website (lakeinfo.tva.gov), or call the TVA hotline (1-800- 238-2264) and enter code 22 for the Hiwassee. Releases take about three hours to get down to Railroad Bridge in Reliance. When TVA is not running generators, in most sections of the river you can wade across with care. (Caution: Don't get caught on the opposite side of the river from your transportation.)

Hub Cities

RELIANCE

Population 972

ACCOMMODATIONS

Hiwassee Angler, 179 Tellico Road / 423-338-8500 / www.hiwasseeangler.com / Rental cabins on the river

Mountain Stream Creekside Lodging, 1370 Childers Creek Road / 423-338-1072 / www.mountainstreamlidging.com

CAMPGROUNDS/RV PARKS

Black Bear Cove Lodge, Campground and RV Park, 5842 Highway 30, Benton / 866-438-4399 / www.blackbearcoce.com / On the banks of the Hiwassee River

Hiwassee Outfitters / 423-338-8115 / www.hiswasseeoutfitters.com / Cabins, campground and general store

GUIDES & FLY SHOPS

Bob Borgwat's Reel Angling Adventure / 866-899-5259 / www.reelanglingadventures.com

Southeastern Anglers / 866-558-7688 / www. southeasternanglers.com

Hiwassee Angler, 179 Tellico Road / 423-338-8500 / www.hiwasseeangler.com

Reliance Fly & Tackle / 423-338-7771 / www.relianceflyshop.com

ETOWAH

Population 3,488

ACCOMMODATIONS

Red Roof Inn, 600 Tennessee Avenue / 866-460-7454

Caney Creek Village Cabins, 5859 Highway 360, Tellico Plains / 423-253-3670 / www.caneycreekvillage.com

CAMPGROUNDS/RV PARKS

Cherokee/Lost Creek, National Forest / 423-263-5486

RESTAURANTS

The Farmhouse Restaurant, 1210 Ohio Avenue / 423-263-3276

Tony's Italian Restaurant, 718 Tennessee Avenue / 423-263-1940

Tom Thumb Diner, 110 5th Street / 423-263-1150

AIRPORT

Chattanooga Airport, 1001 Airport Road, Chattanooga / 423-855-2202 / www.chattairport.com

MEDICAL

Internal Medicine Associates, 301 Grady Road / 423-263-2444

FOR MORE INFORMATION

Etowah Area Chamber of Commerce / 423-263-2228 / www.etowahcoc.org

Rafting the Hiwassee River. Photo courtesy Bob Borgwat/Toccoa Bend Images LLC.

North Carolina

NORTH CAROLINA FACTS

Area: 53,821 square miles, 28th largest state
Population: 9,656,401
State Fish: Southern Appalachian brook trout

TROUT FISHING LICENSE

www.ncwildlife.org / 888-248-6834
Resident annual fee: $20.00
Non-resident annual fee: $30.00
Non-resident 10-day fee: $10.00

STATE RECORD TROUT

Brook trout, 7 pounds, 7 ounces by G. L. Marshall / May 15, 1980 / Raven Fork River
Brown trout, 24 pounds, 10 ounces by Robert Lee Dyer / April 17, 1998 / Nantahala River
Rainbow trout, 20 pounds, 3 ounces by Leah Johnson / January 28, 2006 / Horsepasture River

With over 4,500 miles of trout streams and rivers, North Carolina has more trout water than any state in the Southeast. North Carolina's trout waters vary from small freestone streams in the Great Smoky Mountains, which harbor small native brook trout and stream-bred brown and rainbow trout, to massive tailwater rivers which harbor some monster trout like the 24-pound, 10-ounce trophy landed by Robert Dyer on the Nantahala River. Let's take a look at my two favorite North Carolina tailwaters, the Nantahala (Nan) and Tuckasegee (Tuck) rivers. The Nantahala currently holds the state trout record, which was previously held by the Tuckasegee – if you like big trout, you will love the Nan and the Tuck.

Drift boats are a great way to fish the Tuckasegee River.

NANTAHALA RIVER

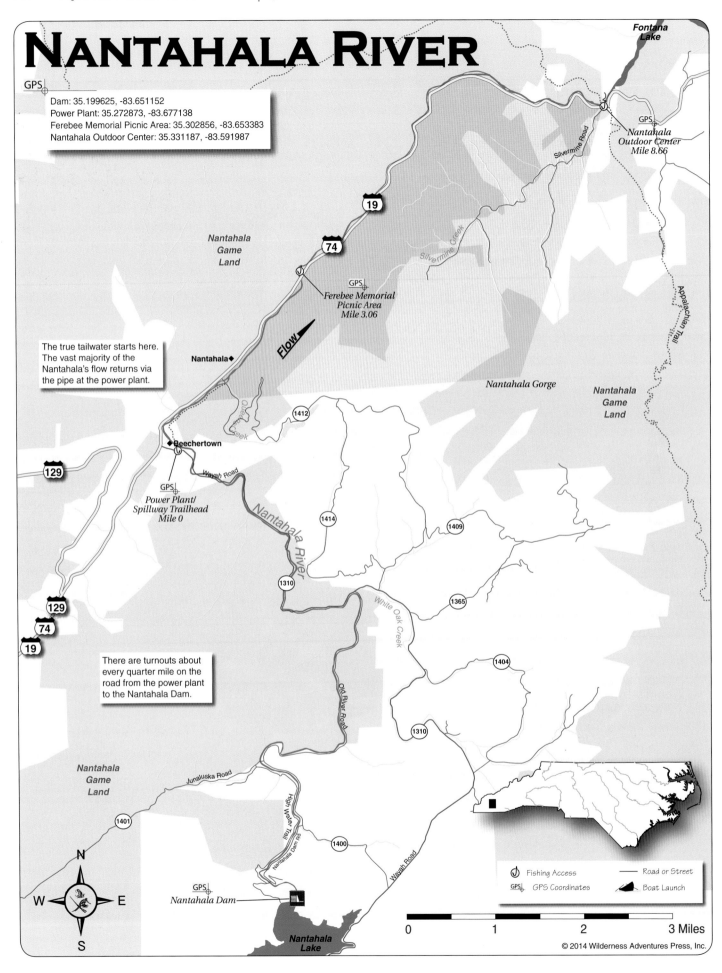

GPS

Dam: 35.199625, -83.651152
Power Plant: 35.272873, -83.677138
Ferebee Memorial Picnic Area: 35.302856, -83.653383
Nantahala Outdoor Center: 35.331187, -83.591987

Fontana Lake

GPS

Nantahala Outdoor Center Mile 8.66

19

74

Nantahala Game Land

GPS

Ferebee Memorial Picnic Area Mile 3.06

Flow

The true tailwater starts here. The vast majority of the Nantahala's flow returns via the pipe at the power plant.

Nantahala◆

Nantahala Gorge

Nantahala Game Land

1412

◆**Beechertown**

Wayah Road

129

GPS

Power Plant/ Spillway Trailhead Mile 0

1414

Nantahala River

1409

1310

1365

129

74

White Oak Creek

1404

19

There are turnouts about every quarter mile on the road from the power plant to the Nantahala Dam.

Old River Road

1310

Nantahala Game Land

Junaluska Road

High Water Trail

1401

1400

Nantahala Dam Rd

Wayah Road

N

W **E**

S

GPS

Nantahala Dam

Nantahala Lake

Fishing Access | Road or Street
GPS — GPS Coordinates | Boat Launch

0   1   2   3 Miles

© 2014 Wilderness Adventures Press, Inc.

NANTAHALA RIVER (FOUR STARS)

The tailwater section of the Nantahala River is located in western North Carolina just outside Great Smoky Mountains National Park, near Bryson City and Cherokee. The Nantahala gets its name from the Cherokee Indians of western North Carolina – Nantahala means "land of the midday sun", as the steep mountains through which the Nantahala flows block the sun from reaching the river until early afternoon.

The Nantahala is probably the best-known river in North Carolina, but not because of its trout fishing. As I discovered on my first trip to the river, it is not just an angler's paradise but also a haven for whitewater enthusiasts. On that first visit, there were literally hundreds of kayakers, from the novice level to professional, testing their skills on the kayak obstacle course in front of the Nantahala Outdoor Center at the lower end of the Nantahala River Gorge. My fishing partner Joe Darcy and I elected to drive upstream to the power station and the beginning of the tailwater. For a short while, Darcy and I had the river to ourselves and were enjoying catching some nice-sized trout in the beautiful wilderness setting of the Nantahala River Gorge. Then one by one, big yellow school buses drove past us going upriver. It didn't take long for us to realize that they were not carrying students, but rather "rafters". Soon we were being mobbed by dozens of rafts – they were being "navigated" (so-to-speak) by folks who acted like they had never been on a river before. It was all we could do to get to shore without getting knocked underwater. I have a picture of Darcy waving his finger at them – I'll let you guess which finger.

The Nantahala River tailwater probably gets less angling pressure than any stream of its caliber in the Southeast, especially when you factor in the good number and size of the river's trout populations. In addition to competing with the whitewater enthusiasts, the Nantahala has to compete with dozens upon dozens of nearby high-quality trout waters in Great Smoky Mountains National Park and the adjacent national forests.

As with all tailwaters, when you are fishing the Nantahala Gorge below the powerhouse, it's important to check the discharge rates and schedule. You don't want to get caught wading out in the middle of the stream when the water suddenly rises. You also don't want to get run over by one of the many rafts or kayaks which launch right after the power company discharge starts. When they are generating power during the summer, normally the only time you can wade this section of the river is early in the morning before they start generating and late in the day when the discharge is over.

While browns and rainbows reproduce in the river, the state liberally supplements the river with catchable-size fish every year. The state stocks brown, brook, and rainbow trout from late winter into early summer. While most of the trout you will catch will be small, occasionally some monster browns are taken, like the 24-pound, 10-ounce trout landed on April 17, 1998. This fish was landed in the outflow channel from the Nantahala Power Plant by Robert Lee Dyer. The public is not allowed to fish the channel, but Dyer works for the power company and had permission to fish it. This fish bested the previous state record 15-pound brown trout landed in the tailwater section of the Tuckasegee River.

DIRECTIONS/ACCESS

The Nantahala River is easy to access from Great Smoky Mountains National Park by taking Route 19/74 south to the Nantahala Outdoor Center, which is located on the river. Route 19/74 closely follows the river upstream some eight miles to the power plant. At the Nantahala spillway there is a foot bridge over the stream and an access trail on the other side of the river.

Angler Joe Darcy fishes the Nantahala River just before the tailwaters are released.

STREAM FACTS

Seasons/Regulations

The Nan is open to year-round fishing under hatchery-supported trout regulations which have no size or bait restrictions and allow a creel limit of seven trout per day. To my knowledge, the Nantahala is the only river in North Carolina that is open to night fishing. There are delayed-harvest regulations from October 1 to the first Saturday in June from the generator upstream to Old River Road along Wayah Road. The upper river is hatchery supported from Wayah Road to Nantahala Dam, and from the generator downstream to Nantahala Outdoor Center.

Fish

While browns and rainbows reproduce in the river, the state liberally supplements the river with catchable-size fish. The state stocks brown, brook, and rainbow trout from late winter into early summer. The Nantahala is open to night fishing, and you have a real shot of hooking into a trophy nocturnal brown trout by using big streamers or wet flies. For this type of fishing, I would use a 6-weight or heavier rod and a minimum of 10-pound test tippet. If you night fish on any body of water, arrive well before dark and familiarize yourself with the surroundings. Do not fish at night if they are going to release water.

River Characteristics

The Nantahala River is a wild trout stream far upstream above Nantahala Lake, where it flows through Nantahala National Forest. Below the lake, when the water leaves the dam, it travels some eight miles through a pipeline to the Nantahala powerhouse. From the outflow of the powerhouse, the river runs through Nantahala Gorge for the next eight miles. When they are not releasing water, the river is very wadeable along most of this section. Low water is usually found in the evening and early morning before power generation starts.

What's in a Name?

The Nantahala gets its name from the Cherokee Indians of western North Carolina. Nantahala means "land of the midday sun", as the steep mountains through which the Nantahala flows block the sun from reaching the river until early afternoon.

What the Experts Say

Tom Hopkins of Western North Carolina Guides describes the Nantahala this way, "This spectacular tailwater is more geared to the whitewater sportsman than the flyfisherman. That said, there are some real opportunities to be found. Most mornings they will be generating power. Needless to say, there is a lot of water to fish before and after the generation. In the morning it is better to fish downstream towards the Nantahala Outdoor Center to get the longest time before the heavy water arrives. And the opposite is true of when the generation stops...be near the generator. Some huge surprises can occur during these times.

"Above the generator there is a delayed-harvest section about 3.5 miles long, which never disappoints. Fish the tailwater early and late in the day, and the delayed-harvest section during the heavy flow."

Flows

The tailwater section of the river starts at the outflow channel from the power plant, which gets its water via an eight-mile pipeline from Nantahala Lake. From the outflow, the tailwaters flow some eight miles through the rugged and scenic Nantahala Gorge. Wading is relatively easy when they are not discharging water, but when they are generating power it is too dangerous to wade. For a taped release schedule, call Nantahala Power and Light Company 828-369-4556.

Hatches

Unlike most tailwaters, the Nantahala harbors a great diversity of mayflies. Spring fishing can be excellent, with good blue-winged olive, blue quill, quill Gordon, and Hendrickson hatches in April. In May and June there are good hatches of March browns, light Cahills, and green drakes. The best hatches of the fall are the blue-winged olives.

Tackle

A 9-foot, 4-weight outfit is ideal for this river.

Hub City

BRYSON CITY

Population 1,424

ACCOMMODATIONS

The Cabins at Nantahala / 888-447-4436 / www.cabinsatnantahala.com

Nantahala River Lodge / 800-470-4718 / www.nantahalariverlodge.com

Relax Inn, 40 Highway 19 South / 828-488-2127 / www.brysoncitymotel.com

Riverbend Lodging, 470 Highway 19 South / 877-272-3155 / www.riverbendlodging.com

Nantahala Village, 9400 Highway 19 West / 828-488-9000 / www.nantahalavillage.com

Lakeview at Fontana Mountain Inn & Spa, 171 Lakeview Lodge Drive / 828-488-3727 / www.lakeviewatfontana.com

Deep Creek Lodge, 1881 West Deep Creek Road / 828-488-2587 / www.deepcreeklodgetubing.com

Two Rivers Lodge, 5280 Ela Road / 828-488-2284 / www.tworiverslodgenc.com

Panther Creek Cabins, 3515 Wrights Creek Road, Cherokee / 828-497-2461 / www.pantercreekresort.com

CAMPGROUNDS/RV PARKS

Deep Creek Campground, 1090 West Deep Creek Road / 828-488-6055

P & J Campground, 160 Ashe Lane / 828-488-6841

Ela Campground & RV Park, 510 Ela Road / 828-488-2100 / www.elacampground.com

Adventure Trail Campground, Camp Creek Road, Cherokee / 828-497-3651 / Open May to October

RESTAURANTS

Pasqualino's Italian Restaurant, 25 Evertt Street / 828-488-9555

Fryemont Inn Restaurant & Bar, 245 Fryemont Street / 828-488-2159 / www.fryemontinn.com

Riverside Bar & Grill, 1341 Main Street / 828-226-2375

The Village Bistro, 9400 Highway 19 / 828-488-9000

FLY SHOPS & GUIDES

Fontana Guides, 3336 Balltown Road / 828-736-2318

Western North Carolina Guide / 828-342-6480 / www.westernncflyfishingguide.com

Nantahala Fly Company, 4221 Tallulah Road, Robbinsville / 828-479-8850 / www.flyfish24-7.com

Nantahala Fly Fishing Co. / 828-479-8850 / www.flyfishnorthcarolina.com

AIRPORTS

McGhee Tyson Airport, 2055 Alcoa Highway, Knoxville, TN / www.tys.org

MEDICAL

Swain County Medical Center, 45 Plateau Street / 828-488-4205

FOR MORE INFORMATION

Swain County Chamber of Commerce / 800-867-9246 / www.greatsmokies.com

Rafting the Nantahala during a release.

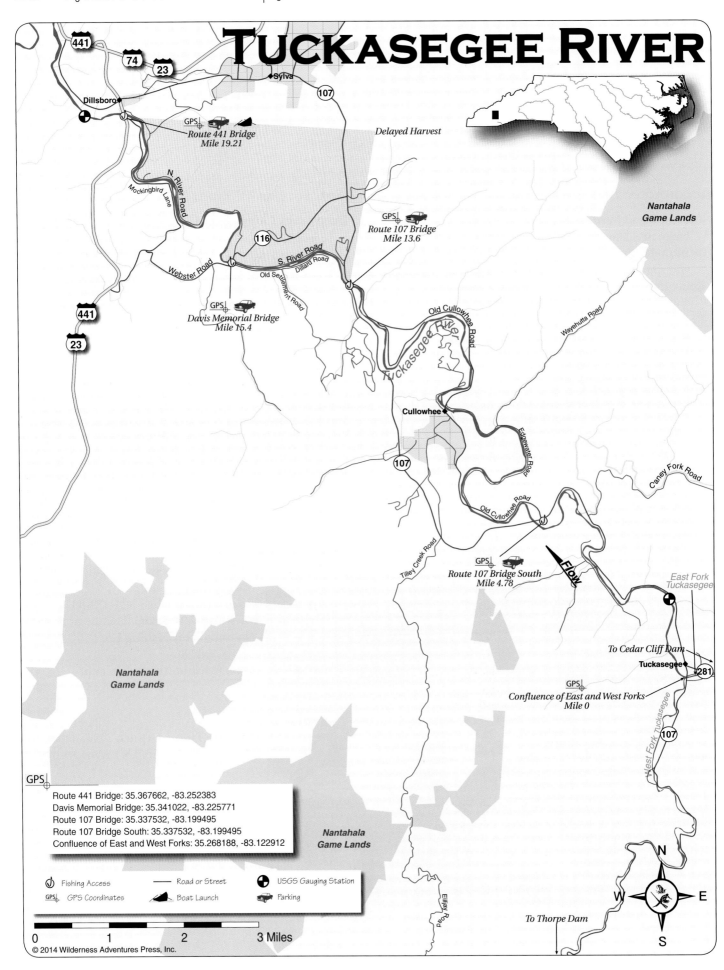

TUCKASEGEE RIVER

GPS
Route 441 Bridge
Mile 19.21

Delayed Harvest

N. River Road

Mockingbird Lane

Webster Road

S. River Road

Old Settlement Road

Dillard Road

GPS
Route 107 Bridge
Mile 13.6

GPS
Davis Memorial Bridge
Mile 15.4

Nantahala
Game Lands

Sylva

Dillsboro

441
74
23
107
116

Tuckasegee River

Old Cullowhee Road

Wayehutta Road

Cullowhee

107

Edgewater Road

Old Cullowhee Road

Caney Fork Road

Tilley Creek Road

GPS
Route 107 Bridge South
Mile 4.78

Flow

East Fork
Tuckasegee

To Cedar Cliff Dam

Tuckasegee

281

GPS
Confluence of East and West Forks
Mile 0

West Fork Tuckasegee

107

Nantahala
Game Lands

Nantahala
Game Lands

Ellijay Road

To Thorpe Dam

GPS
Route 441 Bridge: 35.367662, -83.252383
Davis Memorial Bridge: 35.341022, -83.225771
Route 107 Bridge: 35.337532, -83.199495
Route 107 Bridge South: 35.337532, -83.199495
Confluence of East and West Forks: 35.268188, -83.122912

Fishing Access
Road or Street
USGS Gauging Station
GPS GPS Coordinates
Boat Launch
Parking

0   1   2   3 Miles
© 2014 Wilderness Adventures Press, Inc.

N
W   E
S

TUCKASEGEE RIVER (FOUR STARS)

The Tuckasegee River gets its name from the Cherokee Indian word tuckasegee which means "crawling terrapin" – obviously it was named before the creation of this great tailwater fishery. The mainstem of the Tuckasegee River begins in the western North Carolina mountains just outside the town of Dillsboro. The tailwater section is formed by the bottom releases from dams on both the East and West Forks of the Tuckasegee (the East Fork is referred to as just the Tuckasegee on many maps). The two coldwater discharges combine to form the Tuck tailwater, which provides a suitable habitat for trout most of the year. The Tuckasegee is a medium to large tailwater, as wide as 75 yards in places.

When water is not being released, you can wade across the river in many locations. There are numerous rock ledges crossing the river creating lots of riffles, and where there are breaks in the ledges, long, deep pools develop. These deep pools are perfect places for the trout to stage and feed and for you to fish a dry fly. There are several areas where the water is shallow in one area and, just a few feet away, it drops off into deep holes. Most of the river is wadeable with care when power is not being generated. If only one dam is generating power, there is still a lot of wadeable water; but if both Cedar Cliff and Thorpe Dams are releasing water, don't attempt to wade. However, float fishing from a driftboat at this time can make for some fantastic fishing. The Tuckasegee River is open to year-round fishing under hatchery-supported trout regulations, which have no size or bait restrictions and have a creel limit of seven trout per day. The Tuck also has a delayed-harvest section which is regulated as catch-and-release, artificial-lures-only from October 1 until the first Saturday in June. Starting with the first Saturday in June and continuing until the end of September, hatchery-supported trout regulations apply. The delayed-harvest section runs from Route 107 bridge downstream 5.5 miles to the low-head dam in Dillsboro.

Most years the state stocks over 40,000 trout – brookies, browns and rainbows – making the delayed-harvest section the most heavily-stocked section of river in North Carolina. Anglers have a real shot at getting a "trout slam", a brook, brown, and rainbow trout in one outing, which I have done on several occasions on the Tuck. In addition, the river has a good holdover rate, and many large brown trout have been taken, including the former state brown trout record, a monster weighing a little over 15 pounds.

The state stocks in the spring and again in the fall, and these are the best times of the year to fish the Tuck, but winter fishing can be excellent on all but the coldest days of the year. Avoid fishing it in the summer months, as the water warms and puts a stress on the trout.

DIRECTIONS/ACCESS

From Bryson City and Cherokee, take Route 441 south to Dillsboro. In Dillsboro, Route 441 crosses the Tuckasegee a short distance downstream of the delayed-harvest section. Just before reaching the bridge, make a left turn onto River Road. River Road follows the Tuck upstream for about five miles. The delayed-harvest section begins at the low-head dam just upstream from the Route 441 bridge and runs upstream about 5.5 miles to the Route 107 bridge. Above the bridge the Tuck is stocked and managed under hatchery-supported trout regulations. River Road is marked North River Road from Route 441 upstream to the "T" at Webster Road. If you turn right on Webster Road, you'll have two options: You can take the first left, which is South River Road, and you can access the river all the way to the Route 107 bridge. Or you can stay straight on Webster Road (Route 116), cross over the Trooper Robert "Bob" Davis Memorial Bridge, turn left after crossing the bridge onto Old Settlement Road, and drive 0.6 miles to Dillard Road. Bear left onto Dillard, which gives you access to another 0.6 miles of stream. Parking is via roadside pull-offs on Dillard, South River, and North River Roads.

Float fishing can make for some fantastic fishing, especially when both dams are generating.

STREAM FACTS

Seasons/Regulations

The Tuckasegee River is open to year-round fishing under hatchery-supported trout regulations, which have no size or bait restrictions and a creel limit of seven trout per day. The delayed-harvest section is regulated as catch-and-release, artificial-lures-only from October 1 until the first Saturday in June. Starting with the first Saturday in June and continuing until the end of September, hatchery-supported trout regulations apply.

River Characteristics

The Tuckasegee is a medium to large tailwater, as wide as 75 yards in places. When water is not being released, you can wade across the river in many locations. There are numerous rock ledges crossing the river, creating lots of riffles, and where there are breaks in the ledges, long, deep pools are formed.

Fish

The delayed-harvest section is the most heavily stocked section of stream in the state. There are an estimated 9,000 trout per mile in this section – more than any river I am aware of. The river has a good holdover rate and the fish can grow quite large, as evidenced by the former state record trout, a 15-pound brown trout landed just upstream of the delayed-harvest section. According to local guide Eugene Shuler, who has been guiding on the river for almost 20 years, there are fair numbers of wild fish which enter the river from the many adjoining tributaries as well as fish that migrate up from Fontana Lake to spawn.

What's in a Name?

The Tuckasegee River gets its name from the Cherokee Indian word "tuckasegee" which means "crawling terrapin".

What the Experts Say

Shuler reports that the Tuckasegee has a greater diversity of hatches than most tailwaters. He attributes this to the numerous high-quality trout stream tributaries which flow into the Tuck. In addition to common tailwater hatches like midges, blue-winged olives and sulphurs, Shuler reports the Tuckasegee has abundant quill Gordon, March brown, and early black stonefly hatches as well as enormous caddis hatches.

Tom Hopkins, of Western North Carolina Fly Fishing Guides, feels that the Tuck "is a very appealing river for the inexperienced as well as the very seasoned flyfisher. There are nice runs and ledge pools. The least experienced flyfishers find it a little easier to fish the area just above and below the island to the Webster Bridge.

"The fly selection is, well.....it is as you find it anywhere. Season, water condition, and time of day are the dictators of what's working. Sometimes it makes you a star, and sometimes.....not so much. It is what keeps us coming back."

Flows

Most of the river can be waded with care when power is not being generated. If only one dam is generating power, there is still a lot of wadeable water. If both Cedar Cliff and Thorpe Dams are releasing water, don't attempt to wade; however, float fishing at this time can be fantastic. Release schedules for both Cedar Cliff and Thorpe Reservoirs can be obtained by calling Nantahala Power & Light at 828-369-4556.

Tackle

A 9-foot, 4-weight outfit is ideal for this river.

When water is not being released, you can wade across the river in many locations.

Hub City

SYLVA

Population 2,588

ACCOMMODATIONS

Bear Lake Reserve, 503 Harbor Ridge Drive, Tuckasegee / 828-293-7414

Tuckasegee Valley Cabins, 897 Roy Tritt Road / 828-507-1201 / www.tuckcabins.com

Sylva Inn, 2807 Highway 74 East / 828-586-3115 / www.sylvainn.com

Great Smoky Mountain Log Cabins, Olivet Church Road / 828-497-6182 / www.gsmcabins.com

Dillsboro Inn, 146 North River Road, Dillsboro / 828-586-3898 / www.dillsboroinn.com

CAMPGROUNDS AND RV PARKS

Moonshine Creek Campgrounds & Cabins, 2486 Dark Ridge Road / 828-586-6666 / www.moonshinecreekcampground.com

Fort Tatham RV Park, 175 Tatham Road / 828-586-6662 / Open April to November

RESTAURANTS

B & Al's, 1558 West Main Street / 828-586-5686 / The best burger in town

Coffee Shop, 385 West Main / 828-586-2013 / Owned and operated by the Gibson family since 1985 – defines hometown diner and home-cooked meals at reasonable prices.

Speedy's Pizza, 82 West Main Street / 828-586-3800 / One of Sylva's iconic family-owned restaurants – reminds me of "Cheers" bar.

Dillsboro Inn, 146 North River Road / 828-586-3898 / www.dillsboroinn.com / Riverfront dining on River Road.

FLY SHOPS & GUIDES

Eugene Shuler's, Fly Fishing the Smokies / 17 Ela Heights, Whittier / 828-488-7665 / www.flyfishingthesmokies.com

Nantahala Fly Fishing Co. / 828-479-8850 / www.flyfishnorthcarolina.com

Western North Carolina Guide / 828-342-6480 / www.westernncflyfishingguide.com

Hooker's Fly Shop & Guide Service, 546 West Main Street / 828-587-4665

AIRPORTS

McGhee Tyson Airport, 2055 Alcoa Highway, Knoxville, TN / www.tys.org

MEDICAL

Swain County Medical Center, 45 Plateau Street / 828-488-4205

FOR MORE INFORMATION

Jackson County Chamber of Commerce, 773 West Main / 828-586-4887 / www.mountainlovers.com

Joe Darcy wading the Tuckasegee River.

GEORGIA

GEORGIA FACTS

Area: 59,441 square miles – 24th largest state
Population: 9,815,210
State Fish: Largemouth bass

TROUT FISHING LICENSE:

www.gofishgeorgia.com
Resident annual fee: $9.00 plus $5.00 trout stamp
Non-resident annual fee: $45.00 plus $20.00 trout stamp
Non-resident three-day fee: $20.00 plus three-day $10.00 trout stamp

STATE RECORD TROUT

Brook trout, 5 pounds, 10 ounces by Russell Braden / March 1986 / Waters Creek
Brown trout, 20 pounds, 14 ounces by Chad Doughty / Chattahoochee River / July 2014
Rainbow trout, 17 pounds 8 ounces by Mark Cochran / Soque River / May 2004

Most anglers are surprised to learn that Georgia's waters host native brook trout and stream-bred brown and rainbow trout. Georgia has over 1,500 miles of trout production waters in the Blue Ridge Mountains in the northeast corner of the state and the Cohutta Mountains in the northwest part. These streams host native southern Appalachian brook trout and wild and stocked browns and rainbows. Georgia also has two excellent tailwater rivers, the Chattahoochee (or "Hooch," as the locals call it) and the Toccoa. Georgia's general trout season runs from the last Saturday in March through the end of October, but its tailwaters are managed as year-round trout fisheries.

Georgia hosts native brook trout, and wild rainbows and browns like this Toccoa River monster. Photo courtesy Dane Law, Southeastern Angler.

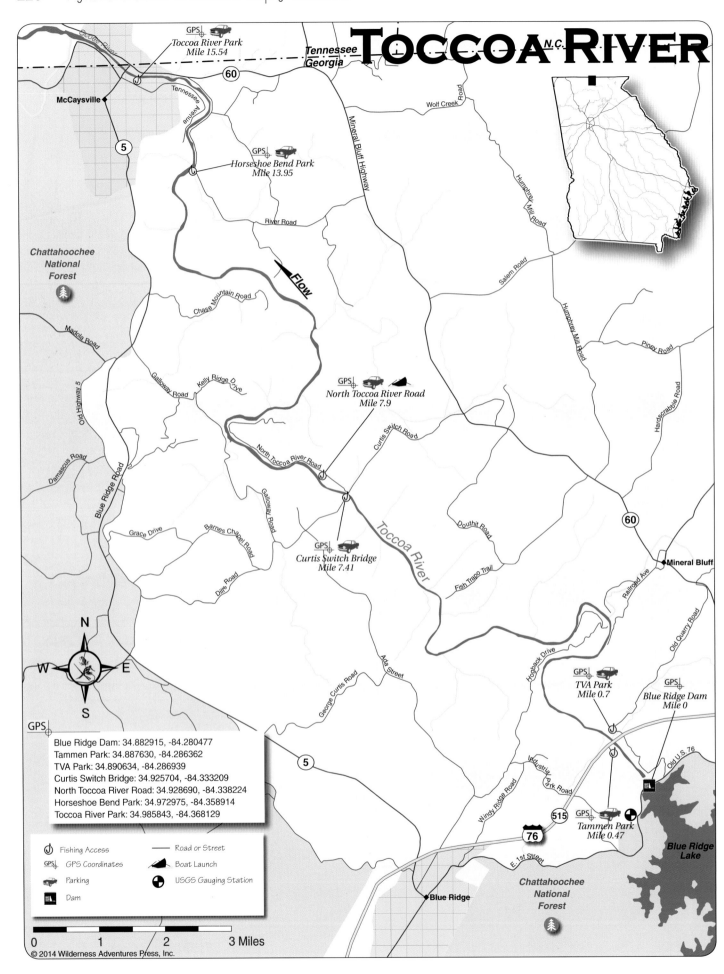

TOCCOA N.C. RIVER

Toccoa River Park
Mile 15.54

Horseshoe Bend Park
Mile 13.95

North Toccoa River Road
Mile 7.9

Curtis Switch Bridge
Mile 7.41

TVA Park
Mile 0.7

Blue Ridge Dam
Mile 0

Tammen Park
Mile 0.47

Blue Ridge Dam: 34.882915, -84.280477
Tammen Park: 34.887630, -84.286362
TVA Park: 34.890634, -84.286939
Curtis Switch Bridge: 34.925704, -84.333209
North Toccoa River Road: 34.928690, -84.338224
Horseshoe Bend Park: 34.972975, -84.358914
Toccoa River Park: 34.985843, -84.368129

Fishing Access
GPS Coordinates
Parking
Dam
Road or Street
Boat Launch
USGS Gauging Station

0   1   2   3 Miles

© 2014 Wilderness Adventures Press, Inc.

TOCCOA RIVER (FOUR STARS)

The Toccoa River tailwater begins at the Tennessee Valley Authority's (TVA) dam in the town of Blue Ridge in the northeast corner of Georgia. The Toccoa River almost did not make the cut for this book, as there was a major fish kill in 2010. In order to repair the dam, the TVA had to significantly draw down the lake. Lowering the depth of the lake increased the water temperatures in the tailrace and, in the summer of 2010, the temperatures exceeded 75 degrees, causing a major fish kill.

The Georgia Wildlife Resources Division (WRD) and the U.S. Fish & Wildlife Service heavily restocked the river to aid in its recovery, and recover it did! Excellent catch rates and numbers of trophy trout are now being recorded in the Toccoa at pre-2010 levels. Most of the trout stocked are rainbows and browns, and in 2013, the state began stocking brook trout. The state stocks adult, fingerling, and brood stock trout. The coldwater releases from the Blue Ridge Dam provide good flyfishing for 15 miles north to the town of McCaysville on the Tennessee border. There is no trout fishing downstream of McCaysville due to mining contamination. (Note: In Tennessee, the Toccoa River changes its name to the Ocoee River.)

A few years back, the TVA installed a dissolved oxygen injection system at the bottom release outlet from the lake. This was a real boost to the river's biomass. The Toccoa has great insect life which often provides good hatches and very good dry fly fishing. In the dead of winter, you'll find caddis and stoneflies coming off. During late winter through spring, be on the lookout for great black caddis hatches, Hendricksons, March browns, and black or cream midges. In late spring and early summer, the sulphurs and light Cahills become dominant. In mid-summer you will find grey caddis, small sulphurs, and cream midges. Fall provides good dry fly fishing to blue-winged olives and the October caddis hatches.

The river is relatively small in width, averaging about 40 yards, and it is easy to wade when the dam is not releasing water. However, when water is being released, wading can be dangerous and should not be attempted. Most of the stream flows through private lands; so, many anglers prefer to float it.

A float trip enables you to cover more water and to access waters that wading anglers cannot reach. There are five public access points for wading anglers described below.

DIRECTIONS/ACCESS

The Toccoa River has five public access points and a total of about 15 miles of trout water running from Blue Ridge to McCaysville. The first two access points are just below the dam and Route 515. Fannin County maintains Tammen Park on the west side of the river just below the dam and Route 515, and the TVA has a park on the east side of the river below Route 515. This area offers a lot of good wading during low-water periods.

Access to the middle portion of the trout water is off of Curtis Switch Road. From Route 515 East, turn left onto Route 60 North. Turn left onto Curtis Switch Road and follow it to the river. There is limited parking around the bridge, but if you turn right at the bridge onto North Toccoa River Road (unpaved) for about a half mile you will come to the TVA park and boat launch site.

The final two access parks are north in the town of McCaysville. I prefer to fish Horseshoe Bend Park, which is about one mile south of McCaysville off of Route 60 on River Road. It affords about a half mile of easy access and good wading during low-water periods. Toccoa River Park is on the west side of the river in downtown McCaysville off of East Market Street.

The Toccoa has recovered well from a major fish kill in 2010. Photo courtesy Steve Lamb of Georgia Fly Guide.

STREAM FACTS

Seasons/Regulations

The Toccoa River is open to fishing year round with no tackle or bait restrictions, except you cannot fish with minnows. The daily creel limit is eight fish per angler, with no size limit.

Fish

While there is some natural reproduction, the fishery is largely maintained through stocking. Historically, the state has stocked some 20,000 brown and rainbow trout annually. Starting in 2013, it began adding brook trout to the stockings. It stocks adults, brood stock, and fingerling trout. The fingerlings that survive to adult stage act and look more like wild trout. They can be picky and very selective, unlike most stocked tailwater trout. The Toccoa also produces some real trophy fish, like the one the state turned up during its 2009 stream survey, a 28-inch, 14-pound brown trout.

River Characteristics

The river has long and very deep pools and a lot of rocky shoals, which make it difficult to wade. The pools are separated by rocky shoals which stretch across the river. Much of the river flows through private land, but you can float these sections and get out of the boat to wade the shoals.

What the Experts Say

Not only does the Toccoa have a good insect population, but according to guide Steve Lamb, who has been guiding on the river for 40 years, the river is loaded with forage fish, and he has landed many trophy browns by chucking his streamers in low-light conditions early and late in the day with a sink-tip line. The Lambster, as Steve is referred to on the river, has developed a series of killer streamer patterns, which he ties using flashy metallic material. Trust me, they really work! My favorites are his De Silver and De Fools Gold. (You can purchase Steve's streamers on line at www.bigyflyco.com.)

Dane Law of Southeastern Anglers describes the river this way, "The Toccoa River offers a small and personal driftboat experience by TVA standards. The river features many of the major eastern insect hatches and is a favorite for the Hendrickson and sulphur hatches.

Bob Borgwat of Reel Angling Adventures feels the Toccoa is "arguably the best trout fishery in the state. Water temperatures range from low 40s in winter to mid-60s in summer, so it's a year-round fishery.

Floating is a safer option to fish the Toccoa when the dam is releasing water. Photo courtesy Steve Lamb of Georgia Fly Guide.

Flows

The TVA has been very cooperative in working with Georgia's Department of Natural Resources to provide for discharges that help protect the fishery. The discharge schedules provide for fairly stable temperatures throughout the year. Even in the heat of summer, the tailwater section of the Toccoa seldom rises above the mid-60s when the TVA is not generating power. Release Information: Call 1-800-238-2254 (#4, #23) to reach the Blue Ridge Dam information line or visit www.tva.com.

Hatches

Late winter into spring the Toccoa has a great little black stonefly hatch, and blue-winged olive and midge hatches are daily possibilities. These are followed by tons of caddis, then Hendricksons, sulphurs, and light Cahills. Fall provides good dry fly fishing on blue-winged olives and the October caddis. Midges (in cream, grey, or black) and blue-winged olives are found coming off year round on the Toccoa, so you should always have these patterns in your box. Olive Woolly Buggers and the Lambster's deadly streamer patterns will also dredge up fish when nothing appears to be happening on the surface.

Tackle

My favorite method of fishing the Toccoa is with a 9-foot, 3-weight rod, and long, 12- to 15-foot, 5x or 6x leaders. A dry/dropper combination of an Elk Hair Caddis with a small Pheasant Tail or Hare's Ear Nymph dropped about 20 inches off the bend of the hook can be extremely productive. During periods of high water, tossing big streamers with a 7-weight rod and a sink tip fly line can produce some brutes well above 20 inches.

Hub City

BLUE RIDGE

Population 1,290

ACCOMMODATIONS

Reid Ridge Lodge, 30 Overlook Drive / 706-632-4444 / www.reidridgelodge.com

The Blue Ridge Lodge by Comfort Inn & Suites, 83 Blue Ridge Overlook Drive / 706-946-3333 / www.comfortinnofblueridge.com

The Oyster Cast & Blast, 494 East Main Street / 706-374-4239 / www.oysterbamboo.com

A Blue Ridge Vacation Cabin Rentals, 181 Tammen Drive / 706-632-7100 / www.ablueridgevacation.com

Blue Ridge Inn B&B, 477 West First Street / 706-632-0222 / www.blueridgeinnbandb.com

CAMPGROUNDS & RV PARKS

Blue Ridge Mineral Springs RV Park and Tent Camping, 803 Mineral Springs Road / 706-632-5010

Toccoa Valley Campground & RV Park, 11481 Aska Road, 706-838-4317 / www.toccoavalleycampground.com

RESTAURANTS

Harvest on Main, 576 East Main Street / 706-946-6164 / www.harvestonmain.com

Christy Lee's Courtyard Grille, 588 East Main Street / 706-946-5100 / www.christylees.com

The Vine Wine Bar & Bistro, 632 East Main Street / 706-946-8463 / www.thevineofblueridge.com

The Big Pink Pig, 824 Cherry Log Street / 706-632-2403 / www.budspinkpig.com

Pete's Place, 83 Dunbarton Farm, 706-946-0222 / Where the locals eat

FLY SHOPS & GUIDES

Steve Lamb's Georgia Fly Guide / 678-986-0703 / www.georgiaflyguide.com

Bob Borgwat's Reel Angling Adventures / 866-899-5259 / www.reelanglingadventures.com

Southeastern Angler / 866-55-Trout (87688) / www.southeasternanglers.com

Unicoi Outfitters, 7280 South Main Street , Helen / 706-878-3083 / & 490 East Main Street, Blue Ridge / 706-632-1880 www.unicoioutfitters.com

Blue Ridge Fly Fishing Guides, 490 East Main Street / 706-838-5515 / www.blueridgeflyfishing.com

Reel Job Fishing / 770-330-7583 / www.kent-klewein.com

Southern Sweetwater Anglers / 770-530-2228 / www.southernsweetwateranglers.com

Lake and Stream Guide Service / 706-669-4973 / www.ellijayfishing.com

AIRPORTS

Atlanta International Airport, 6000 North Terminal Parkway, Atlanta / 800-897-1910 / www.atlanta-airport.com

MEDICAL

Fanning Regional Hospital, 2855, Old Highway 5 North / 706-632-3711 / www.fanningregionalhospital.com

FOR MORE INFORMATION

Fannin County Chamber of Commerce / 706-632-5680 / www.blueridgemountains.com

A dissolved oxygen injection system has increased the Toccoa's biomass. Photo courtesy Dane Law, Southeastern Angler.

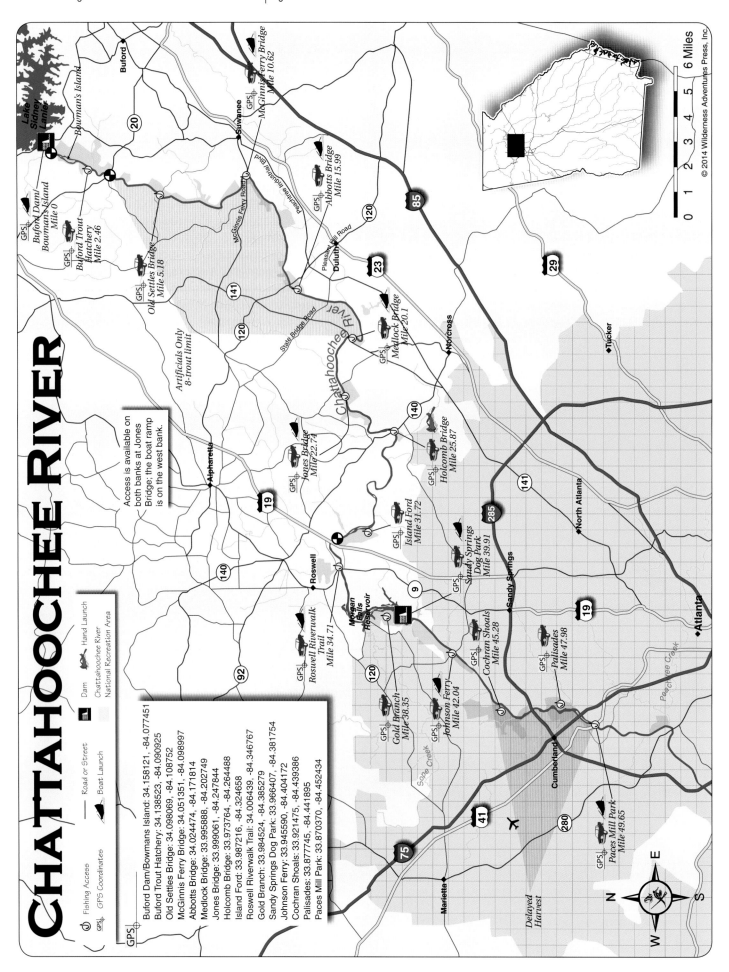

CHATTAHOOCHEE RIVER

Access is available on both banks at Jones Bridge; the boat ramp is on the west bank.

Artificials Only
8-trout limit

GPS

Buford Dam/Bowmans Island: 34.158121, -84.077451
Buford Trout Hatchery: 34.138523, -84.090925
Old Settles Bridge: 34.098069, -84.108752
McGinnis Ferry Bridge: 34.051351, -84.098997
Abbotts Bridge: 34.024474, -84.171814
Medlock Bridge: 33.995888, -84.202749
Jones Bridge: 33.999061, -84.247844
Holcomb Bridge: 33.973764, -84.264488
Island Ford: 33.987216, -84.324658
Roswell Riverwalk Trail: 34.006439, -84.346767
Gold Branch: 33.984524, -84.385279
Sandy Springs Dog Park: 33.966407, -84.381754
Johnson Ferry: 33.945590, -84.404172
Cochran Shoals: 33.921475, -84.439386
Palisades: 33.877745, -84.441895
Paces Mill Park: 33.870370, -84.452434

Fishing Access
GPS Coordinates
Dam
Boat Launch
Road or Street
Hand Launch
Chattahoochee River
National Recreation Area

Lake Sidney Lanier
Bowman's Island
Buford

Buford Dam/
Bowmans Island
Mile 0
Buford Trout
Hatchery
Mile 2.46

Old Settles Bridge
Mile 5.18

McGinnis Ferry Bridge
Mile 10.62

Suwanee

Abbotts Bridge
Mile 15.99

Peachtree Industrial Blvd
McGinnis Ferry Road

Duluth

Pleasant Hill Road

State Bridge Road

Medlock Bridge
Mile 20.1

Norcross

Chattahoochee River

Jones Bridge
Mile 22.74

Alpharetta

Holcomb Bridge
Mile 25.87

Island Ford
Mile 31.72

Roswell

Roswell Riverwalk
Trail
Mile 34.71

Morgan
Falls
Reservoir

Sandy Springs
Dog Park
Mile 39.91

Sandy Springs

Gold Branch
Mile 38.35

Johnson Ferry
Mile 42.04

Cochran Shoals
Mile 45.28

Palisades
Mile 47.98

Sope Creek

North Atlanta

Peachtree Creek

Atlanta

Cumberland

Paces Mill Park
Mile 49.65

Delayed
Harvest

Marietta

Tucker

© 2014 Wilderness Adventures Press, Inc.

0 1 2 3 4 5 6 Miles

N
W E
S

CHATTAHOOCHEE RIVER (FOUR STARS)

"The Hooch" begins as a small, freestone, native brook trout stream in north Georgia's Appalachian Mountains at an elevation of about 2,400 feet, which keeps the river cold enough to support a thriving population of native brookies. Chattahoochee is a Native American word which means "river of painted rocks", referring to the many colorful rock outcroppings near its headwaters. The river flows through wilderness areas in Chattahoochee National Forest and Chattahoochee Wildlife Management Area. By the time it reaches the village of Helen in northeastern Georgia, the water becomes too warm to sustain trout throughout the summer. It remains a put-and-catch fishery as it heads toward Lake Sidney Lanier and the city of Atlanta in north-central Georgia.

In 1957, the Army Corps of Engineers completed Buford Dam on the Chattahoochee River creating Lake Sidney Lanier, which supplies nearly 70 percent of Atlanta's water. The lake gets over 10 million visitors annually, making it the most heavily used impoundment in the country. The cold water released from the bottom of Buford Dam has created a coldwater fishery downstream some 48 miles to Peachtree Creek in Atlanta.

Realizing the unique significance of this natural treasure for the citizens of Atlanta as well as the rest of the nation, Congress in 1978 passed legislation creating the Chattahoochee River National Recreation Area (CRNRA). The park is a series of parklands along the 48-mile stretch of river from Buford Dam downstream to Peach Tree Creek. At the dedication, then-President Jimmy Carter stated, "It's one of the most beautiful places in our country, extremely valuable to all who know it, who live near it, and who appreciate the quiet and seclusion and the beauty and the value of this river... It's a rare occasion when within the city limits of our major cities, one can find pure water and trout and free canoeing and rapids and the seclusion of the Earth the way God made it. But the Chattahoochee River is this kind of place."

My first trip to the Hooch was daunting – flying into Atlanta, renting a car, and negotiating the evening rush hour traffic to get to my sister-in-law's home in Roswell on the outskirts of Atlanta. Within two miles of her house, I crossed a six-lane bridge in stop-and-go traffic over the Chattahoochee River and got my first look at the river. It appeared massive, over 300 feet wide, and it was running high and muddy from the heavy rains the region was experiencing – it certainly didn't look like much of a trout stream to a guy who grew up fishing the freestone mountain streams and spring creeks of central Pennsylvania. Impressed by its size, I thought I must be below the trout section of the river, but I would later find out that I was in fact in the middle of the trout water.

The next morning I opted for an early start. My plan was to drive up the river and start fishing near the base of Buford Dam and work my way downriver while checking out various access points. My journey would take me about 20 miles north of Roswell, mostly on Route 19. On the entire drive north on Route 19, there was a steady stream of headlights coming south as the wall-to-wall commuters headed to work in downtown Atlanta. I had recently retired and felt grateful that I had left behind 45 years of commuting on busy interstate highways to fish, write, and spend time with my grandchildren.

After crossing the dam which created Lake Lanier, I headed down the road to the first public access point at Bowmans Island. The Army Corps was not releasing water, so the water in this section was very wadeable. In fact, a few anglers had worked their way across to the opposite side of the river. The upper river below the dam was very clear and the trout were very cooperative. Fishing a pair of wet flies, I was able to land several freshly stocked rainbows and two beautifully colored browns. I had read that the Hooch was strictly a put-and-catch fishery, but I would later find out that the state had documented reproducing brown trout in the Chattahoochee, and no longer stocked brown trout above Morgan Falls Dam – my browns were wild fish.

As I moved downstream to check out some other access areas, the water began to change color, as the recent rains had washed some of the region's red clay into the river. The farther downriver I went, the more orange the water became.

Wild brown trout like this one make up as much as 15 percent of the total Chattahoochee River trout population. Photo courtesy Davie Crawford, Deep South Fly Anglers.

DIRECTIONS/ACCESS

Bowmans Island

The Bowmans Island public access area is just below Buford Dam. Take Route 19 North about 20 miles from Roswell. Exit Route 19 at Route 20 (Buford Highway), turn left on Market Place Road, and then turn right onto Buford Dam Road, crossing the dam and heading down the road to the first public access point at Bowmans Island. This section is easily waded when no water is being released Extreme caution must be used in this section due to its close proximity to the dam. The National Park Service requires anglers and boaters to wear a personal flotation device from the dam downstream to the Route 20 bridge. The river from the dam down to the Route 20 bridge is managed under Georgia's general regulations.

Buford Trout Hatchery

The next section of river downstream from Bowmans Island was difficult to find but well worth the effort, as I only encountered one other angler. Access to the section behind the Buford Trout Hatchery is through a beautiful upscale housing development. The development is known as the Chattahoochee River Club and is a mile or two west of the river on Route 20. Turn right onto River Club Drive for 0.6 miles to Trout Place Road. After 0.3 miles you will see the entrance to the hatchery. The hatchery is open to the public but there is no access to the river from the hatchery. To access the river, park on the right just outside the hatchery gates and across from house number 3197 on the left. You will see a small sign with a trout and a hook on it. Just past the sign is an inconspicuous trail which circumvents the hatchery fence and takes you to the river after about a quarter-mile walk.

STREAM FACTS

General Regulations

From State Route 141 downstream 12 miles to the Route 9 bridge in Roswell, angling is open to any method of fishing. This section is far enough from the dam that the scouring effects of the water release surges are minimized and aquatic insect life and vegetation increases. Here the river is a caddis factory, with exceptional hatches from early spring into the summer. There is easy access and parking at the Medlock Bridge, Holcomb Bridge, and Island Ford units of the Chattahoochee River National Recreation Area. The Island Ford Visitor Center is a good place to start your visit to the Chattahoochee. At the center you will be able to pick up maps for the national recreation area that are very helpful in finding access areas. To access the visitor center from northbound Route 400 in Roswell, take Exit 6 and turn right over Route 400, then turn right onto Dunwoody Place. Proceed 0.5 miles to Roberts Drive. Turn right and proceed 0.7 miles to the park entrance on the right.

Special Regulations Section

There are two sections of the Chattahoochee River which have special regulations. The 15-mile stretch north of the city of Atlanta from State Route 20 to State Route 141 (Peachtree Parkway) is restricted to artificial-lures-only, with a daily limit of eight trout.

This stretch is best suited for a float trip to access the more remote sections of the river. Wading anglers can access this section of the river at the park service access areas at Settles Bridge, McGinnis Ferry, Suwanee Creek, Abbotts Bridge, and Medlock Bridge.

The tailwater section gets stocked annually with over 250,000 legal size-rainbow trout, plus an additional 750,000 fingerlings. Photo courtesy Davie Crawford, Deep South Fly Anglers.

In 2000, the state implemented a delayed-harvest section which runs from the mouth of Sope Creek downstream to Cobb Parkway (Route 41). The state heavily stocks the delayed-harvest section with both brown and rainbow trout and stocking continues in the general regulation waters downstream to Peachtree Creek in northwest Atlanta. The delayed-harvest season runs from November 1 until May 14, during which time anglers must use single-hook artificials and release all trout. Starting May 15, due to the warm summers in Atlanta, anglers can keep a daily limit of eight trout. There is good wade fishing in the Cochran Shoals and Palisades units of the CRNRA.

The rest of the river has no gear restrictions and a daily limit of eight trout.

Fish

The tailwater section gets stocked annually with over 250,000 legal size-rainbow trout, plus an additional 750,000 fingerlings. The state has also documented wild brown trout making up as much as 15 percent of the trout population and therefore, it no longer stocks brown trout above Morgan Falls Dam. There is a good holdover rate, and several double-digit fish are landed every season, including the current state record trout, a 20-pound, 14-ounce brown which was take in the river in July 2014, besting the old record of 18 pounds, 14 ounces also take in the Chattahoochee River.

River Characteristics

The river is about 200 feet wide below the dam; it grows in size to about 400 feet wide in Atlanta, and it is very deep. While there are numerous sections which are wadeable when the dam is not releasing water, most anglers prefer a float option to reach wade able gravel bars and shoals. I have seen every type of water craft on the river including driftboats, canoes, jonboats, kayaks, and float tubes.

Hatches

Mayfly hatches consist of mostly *Baetis* species or blue-winged olives from size 14 to 26. On overcast days when fish are on the surface, a Parachute Adams is always a good bet. *Plecoptera* stonefly species are prolific on clear, crisp winter days in sizes 12 to 16. Various Stimulator patterns will work during this time. If there is no surface action, Beadhead Pheasant Tail and Hare's Ear Nymphs will produce. Midges hatch all winter, and a great midge dry fly pattern is the Griffith's Gnat size 18 to 22. The spawning season for brown trout lasts well into the mild winter months, and some monster browns are landed every winter on streamer patterns fished slow and deep. Spring brings a hefty assortment of caddis, with black caddis hatches being the heaviest. May has some decent sulphur hatches.

The river is about 200 feet wide below the dam; it grows in size to about 400 feet wide in Atlanta, and it is very deep. Photo courtesy Davie Crawford, Deep South Fly Anglers.

What's in a Name?

Chattahoochee is a Native American word which means "river of painted rocks", referring to the many colorful rock outcroppings near the river's headwaters.

What the Experts Say

Davie Crawford of Deep Fly South Angler states, "My favorite time to be on the water is during fall and winter (October through January). During this time the brown trout are really aggressive. This is also the best time of the year to fish big, black stonefly nymphs and articulated streamers for not only bigger brown trout, but also the feisty holdover rainbows. The lower catch rate is made up for by the quality of the fish."

Flows

Releases are not always predictable. This is one of the few tailwaters that can't be fished during releases, as it flows very high and muddy. Releases can raise the river as much as six to eight feet in a relatively short period of time. For water release schedules, can call the Army Corps of Engineers at Buford Dam at 770-945-1466.

Tackle

For me, the best all-around outfit on the Hooch is a 9-foot, 5-weight with a floating line. For winter streamer fishing I'll use a 9-foot, 7-weight with a sink tip line.

The lower Hooch is officially the southernmost trout water in the United States and a good place to end our journey, which like the Appalachian Trail starts in Maine and concludes its journey in Georgia. I hope you enjoyed the trip through *Eastern Trophy Tailwaters*.

Hub City

ROSWELL

Population 79,334

The hub city of Roswell is a booming, upscale suburb 20 miles north of Atlanta. It has been rated as one of the safest cities and best places to raise a family in the U.S. Roswell is home to many historic homes and sites and it hosts many art and cultural festivals. Roswell's Canton Street is known as Georgia's historic treasure – it is home to historic commercial buildings and homes. This narrow, tree-lined street with brick sidewalks provides a beautiful backdrop for Roswell's many cultural festivals and rich dining experiences. Be sure to visit Canton Street for a superb dining experience.

ACCOMMODATIONS

Towne Place Suites by Marriott, 7925 Westside Parkway, Alpharetta / 770-664-1300

Holiday Inn Express, 2950 Mansell Road, Alpharetta / 512-227-8707

La Quinta Inn, 1350 North Point Drive, Alpharetta / 770-754-7800

Wingate Inn, 1005 Kingswood Place, Alpharetta / 770-649-0955

CAMPGROUNDS & RV PARKS

Shoal Creek Campground, 6300 Shadburn Ferry Road, Buford / 678-482-0332

RESTAURANTS

*Fickle Pickle, 1085 Canton Street / 770-650-9838 / Southern

*Vin 25, 25 Plum Tree Street / 770-628-0411 / American

*Ceviche Taqueria, 963-Canton Street / 678-461-4025 / Mexican

Greenwoods, 1087 Green Street / 770-992-5383 / www.greenwoodssongreenstreet.com / Southern

Harp Irish Pub, 1425 Market Boulevard / 770-645-0118 / www.harpirishpub.com

Little Steak Ally, 955 Canton Street / 770-998-0440 / Steakhouse

Osteria Mattone, 1095 Canton Street / 678-878-3378 / www.osteriamattone.com / Italian

*Recommended by my sister-in-law Katie Langan, who has been a resident of Roswell for almost 40 years.

FLY SHOPS & GUIDES

Deep South Fly Anglers / 678-986-9240 / www.deepsouthflyangler.com

Orvis, 3275 Peach Tree Road NE #210, Atlanta / 404-841-0093 www.orvis.com/atlanta

The Fish Hawk, 3095 Peachtree Road NE, Atlanta / 404-237-3473 / www.thefishhawk.com

River Through Atlanta Guide Service, 710 Riverside Road / 770-650-8630 / www.riverthroughatlanta.com

Cohutta Fishing Company, 39 South public Square / 770-606-1100 / www.cohuttafishingco.com

AIRPORTS

Atlanta International Airport, 6000 North Terminal Parkway, Atlanta / 800-897-1910 / www.atlanta-airport.com

MEDICAL

North Fulton Hospital, 3000 Hospital Blvd. / 770-751-2500 / www.nfultonhospital.com

FOR MORE INFORMATION

www.roswell.org

Index